Leadership for Increasingly Diverse Schools

Leadership for Increasingly Diverse Schools provides both practicing and aspiring leaders with the theory, research, and practical guidance to lead socially just schools. Today's schools are growing more pluralistic and diverse, and leadership is central to reversing long-standing trends of educational inequities, exclusion, and disparate school outcomes. This book helps readers sharpen their awareness of how multiple dimensions of diversity intersect as well as develop strategies for working with students of all socioeconomic statuses, races, religions, sexual orientations, languages, and special needs. *Leadership for Increasingly Diverse Schools* provides school leaders the tools to foster teaching and learning environments that promote educational equity and excellence for all students.

Special Features:

- Each chapter focuses on a specific dimension of diversity and discusses intersectionality across other areas of difference, including ability/disability, linguistic diversity, race, socioeconomic status, sexual orientation, gender, religion, and social frontiers.
- Chapters synthesize literature, provide practical strategies and tools, and include school-level and district-level cases illustrating inclusive leadership.
- End-of-chapter resources point readers toward further discussion of conceptual elements, practice connections, and research applications.
- A companion website features modifiable downloads and further resources for each chapter.

George Theoharis is Chair of the Teaching and Leadership Department and Associate Professor in Educational Leadership and Inclusive Elementary Education at Syracuse University.

Martin Scanlan is Associate Professor in Educational Policy and Leadership at Marquette University.

EDUCATIONAL LEADERSHIP FOR EQUITY AND DIVERSITY

Series Editor: Colleen A. Capper

Leadership for Increasingly Diverse Schools
George Theoharis and Martin Scanlan

Leadership for Increasingly Diverse Schools

Edited by
George Theoharis & Martin Scanlan

NEW YORK AND LONDON

First published 2015
by Routledge
711 Third Avenue, New York, NY 10017

and by Routledge
2 Park Square, Milton Park, Abingdon, Oxon, OX14 4RN

Routledge is an imprint of the Taylor & Francis Group, an informa business

© 2015 Taylor & Francis

Library of Congress Cataloging-in-Publication Data
A catalog record for this book has been requested

ISBN: 978-1-138-78592-2 (hbk)
ISBN: 978-1-138-78593-9 (pbk)
ISBN: 978-1-315-76757-4 (ebk)

Typeset in Aldine 401 and Helvetice Neue
by Apex CoVantage, LLC

Printed and bound by CPI Group (UK) Ltd, Croydon, CR0 4YY

To Ella and Sam—Thank you for your ebullient spirits. Remember, we cannot be silent in the face of inequity.
To my students—I expect great things.
—G.T.

I dedicate this work to Christopher, and to all the other children and families who face uphill battles fighting to be included and embraced in our school communities.
—MKS

Contents

Series Editor Introduction   xiv
Foreword   xvi
Preface   xix
Acknowledgments   xxiv

1   Introduction: Intersectionality in Educational Leadership   1
    Martin Scanlan and George Theoharis

2   Inclusive Leadership and Disability   13
    George Theoharis, Julie Causton, and Casey Woodfield

3   Inclusive Leadership and Poverty   39
    Curt Dudley-Marling and Anne Dudley-Marling

4   Inclusive Leadership and Race   58
    Sonya Douglass Horsford and Christine Clark

5   Inclusive Leadership and English Learners   82
    Isabel Kelsey, Carmen Campuzano, and Francesca López

6   Inclusive Leadership and Lesbian, Gay, Bisexual, Transgendered,
    and Questioning Students   101
    Frank Hernandez and Don Fraynd

7   Inclusive Leadership and Gender   119
    Margaret Grogan and Shamini Dias

8   Inclusive Leadership and Religion   142
     Joanne M. Marshall

9   Inclusive Leadership on the Social Frontiers: Family and
     Community Engagement   162
     Martin Scanlan and Lauri Johnson

10   The Equity Audit as the Core of Leading Increasingly Diverse
     Schools and Districts   186
     Colleen A. Capper and Michelle D. Young

Appendix: Equity Audit Data Collection and Analysis   198
About the Contributors   215
Index   221

Extended Contents

Series Editor Introduction   xiv

Foreword   xvi

Preface   xix

Acknowledgments   xxiv

1   Introduction: Intersectionality in Educational Leadership   1
    Martin Scanlan and George Theoharis

    Core Expectations of School Leaders   1
        Social Justice and Leadership Standards   2
        What Does Social Justice Leadership Look Like?   3
    Pursuing Socially Just Schooling: Leadership *Practices*   4
    Fostering Communities of Practice   5
        What Are COPs?   5
        Who Belongs to My Social Justice Leadership COP?   6
        What Is Our Shared Repertoire?   8
        Building Networked Social Justice Communities   8

2   Inclusive Leadership and Disability   13
    George Theoharis, Julie Causton, and Casey Woodfield

    Part 1: The Current Context of Disability in Schools   13
        What Do People with Disabilities Say? Voices of the Community   14
    Part 2: What We Know About Disability: The Literature   16
        How Does Disability Relate to Other Areas of Difference?
          Intersections and Overrepresentation   16
        The Social Construction of Disability   17
        The Efficacy of Inclusive Services   18
        Response to Intervention (RTI)   19
        We Must Assume Students CAN! Presumption of Competence   19

Part 3: Inclusive Leadership for Students With Disabilities in K–12 Schools   20
   Leaders' Roles in Inclusion and Disability   20
   Case Studies   30
Conclusion   35

3   Inclusive Leadership and Poverty   39
Curt Dudley-Marling and Anne Dudley-Marling

Part 1: The Current Context of Poverty in Schools   39
Part 2: What We Know About Poverty: The Literature   41
   The Impoverished Curricula That Come From Deficit Thinking   42
Part 3: Inclusive Leadership Around Poverty in Schools   43
   Dismantling Tracking and Ability Grouping   44
   Culturally Responsive Theories of Education   46
   High-Expectation Curriculum: Creating Opportunities
    for Engaging Learning Through Rigorous Discussion   49
   Case Study   50
   Equity Audit   53
Conclusion   53

4   Inclusive Leadership and Race   58
Sonya Douglass Horsford and Christine Clark

The Problem of Race in US Schools   58
Purpose and Overview   59
Part 1: The Current Context of Race in Schools   60
   Race and Intersectionality   61
Part 2: What We Know About Race: The Literature   61
   Current Challenges   62
   Strategies   63
Part 3: Inclusive Leadership Around Race in K–12 Schools   64
   Case Studies   64
   Tools and Strategies   68
Conclusion: From Curiosity and Compassion to Inclusion and Justice   76

5   Inclusive Leadership and English Learners   82
Isabel Kelsey, Carmen Campuzano, and Francesca López

Part 1: The Current Context of English Learners in Schools   82
   Meeting the Needs of ELs in the US   83
   What Do English Learners Have to Say? Voices of the Community   84
Part 2: What We Know About English Learners: The Literature   85
   Inclusive, Culturally Responsive Curriculum and Instruction   87
   Academic Rigor via Funds of Knowledge   88
   Accountability   88
   The New Instructional Leader Beyond 21st-Century Practices   89

Part 3: Inclusive Leadership Around English Learners in K–12 Schools   89
    Case Studies   90
    Supporting Leadership Around ELs: Inclusive School Reform   94
Conclusion   96

6   Inclusive Leadership and Lesbian, Gay, Bisexual, Transgendered, and Questioning Students   101
Frank Hernandez and Don Fraynd

Part 1: The Current Contexts for Lesbian, Gay, Bisexual, Transgendered, and Questioning Students in Schools   101
    Speaking From Experience   102
Part 2: What We Know About LGBTQ Students and Perceived-LGBTQ Students: The Literature   104
    Defining the Terms   104
    Intersectionality   105
    Harassment of LGBTQ and Perceived-LGBTQ Youth Relative to
      Social Justice Leadership   105
    The Effects of Name-Calling   107
    LGBTQ Identity-Development Theories and Research   108
Part 3: Inclusive Leadership Around LGBTQ Issues in K–12 Schools   109
    Creating Environments That Support LGBTQ and
      Perceived-LGBTQ Students   109
    Countering Heteronormative Perspectives   110
    Creation of LGBTQ-Supportive Rituals, Celebrations, and Activities   111
    Implementation of a School-Wide Equity Audit Regarding
      LGBTQ Matters   112
    District Policies and Community Involvement   113
    Case Studies   114
Conclusion   115

7   Inclusive Leadership and Gender   119
Margaret Grogan and Shamini Dias

Part 1: The Current Context of Gender in Schools   120
    Voices of the Community   121
    Listening to the Voices in the Community   123
Part 2: What We Know About Gender: The Literature   124
    Legislation   125
    Classroom Pedagogies, Course Content, and Curriculum Materials   126
    Academic Performance, Gendered Career Preparation, and
      Encouragement   127
    Sexual Harassment   129
    Pregnancy and Parenting   129

Part 3: Inclusive Leadership Around Gender in K–12 Schools   130
    From Awareness to Action   131
    A Case Study of Professional Development: Gender as a
        Sustained Theme   132
    Applications Across PreK–12   137
Conclusion   138
Equity Audit Questions   139

8   Inclusive Leadership and Religion   142
    Joanne M. Marshall

    Part 1: The Current Context of Religion in Schools   142
        History, in Brief   142
        Changing Religious Demographics and Non-Homogeneous Groups   143
        Why Religion Is a Hot-Button Issue   144
    Part 2: What We Know About Including Religion and Religious Beliefs:
        The Literature   145
        Including Religion as a Topic in the Curriculum   145
        Including Religious and Non-Religious People   147
        Intersections Across Communities: Religion and Race/Ethnicity,
            Language, and Sexual Orientation   149
    Part 3: Inclusive Leadership Around Religion   152
        Tool 1: Personal Reflection—The Spiritual Autobiography   152
        Tool 2: School-Level Religious Inclusion Equity Audit   153
        Tool 3: District-Level Analysis of Current Practices   154
        Case Studies   154
    Conclusion   157

9   Inclusive Leadership on the Social Frontiers: Family and
    Community Engagement   162
    Martin Scanlan and Lauri Johnson

    Part 1: The Current Context of Social Frontiers in Schools   163
        Intersections: Boundaries and Borders   163
        Advocacy at Intersections   164
        Boundary Spanners, Border Crossers, and Advocates   165
    Part 2: What We Know About Social Frontiers: The Literature   165
        Culturally Responsive Leadership   166
        Parent Engagement   167
        Community Engagement   168
        Intersections   169
    Part 3: Inclusive Leadership on Social Frontiers in Schools   170
        Tripping Equity Traps   170
        Fostering Relational Networks   174
        Building Partnerships   178
    Equity Audit Questions   182
    Conclusion   182

10   The Equity Audit as the Core of Leading Increasingly Diverse
     Schools and Districts   186
     Colleen A. Capper and Michelle D. Young

     Equity Audits as a Focus of Scholarship   187
         Exploring the Use of Equity Audits   187
         Preparing Leaders to Conduct Equity Audits   189
     The Equity Audit Process   190
         *Phase 1: Identifying Integrated/Inclusive Practices as Measured
             by Proportional Representation as the Anchoring Philosophy of
             the Equity Audit*   190
         Phase 2: Establishing the Team to Conduct the Equity Audit   192
         Phase 3: Designing the Audit   192
         Phase 4: Collecting and Analyzing the Data   193
         Phase 5: Setting and Prioritizing Goals Based on the Data   194
         Phase 6: Developing an Implementation Plan   195
     Conclusion   195

Appendix: Equity Audit Data Collection and Analysis   198
About the Contributors   215
Index   221

Series Editor Introduction

The series Educational Leadership for Equity and Diversity aims to publish the primary text for each Pre-K to Grade 12 educational leadership preparation course while educators in schools and districts can rely on the same books for leadership development. I am thrilled to lead off the series with this book, *Leadership for Increasingly Diverse Schools*, edited by esteemed scholars George Theoharis and Martin Scanlan. Both former successful school principals for social justice, Theoharis and Scanlan have assembled a diverse group of the foremost experts in leadership and equity in this collection that can serve as a primary text for preparation courses and leadership development to eliminate educational inequities.

We have learned from research and school and district equity data that responding to increasingly diverse schools by adding special diversity programs and remedial initiatives that circulate around a fundamentally white, middle/upper class culturally unresponsive core instruction does not work. Instead, leading for equity and diversity demands that leaders must rethink and fundamentally transform the entire school/district system:

- from believing that equity pertains to only certain matters in the school to viewing all decisions from an equity lens; to disrupting deficit thinking and replacing that with assets-based perspectives about students and families; to dismantling the myriad of uncoordinated committees and teams, to creating only a leadership team and grade level teams to facilitate the work;
- from promulgating special programs, special classrooms, and pullout programs to reassigning all students and staff to heterogeneous, proportionally representative classrooms and courses; and
- from special education teachers co-teaching with general educators to teams of special education, general education, bilingual, reading, and gifted teachers co-planning and co-educating all students; to redesigning the curriculum to be rigorous, authentic, culturally responsive, and universally designed; to merging funding and policy in support of all students; to changing staff hiring, development, and evaluation to align with this work.

As such, leading for equity and diversity demands that educational leaders must become experts across the range of student differences. These leaders cannot pick and choose which inequities they will address in their schools and which they will ignore. Leaders cannot also delegate or rely on other school or district colleagues to fill their own knowledge/skill gaps when these colleagues themselves may be entrenched and socialized in the historical sort and slot deficit mentality of "dealing with" school diversity.

To meet this demand, this book tackles a fundamental challenge when leading for equity and diversity: how to eliminate inequities across the range of student differences and their intersections. Importantly, many leaders may have strong leadership skills related to one area of difference (e.g., the inclusion and achievement of students with disabilities), but may not be as skilled in other areas of difference (e.g., the education and integration of students who are culturally and linguistically diverse). Related to this, a leader may have confidence in supporting students who are lesbian, gay, bisexual, or transgender (LGBT), yet may not know how to support LGBT students of color whose needs may be different from white LGBT students.

At the same time, most schools and districts promote mission statements that aim for goals such as "achievement of all students." Yet, the outcomes of previous reform efforts and research and equity data show that when, with good intentions, we aim for "all" in equity work without distinguishing among student differences with equity data, goals, or strategies, invariably, white middle/upper class, heterosexual English-speaking students without disabilities benefit the most and, typically, marginalized students are left further behind.

This book breaks this inequitable reform cycle, each chapter providing potential and practicing leaders with not only the literature and research base to support their equity efforts but also a plethora of practical strategies, tools, case studies, and guiding discussion questions that will enable preparation faculty and district leaders to put to immediate use. Each chapter addresses a unique aspect of student identity and at the same time addresses issues and solutions for responding to intersecting differences with that identity. For example, readers will learn the importance of including students with disabilities, and how to do so, and also how to respond to inequities related to the overrepresentation of students of color in special education, or the fact that students of color with disabilities are more often segregated from their peers compared to white students with disabilities. As such, this groundbreaking, seminal text sets the tone and the bar for the Educational Leadership for Equity and Diversity Series to lead the transformation of leadership preparation and development to eliminate inequities.

Colleen A. Capper, Series Editor
University of Wisconsin–Madison

Foreword

The scholarship on leadership is increasingly addressing diversity and equity issues (Tillman & Scheurich, 2013). This is a welcome trend considering the demographic imperative that school systems around the nation face in the XXI century. The urgency of this challenge is heightened by the differential educational outcomes across groups of students that have been documented for decades. Nevertheless, there are substantial limitations in the ways in which diversity has been taken up in the leadership scholarship (Kozleski & Artiles, 2012). Theoharis and Scanlan's edited book makes an excellent contribution to this field of study and it stands out for tackling such limitations. There are at least five distinctive features that distinguish this volume from the bulk of the leadership literature related to diversity. These are (a) framing the volume with an inclusive systems standpoint that is mindful of multiple perspectives, (b) conceptualizing the idea of diversity through a cultural lens, (c) foregrounding intersectional analyses, (d) using conceptual tools that situate identities in cultural historical contexts, and (e) structuring the book with pedagogical tools informed by social constructivist considerations to maximize content learning. I outline these features in the subsequent paragraphs.

Theoharis and Scanlan conceived this volume on leadership for increasingly diverse schools from the perspective of inclusive educational systems. This is a key strength of the volume for several reasons. For instance, the authors did not fall on the trap of limiting leadership for diversity to the creation of initiatives to "fix" learners from subordinate groups. Instead, consistent with an inclusive perspective, the authors argued for the reconfiguration of the entire educational system to be responsive to human variability. An additional strength is that the idea of inclusive education is not limited to learners with disabilities, as we tend to find in the literature on this topic from around the world (Artiles, Kozleski, & Waitoller, 2011). In contrast, the authors challenge us to engage the notion of inclusive education in its broadest connotation so that people, practices, and policies (with their attendant institutional dimensions) are considered. Finally, the authors approached the discussions of various topics from alternative perspectives—administrators, teachers, families, communities, as well as schools and districts. The deliberate attention to the interlocking of schools with districts as a core unit of analysis in inclusive education systems is an important contribution to the inclusive education literature (Kozleski & King Thorius, 2013).

Second, Theoharis and Scanlan's volume transcends the limits of the traditional leadership scholarship that defines diversity in terms of fixed personal characteristics. Such an approach reflects a superficial and often deficit orientation to the idea of diversity that frequently leads to calls for remedial programs that promise to fix what is lacking among diverse individuals and groups. This canonical view neglects the dynamic *cultural dimension* embedded in people's lives. This dimension includes the cultural (material) practices, beliefs, tools and the like that are linked to ethnic, social class, gender and other identity traits. The book is organized around core markers of diversity—disability, social class, race, English learners, LGBTQ, gender, religion—but attention is given to the cultural aspects of these identities. A more dynamic culturally-based perspective on diversity also calls for an acknowledgement of the considerable heterogeneity distributed *within* groups. That is, although members of identity groups share cultural assumptions, practices, beliefs, etc., there is also substantial variability among members of these groups (Artiles, 2015). This is an important reflection for traditional understandings of diversity in the leadership literature tend to assume seamless homogeneity within identity groups. Traditional interventions, therefore, compel leaders to offer distinctive responses according to group membership, since *all* members of such groups are presumed to share the same traits, behaviors, beliefs, etc.—e.g., there are curricular models for English learners, empowerment strategies for girls, and so forth. The authors in this volume challenge the "group unity equals group uniformity" logic commonly found in the leadership literature (Hancock, 2007, p. 65).

The third distinctive feature of Theoharis and Scanlan's volume is closely aligned with the previous one. Just as the book is conceptualized to focus on major identity categories that mediate educational opportunity and stratification, the authors also account for people's intersectional identities. Students are not only racial or beings labeled with disabilities. Likewise, individuals are not defined solely by their social class or sexual orientation. A major trend in this literature is the isolation of people's traits to examine diversity issues and their implications for educational equity. However, an intersectional lens enables us to account for students' multidimensional identities. This framework allows us to debunk the implicit assumption that markers of difference are mutually exclusive categories of everyday experiences—e.g., analysts focus on either racial or gender issues only (Crenshaw, 1989). This means that intersectionality challenges us to transcend essentialist perspectives on people's identity that stress analyses of single axes of experience (Artiles, 2013). Crenshaw explained that *structural* intersectionality reminds us that the location of particular intersections mediates people's experiences in qualitatively unique ways—thus, for example, the meanings, consequences, and correlates of race, gender and social class create unique educational experiences for individuals living at these intersections vis-à-vis the experiences of their counterparts—e.g., boys of color from low income homes with disabilities compared to white middle class boys without disabilities. *Political* intersectionality, in turn, enables us to understand how identity groups pursue their own political agendas, and that a person's intersectional identities could have conflicting agendas. This fragmentation of political drive can contribute to intersectional disempowerment (Crenshaw, 1989). The contributors to Theoharis and Scanlan's book engage issues of intersectionality that shed light on structural and political aspects of this construct. This is an urgently needed perspective in the leadership scholarship.

A fourth complementary feature of this volume is that discussions and analyses of student identities and their intersections are grounded in interdisciplinary theories of identity formation and performance in cultural historical contexts. These include communities of practice, culturally responsive pedagogy, and funds of knowledge, among others. This is a unique strength of this volume for these theoretical frameworks contextualize the implicit psychological bias of early identity theories with an attention to cultural practices.

The result is a perspective that acknowledges the historical gravity of identity markers that shape educational opportunity—disability, social class, race, language, sexual orientation, gender, religion—while it situates the analytical spotlight on the institutional contexts in which these students live, work, and learn. Few scholars in the leadership field have attempted this theoretical move and I commend the editors and contributors for striving to do it.

The fifth distinctive feature of Theoharis and Scanlan's edited book is its structure. The volume is well grounded in inclusive education, diversity and intersectionality, with several subsequent chapters focusing on various identities. This allows readers to have a conceptual foundation that informs discussions of these various identities. In so doing, each of these chapters covers three core sections, namely the research literature, the contemporary contexts of the topic under discussion, and the heart of each of these chapters is devoted to inclusive leadership considerations as applied to the target intersectional identity. The first two sections have a powerful pedagogical force as they enable readers to learn the state of the art on the topic, but contextualize such insights in the current conditions under which the work is being done. The discussion of inclusive leadership in each chapter is full of pedagogical resources that enable readers to engage personally as well as professionally with the topics. Case studies, reflection exercises, equity audits, and the like are included in this section. The goal of balancing theoretical considerations, with personal reflections, and professional considerations of the rich contexts of practice is obvious and compelling. In-depth examinations of family/community engagement and equity audits are included at the end of the volume and can be approached as additional considerations and equity tools for leadership practice.

In conclusion, this edited volume makes a significant contribution to the leadership literature by virtue of its strong theoretical grounding, its innovative framing of the complex dimensions of diversity, and the outstanding pedagogical resources embedded throughout the chapters. Of significance, the authors are to be commended for challenging us to engage diversity as the quintessential trait of human beings, and to organize educational institutions so that the diversity of the human condition is used as a resource for learning and educational opportunity.

Alfredo J. Artiles,
Arizona State University

REFERENCES

Artiles, A. J. (2013). Untangling the racialization of disabilities: An intersectionality critique across disability models. *DuBois Review, 10*, 329–347.

Artiles, A. J. (2015). Beyond responsiveness to identity badges: Future research on culture in disability and implications for RTI. *Educational Review, 67*(1), 1–22.

Artiles, A. J., Kozleski, E., & Waitoller, F. (Eds.). (2011). *Inclusive education: Examining equity on five continents*. Cambridge, MA: Harvard Education Press.

Crenshaw, K. (1989). Demarginalizing the intersection of race and sex: A Black feminist critique of antidiscrimination doctrine, feminist theory, and antiracist politics. *University of Chicago Legal Forum, 140*, 139–167.

Hancock, A. (2007). When multiplication doesn't equal quick addition: Examining intersectionality as a research paradigm. *Perspectives on Politics, 5*, 63–79.

Kozleski, E. B., & Artiles, A. J. (Eds.). (2012). In the smelter: Leading special education in an era of systems redesign. *Journal of Special Education Leadership, 25*(1).

Kozleski, E. B., & King Thorius, K. (2013). *Ability, equity, and culture: Sustaining inclusive urban education reform*. New York: Teachers College Press.

Tillman, L., & Scheurich, J. J. (2013). *Handbook of research on educational leadership for equity and diversity*. Newbury Park, CA: Sage.

Preface

Each individual is a complex, wondrous being. So it comes as no surprise that when we cluster together—such as within classrooms and schools—this complexity is compounded exponentially. This is part of what makes the profession of education at once tremendously fulfilling and perennially frustrating.

We each have multiple aspects of our identities—from race and ethnicity, to gender, to culture and language, to belief systems, to sexual orientation, to social and economic class, to exceptionalities, abilities, and disabilities. Some of these dimensions are readily apparent, others ambiguous, and still others hidden. Since learning is a process that engages our identity (Wenger, 1998), these multiple aspects matter. The context of this diversity presents educators with a dilemma: How do we meet each student's particular needs? How do we ensure that all enjoy ample opportunities to learn? Whether we are teachers or principals or district-level administrators, we wrestle with differentiation.

Effectively educating a diverse population is an old and historic challenge. Indeed, part of the original impetus toward forming a system of public schooling in the United States was a desire to bring unity to culturally, linguistically, and economically heterogeneous masses (Katz, 1987). Schools have always struggled, as organizations, to meet all students' needs. As Deschenes, Cuban, and Tyack (2001) put it, children who perform poorly have been seen as mismatches: "Historically, students, families, inefficiency in schools, and cultural difference have been identified as the sources for failure. In different ways, each of these explanations points to the mismatch between certain groups of students and their schools" (p. 534). Schools have traditionally tried to meet these students needs through separate programs, separate classrooms, and separate schools (Frattura & Capper, 2007).

In this book we address this old challenge of effectively educating a diverse population from the opposite standpoint, focusing on inclusive structures and processes to meet all students' needs. The book is written for school leaders. School leaders include both those with positional authority, such as administrators and department chairs, as well as those with relational authority, such as master teachers who have earned the respect of colleagues.

The goal of the book is to help school leaders build the capacity of their school communities to meet students' diverse needs *inclusively*. Inclusion is increasingly recognized as a human right. A recent report by the United Nations speaks to this:

> Inclusion requires the recognition of all children as full members of society and the respect of all of their rights, regardless of age, gender, ethnicity, language, poverty or impairment. Inclusion involves the removal of barriers that might prevent the enjoyment of these rights, and requires the creation of appropriate supportive and protective environments.
>
> (UNICEF, 2007, p. 1)

The premise of the book is straightforward: schools best serve the common good by eliminating marginalization across students' multiple dimensions of diversity. Thus, the purpose of the book is to help school leaders deepen their knowledge, skills, and dispositions to create such schools. We purposefully argue that seeking to eliminate marginalization requires action, and thus this book contains ideas and strategies for leadership practice.

STRUCTURE

The book is structured to help you look broadly across multiple dimensions of diversity, as well as deeply into each of these. The intent is to foster your appreciation for how these dimensions intersect. As a school leader, it's important to think about how students from diverse races are experiencing your school, and how students with different disabilities and exceptionalities are experiencing your school. But critically, it's important to consider the ways that these aspects of identity intersect. The first chapter introduces this notion.

The eight chapters that form the heart of the book (Chapters 2–9) dig into specific dimensions of diversity: disability, language, race, socioeconomic status, sexual orientation, gender, religion, and social frontiers. Each chapter begins with a background on the context (Part 1) and continues with a summary of empirical literature highlighting best practices with regards to that area of diversity (Part 2). Then, the bulk of each chapter is dedicated to describing the leader's role in creating inclusive schools and districts, highlighting specific tools and strategies to support this work as well as providing examples from the field of what this looks like (Part 3).

In Chapter 2, "Inclusive Leadership and Disability," George Theoharis (Syracuse University), Julie Causton (Syracuse University), and Casey Woodfield (Syracuse University) describe how school leaders are instrumental figures in creating and carrying out a vision for inclusive schools for students with disabilities. Each year since students with disabilities were guaranteed the right to a free and appropriate public education, more students with disabilities are being educated in general education schools and classrooms. Inclusion has evolved over time and increasingly schools are giving students with disabilities access to rich academic instruction, connection to their peers, and full membership in their schools and communities. This, in conjunction with the new era of standards where schools and districts are being held increasingly accountable for the achievement of students with disabilities, has created the need to focus on inclusive leadership with regards to special education. This chapter examines strategies and guiding principles for leaders to create inclusive schools and districts for all students regardless of ability/disability including: school/district policy, service delivery, school structures and staffing, and classroom practices.

In Chapter 3, "Inclusive Leadership and Poverty," Curt Dudley-Marling (Boston College) and Anne Dudley-Marling (University of Dayton) address the issue of students living in poverty. The scarcity of living-wage jobs, the inaccessibility of health care, hunger: these are the challenges low-income families overcome in order simply to attend school. Even in the face of *savage* inequities (e.g., in access to licensed teachers, learning materials, higher-level pedagogies) and despite deficit chatter painting them as incapable, low-income families demonstrate incredible resilience. Still, popular approaches to class equity in schools are focused largely upon remedying perceived deficiencies in low-income communities rather than on drawing from the rich experiences—the "cultural funds"—of low-income communities for insights into how we might remedy educational inequities. This chapter discusses the critical shift from a "deficit" approach to a "cultural funds" approach to class-equitable education and how school leaders can enact this shift. In addition, this chapter can help us to learn about the larger enactment of just leadership and practice by observing the resilience of low-income families.

In Chapter 4, "Inclusive Leadership and Race," Sonya Douglass Horsford (George Mason University) and Christine Clark (University of Nevada, Las Vegas) discuss why racial inequality persists in US education and how flawed conceptions of race undermine efforts to improve academic achievement for all students. Most importantly, it puts forth the concept of racial literacy courageous conversations, as well as other practical approaches to improving school leadership practices and their implications for student learning and achievement in racially diverse school communities.

In Chapter 5, "Inclusive Leadership and English Learners," Isabel Kelsey (University of Arizona), Carmen Campuzano (Davis Bilingual Magnet School), and Francesca López (University of Arizona) describe team and instruction practices that support an inclusive education for English learners (ELs). An increasing number of schools and districts are replacing separate means of providing services, such as segregated pullout classes and teaching English as a separate subject, with more inclusive learning supports, such as co-teaching in heterogeneous general education classes and teaching English through academic content. This chapter provides a multi-faceted rationale for this reform and outlines what has been learned in the experience of several school districts across the nation. It examines the factors that contribute to creating and sustaining successful inclusive and collaborative models for supporting learning of ELs.

We then turn to dimensions of diversity that are no less important, but often addressed much less: sexual orientation, gender, religion, and social frontiers. Since schools are *not* required to report out on these dimensions with the same level of transparency, these dimensions are more frequently ignored. Yet inclusive leadership demands that they be addressed as well.

In Chapter 6, "Inclusive Leadership and Lesbian, Gay, Bisexual, Transgendered, and Questioning Students," Frank Hernandez (University of Texas, Permian Basin) and Don Fraynd (TeacherMatch) focus on students who identify as lesbian, gay, bisexual, transgendered, or questioning (LGBTQ). This chapter (by a school administrator and a professor who both are openly gay) expands the discussion on what it means to lead for social justice by focusing specifically on changes that need to occur for leaders to meet the needs of LGBTQ students.

In Chapter 7, "Inclusive Leadership and Gender," Margaret Grogan (Claremont Graduate University) and Shamini Dias (Claremont Graduate University) address gender. Gender plays a key role in K–12 schools and impacts the lived reality of students and adults in schools. Grogan and Dias provide a sharp focus on dismantling female stereotypes and inequities. This chapter discusses the ways gender is played out in schools and ways in which leaders can enact gender inclusivity.

In Chapter 8, "Inclusive Leadership and Religion," Joanne Marshall (Iowa State University) discusses the often ignored dimension of diversity: religious identity. Since US schooling is rooted historically in Protestant Christianity and about 75% of the US adult population currently identifies as Christian, it is not surprising that some school practices explicitly or implicitly privilege Christianity. This chapter provides examples of how Christianity is the norm within schools, analytical questions social justice leaders can ask about the practices embedded in their own schools, and suggestions for making schools more inclusive around religion. Social justice leaders can be religiously inclusive without violating the religion clauses of the First Amendment.

In Chapter 9, "Inclusive Leadership on the Social Frontiers," Martin Scanlan (Marquette University) and Lauri Johnson (Boston College) link inclusive schooling with broader connections to families and community members. This chapter is not about a specific area of difference within students in K–12 schools, but in differences in systems/agencies that serve those students. A key aspect of 21st-century inclusivity is working cross-sectors between schools and other agencies and among groups of agencies working with K–12 students and their families.

Conclusion

We conclude with Chapter 10, "The Equity Audit as the Core of Leading Increasingly Diverse Schools and Districts." Here Colleen A. Capper (University of Wisconsin–Madison) and Michelle D. Young (University of Virginia) describe how the equity audit provides a core practice for enacting inclusive social justice leadership. This chapter serves to synthesize Chapters 2–9 to provide a comprehensive equity audit tool. We urge readers to use this tool.

KEY FEATURES

This book aspires to help you see the intersectionalities inherent to the pursuit of social justice schooling by balancing breadth with depth. A key strength of this book—one that we wish to highlight here—is that these chapters bring together diverse voices within this common theme of inclusive leadership. The perennial risk of creating an edited volume is ending up with an amalgamation that lacks cohesion. But the *possibility* it provides is uniting a rich array of voices. We contend that this diversity of perspectives is necessary for accomplishing the work of inclusive leadership.

Woven into each chapter you will find tools and strategies as well as case studies highlighting individual school leaders. The tools and strategies serve to provide concrete guidance for action, while the case studies are intended to help you ground the ideas presented in concrete narratives. As you read, attend to both of these aspects—the characteristics of the leaders and the leadership practices.

Finally, complementing each chapter is an online companion with links to specific tools described in the chapter, references, documents, and extensions. This companion website is intended as a flexible tool to engage you in your leadership practice and link you with companions who are committed to leading toward socially just schooling.

We hope this book with help you learn to engage in leadership practices leading toward more inclusive, socially just schooling. This is both necessary and urgent work.

REFERENCES

Deschenes, S., Cuban, L., & Tyack, D. (2001). Mismatch: Historical perspectives on schools and students who don't fit them. *Teachers College Record, 103*(4), 525–547.

Frattura, E., & Capper, C. (2007). *Leadership for social justice in practice: Integrated comprehensive services for all learners*. Thousand Oaks, CA: Corwin Press.

Guinier, L. (2004). From racial liberalism to racial literacy: Brown v. Board of Education and the interest-divergence dilemma. *Journal of American History, 91*(1), 92–118.

Katz, M. (1987). *Reconstructing American education*. Cambridge, MA: Harvard University Press.

UNICEF. (2007). *Promoting the rights of children with disabilities*. Florence, Italy: The United Nations Children's Fund (UNICEF).

Wenger, E. (1998). *Communities of practice: Learning, meaning, and identity*. New York, NY: Cambridge University Press.

Acknowledgments

School leadership for equity and diversity requires a bold vision, significant knowledge and skills, as well as collaboration of many people. We want to thank and offer our gratitude to school leaders who engage in the tiring, often thankless but essential work of creating more inclusive schools. Over our careers of working on equity issues relating to the many areas of difference, we know that as schools and as a society we do not move toward a more equitable education system without school leadership. We appreciate those who work day in and day out to seek this goal.

While we had a vision of a book that centered leadership for increasingly diverse schools in the ideals and practices of equity, inclusivity and social justice, this book is the product of a wealth of knowledge and collaboration with an esteemed group of scholars. We want to show our deepest sense of gratitude to the chapter authors whose expertise and understanding of equity makes this book come alive and provides school leaders with essential knowledge. We so appreciate the work of Carmen Campuzano, Colleen A. Capper, Julie Causton, Christine Clark, Shamini Dias, Sonya Douglass Horsford, Anne Dudley-Marling, Curt Dudley-Marling, Don Fraynd, Margaret Grogan, Frank Hernandez, Lauri Johnson, Isabel Kelsey, Francesca López, Joanne M. Marshall, Casey Woodfield, and Michelle D. Young who created such rich and useful chapters.

We thank Colleen A. Capper, the series editor, for encouraging us to do this book and publish it as part of the Educational Leadership for Equity and Diversity Series. In addition to her insightful and exacting editing, we appreciate how Colleen's work and mentorship teaches us and the larger field that issues of equity and justice are inseparable from educational leadership theory and practice.

We appreciate the on-going support, suggestions, and guidance of Heather Jarrow, Samuel Huber, and the impressive team at Routledge/Taylor and Francis Group. Given that we ground this book in the idea that leadership needs to purposefully engage areas of difference in specific and intersecting ways that have not been central to the history of the field, we thank them for making this work better, consistently structured, and a part of the education leadership discussion.

We hold a deep sense of appreciation and gratitude to the larger communities of scholars that have both supported this work and nourished us professionally. We are motivated and enriched to be in the company of Leslie Hazel Bussey, Madeline Hafner, Latish Reed, Sharon Radd, Jeff Brooks, Doug Biklen, Marcelle Haddix, John Rogers, Nancy Cantor, Gretchen Lopez, Tim Eatman, Tara Affolter, Steve Hoffman, Deb Hoffman, Pete Miller, Rich Halverson, and Catherine Lugg.

Finally, families—both immediate and extended—who keep us grounded in the importance of family time, morning routines, school activities, seeking a better educational system for those who have been left behind, and expanding opportunities for each and every child. Thank you for your care and time to encourage, support, push, eat, and play with us.

CHAPTER 1

Introduction

Intersectionality in Educational Leadership

Martin Scanlan and George Theoharis

In the 21st century, elementary and secondary school communities are growing more pluralistic across multiple dimensions of diversity, such as race, ethnicity, language, religion, sexual orientation, and socioeconomic status (Taylor, 2014). Schools in the United States have historically responded to dimensions of diversity by privileging some and marginalizing others. Dimensions of diversity that have enjoyed privilege include being White, of European heritage, of moderate to high socioeconomic status, Christian, heterosexual, native English speaking, and without disability. By contrast, dimensions of diversity that have been marginalized include being of color; of non-European heritage; of low socioeconomic status; non-Christian; lesbian, gay, bisexual, transgender, or questioning (LGBTQ); of limited proficiency in English; or with a special need or disability. If schools are to serve the common good and promote social justice, school leaders need the knowledge, skills, and dispositions to create schools that eliminate marginalization across these multiple dimensions of diversity. The purpose of this book is to help leaders accomplish this.

CORE EXPECTATIONS OF SCHOOL LEADERS

Across sectors (public, private) and regions (urban, suburban, rural), schools consistently fail to provide equitable educational opportunities to students across these dimensions of diversity (Deschenes, Cuban, & Tyack, 2001; Duncan & Murnane, 2011; Gamoran & Long, 2006). School leaders—including both those with positional authority, such as school principals, department chairs, and formal teacher leaders, as well as those lacking positional authority who are viewed as leaders by peers, such as revered teachers—play a central role in eliminating these educational inequities. Effective school leaders set directions for school communities to be academically ambitious and ensure that the organizational structures support these ambitions—such as by building the instructional capacity of the faculty and staff and including various stakeholders (e.g., teachers, parents) in decision-making (Leithwood & Riehl, 2005). While school leaders are key drivers of organizational learning

(Bryk, Sebring, Allensworth, Luppescu, & Easton, 2010), effective leadership is not a solitary charge, but rather a collective enterprise engaging multiple individuals (Darling-Hammond, LaPointe, Meyerson, Orr, & Cohen, 2007). It entails scaffolding structures and routines across the school community.

Social Justice and Leadership Standards

Generally speaking, standards of the field—the Interstate School Leaders Licensure Consortium (ISLLC) Standards (Council of Chief State School Officers, 2008, 2014)—charge school leaders with engaging in an array of responsibilities. The ISLLC Standards are valuable in articulating the leadership responsibilities in broad brushstrokes (Table 1.1, column 1). However, they have historically fallen short of providing concrete guidance for school leaders on how to carry out these responsibilities through the lens of social justice (Table 1.1, column 2).

By fleshing out these distinctions, this book provides school leaders clear, cogent guidance for enacting social justice leadership. We assert that these social justice distinctions are not peripheral, but rather are core aspects of school leadership in increasingly diverse schools. Consider the ISLLC 2008 Standard, involving a vision for learning in the

Table 1.1 Extending ISLLC Standards to Social Justice Leadership

2008 ISLLC Standards★	Distinctions of social justice leadership
1. Setting a widely shared vision for learning	• Vision foregrounds a critical analysis of educational inequities and the intersectionality of these across multiple dimensions of diversity
2. Developing a school culture and instructional program conducive to student learning and staff professional growth	• School culture and instructional program are inclusive, students across areas of difference have authentic access to heterogeneous peers and the core instruction, affirming each student as an integral member of the school community
3. Ensuring effective management of the organization, operation, and resources for a safe, efficient, and effective learning environment	• Learning environment integrates the delivery of support services into the classrooms; prioritizing access and opportunity over separation
4. Collaborating with faculty and community members, responding to diverse community interests and needs, and mobilizing community resources	• Faculty and staff embrace shared responsibility for the education of all students, building capacity to collectively and collaboratively meet each students' needs; families and community members are engaged in authentic partnerships
5. Acting with integrity, fairness, and in an ethical manner	• Ethical commitment places emphasis on eliminating educational inequities and eliminating structural "isms"
6. Understanding, responding to, and influencing the political, social, legal, and cultural contexts	• Prioritizing the provision of educational opportunities for all students across these contexts

★Council of Chief State School Officers (2008).

school. Socially just school leaders do not first focus on cultivating this vision, and then consider how issues of race, ethnicity, language, religion, socioeconomic status, disability, gender, and sexual orientation fit into it. Rather, eliminating marginalization and promoting educational opportunities for all is central to the vision. In a similar manner, each of these standards needs to be tuned and refined by school leaders to place a preferential option on those who are marginalized.

As this book was being published, the ISLLC Standards were in the process of being reauthorized (Council of Chief State School Officers, 2014). Preliminary drafts suggest that the reauthorized standards place more emphasis on the interconnections of community, justice, and school improvement, as well as on cultural relevance. For instance, several additional standards are included in this revision, including one emphasizing communities of engagement for families and another emphasizing equity and cultural responsiveness. We are encouraged that the standards of the field of school leadership seem to be evolving in this manner. This underscores the relevance of this book for future educational leaders.

Another way of making this point is to say that enacting social justice is a holistic endeavor. Social justice leadership entails attending simultaneously not only to the multiple dimensions of diversity, but also to multiple aspects of leadership: from student achievement to school structures to curriculum and instruction to culture and community (Theoharis, 2007). Teachers have the most direct influence on student learning, since they are at the heart of the instructional core—the intersection of teachers, students, and content. By influencing teachers and the conditions of the schools in which teachers work, school leaders affect student learning (Wahlstrom, Louis, Leithwood, & Anderson, 2010). Since school leaders are increasingly held accountable for the academic outcomes of *all* students, school leaders must be mindful of and responsive to how these multiple dimensions of diversity *intersect* with one another in manners that affect student learning (Scanlan & Theoharis, 2014).

What Does Social Justice Leadership Look Like?

One way to summarize these core expectations of school leaders is to say that effective leaders engage in practices that create socially just schooling. Socially just schooling is evident when educational opportunities abound for all students, when ambitious academic goals are held and met by all students, when all students and families are made to feel welcome in the school community, when students are proportionately distributed across all groupings in the school, and when one dimension of identity (such as one's race or home language or gender or sexual orientation) does not directly correlate with undesirable aspects of schooling (such as being bullied, struggling academically, or dropping out of school). As these outcomes suggest, socially just schooling is both a tangible reality that one can describe and create, and at the same time an ideal goal to which we are always aspiring. In this sense, it is analogous to our personal health. We can at once be accurately described as a healthy person while at the same time recognize that there are aspects of our health that can be improved. So too with socially just schooling. We can point to schools as exemplars and at the same time recognize within these exemplars areas for continued growth and improvement.

One way to parse social justice school leadership is across four outcomes: (a) raising student achievement, (b) improving school structures, (c) recentering and enhancing staff capacity, and (d) strengthening school culture and community (Theoharis, 2007). Empirical literature addressing the intersectionality of various dimensions of diversity (namely race, ethnicity, language, religion, sexual orientation, and socioeconomic status) addresses each of these outcomes.

First, raising student achievement—as evidenced by multiple measures of student learning outcomes—is often a core objective for leaders focusing on these various dimensions of diversity. Federal legislation—such as Title IX, the No Child Left Behind Act of 2001 (NCLB), and the Individuals with Disabilities Education Improvement Act of 2004 (IDEA 2004)—have directly spurred schools to attempt to develop rigorous academic environments that expect and foster high achievement for all. Results are mixed. For instance, despite significant gains by girls in the areas of math and physics in K–12 settings that have resulted in parity with boys (Hyde & Lindberg, 2007), gender inequities persist (Grogan & Dias, this volume). As another example, school leaders are increasingly focused on how all learners—regardless of disability labels—can meet high academic standards (Hardman & Dawson, 2008), yet students with such labels continue to be underserved, and disability labels continue to be disproportionately assigned to students of color (Artiles & Klingner, 2006; Artiles, Rueda, Salazar, & Higareda, 2005).

Second, school structures—particularly those shaping service delivery—directly affect the degree to which students' needs are met holistically. We know school leaders drive organizational change around school structures (Bryk, Sebring, et al., 2010) and that the integrated arrangement of these services is essential for maximizing student achievement and belonging (Frattura & Capper, 2007).

Third, the literature directs school leaders in recentering and enhancing staff capacity. For instance, research shows that school leaders can build the capacity of all teachers to effectively educate culturally and linguistically diverse students through integrating language supports into general education settings (Scanlan & López, 2012, 2014). Clearly, it is important for leaders to know this and to facilitate it happening.

Finally, the literature shows that addressing intersectionality is tied directly to the broader structures of strengthening the school culture and community. This entails building partnerships across dimensions of diversity, such as race and ethnicity (Horsford, 2011) as well as school / family / community (Auerbach, 2012; Warren, 2005; Warren & Mapp, 2011).

PURSUING SOCIALLY JUST SCHOOLING: LEADERSHIP *PRACTICES*

To aid the pursuit of socially just schooling, this book focuses on leadership *practices*, not just characteristics of leaders. To enact socially just school leadership it is essential to develop knowledge, skills, or dispositions. But these are not simply characteristics that leaders either have or don't have. They can be learned. Leaders need to enact these in manners that are responsive to the dynamic context of the local school community. Leadership *practices*— what leaders *do*—matter most. Put differently, to create socially just schooling, we must develop social justice leadership practices.

Throughout this book the authors detail specific socially just leadership *practices*. Each chapter contains both key leader characteristics—knowledge, skills, and dispositions—as well as leadership practices. We recognize that skills and practices might appear to be the same or at least similar. We see skills as having the ability to do something and practices as the work / strategies / structures that leaders actually do.

Leaders need to attend to both characteristics and practices. It's not enough to simply develop certain characteristics as a socially just school leader and then presume to be enacting socially just leadership practices. Socially just school leaders can be characterized as many things, including critically reflective, courageous, innovative, and bold. But as we all know, certain characteristics are manifest at times but hidden at others. We are critically reflective in certain situations, while in other contexts we act unreflectively. We are some-times courageous and at other times timid. We act in innovative or bold manners on some occasions and in pedestrian or shy manners on others. The intent of this book is not to sim-ply focus on whether you are or are not a "socially just school leader," but rather to support you, as a school leader, to strengthen your leadership practices toward socially just ends.

This book attempts to balance a broad look across multiple dimensions of diversity with a deep look into each. Woven into the third part of each chapter you will find tools and strategies as well as small case studies highlighting individual school leaders. The tools and strategies serve to provide concrete guidance for action, while the cases are intended to help you ground the ideas presented in concrete narratives. As you read, attend to both of these aspects—the characteristics of the leaders and the leadership practices.

FOSTERING COMMUNITIES OF PRACTICE

A final notion to consider as you read this book is that you do not learn to engage in social justice leadership practices as an isolated individual, but rather within communities of prac-tice. The sociocultural learning theory of communities of practice (COPs) holds that much of what we learn occurs through purposeful interactions with others (Lave & Wenger, 1991; Wenger, 1998). We do not learn primarily as isolated individuals. Rather, our learning is powerfully affected by those around us as well as by contextual influences. The learning theory of COPs is congruent with and, we would argue, directly supportive of and a pre-requisite for social justice leadership (Scanlan, 2013).

What Are COPs?

A productive way to think about COPs is in terms of three dimensions: what, who, and how (see Table 1.2). The first question is: What are we learning to pursue? This aspect, described as the "joint enterprise," articulates the key purpose of learning that unites members. The second question is: Who is engaged in this learning? This aspect, described as "mutual engagement," defines the parameters of membership. Some individuals are central, others are peripheral. Some are on trajectories inward, some outward. Regard-less of positioning and direction, all are engaged with one another in the shared learning pursuit. The third question is: How are we pursuing this? This aspect, described as the "shared repertoire," identifies the tools, artifacts, stories, and other means through which we learn the pursuit.

In Table 1.2 we use the lighthearted (and, for Martin, true to life) example of learning to homebrew to illustrate the concept of COPs. Martin is a homebrewer, and he learns

Table 1.2 Community of Practice: Homebrewing

Joint Enterprise	*Mutual Engagement*	*Shared Repertoire*
What are we learning to pursue?	*Who is engaged in this learning?*	*How are we pursuing this? (a few examples)*
How to brew beer	Homebrewers - Face-to-face and virtually - Informally and formally	- Swapping recipes - Sharing equipment - Discussing (and imbibing) successes and failures

how to do this with and from others. The joint enterprise (column 1) is learning to brew beer. Those who are mutually engaged in this pursuit (column 2) are homebrewers. Notice that there are many ways in which one might meet fellow members of this COP—both face-to-face and virtually (such as through an online forum or listserv), both informally and formally (such as through a local homebrewing club). Through all these means, home-brewers share a repertoire allowing them to pursue this craft, a few examples of which are provided (column 3).

As this example suggests, discussing a COP is not synonymous with identifying membership in a formal grouping. The COP of homebrewers is more than simply a list of who belongs to the homebrew club. The concept is more expansive, describing the relationships that influence our learning. Some key members of the COP may also be card-carrying members of the local chapter of Homebrewers United, while others may not (Martin isn't). The concept of COPs is also fluid. For instance, whom one person identifies as key in a COP of homebrewers might be somewhat different from whom others identify. For instance, Martin may be good friends with Javier, who also homebrews. Javier and Martin might talk homebrewing all the time, and Martin may be learning a lot from Javier. Javier is clearly a part of Martin's homebrewing COP (and vice versa). Unlike Martin, however, Javier may also be an avid member of Homebrewers United, and learning a lot from his fellow club members. Consequently, they would be considered central members of Javier's COP, but peripheral, or even non-members, of Martin's COP.

Who Belongs to My Social Justice Leadership COP?

Now we apply this concept of COPs to the more substantive example of school leadership for social justice (Table 1.3). Again, begin with the three core dimensions: what, who, and how. The joint enterprise (column 1) identifies *what* we are learning in our social justice leadership COP. We are learning to create, support, and sustain socially just schooling. Those who are mutually engaged in this pursuit (column 2) are fellow school leaders. Again, notice that there are many ways in which one might meet fellow members of this COP. For instance, this can happen both face-to-face (e.g., in district-level meetings, at professional development workshops) and virtually (such as through an online forum or listserv). It can happen both informally (e.g., over a cup of coffee) and formally (e.g., in a graduate class as you pursue your administrative license). Through all these means, school leaders committed to social justice develop and share a repertoire of tools, artifacts, stories, and other resources allowing them to pursue this goal, a few examples of which are provided (column 3).

Table 1.3 Community of Practice: Social Justice Leadership

Joint Enterprise	*Mutual Engagement*	*Shared Repertoire*
What are we learning to pursue?	*Who is engaged in this learning?*	*How are we pursuing this? (a few examples)*
How to create, support, and sustain socially just schooling	School leaders - Face-to-face and virtually - Informally and formally	- Sharing resources - Participating in critical friends groups - Assisting on conducting equity audits and school climate surveys

Table 1.4 Creating a COP Sociogram

Supplies: small Post-it notes, large poster or whiteboard, markers and pens

Directions:

Step 1—Begin with the question: In my role as a socially just school leader, to whom do I turn for help, advice, direction, or feedback when I am wrestling with various questions? You can pose this question in general terms, and then think about it more specifically with regards to questions about specific issues of social justice in your leadership practice. Generate an initial list of names, writing one name on each Post-it.

Step 2—After you have created an initial list, go back to each Post-it and add two details.

1. Put a shape to correspond with various roles. For instance, put a circle for a teacher, a square for an administrator, a triangle for a central-office administrator, and a diamond for "other." (Choose whatever shapes and roles seem most salient to you.)
2. Inside each shape add a number from 1 to 4 to signify the relative strength of each relationship. Use a 1 to signify a weak relationship for a person whom you don't talk with very often. Use a 4 to signify your strongest, most reliable and frequent contact to whom you turn for help, advice, direction, or feedback. Use a 2 or 3 to signify those in the middle of these two poles.

Each Post-it should now look something like these examples. Add more Post-its if more names have occurred to you in this process. Also create one Post-it with your own name on it, with a shape signifying your role.

Step 3—Place and arrange these Post-its on the poster or whiteboard, with a Post-it with your name on it in the center. With the markers, draw two double-thick lines from yourself to anyone who you rated a 4, draw one solid line from yourself to anyone you rated a 3, a dashed line to a 2, and a faint dotted line to a 1.

Step 4—Stand back and look at this initial sociogram. Consider these reflection prompts:

- What do you notice about the number of individuals you have identified, the variation of roles they represent, and the relative strength of these relationships?
- Who could be added to this sociogram if you took some of the individuals on it and asked them the same question, adding Post-its and lines to signify their contacts?
- What dimensions of diversity are hidden on this sociogram? (Think: How diverse is my network by race and ethnicity? By gender? By religion?)
- How has the composition of this sociogram changed over time? How would you like it to change in the coming year?

Just as with the previous example, describing this social justice leadership COP is not a matter of identifying who belongs to a formal group, committee, or council. The concept is expansive and flexible, striving to capture the *contours of the relational networks influencing one's learning.* So in this case, who influences your learning to pursue socially just schooling? A good way to get a sense of who is at the core of your social justice leadership COP is to begin by creating a sociogram to visually show it. In Table 1.4 we describe a process for doing this.

An activity like the one we describe here (Table 1.4) allows you to see the organic nature of COPs. The heart of this learning theory is in the people with whom we are *learning to become social justice leaders.* These may be people with whom we are in formal relationships and from whom we are supposed to be learning. For instance, maybe you are reading this book as part of a formal class in leadership preparation and are part of a cohort of students who have been working together for several semesters. Many—perhaps all—of these classmates might be on your sociogram. Or perhaps you are a new principal and have been assigned a mentor by the central office. This individual may well be on your sociogram. But the point is that these individuals with whom you are formally connected are not where you begin identifying members. These people are not a de facto COP just because of this role. Rather, the starting point is the question about who is influencing your *learning about equity and justice* (see Table 1.4, step 1): In my role as a school leader, to whom do I turn for help, advice, direction, or feedback when I am wrestling with various equity questions?

An activity like this in which you begin thinking about whom you would count as core and peripheral members of your social justice leadership COP will help you as you dig into this book. These are your peers, colleagues, confidants, friends, and allies. You want to read this book *with* them, bouncing ideas back and forth, arguing, commiserating, and critically reflecting.

What Is Our Shared Repertoire?

Return to the three aspects of COPs: the what, who, and how questions (Table 1.3). *What* you are doing is learning to create, support, and sustain socially just schooling. *Who* is helping you learn to do this is visually represented on your sociogram. The final aspect, *how* you are learning to create, support, and sustain socially just schooling, is the subject of this book. Reading this book will help you build this repertoire of tools, artifacts, stories, and other resources. Our intention is that this book is primarily a catalyst for helping you strategize.

In this book we strive to help you lead toward socially just schooling. Chapter by chapter, the authors provide clear, compelling directions for pursuing this across different dimensions of diversity. But more than this, across the book we aspire to help you think differently about your leadership—to delight and marvel in the intersectionality of identities, and to thrive on creating innovative responses that expand educational opportunities amidst this rich diversity.

Building Networked Social Justice Communities

Toward this end, we provide one example here of a meta-strategy that extends across each of the forthcoming chapters: creating a networked social justice community (Bryk, Gomez, & Grunow, 2010). Networked social justice communities are structured communities of practice that "endorse shared, precise, measureable targets" (p. 11) to address complex problems of equity practice. The strategy of forming networked social justice communities is a pragmatic step for you, as a school leader, to bear in mind as you read this book.

Networked social justice communities can be thought of as guided by three basic questions:

1. What equity problem(s) are we trying to solve?
2. Whose expertise is needed to solve these equity problems?
3. What are the social arrangements that will enable this equity work?

Corresponding to these questions, four characteristics of productive networked social justice communities emerge (see Table 1.5, row 1). First, in identifying the equity

Table 1.5 Guiding Questions and Key Characteristics of Networked Social Justice Communities

Networked Social Justice Communities ask:	*Networked Social Justice Communities are:*
1. What equity problem(s) are we trying to solve?	• Focused on well-specified common equity goals
2. Whose expertise is needed to solve these equity problems?	• Guided by a deep understanding of the equity problem and the system that produces it
3. What are the social arrangements that will enable this social justice work?	• Disciplined by the rigor of improvement science, and • Networked to develop, test, and refine tools, strategies, and interventions

Adapted from Bryk, Gomez, and Grunow (2010); Earl, Katz, Elgie, Jaafar, and Foster (2006); and Park and Takahashi (2013).

problem(s) with specificity, networked social justice communities articulate a common aim. While all COPs share this, the distinction here is in the focus on addressing an equity problem directly. Accordingly, networked social justice communities have specific, time-delineated equity goals that they are working to accomplish. Second, to identify the expertise to address the equity problem, a comprehensive equity analysis is needed (Table 1.5, row 2). These analyses lead directly to the third question—creating social arrangements to respond in transformative ways to the equity issues (Table 1.5, row 3). This response is characterized by: a) improvement science (the process of systematically gathering, analyzing, and responding to equity evidence in an iterative cycle of working toward socially just ends); and b) networking (the relational networks engaged in this equity work).

Chapter by chapter, you can use this meta-strategy to guide your analysis and response to equity issues in your setting. For the first question—what equity problem(s) are we trying to solve? (Table 1.5, row 1)—a key tool provided throughout this book is an equity audit (Frattura & Capper, 2007; Johnson & La Salle, 2010). Each chapter incorporates equity audit questions, and the final chapter provides this tool in a central and elaborated format. These are available at the companion website in editable document form as well.

For the second question—whose expertise is needed to solve these equity problems? (Table 1.5, row 2)—each chapter provides a concise overview of the particular dimension of diversity (Part 1, Current Context) and the pertinent research literature (Part 2, Literature).

For the third question—what are the social arrangements that will enable this social justice work? (Table 1.5, row 3)—each chapter provides a thorough description of leaders' roles in creating inclusive socially just schools and districts (Part 3, Inclusive Leadership). These include specific tools and strategies as well as case studies incorporating the voices and narratives of leaders. These are organized with reflection questions to guide your understanding of the issue so that you can thoughtfully identify whom you should include in addressing it. Selecting and applying these tools with the disciplined rigor of improvement sciences means that rather than implementing these tools in a haphazardly, idiosyncratic, or anecdotal manner, you are conscientiously, carefully, and thoughtfully applying them. Being networked with others in this equity work ensures that as you develop, test, and refine these tools, strategies, and interventions, you are learning with and from others.

Deliberately creating networked social justice communities is a meta-strategy in that it guides how you engage in the work of this book. It emphasizes that developing your knowledge and skills at creating, supporting, and sustaining socially just schooling is not a solitary

., but one that you must engage in with others. Further, it provides a framework for .ing this pursuit into addressing specific equity challenges in a systematic manner.

In sum, leaders must play a role in creating and maintaining schools that are inclusive of multiple areas of difference and aspects of diversity at the same time. There are moments and initiatives that foreground particular areas of difference, but issues of equity and justice require that leaders keep the intersections of difference and identities foregrounded in their values and practice. Recognizing that leaders cannot engage in this inclusive, socially just work alone, we stress the ideas of COPs and networked social justice communities as key strategies to engage in this thinking, this work, this practice and the ideas in this book in a broader and potentially supportive manner.

REFERENCES

Artiles, A., & Klingner, J. (2006). Forging a knowledge base on English language learners with special needs: Theoretical, population, and technical issues. *Teachers College Record, 108*(11), 2187–2194.

Artiles, A., Rueda, R., Salazar, J. J., & Higareda, I. (2005). Within-group diversity in minority disproportionate representation: English language learners in urban school districts. *Exceptional Children, 71*(3), 283–300.

Auerbach, S. (2012). Conceptualizing leadership for authentic partnerships. In S. Auerbach (Ed.), *School leadership for authentic family and community partnerships: Research perspectives for transforming practice* (pp. 29–51). New York, NY: Routledge.

Bryk, A., Gomez, L., & Grunow, A. (2010). *Getting ideas into action: Building networked improvement communities in education.* Stanford, CA: Carnegie Foundation for the Advancement of Teaching.

Bryk, A., Sebring, P. B., Allensworth, E., Luppescu, S., & Easton, J. (2010). *Organizing schools for improvement: Lessons from Chicago.* Chicago, IL: University of Chicago Press.

Council of Chief State School Officers. (2008). *Interstate School Leaders Licensure Consortium (ISLLC) Standards for school leaders.* Retrieved from http://www.ccsso.org/Resources/Publications/ Educational_Leadership_Policy_Standards_ISLLC_2008_as_Adopted_by_the_National_Policy_ Board_for_Educational_Administration.html

Council of Chief State School Officers. (2014). *Interstate School Leaders Licensure Consortium (ISLLC) Standards for school leaders.* Retrieved from http://www.ccsso.org/documents/2014/Draft% 202014%20ISLLC%20Standards%2009102014.pdf

Darling-Hammond, L., LaPointe, M., Meyerson, D. E., Orr, M. T., & Cohen, C. (2007). *Preparing school leaders for a changing world.* Stanford, CA: Stanford University Press.

Deschenes, S., Cuban, L., & Tyack, D. (2001). Mismatch: Historical perspectives on schools and students who don't fit them. *Teachers College Record, 103*(4), 525–547.

Duncan, G., & Murnane, R. (2011). Introduction: The American dream, then and now. In G. Duncan & R. Murnane (Eds.), *Whither opportunity?* (pp. 3–23). New York, NY: Russell Sage Foundation.

Earl, L., Katz, S., Elgie, S., Jaafar, S. B., & Foster, L. (2006). *How networked learning communities work.* Toronto, ON: Aporia Consulting, Ltd.

Frattura, E., & Capper, C. (2007). *Leadership for social justice in practice: Integrated comprehensive services for all learners.* Thousand Oaks, CA: Corwin Press.

Gamoran, A., & Long, D. (2006). *Equality of educational opportunity: A 40-year retrospective.* Madison: Wisconsin Center for Education Research.

Hardman, M. L., & Dawson, S. (2008). The impact of federal public policy on curriculum and instruction for students with disabilities in the general education classroom. *Preventing School Failure, 52*(2), 5–11.

Horsford, S. D. (2011). *Learning in a burning house: Educational inequality, ideology, and (dis)integration.* New York, NY: Teachers College Press.

Hyde, J., & Lindberg, S. M. (2007). Facts and assumptions about the nature of gender differences and the implications for gender equity. In S. Klein, B. Richardson, D. A. Grayson, L. H. Fox,

C. Kramarae, D. Pollard, & C. A. Dwyer (Eds.), *Handbook for achieving gender equity through education* (2nd ed., pp. 19–32). Mahwah, NJ: Lawrence Erlbaum Associates.

Johnson, R., & La Salle, R. A. (2010). *The wallpaper effect: Data strategies to uncover and eliminate hidden inequities*. Thousand Oaks, CA: Corwin.

Lave, J., & Wenger, E. (1991). *Situated learning: Legitimate peripheral participation*. New York, NY: Cambridge University Press.

Leithwood, K., & Riehl, C. (2005). What we know about successful school leadership. In W. Firestone & C. Riehl (Eds.), *Directions for research on educational leadership* (pp. 22–47). New York, NY: Teachers College Press.

Park, S., & Takahashi, S. (2013). *90-day cycle handbook*. Stanford, CA: Carnegie Foundation for the Advancement of Teaching.

Scanlan, M. (2013). A learning architecture: How school leaders can design for learning social justice. *Educational Administration Quarterly, 49*(2), 348–391.

Scanlan, M., & López, F. (2012). ¡Vamos! How school leaders promote equity and excellence for bilingual students. *Educational Administration Quarterly, 48*(4), 283–625.

Scanlan, M., & López, F. (2014). *Leadership for culturally and linguistically responsive schools*. New York, NY: Routledge.

Scanlan, M., & Theoharis, G. (2014). Inclusive schooling and leadership for social justice. *Theory into Practice, 53*(2).

Taylor, P. (2014). *The next America*. Washington, DC: Pew Research Center.

Theoharis, G. (2007). Social justice educational leaders and resistance: Toward a theory of social justice leadership. *Educational Administration Quarterly, 43*(2), 221–258.

Wahlstrom, K., Louis, K. S., Leithwood, K., & Anderson, S. (2010). *Investigating the links to improved student learning: Executive summary of research findings*. Washington, DC: Wallace Foundation.

Warren, M. (2005). Comunities and schools: A new view of urban education reform. *Harvard Educational Review, 75*(2), 133–173.

Warren, M., & Mapp, K. L. (2011). *A match on dry grass: Community organizing as a catalyst for school reform*. New York, NY: Oxford University Press.

Wenger, E. (1998). *Communities of practice: Learning, meaning, and identity*. New York, NY: Cambridge University Press.

CHAPTER 2

Inclusive Leadership and Disability

George Theoharis, Julie Causton, and Casey Woodfield

This chapter focuses on what leaders need to know and be able to do in order to create schools that meet the needs of students with disabilities. It is important to note that disability is often the first and only dimension of diversity that people associate with inclusion and issues of inclusivity. While for some readers this chapter will resonate with notions of inclusion and special education in schools, disability does not exist in a vacuum but in a world full of intersections between disability and other areas of difference. When we think about inclusive schooling, we are talking about shifting the way we see education—a paradigm shift, a sea change, a philosophy that undergirds planning and decision-making. In terms of disability, inclusive education at its core means *all* students with disabilities are learning and socializing in general education settings, and educators are providing inclusive services to meet their needs while eliminating pullout or self-contained special education programs. It is a constant effort to reject partial attempts and get beyond segregated lives, classrooms, and communities. This means we see *each and every* child, regardless of disability or need, as a fundamental and valued member and participant of the general education heterogeneous classroom community. This necessitates a team of professionals working together to adapt, modify, and differentiate for all students to get beyond a one-size-fits-all approach. This chapter focuses on inclusive leadership and disability. We begin with the current context of disability in schools, then proceed to summarize the research literature relating disability to the needs of school leaders, and finally detail what inclusive leadership around disability looks like with tools and case studies.

PART 1: THE CURRENT CONTEXT OF DISABILITY IN SCHOOLS

The provision of special education services for the 6.5 million school-aged students labeled with disabilities in the United States is driven and mediated by the Individuals with Disabilities Education Improvement Act of 2004 (IDEA 2004). Since this federal special education law's least restrictive environment (LRE) principle ensures that "to the maximum

appropriate, children with disabilities . . . are educated with children who are not
ed . . . with the use of supplementary aids and services" (IDEA 2004, 20 U.S.C. §1412
(B) *et seq.*), students with disabilities are increasingly being educated and provided those
supports in heterogeneous general education classrooms (US Department of Education,
Office of Special Education Programs, 2011). Based on the foundation of equitable access
established by these provisions, general education, with meaningful access to the academic
and social aspects of schooling, is considered the preferred placement for students with disabilities to receive special education and related services.

Under IDEA 2004, the Individualized Education Program (IEP) must direct these
services and supports for students with disabilities; a guiding document collaboratively
designed by a multidisciplinary team that includes the student him/herself, general education teacher, special education teacher, administrative designee, psychologist, parent/
guardian, and any other individuals who are knowledgeable about the student. As members
and key contributors to IEP teams, school administrators can not only help to make these
placement and service decisions for students with disabilities, but they also can be crucial to
cultivating a school-and district-wide culture that hinges on inclusive and equity-oriented
special education service delivery options. School leaders' absence from this role almost
certainly precludes the development of inclusive and equity-oriented special education service delivery.

Over the past two decades many schools have shifted their service delivery to comply
with the LRE requirement by unifying previously separate general and special education
environments to establish cohesive services that benefit all students (Causton-Theoharis &
Theoharis, 2008; Frattura & Capper, 2007). As research suggests, inclusive service delivery
goes beyond implications for only students with disability labels and extend into the experiences of *all* students (McLeskey & Waldron, 2006; Giangreco, Dennis, Cloninger, Edelman, & Schattman, 1993). These benefits are social and academic, but also more global as
students learn to live, work, and play side-by-side.

The education of students with disabilities in this country has an exclusionary past
that has been, and continues to be, rewritten through the implementation of this federal
legislation that holds all learners to high academic standards (Hardman & Dawson, 2008).
These expectations are inherent in the accountability measures sanctioned by the No Child
Left Behind Act of 2001 (NCLB). A standards-based reform, NCLB fosters educational
accountability through the use of evidence-based practices; students are expected to meet
grade-level benchmark standards, as measured by standardized assessments. Both this act
and IDEA 2004 are united in their call for highly qualified teachers, academic goals for students with disabilities that are attached to standards, and the systematic measurement and
reporting of academic progress (US Department of Education, 2007; Rosenberg, Sindelar, &
Hardman, 2004). The culture of accountability established by these mandates pushes
schools to move beyond just providing access for students with disabilities, holding them
responsible for developing rigorous academic environments that expect and foster high
achievement for all. School administrators initiate, monitor, and maintain patterns of action
to build this culture.

What Do People With Disabilities Say? Voices of the Community

Of course, the high expectations that run through these accountability measures and
legal provisions do not automatically translate into improvements in the education and
services directed toward students with disabilities. Developing inclusive spaces based on
collaboration and respect among staff and between students requires commitment at all
levels—actions that should include and involve student perspectives as well. Yet the voices

of professionals and parents continue to be utilized as the primary means of interpreting students' experiences with disability and education, rather than seeking feedback from individuals with disabilities themselves (Robledo & Donnellan, 2008; Wickenden, 2009). It is not surprising, then, that this predisposition for the professional perspective is also reflected in practice (Ashby & Causton-Theoharis, 2009; Connor, 2007). Here in this chapter, and in practice, we would like to change that.

Consider feedback from students. Too many students with disabilities have stories to share of instances where inclusion was not made a priority and their accounts are often as powerfully instructive as they are disheartening. These students have much to teach us from our own—historical and current—missteps and it is our commitment as scholars and teacher educators to rely on their experiences as resources. For example, the following poetic representation of Michael's perspective, an adult labeled Learning Disabled (LD), provides a retrospective on what could have made his experience better:

> I think they should get rid of the title "special ed." . . .
> It should be just forgotten about.
> Before I got into special ed.
> I'd just sit there, playing around, lolly-gagging.
> Then in junior high school I was just falling down, so
> they was like
> *"Michael's not catching up with the class . . . "* da-da-da
> My resource room teacher said, *"Maybe you should get
> him tested."*
> Then I was tested some more, so I was being tested,
> tested, and they said,
> *"You can either get left back . . . or you gotta go to special ed."*
> I hated it.
> That's the most embarrassing thing to a kid.
> Everyone thinks you're slower than everyone else.
> When I was in there I was like *"Oh man, you have to get
> out . . . "*
>
> (Connor, 2006, p. 15)

Like many other students with disabilities with similar educational experiences, the stigma associated with labeling and exclusion that Michael describes is real. His preoccupation with embarrassment, measuring his own performance against his peers, and "get[ting] out" of special education suggests that these feelings fostered during his junior high and high school years have stuck with him even in his adult life. Is that what school is intended to be? His critique of special education is compelling and candid: "it should just be forgotten about"; perhaps an artful, and productive, twist on his own stated feelings as a student.

In a published version of a conversation between himself and Doug Biklen (a professor), Jamie Burke, a high school student with autism who types and reads aloud his text to communicate, poses questions that breathe life to Michael's previous critique. He notes, "Segregation equals a distinction of lesser ability. Am I lesser because I get nervous about an exam? Am I deemed less intelligent because my feelings only make passing a higher stakes? I again ask you to think of who is it that has placed this way of evaluating worthiness? Have they placed their feet in my shoes? I would enjoin them to try, and to allow me to view the straightness of their path" (Biklen & Burke, 2006, p. 172). Together, Michael and Jamie's perspectives testify to the inequity of exclusion typical of segregated special education; important realities to consider as we work to determine placements and service

the students with disabilities that follow them. As Jamie goes on to note, doing
us, but critical:

the idea of school inclusion can be as a lousy or lovely happening. It's really all in the
hands of the teachers along with the permission from the big boss, the superintendent.
Teachers must be willing to not just give me a desk and then leave me to fill the chair.
I need to be asked questions, and given time for my thoughtful answers. Teachers need
to become as a conductor, and guide me through the many places I may get lost.

(p. 172)

Informed by his own school experiences, Jamie's example not only sheds light on what
it may have felt like for him to navigate an educational system not designed with him in
mind, but also pushes educators and administrators to ask, "How could we do better?" As
Jamie and Michael's words suggest, "inclusive" is not an acquired status, it a collaborative,
ongoing, and malleable journey grounded in commitment to students. Thus, listening to
these experiences of individuals whose ways of moving in and interacting with the world
often in and of themselves challenge the normative expectations of the spaces and people
they encounter holds much promise for movement toward more inclusive opportunities
(Ferri, 2009).

PART 2: WHAT WE KNOW ABOUT DISABILITY: THE LITERATURE

In this section, we review and synthesize four key aspects of the research literature that
inclusive leaders need to understand: intersections and overrepresentation, social construction of disability, efficacy of inclusive services, response to intervention, and presuming
competence.

How Does Disability Relate to Other Areas of Difference? Intersections and Overrepresentation

Although our chapter focuses on disability, disability cannot be examined in isolation,
since many areas of difference overlap with and in it. The over-representation of students of color in special education represents an area in which complex intersections of
race, class, and ability translate into marginalization and exclusion. Due to this subjective
nature of labeling, Black and Latino students are currently represented three times more
frequently than their White peers in special education (Ferri & Connor, 2006; Losen &
Orfield, 2002).

The over-representation of students of color in special education is confounded by the
fact that students of color are more than twice as likely to be living in poverty (Macartney,
Bishaw, & Fontenot, 2013) and often have less access to quality prenatal and early childhood
medical care and early intervention services resulting in manifestation of developmental
and cultural characteristics that can be misinterpreted as disability (Dudley-Marling &
Dudley-Marling, this volume; see further Donovan & Cross, 2002) and/or be complicated
by an absence of culturally relevant support (Artiles, Kozleski, Trent, Osher, & Ortiz, 2010;
Blanchett, Klingner, & Harry, 2009). Moreover, the disproportionate representation of children from diverse cultural and linguistic backgrounds in special education has been a problem for over 20 years (Garcia & Ortiz, 2011).

Importantly, once students from lingustically and culturally diverse groups are labeled, they are more likely to be in segregated placements than their White classmates who carry the same disability label (Cartledge, Singh, & Gibson, 2008; National Center for Education Statistics, 2014). This over-representation of students of color often occurs in the categories of emotional and behavioral disturbances, intellectual disabilities, and learning disabilities (Parrish, 2002), and these categories are more likely to be segregated (US Department of Education, Office of Special Education Programs, 2012). More specifically, 21.7% of Black students across disability labels and 21.8% of Asian and Pacific Islanders spend less than 40% of their day in general education, compared to 11.9% of their White counterparts (US Department of Education, Office of Special Education Programs, 2012).

The over-representation of students of color in special education is also complicated by gender. Roughly two-thirds of students with disabilities between the ages of 6 and 17 served under the IDEA are male (US Department of Education, 2007). Within that group, the most heavily male-dominated disability categories include emotional disturbance (80% male ages 6–12; 77% male ages 13–17) and autism (83% male ages 6–12; 84% male ages 13–17). This disproportionality should not be interpreted to mean that disabilities are more common in boys than girls. Just as is the case with the overrepresentation of students of color in special education—many of whom, we can see from the data, are boys—the subjective nature of labeling must be considered as well. Behavioral expectations and ideas about normative performance are important to consider in light of these statistics, which tell us only that males tend to be labeled with disabilities more often than girls. As school leaders, what we do with these numbers, and how we move toward more equitable delivery of services, has to do first with how we conceptualize disability itself.

The Social Construction of Disability

Leaders for inclusive schooling must consider how individuals with disabilities have historically been regarded in medical, professional, educational, and general parlance. The understanding of disability, and the institutionalized responses to it, have traditionally and pervasively been associated with a medicalized, deficit-based perspective that positions disability as an inherent, negative trait within an individual. Disability, and therefore the student with a disability, has been seen as a problem to be fixed. Yet scholars in the fields of disability studies (DS) and disability studies in education (DSE) reveal other factors at play, too, in our current understandings of what disability is and whom it impacts. The notion of disability as a social construction holds that meaning is and has been made by human beings in interactions with one another and the world around them (Taylor, 2008; Shakespeare, 2010). Therefore, "disability" is a concept representative of the contextual nature of the way that individuals with impairments experience, and are marginalized by, social, structural, emotional, institutional, historical, and political aspects of the world (Garland-Thomson, 1997). Not only is this framework a key tenet of DS and DSE as academic fields, but a helpful way of thinking about disability in relation to inclusive educational opportunities and practices.

Through the lens of the social construction of disability, disability categories are not only created through a combination of medical, professional, research-based, educational, and federal governmental conceptions, but they also can and have changed over time. For example, the category of intellectual disability (or mental retardation, as it has been referred to until recently) and associated assumptions about intellectual ability and competence that accompany it have evolved and changed over time, showing that a disability category is not fixed, objective, or static (Bogdan & Taylor, 1976; Danforth, 1997). Prior to 1973, individuals with an IQ of 80 or below qualified for a label of what was then known as mental retardation. Yet during 1973 the federal government lowered that diagnostic criteria measure to 70 or below. With the swift stroke of a pen, hundreds of thousands of individuals who went to bed one night labeled mentally retarded were essentially "cured" the very next day (Blatt, 1987).

Perhaps most significantly, once created, these disability categories are reinforced and marked by assumptions that accompany them. Simply put, people see what they are looking for. And what they are looking for is based on characteristics associated with the diagnostic criteria of a disability label. Once labeled, students with disabilities often become understood—particularly by educators—almost exclusively through the lens of their perceived deficits (Baglieri, Bejoian, Broderick, Connor, & Valle, 2011).

We see this personified in our work with schools constantly (Causton & Theoharis, 2014). For example, while observing in a third-grade classroom we noted how these negative perceptions of students labeled with disabilities translate into lived consequences for students. While the classroom was bustling with students talking as they completed art projects, the teacher shouted over the noise, "Seth, that is the last time." She walked to the chalkboard and wrote his name, on display for the rest of his classmates to see. Yet the noise in this classroom came from the combination of many students talking at the same time. From where we were sitting, Seth's behavior looked no different than his classmates'. So why was Seth—a student who carries the label of emotional disturbance—the only student whose actions were considered problematic? Could it be that the answer is as simple as, "because he was expected to be"?

As is evident in the historical revision of criteria for intellectual disability labels, as well the example of Seth's seemingly unwarranted disciplining, the "creation" of disability categories has implications for the lived realties of those so labeled; experiences over which, often, they have no control. These categories are developed, amended, and attached in relation to individuals' lives through the determinations made by external others of whether they "qualify" or not. The social construction of disability means that disability labels are not static; they are not made up of hard and fast rules that describe certain types of people. In contrast, they are merely reflections and indicators of patterns of difficulty for individuals, the meaning of which has been made by other people and throughout history. Understanding this can drive us to be more accountable for and critical of our own biases, and lead to a more individualized, assets-based rather than categorical, deficits-based approach to educating students with particular needs.

The Efficacy of Inclusive Services

Research has shown that when students with significant disabilities are educated in general, rather than special, education settings, their academic outcomes increase and instances of challenging behavior decrease (Dawson et al., 1999). Further, a review of 50 studies comparing academic performances of students with mild disabilities included in general education with those who were not indicated that students in the inclusive setting had higher average academic growth (80th percentile) than those who were segregated (50th percentile) (TASH, 2009). Research suggests that students with disabilities in inclusive settings earn better standardized assessment scores and achieve higher grades overall, as compared to their counterparts in segregated special education settings (Rea, McLaughlin, & Walther-Thomas, 2002).

The academic and social benefits of inclusive education extend beyond just students with disabilities to impact those without disabilities as well (Cole, Waldron, & Majd, 2004; Fisher & Meyer, 2002; Freeman & Alkin, 2000; Kennedy, Shulka, & Fryxell, 1997; Sharpe, York, & Knight, 1994; Waldron & McLeskey, 1998). Studies have revealed increased academic performance of students without disabilities placed in inclusive classroom settings

(TASH, 2009) and found achievement for students without disabilities to be equal to or better academically when in inclusive settings (Salend & Duhaney, 1999). Research has revealed that placing students with disabilities in inclusive classrooms had no impact on amount or disruption of instruction time (Staub & Peck, 1995), an argument commonly made against inclusive schooling. In this achievement-based era of accountability, school leadership must make certain to provide all learners (particularly students with disabilities) opportunities to academically advance. Inclusive education has proven to be a vehicle of such equitable and positive outcomes.

Response to Intervention (RTI)

There has been ongoing debate, resulting in an abundance of reforms, around the best ways to educate students who receive special education services (Gersten & Dimino, 2006). Currently, schools have implemented Response to Intervention (RTI) as a mechanism for delivering services. RTI is a three-tiered model based on a student's "response to interventions" that increase in intensity at each level. At its core, RTI aims to alter contextual variables through intensity of instruction (i.e., explicit instruction, increase frequency, lengthen duration, creating homogeneous groups, remediation of skills) in an effort to remediate skills based on the perceived deficits of students considered to be "at risk" for academic failure. While the premise of providing support to students when they struggle as opposed to waiting for them to fail is promising, there are elements of the model that, in practice, work against inclusive schooling.

For instance, while Tiers I and II involve intensifying interventions within the classroom, Tier III includes the provision of individualized interventions for students who have failed to respond to previous interventions, thus suggesting that for those students, separate classroom settings are acceptable. Moreover, students of color and students who are culturally and linguistically diverse are often over-identified for RTI and, as a result, are again more segregated from their peers than White students (Artiles, Bal, & Thorius, 2010; NCCRESt, 2005).

RTI interventions, in theory, are designed to be useful for the majority of students, yet frequently steps are not taken to mold them to students' particular needs or social, cultural, personal, or classroom contexts (NCCRESt, 2005). Thus, while on its surface this model encourages advocacy and appropriate services for students with disabilities—a key element in establishing socially just schools—this generalized approach to reform threatens to perpetuate dominant ideas about segregated learning environments being suitable placements for students who fail to measure up to standardized academic and behavioral expectations. This idea feeds into the histories of segregating students, an idea and practice from which an inclusive education philosophy aims to move away (Artiles et al., 2010; Ferri, 2012). Additionally concerning is that once a student is placed into special education, further research on how progress monitoring should be conducted is not part of the RTI model (Ferri, 2012); all we know is that the student did not respond to the interventions implemented prior to their designation. As Artiles and colleagues (2010) make note: "Framing RTI as a solely technical endeavor in which oppression does not exist will ultimately exacerbate the possibilities of reproducing past inequities for the next generation" (p. 256).

We Must Assume Students CAN! Presumption of Competence

The fourth area of literature that should undergird leadership in increasingly diverse schools centers on the presumption of competence, a conviction that asserts the importance of fundamentally believing in all students' ability to learn (Biklen & Burke, 2006). For many students, but particularly for students with significant disabilities, notions of competence and intelligence are too often called into question. Students with complex support needs pose unique challenges for educators related to the assessment, communication, and determination of their learning. The presumption of competence provides a clear response to this perceived quandary: no one can definitively know another person's thinking unless the other person can (accurately) reveal it. Given this, presuming competence can be considered what Anne Donnellan (1984) has termed the *least dangerous assumption*. It is less harmful to assume that students can learn—and support them to do so—than to expect that they cannot.

Over the course of history students with disabilities have revealed time and again that professionals have been wrong about how and what they can learn or gain from educational opportunities. We have continually been surprised by what students can communicate, learn, share, and do. And yet students with disabilities have perpetually been excluded from the educational opportunities they deserve. That we continue to be caught off guard by such realizations—that students continue to have to prove us wrong—is an unfortunate reality, as it reflects a systematic unwillingness to shift, change, and grow based on lessons learned. Presuming competence for all (students with disabilities, students who speak English as a second language, students from all races and socioeconomic status), then, pushes us not only to expect that students can and will learn, but also to place them in inclusive settings that provide challenging, interesting, age-appropriate experiences as well as opportunities, supports, and expectations for success.

In sum, inclusion is not a program to be offered to some students in some classrooms. Instead, inclusion forms an underlying philosophy or way of seeing the world. Inclusion is a way of leading schools that embraces *each and every* student as full members of the general education academic and social community. Thus, while this chapter is focused on disability, this understanding of inclusion is much broader and applies across all areas of difference. We know that it is the leaders who need to make this happen, and we now turn to the tools and strategies to make inclusion possible.

PART 3: INCLUSIVE LEADERSHIP FOR STUDENTS WITH DISABILITIES IN K–12 SCHOOLS

> Systemic change toward inclusive education requires **passionate visionary leaders** who are able to build consensus around the goal of providing quality education for all learners. . . . . . [Study after study found] **administrative support and vision to be the most powerful predictor** of success of moving toward full inclusion.
> —Villa and Thousand (2003, p. 13)

Villa and Thousand (2003) challenge us to realize that more than anything else, the role of school leaders is paramount to create and maintain inclusive schools. Here, we review the leader's role in including students with disabilities through a process for leaders to use in moving their schools to become more inclusive (inclusive school reform). We conclude with case study examples of a school and district engaged in this work.

Leaders' Roles in Inclusion and Disability

There are many contributing factors to inclusive schools and the benefits students with and without disabilities, staff, teachers, parents, and communities realize. However, it is the leaders who ultimately make or break efforts to be inclusive and to transcend from the rhetoric of inclusion to the reality of embracing the full range of students with and without disabilities as members of the general education learning and social community.

This section brings together the practice of school leaders and the research examining the role leaders play in creating inclusive schools for students with disabilities (see Capper & Frattura, 2008, McLesky & Waldron, 2006, Riehl, 2000, Theoharis, 2009), and focuses on providing leaders additional tools and strategies—in the form of a *process*—to create (or recreate) more inclusive contexts for all students. We refer to this approach as inclusive school reform. Consistently, leaders who are successful at leading or moving toward fully inclusive schools do the following:

- Set a bold, clear vision of full inclusion
- Engage in collaborative planning and implementation with their staff
- Conduct an equity audit
- Map current service delivery
- Set goals based on the vision
- Realign school and staffing structure
- Build instructional teams
- Transform classroom practice
- Reduce fragmentation of initiatives
- Monitor, adjust, and celebrate

Set a Bold, Clear Vision of Full Inclusion

A strong leadership vision of inclusive schooling is vital for the successful implementation of inclusive practices. Perhaps the most difficult, but most important, of all the leadership for inclusive education strategies, leaders need to be visible and consistent in their vision to move toward fully inclusive schools. Successful inclusive leaders do not accept some segregation or partial inclusion as the goal, nor do they talk in platitudes like "all children can learn." They are specific and firm in their vision for inclusive schooling, returning to it to drive planning and to make decisions for the school. Assistant Superintendent Lisa describes the bold direction for her district:

> We know that inclusive services are best for students with and without disabilities. This requires teams of professionals working in inclusive classrooms to meet the needs of each learner in the classroom. I believe that each student in this district deserves authentic access to general education, peers, and the general education teachers. We can and will successfully include all students who come to us. We will figure out how to do this together, but we will do this.

Principal Janice also provides a powerful example of maintaining a focus on the vision during the transition to a fully inclusive model. After months of planning about how to eliminate self-contained and pullout programs and fully include students with the proper supports in general education across her K–8 school, the leadership team unveiled the service delivery plan at a Spring staff meeting. After the plan was discussed, principal Janice got up and said:

> This is where we are going. We are not going back to the segregated ways of our past. This team has worked very hard to come up with the best plan for next year. I recognize we all need support to do this. I also recognize that some of you have serious reservations about this direction. I ask that you come with us as we work to make this school a model of inclusion, but if you feel this is not a direction you can head I will

help you find a position where you can be successful. No one here will be allowed to sabotage our efforts . . . We will become a model of inclusion; if you can't be part of that, I have a stack of transfer forms right here.

In the years that followed, she worked on developing a shared vision with the staff. She also held people to that vision and was often heard asking, "How does that fit with our commitment to inclusive education?" about decisions around how to meet the needs of students. Her insistence that inclusivity for all students not get sidelined by other matters and instead drive decisions helped her maintain a bold vision at the forefront of her school.

The inclusive vision of school leaders needs to drive a collaborative process that leads toward a shared inclusive vision in the school; however, in our experience there are not many schools where there is an initial shared vision of inclusion across school staff. The leadership needs to drive the inclusive vision and build a collaborative planning process that meaningfully engages diverse stakeholders.

Engage in Collaborative Planning and Implementation

In all of the schools and districts we have studied on their journeys to creating fully inclusive services, identifying the best ways to create inclusive services was a collaborative process. The leader should facilitate the planning process in a democratic and transparent manner with a representative leadership team consisting of school administrators, general education teachers, special education teachers, and other staff members. The team should also check in and communicate with the entire staff throughout the process.

The leaders may have provided a direction, but she or he or they brought staff together—special education teachers, general education teachers, support staff, and paraprofessionals—to figure out how the people in their school could make that happen. The planning and implementation was democratic.

In one case, the district administration pushed all the schools in a more inclusive direction. Special Education Director Mike and Superintendent Carol helped support service delivery changes at all schools. For example, Principal Olivia, working with the special education administrator, created a service delivery leadership team to examine their special education service delivery. She made this team open to all who wanted to join. The team created a variety of options for using their existing human resources to become fully inclusive and eliminate self-contained and pullout services, working together to make a coherent service delivery plan for the following year. The team, not the principal, then presented it to the staff to gain broader support.

As with all new initiatives, there were bumps in the road. Principal Olivia made sure the school stayed the course after the first concerns were voiced at the beginning of implementation and a number of staff members got nervous and wanted to return to the way things used to be. Olivia brought teachers together to problem solve, but she was clear that the school was not turning back. Every January this service delivery team begins its work in planning for the following year, collaboratively looking at the projected students, needs, and grade levels for the next year. Principal Olivia makes sure this process happens, but does not control it. She has the literacy coach facilitate the service team meetings.

While many specific attributes for collaborative planning are unique to Principal Olivia's school, there are some key salient ideas for all schools. First, the staff worked together to make an implementation plan over a series of months. Second, the plan was not abandoned at the first or second or third implementation bump. And finally, given lessons learned and changes in students and staff, each year a team of staff members begins thoughtfully planning how to implement a fully inclusive philosophy for the following year.

This key component of successful inclusive services involves the collaborative planning that brought different stakeholders to the table to develop and fine-tune implementation for a school-wide plan. It is important to get buy-in but also different perspectives on an inclusive service delivery plan for the school.

Part of collaborative planning and implementing inclusive reform is creating a climate of belonging. This means working with all stakeholders at school to presume competence and value of all students, building community purposefully in each classroom throughout the year, adopting a school-wide community-building approach, and enhancing the sense of belonging for all students, staff, and families. It is essential that throughout this process inclusion is looked at broadly, keeping in mind the intersections of disability, race, class, and gender. (See the online companion website, www.routledge.com/cw/theoharis, for the belonging observational tool.)

Conduct an Equity Audit to Understand Current Realities

Equity audits are becoming a more widely used tool for school leaders to understand and gather local data about their schools. Many educators feel their school operates in an equitable manner overall, but equity audits provide concrete data to reflect operational realities and identify disproportionate areas to address. The final chapter of this text describes a comprehensive equity audit process. See the disability section and full equity audit detailed in Chapter 10 and online (www.routledge.com/cw/theoharis). Conducting an audit can achieve a number of goals, like making a case for changing service delivery, strengthening the vision of inclusion, and providing data for a collaborative planning process.

Create Service Delivery Maps

Teams examine the existing way services are provided, human resources are used, and where students receive which services. This process requires that school teams map out current service delivery and human resource distribution in efforts to meet the range of student needs. This involves creating a visual representation of the classrooms, special education service provision, general education classrooms, and how students receive their related services. An essential part of creating service maps is to indicate which staff pull students from which classrooms, which students learn in self-contained spaces, and which paraprofessionals are used where—a complete picture of how and where all staff at the school work.

Figure 2.1 provides an example of this kind of visual map of the service delivery model before inclusive school reform. The rectangles around the edge represent the general education classrooms. The ovals in the middle labeled "resource" represent resource special education teachers who worked with students with disabilities in many classrooms (as indicated by the lines) through a pullout model. The circles labeled self-contained had a multi-aged group of students with disabilities who spent the entire day together, separate from general education peers. There is one oval marked with "inclusion 20+10." This represents what was previously called an "inclusive" classroom. This room had about 20 general education students with an additional ten students with disabilities. This old service delivery plan segregated students with intense needs into certain classrooms, while other classrooms lacked students with disabilities and additional adult support. Some students were excluded and removed from the general education curriculum, instruction, and social interaction with general education peers for some or all of each school day.

We see the visual mapping of services as a key way to understand the patterns and who gets which kinds of services and where these services happen. Visual mapping of services can also allow leaders and teams to see racial and economic patterns of student composition in classes and services (see Figure 2.2). Creating service maps and identifying the race,

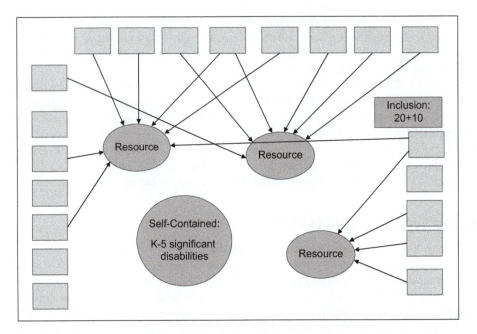

Figure 2.1 Special Education Service Delivery Prior to Inclusive Restructuring

Note: Rectangles = elementary general education classrooms K–5. Circles/ovals = special education teachers. Resource = special education teachers who pull students from their general education classroom. Inclusion 20+10 = a classroom where a general education teacher is team teaching with a special education teacher where there are 20 general education students and 10 special education students. Self-contained: K–5 significant disabilities = a special education classroom where all students who have significant disabilities receive their instruction and spend the majority of their school day.

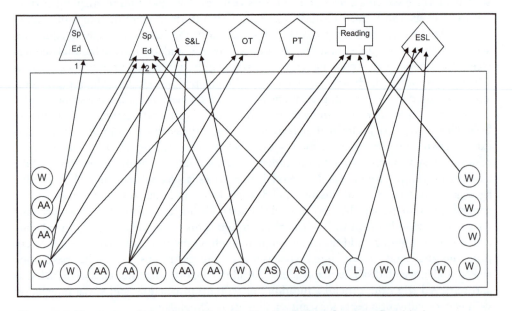

Figure 2.2 Elementary Classroom—Disrupted by the Pullout Services Provided

Note: Shapes on top represent staff members and their corresponding pullout program: Sp Ed = special ed teacher. S&L = speech & language therapist. OT = occupational therapist. PT = physical therapist. Reading = Title I reading teacher. ESL = English as a Second Language teacher. Circles on the sides and bottom represent the students; labeled by race: AA = African American, AS = Asian, L = Latino, W = white.

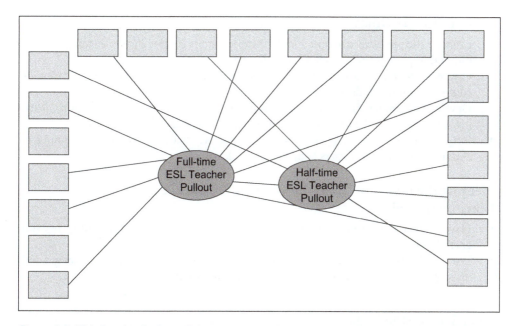

Figure 2.3 ELL Service Delivery Prior to Inclusive Restructuring

Note: Rectangles = elementary general education classrooms. Ovals = ESL teachers. Pullout = ESL teacher taking ELL students to an ESL resource room to provide instruction. Lines = the classrooms from where the ESL teachers pull students for the ESL program.

social class, gender, or language of students who are being pulled out of classrooms and the students who remain in the classroom visually shows the ways that segregating students typically marginalizes students of color, students who are linguistically diverse, low-income students, and privileged White and middle class students. These maps then allow leaders and school teams to have conversations about these inequitable patterns. For example, Figure 2.2 shows one classroom of elementary students, with the circles on the bottom representing students and the individual students who were pulled out prior to inclusive reform.

While this process for inclusive school reform was designed for inclusion of students with disabilities, we have used the same process for creating more inclusive services for students who are culturally and linguistically diverse. In those cases, the teachers of and service providers for students who are labeled English-Language Learners (ELLs) were represented on the service maps instead of special education teachers. See Figure 2.3.

Set Goals Based on the Vision

Operating with a bold vision of inclusion and an understanding of the current service delivery, the team sets goals for the school reform initiative around three areas: (1) school structure—how we arrange adults and students, (2) school climate, and 3) meeting the needs of all in the general education classroom. Below is an example of goals that a K–8 school created during the inclusive school reform work. They include:

Structure Goals (How We Arrange Adults and Students)

- Students will be placed in classrooms in natural proportions with positive role models.
- Designated person will facilitate efficient monthly communication meetings for staff to discuss various topics surrounding inclusion.

School Climate Goals

- Examine the physical structure to determine locations conducive to planning, supporting, and implementing inclusion at each grade level.
- Create a schedule that promotes consistent and common planning time for ongoing communication and dialogue.
- Develop and implement approaches and procedures that promote a professional learning community (collaboration, consensus, agree to disagree respectfully).
- Purposefully build a classroom and school climate that is warm and welcoming for children and staff and fosters active/engaging learning.

Meeting the Needs of All in the General Education Classroom Goals

- Have planned opportunities for vertical communication to provide continuity between grade levels.
- Provide child-centered, differentiated, research-based instruction that challenges children of all abilities, supported by targeted staff development.

Align School Structures

This step involves rethinking structures and the use of staff to create teams of professionals to serve all students inclusively; in other words, creating a new service delivery map. The staff develops a new inclusive service delivery plan by redeploying staff to make balanced and heterogeneous classrooms where all students are included. Figure 2.4 provides

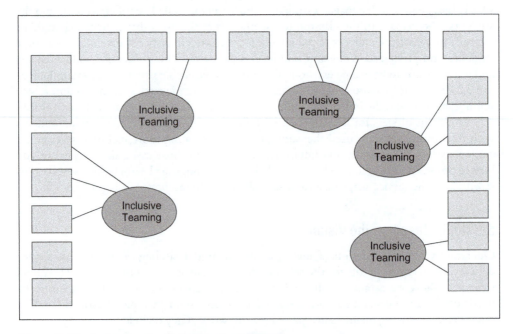

Figure 2.4 Inclusive Service Delivery—Post-Reform

Note: Rectangles = elementary general education classrooms. Circles/ovals = special education teachers. Inclusive teaming = a special education teacher teaming with two to three regular education teachers to meet the range of student needs within the classroom. Each team has one paraprofessional assigned as well.

an example of inclusive service delivery, where teachers and administrators reconfigured the current use of staff (from Figure 2.1) to form teams of specialists and general education teachers to create inclusive teams that collaboratively plan and deliver instruction to heterogeneous student groups (seen in Figure 2.4). In this example the school chose to pair special education teachers as part of inclusive teams with two to three general education classrooms and teachers.

This was not about "dumping" students with needs into a particular classroom, it was about creating heterogeneous spaces. This necessitated focusing each year on creating heterogeneous classrooms that balanced student need across all rooms or sections, and kept the natural proportion front and center. Natural proportions means that if 13% of the students at the school have disabilities, then the student placement process should mirror that density of students with disabilities in each classroom. Classrooms should not be created such that students with disabilities (and thus a need for additional support) are highly concentrated in some spaces and not in others. Part of creating classes at any level is to not segregate students with special education needs into one room or section. Using natural proportions as a guide, it is important to strive for balanced/heterogeneous classes that mix abilities, achievement, behavior, and other learning needs.

Build Instructional Teams

Re-thinking staff involves creating teams of general education teachers, specialists (i.e., special education teachers, ELL teachers, etc.), and paraprofessionals to serve all students inclusively. In the example in Figures 2.1 and 2.4, the special education teacher who was formerly a teacher in the self-contained classroom (Figure 2.1) is now part of a teaching team and co-plans and co-delivers instruction with two general education teachers (Figure 2.4) and a paraprofessional. An essential component of this step is placing students into classrooms using the school's natural proportions of students with special education needs or other needs (like ELL) as a guide as previously defined.

Leaders of inclusive schools develop instructional teams of specialists and generalists. These teams are the ones who provide services, teach, and carry out the plan described in the previous section. Developing teams takes on different forms, but at its core involves bringing together professionals who will share responsibility to work together to inclusively meet the needs of the range of learners under their joint care. This requires revising the roles many professionals have previously played in their schools and building trust between those members. It is essential that in addition to developing teams the leader supports those teams and provides them common planning time.

In an effort to develop instructional teams at her high school, Principal Natalie assigned special education teachers to be content-area special education teachers. This change meant her school no longer provided classes of specific content areas that were only for students in special education and no longer maintained self-contained special education programs. Now, all special education staff support students in general education by co-planning and co-delivering instruction. It is important to note that at this school and others described in this chapter, co-teaching or team teaching was not the goal. Too often co-teaching leads to segregating students with disabilities into one classroom. The goal at Principal Natalie's school (and the others in this chapter) was for shared ownership of students and teachers co-planning and increasing their capacity with and from one another. Principal Natalie ensured special education teachers had common planning time with the content teachers with whom they were working and she treated those special education teachers as part of the content team. She provided time for each special education teacher over the summer to meet with, get to know, and become familiar with the content teachers and the yearly curriculum. Principal Natalie found funds to pay her staff for this time. As time passed, the special education teachers became integral parts of many content-area teams.

Middle School Principal Tim provided support and common planning time as well. During this process he made sure staffing was such that all students with disabilities are in general education, eliminating sections of pullout classes for special education students or self-contained special education programs. He utilized general and special education staff to provide teams who would co-plan and co-deliver instruction. He spread his special education support across enough rooms so students with disabilities are not over-represented into one section, and balanced that with a reasonable number of general education teachers for his special education staff to plan with. He gathered feedback from his staff to drive this process. He carefully worked the schedule and staffing plan, creating common planning time for grade-level teams and, perhaps more importantly, for smaller instructional teams of special and general educators.

Additionally, we have seen a number of leaders who brought in outside expertise to help develop instructional teams. Tracy wrote a grant to provide a 1/3-time collaboration facilitator who met with teams helping them learn to work together, use planning time efficiently, and become a more effective team. Other leaders offered team development workshops led by collaboration experts over the summer to help develop teams for the following year. Some provided ongoing collaboration courses for professional development credit. Others worked with local universities to tap into courses being offered. Some worked with district or regional professional developers to offer similar professional development. Regardless of approach, each inclusive school leader realized that adults must work together in profoundly new ways and that most are not well equipped to do this. Thus, the leaders' work developing teams and providing support plays a key role in the success of inclusive schools.

Transform Classroom Practices

It is important to transform the daily classroom practices supported by teaching teams. This involves creating and carrying out a professional development plan for teachers, paraprofessionals, and administrators. Schools are recommended to consider topics such as collaboration, team teaching, differentiated instruction, working with challenging behavior, inquiry-based instruction, ELL methods, and literacy, among others. In our experience, all the schools that have become more inclusive through this process have spent significant professional development time and energy learning about collaboration, teaching teams, and differentiation.

Certainly an important component of transforming classroom practices and the professional development required to do that involves school leaders setting expectations and providing feedback to their staff. We have created a number of tools to assist school leaders with providing this feedback.

See the online companion website (www.routledge.com/cw/theoharis) for tools to assist leaders during walk-throughs and observation in providing feedback to their staff. These include forms focusing on teaching teams, classroom environment, behavior, and belonging. These tools provide a framework for leaders to employ when in classrooms to address key components of effective inclusive classrooms.

Reduce Fragmentation of Initiatives

Previously we stated that inclusion is not a program, but a guiding philosophy for making decisions about where and how we educate students. Thus, when schools move toward fully including all students, this decision cannot be separate from other changes and programs of the school. Leadership is important in two ways in reducing fragmentation of initiatives. First, leaders act as gatekeepers knowing that they could not ask their teachers to do too many new things at once. As they move toward fully inclusive services, they reduce the other new initiatives or programs that are rolled out in their school. This means that the district- and school-level leaders are careful about not initiating other changes during the early years of fully inclusive services. In order to sustain the move toward inclusive education, leaders make sure that as new staff members join the school they understand the philosophy and the inclusive expectations.

Second, successful leaders of inclusive practice reduce fragmentation of initiatives by making sure their commitments to inclusion are part of everything at their school, from new curriculum and instructional approaches to extra-curricular activities and programs. For example, when a new math series was adopted at Principal Steve's high school, he made sure the special education teachers who were co-planning and co-delivering instruction in math attended training about the new math series with the other math teachers. He also made sure they all had teacher manuals and enough materials (calculators, etc.) to be used in large- and small-group inclusive instruction.

In the midst of many state changes and mandates, Superintendent Carol ensured that her district did not lose sight of its inclusive direction, stating: "Our primary focus this year and next is collaboration to support our inclusive services. Teacher time and energy for change is a finite quantity. So, of course, we are working toward the new common core math, but to be honest we have to be cognizant of that finite reality and so we are doing much less with that math change as we have to say focused."

In addition to ensuring inclusion is central to improving teaching and learning, successful leaders make sure inclusion is infused into extra-curricular activities as well. At Principal Meg's elementary school, the district brought in a local non-profit to run after-school programming. Meg would not accept the non-profit organization's hesitance to serve students with significant disabilities and worked with them to ensure students with disabilities had access to the program. She also insisted on, and provided guidance around, students with disabilities being seen as authentic members of the after-school program, being treated as such, and not being separated from their peers.

These leaders provide examples of how reducing fragmentation allows the inclusive philosophy to blossom in their schools and across districts. In so doing, educators view inclusion not as a program that will come and go, or a service for only some students, or a plan that is thrown out when a new initiative comes along. Instead, inclusive education forms the core of a collaboratively developed plan that reflects "the way we do things around here."

Monitor, Adjust, and Celebrate

The next component of the inclusive reform process is to monitor and adjust the plan with attention to obtaining feedback from all staff, students, and families, but without abandoning the plan at the first moment of struggle or resistance. During the summer and into the first few weeks of the year it is important to iron out logistics and adjust teaching schedules as needed. This often means that the leadership team begins to plan for the following year midway through each school year. Additionally, this component involves making time to honor the hard work of school reform—specifically, the new roles and responsibilities that teaching teams have had to adopt—and celebrating successes along the way. Schools going through this process have created a variety of activities to this end: mid-Fall celebrations for staff to keep momentum, banner-raising celebrations to declare a commitment to this effort while inviting local officials and the press, and end-of-year celebrations to end the year on a positive note.

Case Studies

This final section features case studies. The first is about two schools and the final one is about a district. All of the case studies focus on the work and experience of leading inclusive reform.

School Case Studies

This section of the chapter highlights two schools, located in Central New York, that have created more inclusive services for their students with disabilities.[1] Summer Heights (a K–6 school) and River View (a PreK–8 school) both used an inclusive school reform process similar to that described previously. Adopting this inclusive school reform and getting the commitment from staff and administration to move in this direction took a year of planning. This process began with helping the school staff to learn about the philosophy and practice of inclusion, forming a leadership team, examining the current service delivery model, comparing the service delivery model with inclusive philosophy, incorporating changes into a new service delivery model, implementing the model, and monitoring and adjusting annually. At both schools, 23% of the student body are students labeled with disabilities; this group consists of students with mild, moderate, and significant disabilities. We organize these cases around a few of the steps in the 10-step inclusive school process.

Collaborative Planning Process

An essential component of the inclusive reform of both schools was the planning process and examining the existing data. Each school mapped out its current service delivery models and their use of human resources in an effort to meet the range of student needs, just as described previously. At Summer Heights, the leadership team created and presented this visual so all staff could see and understand the birds-eye view of how human resources were being utilized.

The staff then examined these maps with the focus on creating more inclusive services and, their goals in mind, aiming to identify ways to redeploy staff to create balanced classrooms of students where all students were included. At Summer Heights, teams of teachers created drafts of how to rearrange staff, create new teaching teams, and rethink student placements to enhance inclusion and belonging. These drafts were then shared and the leadership team used them in developing a final plan (like Figure 2.4). Following the service delivery changes, a teacher from Summer Heights shared her beliefs that reject the physical removal of students for separate related services: "With this new model I no longer have the students with the most significant needs missing the most instruction . . . wasting so much time in transition, missing valuable core curriculum. Now these services are brought into the classroom seamlessly and everybody benefits . . . let's not forget the social stigma associated with pullout programs. These kids now finally belong somewhere . . . all day long."

Creating Instructional Teams: New Roles and New Skills

All teachers in both schools now have new roles and responsibilities. Special education teachers no longer pull students out into resource rooms. They are expected to co-plan and co-teach with general educators. General education teachers are no longer only responsible for general education students. Instead, Riverview and Summer Heights sought to create a more unified education system where all teachers are responsible for all students. Teachers received extensive professional development on creating inclusive communities, effective adult collaboration, delivering instruction with multiple adults, differentiation of curriculum, and adaptations to the general education curriculum. This professional development is essential to helping teachers make these changes.

All Students Can Achieve More

Reviewing and monitoring data on student outcomes has been an on-going process for each school. Both witnessed basically no change in achievement after the first year of implementation while changing service delivery, having adults take on new roles, and including students with significant and mild disabilities. Since then, however, both schools have seen improvement in student achievement (see Tables 2.1 and 2.2).

At these schools, including the students with the most significant needs in general education has resulted in a more effective education for all. As one of the teachers involved summarized, "While not everybody loves the way we are doing this new inclusion, it has made us better teachers. In thinking about the students with the greatest challenges, we

Table 2.1 Literacy Achievement—Percent at or Above Grade Level

Students	Before	2 years later
Summer Heights 4th grade—all students	50%	58%
Summer Heights 4th grade—students with disabilities	20%	42%
Summer Heights 5th grade—all students	44%	58%
Summer Heights 5th grade—students with disabilities	20%	30%
Summer Heights 6th grade—all students	50%	72%
Summer Heights 6th grade—students with disabilities	25%	35%

Table 2.2 Math Achievement—Percent at or Above Grade Level

Students	Before	2 years later
River View 5th grade—all students	55%	66%
River View 5th grade—students with disabilities	18%	43%
River View 6th grade—all students	54%	72%
River View 6th grade—students with disabilities	18%	53%
River View 7th grade—all students	56%	78%
River View 7th grade—students with disabilities	29%	70%
River View 8th grade—all students	48%	62%
River View 8th grade—students with disabilities	8%	40%

Note: The data reported in both Tables 2.2 and 2.3 follow the same student cohorts. While both schools have made gains on NCLB measures (i.e., comparing one fifth-grade class to the next fifth-grade class), the teachers at Summer Heights and River View felt the most important data required comparing the same group of students to itself as the students progress through the grades.

are doing a better job challenging everybody. It's tough work, but in the end it is the right work."

SCHOOL CASE STUDY GUIDING QUESTIONS

1. What is surprising about the approaches that Summer Heights and River View took in the process of becoming more inclusive?
2. Discuss the importance of collaboration to this process and the potential consequences of an absence of it.
3. What can you take away from these examples and replicate in your own schools?
4. What knowledge, skills, and beliefs are required to lead these changes?

District Case Study

The ten steps toward inclusive school reform discussed previously provide a framework for creating inclusive schooling at the building level; however, many district administrators inquire about how to create an entirely inclusive district. Some district administrators engage in the ten-step inclusive school reform process a school-by-school basis, while others undergo a large-scale approach. Figure 2.5 outlines some guidelines and identifies common pitfalls to avoid when moving an entire district to become more inclusive.

In Wisconsin, the Homesfield district began working toward creating an authentically inclusive district during the 2008–09 school year. They started with an equity audit and quickly realized that their students with disabilities were facing a variety of inequities in achievement, opportunities for participation, and the breadth of school activities. They focused on revising their service delivery by involving the entire administrative team as well as special education and general education teachers. By the Fall of the 2009–10 school year, they had eliminated the self-contained special education rooms and were moving rapidly away from pullout services. Using the teacher mantra of "do it afraid—there is no manual," they redeployed teachers to eliminate the former special education rooms. Their focus on service delivery positioned teams of adults to take on new roles together. This meant recreating classroom environments that met the range of students' needs.

This commitment took many forms, not the least of which were structural district-wide changes to eliminate barriers that kept special education and students with disabilities separate. They combined the teaching and learning (or curriculum decisions) department with the special education department. The learning of students with disabilities became inherently connected to the teaching and curriculum across the district. They also eliminated a significant number of special education paraprofessionals. Using those same funds they hired certified special education teachers (three to four teachers for every ten aides). This allowed for greater teacher collaboration and reduced caseloads for special education teachers.

The Assistant Superintendent, Donna Hooper, believes, "We are not perfect and we have work to do, but we are at a much deeper place than we were four years ago. We are working now on how to co-teach better and how to differentiate better. We are no longer worrying about if this student or that student should be here. People know and expect all of our students to be in general education." She also points to their data. In 2008, students with disabilities started elementary school performing better than their peers across the state, but by the time they were through middle school they lagged behind their peers. After four years, this is no longer true. Students with disabilities achieve at higher rates than the state average.

The following guidelines are for administrators to use when making student placement decisions and policies. While not exhaustive, they represent a range of key decisions that can foster inclusion, belonging and learning.

These guidelines can be used to avoid common administrative pitfalls that set up structures impeding achievement and creating seclusion. They are not meant to be a recipe, but are intended to help put structures and policies in place to create truly inclusive schools.

Home District: All students are educated within their school district.

No students (including students with significant disabilities, students with challenging behaviors, students with autism, etc.) are sent to other districts or cooperative programs outside of the home school district.

Home School: All students attend the schools and classrooms they would attend regardless of ability/disability or native language.

There are no schools within the district set aside for students with disabilities.

General Education Member: All students are placed in chronologically age-appropriate *general education classrooms*.

This is a legal entitlement, not based on staff preference or comfort level. Each classroom represents a heterogeneous group of students. Special education is a service, not a place. No programs, schools-within-a-school or classrooms are set aside for students with disabilities. Students with disabilities are not slotted into predetermined programs, schools, or classrooms. Particular classrooms are not designated, as inclusive classrooms while others are not.

Density Check: Strive for classroom sections that represent *natural proportions* of the school building.

Natural proportions refer to the percentage of students with disabilities as compared to the entire student body. If you have 10 students with disabilities and 100 students in the school, that natural proportion is 10 percent. The national average of students with disabilities is 12 percent.

Special Education Teacher's Caseloads: Assignment of students with disabilities balances the intensity of student need and case-management responsibility.

This moves away from certain special educators being the "inclusive," "resource," "self-contained" or "emotionally disturbed" to all special educators having similar roles and case loads. Students with disabilities with similar labels are not clustered together.

Team Arrangements: All teachers (general education, special education, ELL, reading, etc.) are assigned to instructional teams on the basis of shared students.

Special education teachers are assigned to collaborate with 2-3 classroom sections or teachers to promote collaboration, communication and co-planning. Creating effective teams of adults who work with the same students is essential; consider grouping compatible adult team members as well as building capacity in all staff members to work with all students. Professional development is needed for adults to embrace these new roles, collaborate well and effectively use meeting time.

Related Services: Related services are portable services that come to the student.

Therefore, related service teachers consult with classroom teams, demonstrate skills and techniques and provide instruction/support within the context of general education. Related service providers need to be a part of the placement of students into general education classrooms process and the daily general education planning and program.

Daily Schedule: Use the schedule to support instructional blocks, time for collaborative planning and problem solving and daily direction and training for paraprofessionals.

The master schedule is used as a tool to leverage the vision of collaborative inclusion. Creating sacred planning time for teams of general educators and special educators is essential.

Service Delivery Teams: District and school-level teams meet regularly to reconfigure resources and to revise service delivery on an annual basis.

Schools engage in an ongoing process to plan for the specific needs of their students. This involves re-examining the current way staff are used, how teams are created, the class placement process and the master schedule.

Figure 2.5 District/School Guidelines for Inclusive Student Placement

Table 2.3 Misguided Practices Inclusive Schools Work to Avoid

Practice That Undermines Inclusion and Student Success	Problematic Issues With This Practice
Pullout programs	• Students miss important content. • Social stigma and social isolation. • Over-identification of African American and low-income students in pullout programs.
Self-contained programs	• Very limited access to general education peers, curriculum, or teachers. • Tend to be used for students with the most complex needs. • Do not employ special methods or individualization. • Result in higher teacher burnout rates. • Result in low post-secondary employment rates and independent living. • Have an over-representation of students of color and low-income students. • Rely on an increased use of physical restraint on students.
Dense clustering of students with needs	• Indicate an effort to create "inclusive" classrooms, but the proportions are unnatural. • Disproportionate amount of needs can make these classrooms very much like special education classrooms.
One-on-one support	• Often the least trained and expected to work with students with the most significant needs. • Results in less direct teacher involvement. • Unnecessary dependence. • Interference with peer interaction. • Loss of personal control. • Provocation of negative behaviors.
Age-inappropriate placements	• Performing at grade level is not a requirement to receive modification at an age-appropriate curriculum. • Risk of students being seen as perpetual young children and not developing students with complex emotions and desires. • Lose opportunities to develop an authentic community where students progress through the grades together, learning from and with one another.
Tracking	• Not authentic and meaningful inclusion. • Results in dense clustering of student needs. • Curriculum is usually slower paced, thus getting through less of the general curriculum. • Contributes to lower learning and future possibilities.

DISTRICT CASE STUDY GUIDING QUESTIONS

1. What is surprising about the approaches that the Homesfield School District took in the process of becoming more inclusive?
2. What were some key principles and strategies involved in this change?
3. What can you take away from these examples and replicate in your own school districts?
4. What knowledge, skills, and beliefs are required to lead these changes?

Important Lessons From These Case Studies

When it comes to working toward inclusive education, we see that many schools and districts engage in well-intentioned, but arguably misguided, practices. Table 2.3 briefly illustrates six common practices that undermine inclusion and student success that Summer Heights and River View schools, as well as the Homesfield district, worked to avoid. Awareness of these potential pitfalls, as well as implementation of the strategies we have laid out previously, can help to shape more intentional, effective, and productive approaches for leaders to model when implementing inclusive school reform. We believe that a combination of learning from others' trials and triumphs, as well as having the right tools to chart their own paths, sets the stage for ongoing problem-solving, development, and collaboration as we work toward more inclusive contexts for all.

CONCLUSION

Given the current contexts of schools, school leaders need to not only spend time and energy on issues relating to disability, but they also must have a vision of how to serve inclusively all students, and in particular students with disabilities. Inclusive school reform is a pivotal endeavor, one in which administrators play the critical role to inclusive school success. This inclusive leadership requires both an understanding of and ability to lead a ten-step inclusive leadership process. Throughout this chapter, we have set the stage by describing the present educational conditions and provided a ten-step process with tools and examples of how to implement inclusive school reform in all schools and districts.

NOTE

1   Pseudonyms are used throughout this chapter to protect the privacy of these schools.

REFERENCES

Artiles, A. J., Bal, A., & Thorius, K. A. K. (2010). Back to the future: A critique of response to intervention's social justice views. *Theory into Practice*, *49*, 250–257.

Artiles, A. J., Kozleski, E. B., Trent, S. C., Osher, D., & Ortiz, A. (2010). Justifying and explaining disproportionality, 1968–2008: A critique of underlying views of culture. *Council for Exceptional Children, 76*(3), 279–299.

Ashby, C. E., & Causton-Theoharis, J. N. (2009). Disqualified in the human race: A close reading of the autobiographies of individuals identified as autistic. *International Journal of Inclusive Education, 13*(5), 501–516.

Baglieri, S., Bejoian, L., Broderick, A.A., Connor, D.J., & Valle, J. (2011). [Re]claiming "inclusive education" toward cohesion in educational reform: Disability studies unravels the myth of the normal child. *Teachers College Record, 113*(10), 2122–2154.

Biklen, D., & Burke, J. (2006). Presuming competence. *Equity & Excellence in Education, 39*(2), 166–175.

Blanchett, W.J., Klingner, J.J., & Harry, B. (2009). The intersection of race, culture, language, and disability: Implications for urban education. *Urban Education, 44*(4), 389–409.

Blatt, B. (1987). *The conquest of mental retardation.* Austin, TX: Pro-Ed.

Bogdan, R., & Taylor, S. (1976). The judged, not the judges: An insider's view of mental retardation. *American Psychologist, 31*(1), 47–52.

Capper, C.A., & Frattura, E. (2008). *Meeting the needs of students of all abilities: Leading beyond inclusion* (2nd ed.). Thousand Oaks, CA: Corwin Press.

Cartledge, G., Singh, A., & Gibson, L. (2008). Practical behavior-management techniques to close the accessibility gap for students who are culturally and linguistically diverse. *Preventing School Failure, 52,* 29–38.

Causton, J., & Theoharis, G. (2014). *The principal's handbook to leading inclusive schools.* Baltimore, MD: Brookes Publishing.

Causton-Theoharis, J., & Theoharis, G. (2008). Creating inclusive schools for all students. *The School Administrator, 65*(8), 24–30.

Cole, C.M., Waldron, N., & Majd, M. (2004). Academic progress of students across inclusive and traditional settings. *Mental Retardation, 42*(2), 136–144.

Connor, D.J. (2006). Michael's story: "I get into so much trouble just by walking": Narrative knowing and life at the intersections of learning disability, race, and class. *Equity & Excellence in Education, 39*(2), 154–165.

Connor, D.J. (2007). *Urban narratives: Portraits in progress, life at the intersections of learning disability, race & social class.* New York, NY: Peter Lang.

Danforth, S. (1997). On what basis of hope? Modern and postmodern possibilities. *Mental Retardation, 35*(2), 93–106.

Dawson, H., Delquadri, J., Greenwood, C., Hamilton, S., Ledford, D., Mortweet, S., . . . Walker, D. (1999). Classwide Peer Tutoring: Teaching Students with Mild Retardation in Inclusive Classrooms. *The Council for Exceptional Children 65*(4), 524–536.

Donnellan, A. (1984). The criterion of the least dangerous assumption. *Behavioral Disorders, 9,* 141–150.

Donovan, S., & Cross, C. (Eds.). (2002). *Minority students in special and gifted education.* Washington, DC: National Academy Press.

Ferri, B.A. (2009). Doing a (dis)service: Reimagining special education from a disability studies perspective. In W. Ayers, T. Quinn, & D. Stovall (Eds.), *Handbook of social justice in education* (pp. 377–399). New York, NY: Routledge.

Ferri, B.A. (2012). Undermining inclusion? A critical reading of response to intervention (RTI). *International Journal of Inclusive Education, 16*(8), 863–880.

Ferri, B.A., & Connor, D.J. (2006). *Reading resistance: Discourses of exclusion in desegregation and inclusion debates.* New York, NY: Peter Lang.

Fisher, M., & Meyer, L. (2002). Development and social competence after two years for students enrolled in inclusive and self-contained educational programs. *Research & Practice for Persons With Severe Disabilities, 27*(3), 165–174.

Frattura, E., & Capper, C.A. (2007). *Leading for social justice: Transforming schools for all learners.* Thousand Oaks, CA: Corwin Press.

Freeman, S., & Alkin, M. (2000). Academic and social attainments of children with mental retardation in general education and special education settings. *Remedial and Special Education, 21*(1), 3–18.

Garcia, S.B. & Ortiz, A.A. (2011). Intersectionality as a framework for transformative research in special education. *Multiple Voices for Ethically Diverse Exceptional Learners, 13*(2).

Garland-Thomson, R. (1997). *Extraordinary bodies: Figuring physical disability in American culture and literature.* New York, NY: Columbia University Press.

Gersten, R., & Dimino, J.A. (2006). Response to intervention: Rethinking special education for students with reading difficulties (yet again). *Reading Research Quarterly, 41*(1), 99–108.

Giangreco, M. F., Dennis, R., Cloninger, C., Edelman, S., & Schattman, R. (1993). "I've counted Jon": Transformational experiences of teachers educating students with disabilities. *Exceptional Children, 59*(4), 359–372.

Hardman, M. L., & Dawson, S. (2008). The impact of federal public policy on curriculum and instruction for students with disabilities in the general education classroom. *Preventing School Failure, 52*(2), 5–11.

Individuals with Disabilities Education Improvement Act of 2004, 20 U.S.C. 1401 *et seq.*

Kennedy, C., Shulka, S., & Fryxell, D. (1997). Comparing the effects of educational placement on the social relationships of intermediate school students with severe disabilities. *Exceptional Children, 64*(1), 31–48.

Losen, D., & Orfield, J. (2002). *Racial inequity in special education.* Cambridge, MA: Harvard Education Press.

Macartney, S., Bishaw, A., & Fontenot, K. (2013). Poverty rates for selected detailed race and Hispanic groups by state and place: 2007–2011. *American Community Survey Briefs.* Retrieved from http://census.gov

McLeskey, J., & Waldron, N. L. (2006). Comprehensive school reform and inclusive schools. *Theory Into Practice, 45*(3), 269–278.

National Center for Education Statistics. (2014). *The condition of education 2014.* Retrieved from http://nces.ed.gov/pubs2014/2014083.pdf

NCCRESt. (2005). *Cultural considerations and challenges in response-to-intervention models.* Retrieved from http://www.nccrest.org/PDFs/rti.pdf?v_document_name=Culturally%20Responsive%20RTI

No Child Left Behind Act of 2001, Pub. L. 107–110, 115 Stat. 1425.

Parrish, T. (2002). Racial disparities in the identification, funding, and provision of special education. In D. J. Losen & G. Orfield (Eds.), *Racial inequality in special education* (pp. 15–37). Cambridge, MA: Harvard Education Press.

Rea, P. J., McLaughlin, V. L., & Walther-Thomas, C. (2002). Outcomes for students with learning disabilities in inclusive and pull-out programs. *Exceptional Children, 72*, 203–222.

Riehl, C. J. (2000). The principal's role in creating inclusive schools for diverse students: A review of normative, empirical, and critical literature on the practice of educational administration. *Review of Educational Research, 70*(1), 55–81.

Robledo, J. A., & Donnellan, A. M. (2008). Properties of supportive relationships from the perspective of academically successful individuals with autism. *Intellectual and Developmental Disabilities, 46*(4), 299–310.

Rosenberg, M., Sindelar, P., & Hardman, M. (2004). Preparing highly qualified teachers for students with emotional and behavioral disorders: The impact of NCLB and IDEA. *Behavioral Disorders, 29*, 266–278.

Salend, S., & Duhaney, L. (1999). The impact of inclusion on students with and without disabilities and their educators. *Remedial and Special Education, 20*, 114–126.

Shakespeare, T. (2010). The social model of disability. In L. J. Davis (Ed.), *The disability studies reader* (3rd ed., pp. 266–273). New York, NY: Routledge.

Sharpe, M. N., York, J. L., & Knight, J. (1994). Effects on inclusion on academic performance of classmates without disabilities. *Remedial and Special Education, 15*(5), 281–287.

Staub, D., & Peck, C. A. (1995). What are the outcomes for nondisabled students? *Educational Leadership, 52*(4), 36–40.

TASH. (2009, July). *Inclusive education and implications for policy: The state of the art and the promise.*

Taylor, S. (2008). Before it had a name: Exploring the historical roots of disability studies in education. In S. Danforth & S. L. Gabel (Eds.), *Vital questions facing disability studies in education* (pp. xiii–xxiii). New York, NY: Peter Lang.

Theoharis, G. (2009). *The leadership our children deserve: 7 keys to equity, social justice, and school reform.* New York, NY: Teachers College Press.

US Department of Education. (2007). *IDEA regulations: Alignment with the No Child Left Behind (NCLB) Act.* Retrieved from http://idea.ed.gov/explore/view/p/%2Croot%2Cdynamic%2CTopicalBrief%2C3%2C

US Department of Education, Office of Special Education Programs (OSEP). (2011). *Thirtieth annual report to Congress on the implementation of the Individuals with Disabilities Education Act*. Washington, DC: Author.

US Department of Education, Office of Special Education Programs (OSEP). (2012). *Thirty-first annual report to Congress on the implementation of the Individuals with Disabilities Education Act*. Washington, DC: Author.

Villa, R. A., & Thousand, J. S. (2003). Making inclusive education work. *Educational Leadership, 61*(2), 19–23.

Waldron, N., & McLeskey, J. (1998). The effects of an inclusive school program on students with mild and severe learning disabilities. *Exceptional Children, 64*(2), 395–405.

Wickenden, M. (2009). Talking to teenagers: Using anthropological methods to explore identity and the lifeworlds of young people who use AAC. *Communication Disorders Quarterly, 32*, 151–163.

CHAPTER 3

Inclusive Leadership and Poverty

Curt Dudley-Marling and
Anne Dudley-Marling

It's such a Bore Being always Poor.

(Hughes, n.d.)

PART 1: THE CURRENT CONTEXT OF POVERTY IN SCHOOLS

As the Langston Hughes quote reminds us, it isn't easy being poor. For the 46.5 million Americans living below the poverty thresholds established by the US Census Bureau (2013),[1] 16 million of whom are children, living in poverty means living with less. But the effects of being poor go well beyond the inability to purchase the small luxuries that most Americans take for granted. There are serious consequences of living in poverty, especially for children. Books (2004) notes that

> Poor children bear the brunt of almost every imaginable social ill. In disproportionate numbers, they suffer hunger and homelessness; untreated sickness and chronic conditions such as asthma, ear infections, and tooth decay; lead poisoning and other forms of environmental pollution; and a sometimes debilitating level of stress created by crowded, run-down living spaces, family incomes that fall short of family needs, and ongoing threats of street violence and family dissolution.
>
> (p. 5)

Adverse experiences in early childhood, including poverty, have even been shown to have a lasting impact on children's developing brains, including the capacity to learn new skills, the ability to regulate stress, and the ability to make healthy adaptations to future adverse situations (Juster, McEwen, & Lupien, 2010; Shonkoff & Garner, 2012).

Given the material effects of "being always poor" it should surprise no one that children living in poverty are at a much higher risk for school failure than their more affluent peers. According to the most recent data from the National Assessment of Educational Progress

(NAEP) (2013), students eligible for free lunch, a commonly used index for poverty, are far more likely to achieve at *below basic* levels in math and reading and less likely to reach *proficient* or *advanced* levels in these same subjects compared to their peers. For example, among fourth-grade students eligible for free lunch, 48% scored in the *below basic* range in reading and only 18% reached *proficient* or *advanced* levels. Conversely, 51% of fourth-grade students not eligible for free lunch scored at the *proficient* or *advanced* levels and only 17% were *below basic* in reading. Despite the promise of the No Child Left Behind Act (NCLB, 2001), the NAEP data indicate that the achievement gap between children living in poverty and their more affluent peers has not diminished over the last decade (NAEP, 2013).

Exacerbating this "achievement gap" between poor students and students not living in poverty is the finding that poor students are more likely to attend underfunded schools with fewer instructional resources (Books, 2004). A publication from the Education Trust observes that

> We take the kids who have the least in their homes and communities, and we give them *less* in school, too. Indeed, poor children receive less of everything that research and experience tell us would boost their achievement and improve their chances of succeeding in school and beyond.
>
> (Hall & Ushomirsky, 2010, p. 1)

Kati Haycock (1999), director of the Education Trust, is among those who are critical of the attention given to the issue of poverty by many urban educators who, she believes, excuse teachers in high-poverty schools who fail to teach effectively. However, as Diane Ravitch (2013) observes, "poverty is not an excuse. It is a harsh reality. No one wants poverty to be any child's destiny. Public schools exist to give all children equal educational opportunity, no matter what their zip code" (Ravitch, 2013, Loc. 4574). Ravitch then offers an outline of a program for reducing poverty that includes good prenatal care, high-quality early childhood education, and a rich, balanced, high-quality curriculum.

In reality, poor students are much less likely to be offered the same rich, engaging learning opportunities commonly provided to students in more affluent, high-achieving schools and classrooms. In particular, poor children are more likely to experience an impoverished curriculum that focuses on low-level skills and abilities (Allington, 2000; Oakes, 2005; Watanabe, 2008), what Haberman (1991) has referred to as a "pedagogy of poverty." From this perspective, students in high-poverty schools and classrooms learn less because they are taught less.

In this chapter we argue that the antidote to the pedagogy of poverty that plagues the schooling of poor students is the sort of rich, engaging, high-expectation curriculum commonly found in high-achieving schools and classrooms. Inclusive, socially just leadership ensures that poor students receive such educational opportunities. A high-expectation curriculum is not sufficient to completely overcome the debilitating effects of poverty, but a rich, challenging curriculum is a necessary component in a comprehensive program aimed at improving the academic performance of students in poverty. In keeping with the theme woven throughout this text, we address the intersections of poverty with other dimensions of diversity. Although our focus here is on how leadership ensures opportunities to learn for poor students, the categories of race, gender, language, and disability frequently overlap with poverty. No one is ever *just* poor. People living in poverty are also raced, classed, and gendered, speak a particular language, and are members of particular ethic and cultural groups. Notably, Black Americans, women, second-language learners, and people with disabilities are disproportionately represented among children and adults living in poverty.

In the next section we review salient literature regarding how low-level, basic skills curricula limit poor students' affordances for learning. In Part 3, we then discuss how school leaders can draw on the power of high-expectation pedagogies that build on students' existing knowledge and culture while challenging them with the rich, engaging curriculum common in high-achieving schools and classrooms.

PART 2: WHAT WE KNOW ABOUT POVERTY: THE LITERATURE

For the past 50 years, the dominant view for explaining high levels of school failure among children living in poverty has focused on presumed deficiencies in children's language, culture, families, and communities that leave them ill prepared for the academic demands of schooling. Writing in the mid-60s, Bereiter and Engelmann (1966) asserted that the lives of poor children were deficient in opportunities for acquiring "the knowledge and ability which are consistently held to be valuable in school" (p. 24). Poor Black children in particular, Bereiter and Engelmann argued, lacked the ability to use language "to explain, to describe, to instruct, to inquire, to hypothesize, to analyze, to compare, to deduce, and to test . . . the uses [of language] that are necessary for academic success" (p. 31). (For further discussion of deficit orientations regarding language, see Kelsey, Campuzano, & López, this volume; for further discussion of intersections of racism and classis, see Douglass Horsford & Clark, this volume).

Nearly 30 years later, Hart and Risley (1995) published the results of a longitudinal study of language use in families in various socioeconomic groups including six families living in poverty. Based on their analysis of data from this limited sample of six families, all of whom were Black, Hart and Risley concluded that poor children are deficient in language, particularly vocabulary development, and the responsibility for this situation rests with parents who fail to provide their children the quality and quantity of language experiences common in homes of more affluent families. According to Hart and Risley (1995),

> by age 3 the children in professional families would have heard more than 30 million words, the children in working-class families 20 million, and the children in welfare families 10 million" (p. 132). Compared to the welfare families, the professional parents not only exposed their children to more words, they displayed more words of all kinds to their children, "more multiclause sentences, more past and future verb tenses, more declaratives, and more questions of all kinds.
>
> (pp. 123–124)

Although the Hart and Risley study has been criticized for its small sample sizes and ethnocentric bias (see Dudley-Marling & Lucas, 2009), it has had enormous influence on how children in poverty are perceived.

Ruby Payne's "culture of poverty" further illustrates the dominance of deficit thinking as a lens for understanding the academic struggles of poor children. Payne (2005) has created an immensely popular professional development program based on her foundational belief that the lives of poor children are deficient in the cognitive, linguistic, emotional, and spiritual resources needed to escape poverty and move into the middle class (Gorski, 2008). Payne's claims about people living in poverty have been severely criticized for pathologizing the language and culture of people living in poverty (for a summary of critiques of Payne's program, see Gorski, 2008) and for a complete absence of research support (Bomer, Dworin, May, & Semingson, 2008). Moreover, the culture of poverty model upon which

Payne bases her claim that the poor share a common (pathological) culture has been thoroughly discredited (Foley, 1997). Yet, Payne may be one of the most influential figures in urban education in the United States today (Gorski, 2008).

Because of these patterns in the literature, it is incumbent upon educational leaders to resist deficit thinking that pathologizes students in poverty. This is a pedagogical matter and an issue of social justice. No child, whether poor, a member of a racial, ethnic, or linguistic minority, or a student with disabilities, is well served by a system of schooling that begins with the assumption that there is something fundamentally wrong with them, their language, families, culture, or the communities from which they come. But it isn't deficit thinking per se that harms poor children as much as what comes from this stance and, typically, the result of deficit thinking is an impoverished pedagogy of poverty (Haberman, 1991) that limits poor children's opportunities for learning.

The Impoverished Curricula That Come From Deficit Thinking

Snow, Burns, and Griffin (1998) concluded that, "children living in high-poverty areas tend to fall further behind, regardless of their initial . . . skill level" (p. 98) a finding that led Gee (2004) to ask,

> What is it about school that manages to transform children who are good at learning . . . regardless of their economic and cultural differences, into children who are not good at learning, if they are poor or members of certain minority groups?
>
> (p. 10)

We believe that the answer to Gee's question lies in the quality of curriculum provided to students perceived to be "at risk" for academic failure, including students living in poverty. Students in lower academic tracks and ability groupings, places overpopulated by poor children (Oakes, 2005), are far more likely to experience qualitatively inferior curricula compared to their higher-achieving peers.[2] Students in poverty—and other children viewed through the lens of deficit thinking—learn less because they are taught less.

This conclusion is not new. Writing over 30 years ago, Jean Anyon (1980) reported that children from different socioeconomic groups experience qualitatively different forms of schooling that affect students' educational and vocational aspirations. Anyon found that the curricular experiences of students attending working-class schools were likely to emphasize low-level, mechanical, rote skills. This finding contrasted sharply with the practices that Anyon observed in affluent, professional schools where students experienced a challenging curriculum in which schoolwork was carried out creatively and independently and where students were "continually asked to express and apply ideas and concepts" (p. 79).

Anyon's findings are reinforced by recent work on curricular tracking. Watanabe (2008), for instance, reported that, compared to students in lower academic tracks, students in "academically gifted tracks" spend less time on explicit test preparation, giving them more time to engage in other curricula that teachers deem important; receive more opportunities to practice a wider range of reading and writing skills; engage in more challenging instruction and assignments; receive more written and immediate feedback on essay assignments; and, generally, do more reading and writing in their classes. Additional evidence of differential curricular practices in higher and lower academic tracks and ability groups can be found in Oakes' (2005) comprehensive study of tracking. Crucially, poor and minority students are far more likely to be placed in lower academic tracks or ability groups and less likely to be placed in higher academic tracks than their more affluent peers (Oakes, 2005).

A recent study of mathematics curriculum in different settings by Schmidt and McKnight (2012) offers further support for the finding that students in high-poverty settings tend to have fewer opportunities to learn high-level academic content. They compared schools by socioeconomic status (SES)—the social standing of individuals or groups measured as a combination of education, income, and occupation. Based on their analysis of mathematics curriculum across states and school districts in the US, Schmidt and McKnight (2012) conclude that students in low-SES schools and classrooms are offered fewer opportunities to learn challenging mathematics content than their peers in higher SES settings. They found, for example, that eighth-grade children in high-SES school districts "were more often in classes that focused on algebra and geometry, while children in lower SES districts took more basic mathematics" (p. 67). Schmidt and McKnight's findings are consistent with earlier research by Oakes, Ormseth, Bell, and Camp (1990), who found that low-income students have fewer opportunities to learn science and mathematics. Poor students, according to Oakes and colleagues, have less access to science and mathematics content knowledge in their classrooms, fewer resources, less engaging learning curriculum, and less qualified teachers.

The primary rationale for tracking and ability grouping is based on the assumption that instruction for students in lower academic groupings needs to focus on the basic, presumably foundational skills (phonics or computational skills, for example) that they need to master if they are going to succeed in school without holding back students perceived as more able. These practices are often presented as best practices. But students learn what they are taught and, conversely, students do not learn what they are not taught (Allington, 1983); therefore, students in lower and higher ability groups are often taught—and learn—very different academic content. While elementary students in high-ability reading groups engage in reading and discussing interesting, challenging texts, for example, their peers in low-ability groups focus on low-level decoding skills (Finn, 2009).

In general, students in lower ability groups experience a circumscribed curriculum that limits their educational and, ultimately, vocational opportunities (Duncan & Murnane, 2014). When the learning of students in the lower tracks is assessed, these students will be faulted for what they have not learned; that is, they have not learned as much or as deeply as the students in the higher tracks. This finding appears to justify the whole enterprise of tracking and ability grouping. However, students in lower academic tracks do not learn as much or as deeply as students in the higher tracks because they simply aren't taught as much or as deeply. This explains the finding that even relatively able students will have difficulty escaping from lower tracks (Slavin, 1990).

We are not claiming that all students will achieve at the highest academic levels, nor are we arguing that basic skill instruction is unnecessary. What we are asserting, however, is that students whose education is limited to low-level skills will learn *only* low-level skills. Therefore, effective, socially just leadership demands creating inclusive spaces where students in poverty have opportunities to learn the highly valued content associated with the highest levels of academic achievement.

PART 3: INCLUSIVE LEADERSHIP AROUND POVERTY IN SCHOOLS

Our basic argument is that the high levels of school failure experienced by students in poverty is a socially constructed phenomenon. In addition to coping with the material effects of poverty, poor students are burdened by a qualitatively inferior curriculum that severely constrains their affordances for learning. For educational leaders, the antidote to the low-level, skills-based curricula common in high-poverty schools and classrooms is creating inclusive spaces where *all* students experience the rich, engaging curriculum found in high-achieving schools and classrooms. A high-expectation curriculum affords poor students access to high status learning while simultaneously making challenging content relevant, meaningful, and accessible by situating learning in students' language, culture, and experiences. A high-expectation curriculum provides meaningful and culturally relevant pedagogy. It sharply contrasts with low-level, decontextualized, basic skills instruction that, paradoxically, makes learning more difficult by denying students access to the background knowledge and experiences that support learning new things (Smith, 1998). An important point we want to underscore throughout is that implementing high-expectation curricula is a key socially just leadership priority for reaching *all* students, including not only those living in poverty, but others as well, including culturally and linguistically diverse students, students with disabilities, and others.

Implementing high-expectation curricula for *all* students requires thoughtful leadership focused on systemic change. Specifically, transforming the low-expectation curriculum typically provided to students in poverty begins with dismantling the practices of tracking and ability grouping. Such practices are based on the assumption that children presumed to be at risk require qualitatively different instruction.

In the following sections we discuss three areas of focus for educational leaders seeking to create inclusive learning environments for students in poverty and other children plagued by deficit thinking: detracking and heterogeneous ability grouping; creating culturally relevant instruction that builds on students' background knowledge and experience; and illustrations of high-expectation curriculum in high-poverty schools.

Dismantling Tracking and Ability Grouping

Tracking and ability grouping are widely accepted practices in elementary and secondary schools in the United States. Ability grouping typically begins with first-grade reading groups and extends to high schools that offer a range of academic tracks based on presumed student ability. Yet, "study after study . . . finds no positive effect of ability grouping in any subject or at any grade level, even for the high achievers most widely assumed to benefit from grouping" (Slavin, 1990, p. 491). In general, homogeneous grouping has been found to be ineffective in improving academic achievement and often results in an inferior quality of education with respect to "instructional practices . . . classroom climate . . . and the resulting student attitudes" (Dawson, 1987, p. 349). On the other hand, a substantial body of literature supports the efficacy of heterogeneous, detracked classrooms (Oakes, 2008; Thompson, 2001).

School leaders need, first and foremost, to be well versed in the literature describing detracked schools. Burris, Wiley, Welner, and Murphy (2008), for instance, examined patterns of student achievement in a school district that gradually detracked its middle and high school curricula by offering all students a rich, challenging mathematics curriculum in mixed-ability classrooms. When all middle school students were offered the accelerated math curriculum previously reserved for the school's highest achievers, more than 90% of students in heterogeneously grouped classes entered high school having passed the first New York Regents mathematics exam. Moreover, the percentage of Black and Latino students passing this exam more than tripled (from 23% to 75%). At the high school level, being a member of a detracked cohort substantially increased the odds of a student attaining a Regents diploma; increased by 70% the odds of attaining an International Baccalaureate diploma; and resulted in a decrease in school dropouts. Gains in these areas were particularly strong for Black and Latino students.

The Preuss School is another example of a successful detracked school. The Preuss School is a single-track, college-preparatory public charter high school on the University of California, San Diego (UCSD) campus that provides a rigorous curriculum to low-income students whose parents or guardians have not graduated from a four-year college or university (Mehan, 2013). The school selects through a lottery low-income students with high potential but "under-developed" skills. Seventy-five percent of Preuss students are Black or Hispanic. The school's curriculum, which emphasizes project-based learning informed by a portfolio of assessments, fulfills or exceeds the entry requirements of the University of California and California State University systems. In addition to its rigorous curriculum, the school also seeks to create a college-going culture reinforced by its location on the UCSD campus. An average of 84% of the graduates of the first classes at Preuss (2004–2009) attended four-year colleges and Preuss was among the highest ranked high schools in the district in 2009, 2010, and 2011, outpacing many schools with a much lower proportion of students living in poverty. In 2009 Preuss was named by *Newsweek* as its "Top Transformative High School" ("High School Rankings 2011," 2011).

Boaler and Staples (2008) offer yet another illustration of the effectiveness of high-expectation curricula in detracked schools. They report on a five-year longitudinal study of approximately 700 students in three high schools: Hilltop High School, a rural school where approximately half the students are Latino and half are White; Greendale High School, situated in a coastal community with little ethnic or cultural diversity; and Railside High School, a diverse, urban high school whose students come from a variety of ethnic and cultural backgrounds and where "lessons are frequently interrupted by the noise of trains passing just feet away from the classrooms" (p. 614). The teachers at Railside created a challenging, problem-oriented mathematics program drawing on reform curricula such as the "College Preparatory Mathematics Curriculum" while the teachers at the other two high schools relied on more traditional math curricula. Additionally, students at Railside were organized into heterogeneous (detracked) classes compared to tracked classes at Hilltop and Greendale. At the beginning of Year 1, students at Railside were achieving at significantly lower levels in mathematics than students at the other two high schools. At the end of Year 1, however, students at Railside were achieving at roughly the same level as students in the other high schools on a test of algebra, and at the end of Year 2 Railside students significantly outperformed students at the other two high schools on a test of algebra and geometry.

Evidence from the literature, such as the examples laid out above, provide a firm foundation from which educational leaders can support the creation of heterogeneous ability groupings that challenge all students with rich, engaging curriculum. Detracking is a key step toward achieving high levels of academic success for all students, dismantling structures of schooling that perpetuate racial and class inequities that have long plagued our schools. In the following sections we build from this, describing how educational leaders promote culturally relevant, high-expectation curricula in mixed-ability classrooms.

GUIDING QUESTIONS

- Who and what present the biggest barriers to eliminating tracking and ability grouping in your school context?
- Who are the biggest allies to eliminating tracking and ability grouping in your school context?
- What are ways that you can envision discussing research evidence regarding tracking and ability grouping in your school context?

Culturally Responsive Theories of Education

Alongside eliminating tracking and ability grouping, school leaders must ensure that class-rooms are crafted that are characterized by both high expectations and strong supports for students to meet these expectations (Duncan & Murnane, 2014; Perry, 2003). In contrast to deficit perspectives that devalue and pathologize the knowledge, language, and culture of children and families living in poverty, culturally responsive educational theories recognize and build upon the wealth of cultural and linguistic knowledge that all students bring to school with them each day. These theories are grounded in the assumption that all children are smart, capable learners who bring rich cultural and familial knowledge with them to their formal education experiences (Gay, 2000; Ladson-Billings, 1992). Culturally respon-sive approaches to education are based on sociocultural learning theories in which learn-ing is seen as a process heavily steeped in and influenced by culture. According to these theories, children learn by interacting with members of their culture and using cultural tools, ways of communicating, and language to frame and support their learning. Culture, in turn, shapes the way that children learn and how they come to perceive their worlds. Children are not "blank slates" or "empty vessels" waiting to be filled with knowledge, but active participants in constructing their own learning (Vygotsky, 1978; Derman-Sparks, 1993–1994).

In practice, (socio)culturally responsive pedagogies draw on student's existing "out-of-school" cultural and linguistic practices, maintaining high expectations for achievement and creating spaces for these practices to permeate the formal curriculum (McIntyre & Hulan, 2013). Culturally responsive leaders work with teachers to adapt their methods and strategies in ways that enable all learners to be successful, including children from poor, culturally diverse backgrounds (Banks, 2003). Below we present two approaches crucial for shaping and informing responsive practices as well as ensuring challenging and meaningful curriculum for all children.

Funds of Knowledge

"Funds of Knowledge" is a culturally responsive approach to teaching that helps educators identify and then build on what children already know. The Funds of Knowledge approach was developed by a group of researchers based on ethnographic studies, interviews, and life histories with families that illuminate the wealth of cultural and intellectual knowledge available to children within their homes and communities (Moll, Amanti, Neff, & Gonza-lez, 1992). This approach is particularly important for children whose households are often viewed as deficient in knowledge and linguistic resources because of their economic status and/or because the cultural heritage of the home is different from the dominant culture. Through a careful examination of the data collected from families, researchers identified "ample cultural and cognitive resources with great, potential utility for classroom instruc-tion" (p. 134) within the homes they analyzed. These cognitive and cultural resources are "historically accumulated and culturally developed" (p. 133) and essential for all families to function, regardless of culture or socioeconomic status.

The "funds of knowledge" identified by Moll and colleagues (1992) encompasses a wide range of skills, proficiencies, and abilities based on the environment (e.g., urban, rural), occupations of family members and families' origins and culture. Funds of knowl-edge include, for example, knowledge of religion (morals, reading the Bible), household management (caring for children, cooking), economics (paying bills, renting an apart-ment), scientific knowledge (weather, baking), and so on (Moll et al., 1992). A study by Riojas-Cortez (2001) that examined the funds of knowledge of very young children in a rural Texas town showed that young children's environmentally based knowledge included visiting ranches and branding animals, preparing for a tornado, and visiting a carnival and local amusement parks. The children also had knowledge related to their parents' professions including working at a restaurant and using a truck for work as well as knowledge of family values and traditions such as giving a bottle to a baby, talking on the phone to relatives, and celebrating birthdays (Riojas-Cortez, 2001).

Funds of Knowledge is a powerful tool for teachers to both gather and understand the knowledge that their students have and support school learning through critical home-classroom connections. Research has shown that building bridges between what children already know and new content can strengthen learning and help to ensure future academic success (Nagy, Anderson, & Herman, 1987). In order to uncover students' funds of knowledge, teachers can take on the role of researcher or learner in the homes of the families they work with, including making home visits; conducting authentic, open-ended interviews with students and family members; and maintaining communication with families to ask for curricular input. This can include having family members come into the classroom to share stories and complete projects with children as well as offer feedback to teachers on how their children's knowledge can be incorporated into the lessons and curriculum (Moll et al., 1992).

Funds of Knowledge in Practice

One example of Funds of Knowledge in practice is the "Family Stories Project," a literacy unit conducted in a fourth-grade, Spanish-English bilingual classroom (Dworin, 2006). The aim of the project was to encourage children's language and literacy development in both English and Spanish by using families as a key cultural resource. The unit began with a collaborative discussion of two bilingual short stories about family get-togethers and celebrations. During the discussion, students were encouraged to speak in both English and Spanish and the teachers responded using the language in which the child had chosen to speak. After the discussion, children were asked to gather similar stories about their own families and to write down one story to be shared with the whole class. Students then listened to their classmates read their stories aloud and responded with questions such as, "Where did this take place?," "More details . . ." and "You didn't say why you were afraid!" (p. 513). Students revised their story drafts several times based on peers' feedback. Once a final draft was achieved, students were asked to translate one another's stories into either Spanish of English depending on which language the student author had chosen. This was done to provide an additional challenge to further develop children's biliteracy skills. Finally, the stories were collected together and published into two classroom books, one in English and one in Spanish (Dworin, 2006).

The Family Stories Project provides an excellent example of using children's cultural and linguistic resources in the classroom. Using family stories and experiences as the basis for the project allowed the teacher to connect to students' funds of knowledge as a means of learning important writing and editing skills. Additionally, by encouraging children to use both Spanish and English in classroom discussions and in writing their stories, teachers showed that they valued children's linguistic resources while helping students to develop language and literacy skills in two languages. The project had the additional benefit of enlightening teachers about the lives of their students outside of the classroom and providing them with important information about the funds of knowledge of the families with whom they worked. This project also illustrates how an approach such as Funds of Knowledge can address multiple, intersecting dimensions of diversity, such as race and ethnicity, language and culture, and socioeconomic status.

Culturally Responsive and Culturally Relevant Pedagogy

Culturally relevant, culturally responsive pedagogies are similar to funds of knowledge in that they value and build on students' culture, language, and experiences as strengths that students bring to the classroom and are worthy of being infused into the curriculum and classroom environment. Culturally relevant and responsive practices also recognize the need for educators to confront social and societal inequities within their classrooms and challenge both personal and institutional biases (Gay, 2000; Ford & Kea, 2009).

According to Ladson-Billings (1995), culturally relevant teaching involves three important tenets. The first tenet is academic success, a stance that all children must experience academic success and responsive educators must finds ways to channel students' strengths in academically meaningful ways. The second tenet is cultural competence. This is the notion that students must maintain their cultural identities and integrity while acquiring the skills necessary for academic success. In order to achieve this, educators can use children's culture and funds of knowledge as a "vehicle for learning" (p. 161). Ladson-Billings offers the example of a teacher who used her second-grade students' love of rap music to teach them about poetry and poetic devices such as rhyme and alliteration. The third tenet of culturally relevant pedagogy, according to Ladson-Billings, is critical consciousness. For her, merely valuing and using children's cultural knowledge to teach academic skills is insufficient. Culturally responsive teaching must instill a broad social consciousness in students and encourage them to question cultural norms and values as well as critique institutions that perpetuate societal inequities (Ford & Kea, 2009; McIntyre & Hulan, 2013). An example of this tenet is a teacher who reads storybooks to her students that challenge stereotypes as a means of engaging students in discussions of issues of equity, cultural awareness, and the celebration of human differences (Morgan, 2009).

Culturally Relevant Pedagogy in Practice

A science unit described by Laughter and Adams (2012) provides an illustrative example of culturally relevant pedagogy in practice. The unit was built around a short story called *The Space Traders* that was used to both engage students in learning about scientific biases and to address broader issues of social justice and societal inequities. The story was embedded in a broader curricular unit about earth and space sciences designed to meet state curricular standards for sixth-grade science. The plot of the story details a group of space aliens who offer gold, chemicals for cleaning up the environment, and a safe nuclear technology to the United States in exchange for all of the African Americans living in the country. The teacher began by sharing examples with students illustrating how bias can affect scientific findings especially with regards to gender and race. The teacher then read *The Space Traders* out loud to the students, asking them discuss it in an anonymous online forum that had been set up for this purpose. Questions for discussion were focused to both gauge students' understanding of the story and to help them begin to make connections to their own experiences. Finally, the sixth-grade students engaged in a whole class discussion of the story, examining biases that might exist within their own families or within their lives as well as questioning whether biases and racism might exist within their school and greater society as a whole (Laughter & Adams, 2012).

Analysis of students' comments over the course of the unit revealed that students made routine connections between scientific and societal biases as well as important connections to their own lives and experiences. They also tackled the broader issues of racism and discrimination. Throughout the lessons, the teacher maintained high expectations for student academic success and created a safe space in which discussions could occur. By using a short story to connect students to academic content, asking them to draw on their own experiences to explore issues of both social and scientific biases, and discussing broader and societal inequities, this unit provided a framework for culturally relevant teaching.

Overall, culturally relevant pedagogies draw and build on students' linguistic and experiential funds of knowledge in order to make learning meaningful, relevant, and accessible. In other words, culturally relevant pedagogies give to children from culturally diverse backgrounds—students overrepresented among poor underachievers—the advantages already available to their more affluent, academically successful peers.

GUIDING QUESTIONS

- What, in your perspective, are the key factors promoting as well as inhibiting the spread of culturally responsive theories of education in your school context?
- How do you see the strategies of enacting culturally responsive theories of education discussed here serving to expand opportunities to learn from those available within tracked and ability-group settings?

High-Expectation Curriculum: Creating Opportunities for Engaging Learning Through Rigorous Discussion

A third way for school leaders to promote inclusion of students in poverty is to ensure their access to the same high-expectation curriculum as all students. This goes hand in hand with enacting culturally responsive theories of education, described above. A high-expectation curriculum is nothing more than the rich, engaging curriculum that is common in affluent, high-achieving schools and classrooms. As with tracking and ability grouping, an important starting point for school leaders is to raise their own awareness of the literature describing what this looks like. Consider, for example, the Optimum Learning Environment (OLE) project (Ruiz & Figueroa, 1995). Beginning with the assumption that the best pedagogy is often found in classrooms for students labeled as "gifted," Ruiz and Figueroa brought the rich pedagogy and curriculum found in classes for the brightest students to urban ESL, special education students with excellent results (Ruiz, 1999; Ruiz & Figueroa, 1995). The OLE curriculum emphasizes progressive pedagogical principles such as student choice, active student engagement in learning, meaningful and authentic purposes for learning, and learning in social contexts that are more often found in gifted classrooms and affluent suburban schools than in poor urban schools (Ruiz, García, & Figueroa, 1996).

Shared Inquiry is another example of a high-expectation practice that engages elementary-age students in teacher-guided, evidenced-based discussions of challenging texts (Great Books Foundation, 2010). The overall goal of Shared Inquiry is for students to participate in rigorous discussion of challenging texts by responding to teachers' questions—or questions posed by other students—by making claims, backing up those claims with textual evidence, and explicating the link between the textual evidence and the claim; that is, stating how the textual evidence supports their claims. Shared Inquiry begins with the selection of a text for which there is some ambiguity and with an interpretive question framed by the teacher that has more than one possible answer and for which there is textual evidence. Teachers draw on a set of tools—in the form of talk moves—to orchestrate discussions and scaffold students' development of evidence-based reasoning. For instance, teachers may ask students to expand or clarify what they've said (e.g., "What did you mean by that?" "Can you say more?"). They may press students for deeper reasoning (e.g., "Why do you think that?" "What's your evidence?"). Or they might encourage students to connect their reasoning to the reasoning of other students (e.g., "Who agrees or disagrees with what Ian has said?") (Michaels & O'Connor, 2011). Crucially, teachers conducting Shared Inquiry discussions are strongly discouraged from any evaluation of students' responses on the assumption that teacher evaluation constrains open discussion by leading students to believe there really is a right answer.

Again, literature discussion practices like Shared Inquiry are common in affluent, high-achieving schools but, in our experience, rare in settings where students are perceived to be deficient in the basic skills of reading. However, there is a modest body of research indicating that Shared Inquiry positively affects the reading achievement of students in high-poverty settings (e.g., Criscuola, 1994; Dudley-Marling & Michaels, 2013; Hait, 2011; Heinl, 1988).

GUIDING QUESTIONS

- Who and what present the biggest barriers to enacting a high-expectation curriculum in your school context?
- Who and what present the biggest allies to enacting a high-expectation curriculum in your school context?
- What are ways that you can envision identifying and sharing research evidence regarding enacting a high-expectation curriculum in your school context?

In this section we have described three areas of focus for educational leaders who are committed to creating and extending inclusive learning environments for students in poverty and other children plagued by deficit thinking: eliminating tracking and homogenous ability grouping, creating culturally relevant instruction, and enacting high-expectation curriculum. We now turn to a case study describing a school leader enacting such strategies.

Case Study

Lexington Elementary (a pseudonym) is a high-poverty school in the South Bronx in New York City. Like most high-poverty schools, the students at Lexington Elementary experienced high levels of school failure. However, following the introduction of Shared Inquiry, Lexington students showed dramatic gains on district reading tests (see Dudley-Marling & Michaels, 2013). This led Curt Dudley-Marling and Sarah Michaels to seek permission to study the practice of Shared Inquiry and its effects on the teachers and students at Lexington Elementary. The principal data sources for this study were video recordings of Shared Inquiry discussions in fourth-grade classrooms at Lexington Elementary. These videos illustrate what happens when low-achieving students in a high-poverty school are given the opportunity to engage in thoughtful discussions of challenging texts. Consider the discussion of a short story, "Cedric" (Jansson, 1962), in Ms. Hernandez's fourth-grade class that is representative of the other discussions Dudley-Marling and Michaels observed at Lexington Elementary. First, students spent several days preparing for this discussion. On Day 1 Ms. Hernandez read the story to students and then gave them time to read the story independently. Day 2 included a rereading of the text followed by an activity in which students had an opportunity to practice making claims about the text and citing textual evidence to support their claims. Day 3 focused on words and phrases in the text with which students had difficulty. The overall goal over these preparatory activities was to insure that the text was accessible to all students prior to the Shared Inquiry discussion.

Below we share an excerpt from a 54-minute discussion of "Cedric" to illustrate the rigor of the discussions we observed at Lexington Elementary. Readers will find it easier to follow the discussion if they first have some idea of the story. "Cedric" is about a boy named Sniff who has a stuffed animal, Cedric, who has topaz eyes and a moonstone on his collar. The text says, "Possibly the moonstones were more important to Sniff than the dog's inimitable expressions." Sniff gives Cedric away but immediately regrets it. Sniff visits Sniffkin who tells him a story about a woman who had beautiful things that she collected to the exclusion of friends or travel. She gets a bone stuck in her stomach and believes she has a short time to live. She has the idea to give all her stuff away (because she's suffocating), sending just the right thing to different people in anonymous parcels. She begins to feel better and gets nicer. Friends start to visit, and one day she laughs so hard that the bone comes out. She's changed, she has friends and goes off to travel the world. Eventually, Sniff finds Cedric but the topaz eyes have been removed and made into earrings and the moonstone on the collar has been lost. But, as the story says, Sniff loves Cedric "all the same," but now "only for love's sake."

Ms. Hernandez launches the discussion with the question, "Why at the end of the story does Sniff love Cedric 'only for love's sake'?" The following sequence takes place about halfway through the discussion.

Derrick:	Um . . . I think he loved him, like I said before, like, because if like (. . .) Cedric because if had the jewelry back, I think he would still miss Cedric.
Ms. Hernandez:	If he had the jewelry back, he would still miss Cedric?
Derrick:	If they gave him the jewelry and not Cedric, I think he would still miss Cedric.
Ms. Hernandez:	Oh, and what makes you think that? I—uh, everyone heard what he said? [Students: No] If they had just given him the jewelry back, go ahead, Derrick. Keep on from there. They didn't hear you.
Derrick:	Like because on page 80, he regret giving Cedric away. . . . So that's what caused me to think that.
Ms. Hernandez:	But tell them what? They didn't hear the first part.
Derrick:	Oh. If they might give him the jewelry back, he'd might still miss Cedric.
Ms. Hernandez:	Meaning, you know, if he just had the jewelry by itself, without Cedric?
Diarra:	I understand what Derrick is saying. He's saying that that . . . if they gave him the jewels as a souvenir, then he—then it would remind him [Sniff] so much of him [Cedric] and he would miss him more and more all the time.
Ms. Hernandez:	What would make you think he would miss him more and more?
Diarra:	Um, I think he would miss more miss him more and more because he didn't . . . maybe since—
Ms. Hernandez:	No "maybe." What in the story do you think it might—What makes you believe from the story, that it might?
Diarra:	On page 79, it—it says, "Now, afterwards, it is hard to understand how that small beast, Sniff, could have ever been persuaded to give that small—to give Cedric away."

Ms. Hernandez: So what does that—OK?

Diarra: That shows that he loved him so much and he'd miss him if he ever got lost. . . . But since he didn't um: really, she gave him away instead of losing it, uh she's [Teacher: he] he um he's prob—he's probably more angry at himself because, um he really loved him . . . and nobody has ever persuaded him, so he really regretted it. And he was probably um, taking it on himself a lot.

Ms. Hernandez: So then if he really loved him and we don't understand how he could have been persuaded, then why is it . . . that he gives him away to begin with then?

Diarra: Oh. Because he—he didn't understand, on page 80 and 81, he didn't understand what Moomintroll (meant when he) said . . . "He told him that if one gives away something, then one will get it back ten times over and feel wonderful afterwards." And he probably thought that it meant that if he gave away the um the most precious thing, then he'll get—then he'll um then he'll gain something that he'll that he'll need, or something. . . . So he misunderstood what Moomintroll was saying.

Over several turns, Derrick developed the claim that it was Cedric, not the jewels, that Sniff cared about. He supports his claim with a reference to the text (p. 80) which he glosses as "he regret giving Cedric away." Diarra expands Derrick's claim in her own words. If Sniff had the jewels and not Cedric, she argued, it would only cause him to miss Cedric more. Crucially, she quotes directly from the text to support her claim. On prompting from Ms. Hernandez, Diarra explained how the textual evidence supported her claim. "That shows that he loved him so much and he'd miss him if he ever got lost," she says. Over several turns, and with the support of her teacher, Diarra makes a claim, cites textual evidence, and then makes explicit the evidentiary warrant for her claim—a very sophisticated interpretive move. When the teacher asks a follow-up question, Diarra cites additional textual evidence along with an explanation of how this evidence further supports her claim stating that, "He misunderstood what Moomintroll was saying."

Over the course of this discussion—and, indeed, all of the discussions observed at Lexington Elementary—students made claims, cited textual evidence to support their claims and, if asked, made explicit the warrant for their claims. By allowing students to use their own language and experience to connect to the text—and each other—the practice of Shared Inquiry created affordances for learning that enabled previously low-achieving students in a high-poverty school, many of whom were second-language learners or had been identified as having special needs, to participate successfully in sophisticated, highly valued reading practices normally associated with the highest achievers. And there was a dramatic improvement in student test scores at the school. In the year before Shared Inquiry was introduced fewer than 25% of the students at Lexington Elementary achieved the levels "meets" or "exceeds" standards for reading. In the year after the implementation of Shared Inquiry over 50% of the Lexington students met or exceeded standards on the district reading assessments.

Unexpectedly, there were also modest increases in the math and science test scores for Lexington students even though Shared Inquiry discussions focused on reading. Based on interviews with the Lexington teachers and work on evidenced-based discussions in other high-poverty schools, we have come to believe that one of the most significant effects of high-expectation curriculum like Shared Inquiry is that it often transforms teachers' perceptions of their students. A high-expectation curriculum offers teachers a window into students' thinking, challenging their assumptions that students in high-poverty schools *need* a low-level, basic skills curriculum. They begin to presume that their students are competent, which affects their interactions in all subject areas. This, in turn, leads teachers to expand students' opportunities to learn across the curriculum, further reinforcing teachers' belief that their students are up to challenging learning. This is the real power of high-expectation curriculum.

Still, overcoming the skepticism of teachers that all students, including students in poverty, are up to the challenge of high-expectation practices like Shared Inquiry requires the commitment of strong educational leaders who demand that every student is provided with the same affordances for learning. It also requires the courage of leaders working in high-poverty schools and districts willing to eschew curricula focused on low-level skills aimed at achieving short-term improvements on high-stakes tests. If we want all of our students to achieve at the highest levels then they must have opportunities to learn challenging academic content. Not every student will excel in all subjects, but no student can excel without opportunities to learn. Finally, learning will always be more difficult if teachers can't find ways to help students connect what is being taught to their existing knowledge and experience, a basic constructivist principle rooted in the work of Piaget (Gruber & Vonèche, 1977).

GUIDING QUESTIONS

- How are key aspects of Shared Inquiry utilized to enhance the learning of students in poverty?
- What are the barriers to engaging in Shared Inquiry in your school?
- Think about your own school, what would it take to engage in Shared Inquiry or other aspects of high-expectation curriculum?

Equity Audit

Engaging with equity audit questions relating to students in poverty and low-achieving students in terms of classroom and learning opportunity is a key strategy in moving toward more socially just and inclusive schools. The final chapter of this text describes a comprehensive equity audit process. See the poverty section and full equity audit detailed in Chapter 10 and online (www.routledge.com/cw/theoharis).

CONCLUSION

At this moment in time, the total number of Americans living in poverty has reached an all-time high and the percentage of US citizens falling below the poverty line is the highest in 20 years (US Census Bureau, 2013). And, although the majority of people living in poverty are White, people of color are overrepresented among the poor as are women, second-language learners, and people with disabilities. In this chapter we have argued that poor children are burdened by the material effects of poverty, underfunded schools, and a pedagogy of poverty that limits their opportunities to learn the high-status knowledge and skills that are key to educational and vocational success. We have further argued that the antidote to the low-level pedagogy of poverty common in high-poverty schools and classrooms is a high-expectation curriculum that affords poor students greater opportunities to learn. Arguably, a high-expectation curriculum is also crucial for broadening learning opportunities for students with disabilities if they are to achieve their academic potential. It is doubtful, however, that more challenging curricula will be sufficient for overcoming the material effects of poverty. Strong leaders and teachers matter but, despite the claims of many educational reforms, excellent teachers supported by strong leaders will never be enough (Berliner & Glass, 2014). It will always be difficult for children living in poverty to achieve to their potential without access to high-quality health care, food security, adequate housing, toxin-free environments, and well-resourced schools. It is worrisome, therefore, that a powerful political discourse in the United States implicates the poor for their life circumstances. In this narrative anti-poverty programs are certain to fail since, ultimately, the poor lack the values and/or ability to climb out of poverty. The social Darwinist perspective of sociologist Charles Murray (see Murray, 2008) is increasingly cited by conservative politicians and commentators to support proposals for deep cuts in programs benefiting the poor.

Ultimately, for educational leaders seeking to help poor students achieve their learning potential this is both a pedagogical and a political project. Educational leaders committed to a socially just society in which all persons have equitable access to the nation's cultural and economic riches must work both to transform schools serving students in poverty and challenge destructive biases that demonize the poor. School leaders are best equipped to address the problems of schooling but must recognize that this will never be enough. Educational leaders will also need to be social activists if they are truly committed to eliminating the scourge of poverty in our nation.

NOTES

1   Although Black and Hispanic Americans are overrepresented among the poor, contrary to popular stereotypes, the largest group of poor Americans are White (US Census Bureau, 2013).
2   Similar low-level curricula are common in classrooms serving second-language learners and students with disabilities, two groups overrepresented among poor and minority students.

REFERENCES

Allington, R. L. (1983). The reading instruction provided readers of differing abilities. *The Elementary School Journal, 83*(5), 548–559.

Allington, R. L. (2000). *What really matters for struggling readers: Designing research-based programs*. New York: Longman.

Anyon, J. (1980). Social class and the hidden curriculum of work. *Journal of Education, 162*(1), 67–92.

Banks, J. A. (2003). Teaching literacy for social justice and global citizenship. *Language Arts, 81*(1), 18–19.

Bereiter, C., & Engelmann, S. (1966). *Teaching disadvantaged children in the preschool*. Englewood Cliffs, NJ: Prentice-Hall.

Berliner, D. C., & Glass, G. V. (2014). *50 myths and lies that threaten America's public schools: The real crisis in education*. New York: Teachers College Press.

Boaler, J., & Staples, M. (2008). Creating mathematical futures through an equitable teaching approach: The case of Railside School. *Teachers College Record 110*(3), 608–645.

Bomer, R., Dworin, J., May, L., & Semingson, P. (2008). Miseducating teachers about the poor: A critical analysis of Ruby Payne's claims about poverty. *Teachers College Record, 110,* 2497–2531.

Books, S. (2004). *Poverty and schooling in the U.S.: Contexts and consequences.* Mahwah, NJ: Erlbaum.

Burris, C.B., Wiley, E., Welner, K., & Murphy, J. (2008). Accountability, rigor, and detracking: Achievement effects of embracing a challenging curriculum as a universal good for all students. *Teachers College Record, 110*(3), 571–607.

Criscuola, M. (1994). Read, discuss, reread: Insights from the Junior Great Books program. *Educational Leadership, 51*(5), 58–61.

Dawson, M.M. (1987). Beyond ability grouping: A review of the effectiveness of ability grouping and its alternatives. *School Psychology Review, 16,* 348–369.

Derman-Sparks, L. (1993–1994). Empowering children to create a caring culture in a world of differences. *Childhood Education, 70*(2), 66–71.

Dudley-Marling, C., & Lucas, K. (2009). Pathologizing the language and culture of poor children. *Language Arts, 86,* 362–370.

Dudley-Marling, C., & Michaels, S. (2013). Shared inquiry: Making students smart. In C. Dudley-Marling & S. Michaels (Eds.), *High-expectation curricula: Helping all students succeed with powerful learning* (pp. 99–110). New York: Teachers College Press.

Duncan, J., & Murnane, R. (2014). *Restoring Opportunity.* Cambridge, MA: Harvard Education Press.

Dworin, J.E. (2006). The family stories project: Using funds of knowledge for writing. *The Reading Teacher, 59*(6), 510–520.

Finn, P.J. (2009). *Literacy with an attitude: Educating working-class children in their own self-interest.* Albany, NY: SUNY.

Foley, D.E. (1997). Deficit thinking models based on culture: The anthropological protest. In R. Valencia (Ed.), *The evolution of deficit thinking* (pp. 113–131). New York: Routledge Falmer.

Ford, Y.D., & Kea, C.D. (2009). Creating culturally responsive instruction: For students' and teachers' sake. *Focus on Exceptional Children, 42*(9), 1–16.

Gay, G. (2000). *Culturally responsive teaching: Theory, research, and practice.* New York: Teachers College Press.

Gee, J.P. (2004). *Situated language and learning: A critique of traditional schooling.* New York: Routledge.

Gorski, P. (2008). Peddling poverty for profit: A synthesis of criticisms of Ruby Payne's framework. *Equity and Excellence in Education, 41*(1), 130–148.

Great Books Foundation. (2010). *What is shared inquiry?* Retrieved from http://www.greatbooks.org/programs-for-all-ages/pd/what-is-shared- inquiry.html

Gruber, H., & Vonèche, J.J. (1977). *The essential Piaget.* New York: Basic Books.

Haberman, M. (1991). The pedagogy of poverty versus good teaching. *Phi Delta Kappan, 73,* 290–294.

Hait, N.A. (2011). *Learning to do shared inquiry in a fourth grade classroom.* Unpublished dissertation. Chestnut Hill, MA: Boston College.

Hall, D., & Ushomirsky, N. (2010). *Close the hidden funding gaps in our schools.* Washington, DC: Education Trust.

Hart, B., & Risley, T.R. (1995). *Meaningful differences in the everyday experiences of young American children.* Baltimore, MD: Brookes.

Haycock, K. (1999). "Letter from Kati Haycock, Director, The Education Trust." In P. Barth, K. Haycock, H. Jackson, K. Mora, P. Ruiz, S. Robinson, & A. Wilkins (Eds.), *Dispelling the myth: High poverty schools exceeding expectations* (p. i). Washington, DC: The Education Trust.

Heinl, A.M. (1988). *The effects of the Junior Great Books program on literal and inferential comprehension.* Paper presented at the Annual Meeting of the National Reading Conference, Tucson, Arizona.

High school rankings 2011: Newsweek ranks America's most transformative. (2011, June 21). *Newsweek.* Retrieved from http://www.newsweek.com/high-school-rankings-2011-newsweek-ranks-americas-most-transformative-67911

Hughes, L. (n.d). Ennui. In L. Hughes, *The collected poems of Langston Hughes* (p. 305). New York: Knopf Doubleday.

Jansson, T. (1962). "Cedric." In *Tales from Moominvalley* (Trans. T. Warburton, pp. 150–161). New York: Farrar, Strauss, Giroux.

Juster, R.P., McEwen, B.S., & Lupien, S.J. (2010). Allostatic load biomarkers of chronic stress and the impact on health and cognition. *Neuroscience and Biobehavioral Reviews, 35*(1), 2–16.

Ladson-Billings, G. (1992). Reading between the lines and beyond the pages: A culturally relevant approach to literacy and teaching. *Theory Into Practice, 31*(4), 312–320.

Ladson-Billings, G. (1995). But that's just good teaching! The case for culturally relevant pedagogy. *Theory Into Practice, 34*(3), 159–165.

Laughter, J. C., & Adams, A. D. (2012). Culturally relevant science teaching in middle school. *Urban Education, 47*(6), 1106–1134.

McIntyre, E., & Hulan, N. (2013). Research-based, culturally responsive reading practice in elementary classrooms: A yearlong study. *Literacy Research and Instruction, 52*(1), 28–51.

Mehan, H. (2013). Detracking: Re-forming schools to provide students with equitable access to college and career. In C. Dudley-Marling & S. Michaels (Eds.), *The high-expectation curriculum: Helping all students succeed with powerful learning* (pp. 15–27). New York: Teachers College Press.

Michaels, S., & O'Connor, C. (2011). *Promoting academically productive talk across the curriculum: A high-leverage practice*. Unpublished paper.

Moll, L. C., Amanti, C., Neff, D., & Gonzalez, N. (1992). Funds of knowledge for teaching: Using a qualitative approach to connect homes and classrooms. *Theory Into Practice, 31*(2), 132–141.

Morgan, H. (2009). Teaching tolerance and reaching diverse students through the use of children's books. *Childhood Education, 85*(2), 106G–106J.

Murray, C. (2008). *Real education: Four simple truths for bringing America's schools back to reality*. New York: Crown Forum.

Nagy, W. E., Anderson, R. C., & Herman, P. A. (1987). Learning word meanings from context during normal reading. *American educational Research Journal, 24*, 237–270.

National Assessment of Educational Progress (NAEP) (2013). *The nation's report card*. Washington, DC: U.S. Department of Education, Institute of Education Sciences, National Center for Education Statistics.

No Child Left Behind Act of 2001, P.L. No. 107–110, § 115, Stat. 1425 (2002).

Oakes, J. (2005). *Keeping track: How schools structure inequality (2nd ed.)*. New Haven, CT: Yale University Press.

Oakes, J. (2008). Keeping track: Structuring equality and inequality in an era of accountability. *Teachers College Record, 110*(3), 700–712.

Oakes, J., Ormseth, T., Bell, R., & Camp, P. (1990). *Multiplying inequalities: The effects of race, social class, and tracking on opportunities to learn mathematics and science*. Santa Monica, CA: Rand Corporation.

Payne, R. K. (2005). *A framework for understanding poverty* (4th ed.). Highlands, TX: Aha! Process, Inc.

Perry, T. (2003). Young, gifted and black: Promoting high achievement among African American students. In T. Perry, C. Steele, & A. Hilliard (Eds.), *Young, gifted and Black: Promoting high achievement among African American Students* (pp. 131–165). Boston: Beacon Press.

Ravitch, D. 2013. *The hoax of the privatization movement and the danger to America's schools* (eBook). New York: Knopf.

Riojas-Cortez, M. (2001). Preschoolers' funds of knowledge displayed through sociodramatic play episodes in a bilingual classroom. *Early Childhood Education Journal, 29*(1), 35–40.

Ruiz, N. T. (1999). Effective literacy instruction for Latino students receiving special education services: A review of classroom research. *Bilingual Review, 24*(1/2), 161–174.

Ruiz, N., & Figueroa, R. (1995). Learning-handicapped classrooms with Latino students: The optimal learning environment (OLE) project. *Education and Urban Society, 27*, 463–483.

Ruiz, N. T., García, E., & Figueroa, R. A. (1996). *The OLE curriculum guide*. Sacramento, CA: California Department of Education.

Schmidt, W. H., & McKnight, C. C. (2012). *Inequality for all: The challenge of unequal opportunity in American schools*. New York: Teachers College Press.

Shonkoff, J. P., & Garner, A. S. (2012). The lifelong effects of early childhood adversity and toxic stress. *Pediatrics, 129*, 1–17.

Slavin, R. E. (1990). Achievement effects of ability grouping in secondary schools: A best evidence synthesis. *Review of Educational Research, 60*, 471–499.

Smith, F. (1998). *The book of learning and forgetting*. New York: Teachers College Press.

Snow, C. E., Burns, M. S., & Griffin, P. (1998). *Preventing reading difficulties in young children.* Washington, DC: National Research Council.

Thompson, S. (2001). The authentic standards movement and its evil twin. *Phi Delta Kappan, 82*(5), 358–62.

US Census Bureau. (2013). *Poverty.* Retrieved from http://www.census.gov/hhes/www/poverty/poverty.html

Vygotsky, L. S. (1978). *Mind in society: The development of higher psychological processes.* Boston: Harvard University Press.

Watanabe, M. (2008). Tracking in the era of high stakes state accountability reform: Case studies of classroom instruction in North Carolina. *Teachers College Record, 110*(3), 489–534.

CHAPTER 4

Inclusive Leadership and Race

Sonya Douglass Horsford and Christine Clark

The story of public education in the United States cannot be told fully without a discussion of race and its role in the education of American schoolchildren. Whether the American Indian boarding schools of the late 19th and early 20th centuries (General Allotment Act (Dawes Act) of 1887; Fletcher, 2009; Indian Child Welfare Act, 1978), prohibition of "Mongolian or yellow race" children from attending all-White public schools (*Gong Lum v. Rice*, 1927), social separation of Anglos and Mexican students (*Mendez v. Westminster*, 1956), or the *separate but equal* schools of the Jim Crow South (*Plessy v. Ferguson,* 1896) until 1954, the exclusion of *colored* students from otherwise public schools has been a long-held practice in America. A tradition codified in law, many states and jurisdictions not only required racial segregation in schools, but also explicitly prohibited the mixing of races in schools and universities. Efforts to change such laws took time, but the courage of parents and students of color willing to serve as plaintiffs in school desegregation cases and the persistence of the civil rights attorneys who represented them proved successful in ending the legal practice of school segregation in 1954, marking the beginning of the Civil Rights Movement in America (Horsford, 2011).

THE PROBLEM OF RACE IN US SCHOOLS

Beyond the historical, legal, and political features of race and its pervasive nature in US schools and society exists the more complex nature of race and the meaning attached to racial groups by both institutions and individuals. In this chapter, we distinguish race from ethnicity largely by scope. The term *race* is generally used to describe humans based on skin color and perceived related phenotypes. There is, however, no scientific basis for race as biological. And although race is a social construct, the inclination to sort and categorize people based on the perception of race as genetic has had and continues to have a socially engineered epic impact (both tragic and fortuitous) in the lives of people, including students. This is why we center race in our discussion. While related to race, *ethnicity* is generally understood relative to race as a subcategory (e.g., a racially White person of Irish or French or Italian ethnicity), although it can stand on its own, especially given its legitimacy in describing actual geographic origins of humans.

Sadly, given the labeling, sorting, and racial discrimination that continues to take place in K–12 schools, students of color themselves become research questions to be answered and problems of practice to be solved. To be sure, such problematizing of racially minoritized[1] students is not solely a 21st century phenomenon. In his seminal text, *The Souls of Black Folk*, Du Bois (1903) described his personal encounters with those who conceptualized his racial identity—his Blackness—as "a problem":

> They approach me in a half-hesitant sort of way, eye me curiously or compassionately, and then, instead of saying directly, How does it feel to be a problem? they say, I know an excellent colored man in my town; or, I fought at Mechanicsville; or, Do not these Southern outrages make your blood boil? At these I smile, or am interested, or reduce the boiling to a simmer, as the occasion may require. To the real question, How does it feel to be a problem? I answer seldom a word.
>
> (pp. 1–2)

Yet, more than a century later, issues around race, racism, and the problems associated with racial "minority" students in schools persist. This reality presents a unique and distinct set of challenges for school leaders focused on improving student learning and academic achievement in ways that leverage the racially diverse backgrounds and experiences reflected in their classrooms and school communities (Wilson & Horsford, 2013).

PURPOSE AND OVERVIEW

In this chapter, we discuss the development of an educational leadership disposition described as *inclusive* around issues of race in PreK–12 public school contexts (Capper & Young, 2014; Theoharis & Causton-Theoharis, 2008; Scanlan & Theoharis, 2014). Framed according to the "problem" of race in Du Bois' (1903) interpretation of the "curious" or "compassionate" gaze toward racially minoritized students as the unspoken question, "How does it feel to be a problem?" (p. 2), we consider, more than a century later, the ongoing and cumulative impact of race and racism in K–12 schools and their implications for educational leadership practice.

Using Horsford's (2011, 2014) multi-step progression of race-consciousness as a guide, we describe the tools and strategies educational leaders can use to address the pervasive and cumulative impact of race and racism in K–12 schools, and through case studies, provide examples of inclusive leadership that demonstrate various dimensions of this typology, which include:

- Step 1: Racial literacy—"ability to understand what race is, why it is, and how it used to reproduce inequality and oppression" (p. 96)
- Step 2: Racial realism—acknowledgement of the "history, pervasiveness, and salience of race and racism" in US society and schools (p. 98)
- Step 3: Racial reconstruction—"process of ascribing new meaning to race" in ways that transform existing assumptions, beliefs, and biases (p. 100)
- Step 4: Racial reconciliation—"process that seeks to heal the soul wounds and damage" resulting from racism in society and schools (p. 103)

We recognize that race does not function in isolation from other dimensions of identity and, by association, identity-based privilege and oppression. Accordingly—and in keeping with the theme of this book—we highlight the significance of not only race's intersection with other dimensions of difference (e.g., class, gender, language, ability, sexuality, religion), but also the interlocking influences of exclusion and discrimination that uniquely exist at these points of intersection (Hill-Collins, 1986; Crenshaw, 1991; Horsford & Tillman, 2014). We begin with an overview of the current context of race and relevant research literature concerning racial equity and justice in US K–12 schools.

PART 1: THE CURRENT CONTEXT OF RACE IN SCHOOLS

The nation's focus on achievement and opportunity gaps by race, resulting largely from data collected and reported as required by the No Child Left Behind Act of 2001 and subsequent proliferation of state- and district-level accountability systems, have introduced new questions and challenges to school leaders tasked with closing these gaps. These include:

- How do we close achievement gaps by race? What are the sources of these gaps? What, if any role, does poverty play in these gaps?
- What about students with disabilities and linguistic minorities? How do their racial backgrounds connect with these other aspects of their learner identities?
- Given the multiple dimensions of diversity in today's schools, how much does race really matter?

To be sure, great strides have been made concerning racial desegregation, fostering racial diversity in schools where there was none before (Wells, Holme, Revilla, & Atanda, 2009). Yet the history of separate and unequal educational opportunities for children and families of color reveal long-held practices grounded in deep-seated assumptions that hold important implications for the work of today's educational leaders. The ways in which school and district leaders manage this diversity requires a set of dispositions and literacy around race that may not have been as essential in formerly segregated or racially homogeneous school communities. The US population is growing more racially, ethnically, and linguistically diverse at the same time that schools are filled with aging, still mostly White and female teachers. The increasing percentages of students of color comes at a time when high-stakes accountability measures by race dominate the education discourse (Feistritzer, 2011). According to the Center for Public Education (2012), "Between 2000 and 2010, 15 states—six of them in the Northeast—saw their non-Hispanic white populations decline . . . while black populations declined in only two states—Alaska and Hawaii—[at the same time] Hispanic and Asian populations grew in every state. Even in states where the non-Hispanic white population increased, growth was larger in other populations" (paras. 23–25). Yet, most colleges of education are not meaningfully preparing teachers and educational administrators—who are predominantly White—for what we describe herein as inclusive leadership.

This form of leadership is modified by the notion of inclusivity: inclusivity of *all* races, as well as by dimensions of identity that intersect with and go beyond race. Most salient to this chapter are research findings on the educational benefits of racial diversity (Gurin, Dey, Hurtado, & Gurin, 2002; Gurin, Gurin, Dey, & Hurtado, 2004; Gurin, Nagda, & López, 2004; Hurtado, 2001; Hurtado, Dey, Gurin, & Gurin, 2003; Milem & Hakuta, 2000). This research reveals that while all forms of demographic, co-curricular, and curricular diversity (e.g., racial, ethnic, linguistic, gender-based, religious, related to sexual orientation, and so forth) improve student learning and employment outcomes, in the absence of robust racial diversity, in which attention to historically underrepresented racial groups figures prominently, the educational benefits of diversity that accrue to students—all students—are weaker. That is, the educational benefits of diversity most durably accrue to all students (across race) only when there is robust racial demographic diversity, which amply includes US domestic racial and ethnic minorities, regardless of all other dimensions of diversity present. So while all forms of diversity enhance these benefits, racial diversity is *foundational* to bringing them about.

Race and Intersectionality

Aligned with the theme of this book, we take an intersectional approach to the analysis of inclusive leadership in PK–12 schools and districts. Toward this end, we focus here on race, yet also seek to engage its intersection with class, gender, and disability to examine the complex manners in which race is bound up with these other dimensions of identity and, thus, their impact on the development of inclusive leaders and inclusive leadership practices (See Scanlan & Theoharis, 2014; Capper & Young, 2014). It is important to note that while the concept of intersectionality has existed in the academy for more than 25 years, its use of late in educational circles tends to conflate it with notions of multiplicity and interdisciplinarity (Anzaldúa, 1999; Hill-Collins, 1986; Weber, 2007; Zinn & Thornton Dill, 1996).

As an analytical tool, intersectionality is not focused simply on the cross-section of two or more dimensions of identity (Crenshaw, 1995). Having multiple dimensions of identity—for example as a Black, working-class woman with a learning disability, or as a White, middle-class, homosexual male—while interesting to tease out in scholarship contexts, is not the same as having an intersectional identity. Likewise, conducting research from a shared (interdisciplinary) point of entry—for example, African American studies, sociology, women's studies, and disability studies—while, again, may be intellectually engaging, is not intersectional scholarship and may not employ intersectional analysis. This is because the purpose of intersectionality is to reveal the interests of those who are rendered invisible by "the system" precisely because they lack power in that system (Crenshaw, 1995).

So, for example, if the system "sees" White and male interests, it can be made to also see White female interests buoyed by race (Whiteness), and Black male interests buttressed by gender (maleness). In so doing, it reveals that it cannot see Blackness and femaleness. With this purpose in mind, in engaging the concept of intersectionality, drawing from and building on intersectional scholarship and employing intersectional analysis, this chapter seeks to bring forth the interests of those who are *persistently unseen* in education: students of color, poor and working class students, female students, and students with disabilities whose educational experiences are, in sum, increasingly captured by the term "school-to-prison pipeline," as they are physically funneled into this pipeline (Alexander, 2012; Bahena, Cooc, Curie-Rubin, Kuttber, & Ng, 2012; Clark, 2012; Davis, 2003; Foucault, 1995; Harry & Klingner, 2006; Kim, Losen, & Hewitt, 2012; Winn, 2011). It is in these students' interests that inclusive educational leadership is imperative to cultivate if those interests are to ever be made discernable and, from there, central to their education.

PART 2: WHAT WE KNOW ABOUT RACE: THE LITERATURE

While changes in federal law prohibiting exclusion, segregation, and discrimination based on race reflect progress, on-going resistance to this progress limits gains (see *Brown v. Board of Education*, 1954; Orfield & Eaton, 1996; *Parents Involved in Community Schools v. Seattle School District No. 1*, 2007). School accountability provisions requiring the disaggregation of student achievement data by race have unearthed gaps in achievement outcomes that have predominated 21st-century education discourses and practices, such as the contemporary trends and conditions of racial segregation within and between schools and classrooms, as well as gaps in both achievement and opportunity by race.

Current Challenges

The mainstream discourse concerning K–12 education in the United States reflects a near obsession with racialized achievement gaps—whereby Black and Latino students are more likely to be in below grade-level classes, less likely to participate in pre- and after-school programs, more likely to leave school sooner (stop out, opt out, drop out, get pushed or kicked out) and in greater numbers, and more likely to have lower literacy rates than White and Asian students. While achievement gap data regularly reported by the National Assessment of Education Progress (NAEP) has revealed long-term gains for all students since 1990, the maintenance of achievement gaps between Black and White (Vanneman, Hamilton, Baldwin Anderson, & Rahman, 2009) and Hispanic and White (Hemphill, Vanneman, & Rahman, 2011) students during that same period, as well as disparities in discipline by race (and its intersection with gender, ability, and language) have also garnered public attention.

Local district, state, and federal initiatives informed by the work of organizations like the Schott Foundation, PolicyLink, and the Children's Defense Fund are designed to provide additional supports to racially minoritized students who are disproportionately impacted by these achievement gaps. These have sparked new questions around how best to frame and address issues of race as they relate to educational opportunity and equity. For example, in 2014, the Obama administration launched its My Brother's Keeper Initiative to support Black and Latino males by providing interventions where they may have the greatest impact to include: (1) entering school healthy and ready to learn; (2) reading at grade level by third grade; (3) graduating from high school ready for college and career; (4) completing post-secondary education or training; (5) successfully entering the workforce; and (6) staying on track and receiving second chances (White House, 2014). Although controversial given its focus solely on boys of color and exclusion of girls (among many other criticisms that fall beyond the scope of this chapter), the aims and rationale of My Brother's Keeper, along with its critiques, reveal the complexity surrounding efforts to address educational challenges that correlate heavily with the ways in which race operates in US schools and society.

The My Brother's Keeper Initiative also provides an example of an initiative that addresses the intersectionality of two dimensions of diversity—here race and gender (see further Grogan & Dias, this volume). Other examples of the intersectionality are frequently embedded in research. As a recent example of this, in March of 2014, a US Department of Education Office for Civil Rights study on school discipline (Office for Civil Rights, n.d.), using 2011–12 school year data, reported the following:

- **Race.** Black children represent 18% of preschool enrollment but 48% of those receiving more than one out-of-school suspension; compared to White students representing 43% of enrollment, but only 26% of those receiving more than one out-of-school suspension. Additionally, Black students are suspended and expelled three times more frequently than White students.
- **Gender.** Although boys represent only 54% of the preschool population, they represent 79% of one-time suspensions and 82% of multiple suspensions.

- **Race and gender.** Among the female population, Black girls are suspended at higher rates (12%) than girls of any other race or ethnicity and most boys. White boys are suspended at half that rate (6%), and the suspension rate for White girls is 2%.
- **Race, gender, and ability.** With the exception of Latino and Asian American students, more than 25% of boys of color with disabilities (served by IDEA)—and nearly 20% of girls of color with disabilities—receive an out-of-school suspension (see further Theoharis & Causton, this volume).

These are just some of the ways race has manifested itself in K–12 schools, holding implications for both racially minoritized students and the school leaders held responsible for their academic achievement and growth. Fortunately, the research literature has provided important insights concerning how educators can begin the work of conceptualizing inclusive leadership around issues of race within their schools, school communities, and school systems in preparation for implementation of such leadership practices.

Strategies

Cultural Ecological Theory has been employed to explore the cultural conflicts that emerge as minority groups seek to successfully negotiate the Eurocentric cultural norms embedded in US schools (Foster, 2004; Luna, 2008; Ogbu, 2008; Valdés, 2001). These norms do not engender recognition of racially minoritized parent involvement in their children's education because the manners of expression of this involvement are culturally informed; for example, the Eurocentric culture of most schools encourages competition, whereas the home culture of many students of color emphasizes cooperation. Additionally, Critical Race Theory in education has been used to examine the sociopolitical consequences of racism in educational settings in the United States (Cammarota, 2007; Delgado Bernal, 2002; Dixson & Rousseau, 2006; Horsford, 2010; Ladson-Billings & Tate, 1995; López, 2003). Eurocentric culture is predicated on two racist assumptions, one covert and one overt. The covert assumption is that *acculturation* to Eurocentric norms is "wise"; the overt assumption is that *assimilation* to these norms should be desired. Thus, students of color who come to school expressing eagerness to learn in culturally reflexive ways are often perceived to be less capable and taught (or not taught) accordingly. Likewise, parents who seek out involvement in their children's schools in manners that reflect their cultural identities are often met with indifference, or worse, hostility.

While Cultural Ecological Theory and Critical Race Theory have provided insights into the experiences of racially minoritized students and parents in educational settings, Culture-Centered Theory (CCT) has been engaged in the development of pragmatic strategies for parlaying these insights into concrete solutions (Delgado-Gaitán, 2004; Howard, 2003; Wortham & Contreras, 2002; Zambrana & Zoppi, 2002). To reconcile the contradiction between the educational support provided to racially minoritized students by their parents, and these students' still persistent lack of academic achievement, CCT emphasizes the need for highly culturally responsive and otherwise robust schooling interventions like race-focused parental involvement programs (Quezada, Díaz, & Sánchez, 2003; Quiocho & Daoud, 2006; Tinkler, 2002; Zarate, 2007). Sadly, most K–12 schools struggle to establish meaningful relationships with parents of color and are therefore unable to foster the types of school-family relations that facilitate improved student achievement (Tinkler, 2002; Zarate, 2007). Even when race-focused parent involvement programs are highly culturally responsive and otherwise robust, a narrow focus on student academic achievement results in incremental improvement of student advancement overall (Clark, Flores, Rivera,

Biesinger, & Morgan, 2012; Nieto & Rivera, 2010; Tinkler, 2002; Zarate, 2007). This is why educational leaders must engage strengths-based approaches (Wilson & Horsford, 2013) on which to transform negative schooling experiences into racially just and inclusive ones (see further Scanlan & Johnson, this volume).

PART 3: INCLUSIVE LEADERSHIP AROUND RACE IN K–12 SCHOOLS

As is discussed throughout this book, inclusive leaders are educational professionals prepared to create and maintain schools that are intellectually and emotionally dialectical spaces in which teachers, learners, and families work together against discrimination to bring about educational equity and justice for all students, especially the most marginalized and problematized. In this chapter, we are particularly interested in not only *why* inclusive leadership around race is important, but also *how* leaders should and do engage in this work. In this section, we present some of the ways in which school leaders can advance inclusive leadership practices around issues of race at the personal, school, and district levels. We frame this according to Horsford's (2011, 2014) multi-step progression of race consciousness (manifest as awareness, disposition, skills or abilities, and knowledge bases or understandings) from literacy, to realism, to reconstruction, to reconciliation. While we describe the progression of race consciousness in a linear fashion to provide conceptual clarity, the lived experience of this progression is more complex. Leaders may, for example, take two steps forward, and then a step backward, because the evolution of such consciousness is a life-long endeavor. To illustrate this progression we begin this chapter with four case studies.[2]

Following these, we present five tools and strategies: (a) dialogue; (b) film/video screenings; (c) book circles; (d) multicultural curriculum transformation seminars; and (e) parent involvement. Collectively, these form opportunities for advancing racially inclusive school and district leadership. As such, the four steps in Horsford's (2011, 2014) typology will structure our review of dialogue (engaging all four steps), film/video screenings (step 1, racial literacy), book circles (step 2, racial realism), multicultural curriculum transformation seminars (step 3, racial reconstruction), and parent involvement (step 4, racial reconciliation), in developmental fashion. Additionally, dialogue is discussed first so that a dialogic posture can be presumed in discussion of films/videos and books, during seminars, and with parents.[3]

Case Studies

A great way for inclusive educational leaders to have their own learning augmented regarding the role of race in schools is through engagement with community case studies (Horsford, 2009; Horsford, Sampson, & Forletta, 2013) and leadership case studies of highly successful inclusive educational leaders (Theoharis, 2009). In this section, we present four case studies, which begin with the story of Meredith Hall, a 35-year-old White elementary school principal in a large urban school district in the Southwest. Her story will be used to illustrate the development of *racial literacy* in inclusive educational leaders. Next will be the story of Mabel Washington, a 55-year-old African American middle school principal in a large suburban/urban school county in the mid-Atlantic region of the United States. Mabel's story will facilitate understanding of how inclusive leaders effectively leverage *racial realism* in education. Third, the story of Carlos Pérez, a 67-year-old Chicano superintendent of a large, unified rural-urban school district in the Southwest, will be used to illustrate inclusive educational leaders' engagement of *racial reconstruction*. The last story is that of Manuel Vargas, a 42-year-old Puerto Rican superintendent of a moderately sized urban public school district in the Northeast. Manuel's story will give inclusive educational leaders ideas for bringing about *racial reconciliation* in diverse school and district contexts.

Principal Meredith Hall

Racial literacy is the "ability to understand what race is, why it [exists (as a social construct)], and how it is used to reproduce inequality and oppression" (Horsford, 2011, p. 96). Meredith Hall exemplifies a *racially literate* inclusive educational leader because of her ability to immediately identify with the recent immigrant experience of the largely Latina/Latino, primarily Mexican, student population at her school.

> Like so many of the students who attend my school, three of my four grandparents were immigrants to the United States and they all spoke a language other than English when they came to this country. This is one of the main reasons I stay at this school: I understand my community. Many of my grandparents' efforts to survive and thrive as new immigrants to the United States—such as advocating for their child to a teacher, seeking out and attempting to use community resources, and building a supportive network—were blocked by cultural and language barriers.
>
> (personal communication, October 15, 2010)

Meredith Hall's school is an "at-risk" Title I inner-city school serving PreK–5 students. Like many schools in the district, the number of students in the school at any given time is over 700, much larger than most elementary school campuses across the nation. Unlike most district schools, over 80% of its students fall below the poverty line and the majority speak English as a second language. Most of the students who speak English as a second language speak Spanish as their first language, though there are 20 other languages spoken as a first language on the campus.

The challenges that Meredith's school faces makes parent involvement vital in its efforts to improve student achievement. In 2005, the Teaching English to Speakers of Other Languages (TESOL) program at Meredith's school obtained a grant enabling it to have one of its teachers trained and certified, through a community-based private, non-profit family leadership program, to implement a Latina/Latino parent engagement curriculum. Prior to 2005, although Latina/Latino parents were often involved in school events and came to parent-teacher conferences, Meredith noted that it was extremely difficult to get them to take on leadership roles within the school, and often scrambled to find parents—any parents, but especially Latina/Latino parents—to join the district's Parent Teacher Association or the school's Improvement Team. Further, when school board members would hold meetings for parent representatives, or Title I meetings in the district called for parent representatives, it was difficult to find any parent willing to attend—again, especially a Latina/Latino parent. As a result of the establishment of the parent engagement curriculum at Meredith's school, by 2010, parent engagement had increased so dramatically that Meredith hired one of the parents who had completed the curriculum to coordinate parent involvement activities at the school on a full-time basis.

> The barriers that my grandparents faced as immigrant parents of school-aged children are substantially diminished if not wholly eliminated by the parent involvement program we have established. I often wonder how my grandparents', parents', and my family's life would be different if we had access to programs like this—programs that impact the lives not only of individuals, but generations. I am humbled by the accomplishments and self-advocacy of the community of parents that at one time remained silent. Having come through the curriculum these parents have found ownership in

the school as *their* school. As a result, they are my most committed educational partners, thus the people I count on to lead the way in voicing concerns and dreams for our students, our children.

(personal communication, October 15, 2010)

Principal Mabel Washington

Racial realism builds from scholarship on Critical Race Theory applied to education Bell, 2004 (Ladson-Billings & Tate, 1995). This step seeks to "acknowledge the history, pervasiveness, and salience of race and racism in US society, including its schools, and the pitfalls associated with liberal education ideology, policy, and practices" (Horsford, 2011, p. 98). *Racial realism* is most evident in Mabel Washington's inclusive educational leadership through the development of her "extended family" school culture. Mabel is a "fixer," the kind of educator that senior administrators "go to" when they have a "problem" school in need of a solid solution. And, so, in 2003, when Mabel's school's county superintendent asked her to assume the leadership of a Title I, urban/suburban school serving 1,500 African American K–6 students so ineffectively that it was facing closure, of course she said, "Yes!"

Mabel's first order of business was to leverage the fact that all the students who attended the school lived within walking distance of it. She did this by personally walking each student home in an effort to meet as many of their parents as she could, and inviting their participation in the school community.

Taking advantage of her "honeymoon" period as the school's "new" principal—the short-lived time period during which the school staff were still on their best behavior for her and, thus, would politely oblige most every request she made—Mabel's second order of business was to hold an early evening "no titles" get-together for teachers and students' parents. The get-together was just that, an opportunity for school personnel and the parents of the students they served to meet, greet, eat, dance, talk, and laugh—in short, simply to get to know one another as people on equal footing.

The third order of business on Mabel's agenda was to enlist her husband's civil servant connections. As a long-time, well-respected local police officer, Mabel's husband had many friends on the force, as well as among the ranks of the county's firefighters and emergency medical technicians. Mabel asked him to call in a favor on her behalf and ask his friends to commit five hours a week to serve as one-on-one mentors to her schools' students. Akin to the spirit of the "no titles" get-together, there was no specific mentorship agenda beyond simply the individualized time shared between mentor and student.

Within the first six months of Mabel's stint as principal, the "extended family" orientation of the school gleaned a 72% drop in absenteeism and an 86% increase in homework completion from the previous school year. These numbers increased another 9% and 3%, respectively, by the end of Mabel's first year. From that point forward, Mabel focused on improving student academic performance, grade completion and promotion, and test scores. By 2005, Mabel's school's metrics in all three of these areas were in the top 4% of elementary schools in the county, and the threat of school closure was permanently off the table.

Superintendent Carlos Pérez

Racial reconstruction is conceived of as a process in which race is ascribed new meaning, "in order to transform the ways [humans] think about and, subsequently, act on . . . racial assumptions, attitudes, and biases" (p. 100). Carlos Pérez is an inclusive leader of another ilk. His approach to *racial reconstruction* as superintendent of a 57-school district in a US-Mexico border city could be described as merciless, take-no-prisoners, and no-holds barred.

In a five-year period, from 1993 to 1998, Carlos took his district from one in which there was no school identified as "exemplary," according to state testing performance categories, to the highest-performing one state-wide. So extraordinary were his accomplishments in this regard that, after years of declining enrollments, the families of 2,000 children living outside the district sought to enroll them in district schools.

While few argue with Carlos' results, many have complained about his two main tactics for achieving those results. The first concern raised was about his directive to teachers to teach however they felt students would learn best. He gave teachers complete academic freedom, with one important caveat: if the students did not perform well academically, the teachers would be held accountable—referred for professional development, docked pay, disciplined, even fired. While many teachers relished the opportunity to teach *not* "to the test," others expressed uneasiness about being held accountable for the academic performance of students they felt "could not learn" because of who they and/or their parents were racially, linguistically, and socioeconomically. The former group of teachers rose to the occasion, while the latter either resigned or were fired—more than 2,000 of them during Carlos' first three years on the job.

The second complaint about Carlos' tactics had to do with the "beat the test" culture he encouraged schools to cultivate. Rather than teach to the test and thereby create alienating and isolating school climates, schools were to promote the idea that, together, they could beat the test by engaging it as the learning community's common enemy. School days were restructured to leave two hours at the end of each school day for students to take "test preparation" courses, not at all focused on test content, rather merely on the mechanics and psychology of test-taking. Thereafter students were coached on how to apply that preparation on a series of practice tests.

Carlos believed that disaggregating content learning from test-taking would bring about students' love for learning and, at the same time, diminish their test anxiety—and he was correct, which turned out to be a problem for him. Initially championed by educational policy-makers on the political right, when the exclusively Chicana/Chicano, Mexican, and Mexican American students in Carlos' district routinely outperformed students in the most economically elite and all White districts in the state, Carlos fell from grace. While Carlos' tactics seem to operate at counter purposes to Tucson Unified School District's (TUSD) Mexican-centric, but open-enrollment, mathematics and English education development program (chronicled in the documentary film, *Precious Knowledge* [Palos, 2011]), the very similar about-face taken by educational policy-makers in Arizona relative to the outstanding success of the Tucson program suggests that both Carlos' and the TUSD efforts were acceptable up until they resulted in Latina/Latino students routinely succeeding in education at higher levels than their White counterparts. Carlos' story is an important reminder that inclusive educational leadership can be treacherous precisely because it is righteous. For that reason, leaders need to build and maintain a resilient disposition if they are to sustain success—as defined herein, not by neoliberal measures (Giroux, 2010).

Superintendent Manuel Vargas

The process of *racial reconciliation* is seeking "to heal the soul wounds" that have occurred and recurred in schools and society related to race and racism (Horsford, 2011, p. 103). Manuel Vargas' inclusive educational leadership disposition inclines him to champion *racial reconciliation*. As the first Puerto Rican appointed superintendent of his very working class district in 1990, Manuel wanted to change the negative perception of Puerto Ricans typically portrayed—especially in the educational arena—in the New England media, but his approach to doing so was to build a multicultural coalition of inclusive educational leaders at the principal level in his district and, through them, promote an educational philosophy that would improve student educational outcomes by shifting thinking about how students actually learn versus how they have been expected to learn. Accordingly, Manuel's first action as superintendent was to fill ten vacant principal positions; he did so, of course, through a competitive employment process, which yielded nine minority hires and one White woman. While not seemingly earth-shattering, in the city in which Manuel's district is situated, fewer than 2% of the elected officials were at that time, *and* continuing to this day, are people of color, though the city's racial demographics are approximately 67% African American and Puerto Rican (roughly equal numbers of both). Manuel understood that inclusive educational leadership is, in fact, about who is included at the leadership table, not just whom White educational leaders include as their subordinates at that table.

Once in place, Manuel presented his leadership team with his vision for restructuring the district's schools. His vision was simple: "I believe that all children can learn." Yet, he realized this vision was anything but simple. First, he had to bring his team around to his vision; then he had to have them do the same with their teams, parents, and students. Next he had to explain what this vision meant for schooling—if all children can learn, all children should, in fact, be learning and if they are not, then something needs to change. At the crux of this explanation was a critique of how schools configure and then assess teaching and learning—on a time clock. He troubled the clock by suggesting that while he believed all students could learn physics, he did not think that they could all learn it in the typically prescribed academic term for so doing. However, he did not believe that in taking more time to learn it, that made a student any less capable in the content area; perhaps, he reasoned, it even made them more capable—perhaps the reason it took them longer to learn it was because they were making deeper connections within the subject matter. Ultimately, Manuel had to engender inclination to educational flexibility such that all students could, in fact, learn anything because the schools in his district were committed to ensuring they were able to do so.

These case studies offer four examples of inclusive leadership practices around issues of race according to Horsford's (2011) multi-step progression from racial literacy to realism, to reconstruction, to reconciliation. Taken together, they highlight voices and dispositions of educational leaders who have successfully supplanted the deficit-oriented gaze of curiosity and compassion with leadership that advances inclusion and racial justice. Accordingly, these cases are educationally instructive for pre- and in-service educational leaders. All four cases foreground Rorty's (1989) notion of identifying with the "other"—using language of "us" and not "them" to demonstrate inclusive leadership dispositions. Meredith arrives at "us" by connecting her own family's immigrant experience to that of her students and their families. Mabel champions "us" in bringing school staff and students' families together solely for "title-free" adult social interaction and, ostensibly, relationship building. Finally, Carlos and Manuel covey the spirit of "us" in communicating, especially to teachers, that to be effective advocates for all children, fidelity to the belief that all students can learn at the highest levels is paramount. With these case studies in mind, we now turn to elaborate five specific tools and strategies for enacting race consciousness as a school leader.

Tools and Strategies

Dialogue

The first—and foundational—strategy for building race consciousness is dialogue. Dialogue is most aptly defined as a structured form of group conversation designed to help participants in it to develop comfort for, and skill with, conversation on difficult, controversial, and forbidden topics, including race (Clark, 2002b, 2005; Nagda, Gurin, & López,

2003; Nagda, Kim, & Truelove, 2004; Nagda & Zúñiga, 2003; Schoem, Hurtado, Sevig, Chesler, & Sumida, 2001). Unlike debate, in which the goal is to "listen to gain advantage" or trump the perspectives of others, as well as discussion or "serial monologue," in which participants talk in front of, rather than to or with, one another about a topic, in dialogue the goal is "listen to understand," but not necessarily to agree or even to find common ground. In essence, dialogue is about learning to walk the talk of democracy—to live, learn, and work productively with others with whom we fundamentally and persistently disagree. Accordingly, dialogue provides opportunities for inclusive leaders to learn how to engage in dialogue themselves (personal level), and to facilitate others in dialogic interaction (school and district level), and fosters the creation of classroom-, school-, and district-level communities in which people of different races join together to combat systemic racism in education. Dialogue involves all four steps in the progression of race consciousness.

Stages of Dialogue

These four consciousness-raising steps dovetail well with the four "stages" of dialogue, colloquially known as forming, norming, storming, and performing (Clark, 2002b, 2005; Nagda et al., 2003; Nagda et al., 2004; Nagda & Zúñiga, 2003; Schoem et al., 2001), as set out in Table 4.1. In stage one of dialogue, the goal is to *form* the dialogue group by creating opportunities for group members to get to know one another. In race-based dialogue, this knowing requires an openness to understand how race has manifested in the lives of people from different racial groups differentially and the impact of those disparate manifestations on members of each group's access to full participation in democracy (or the lack thereof). Next is the *norming* stage of dialogue. Here, dialogue group members are facilitated in the development of group agreements designed to challenge the relations of power that, in race-based dialogue, govern race-based interactions outside of the dialogue context. These norms serve to build racial equity so that past and continuing sociopolitical realities can mediate the sharing of experiences and exchange of ideas inside the dialogue (e.g., the notion of affirmative action as "reverse racism" would be revealed as wholly erroneous).

Stage three of dialogue is *storming*. Here members engage in the sustained exchange of the most complex and controversial ideas—to, in essence, "weather the storm." The goal at this stage of race-based dialogue is to enable people of color to be able to share long-standing concerns about race and racism with White people, and for White people to be able to hear and heed those concerns without the expectation that a comparable round of sharing from, for example, Whites toward Blacks, will ensue. Finally, in the *performing* stage of dialogue, the goal is for all members in the dialogue to come together and act in some meaningful way to continue to challenge on-going manifestations of oppression and discrimination relative to the dialogue focus area—in this case, race and racism.

Facilitating Dialogue

Implicit in the norming stage of dialogue, as described above, is the requirement that dialogues be facilitated. The expectation is that participants do not facilitate themselves but, rather, are co-facilitated by two formally trained non-participant peers. Co-facilitation enables selection of one facilitator of color and one White facilitator who, through their co-facilitation efforts, model racial understanding for participants. Ideally, inclusive leaders would identify two or more members of their school staff to pursue dialogue facilitator training at a local college or university that has a campus dialogue program, or through a national training program offered by, for example, the National Coalition for Dialogue and Deliberation or the Social Justice Training Institute (see Resource List). Staff chosen for this professional development opportunity should have the respect of their peers across race, work well together and, more generally, in collaborative situations, and express a disposition for thoughtful and sustained engagement in conflict negotiation.

Critical legal scholar Charles Lawrence (2005) provides a powerful example of the ways in which race-related dialogue "shows up" relative to schooling using a seemingly innocuous conversation with a colleague as a jumping-off point. Lawrence is African American and his colleague is European American. The colleague, new to the Washington, DC, area, asks Lawrence, who has lived in the area for a while, to recommend a "good" school to him. Lawrence unpacks this request through the lens of what he terms "forbidden conversation" (p. 1353). In short, Lawrence argues that what his colleague was really asking him in a veiled way was about race and class in schooling based on his assumption that because Lawrence is upper middle class himself, he would surely have his children in either a private school, or a public school in an affluent neighborhood in which the majority of students were also White. Lawrence uses this conversation to discuss the larger implications of race and class in public education in the United States and in making a case for child enrollment and active parent involvement in public schools at the immediate neighborhood level as foundational for improving the quality of public schools in all neighborhoods.

Dialogue as a Foundational Strategy

Once race-conscious dialogic dispositions are developed within and cultivated by inclusive leaders, all interactions can and should flow from this point of entry into leading, teaching, and learning. Accordingly, and building from related work by Horsford (2014), all of the following inclusive leadership development activities presume a dialogic starting point. Dialogue is both a foundational strategy for building race consciousness as well as a fundamental way to raise consciousness across *all* dimensions of diversity discussed in this book.

Table 4.1 Dialogue Summary

Stage of Dialogue	Characteristics of Stage for Race-Based Dialogue
1. Form	*Relationship building*: Openness to understand how race has manifested in the lives of people from different racialized groups differentially and the impact of those disparate manifestations on members of each group's access to full participation in democracy (or the lack thereof).
2. Storm	*Group agreements*: Designed to challenge the relations of power that govern race-based interactions outside of the dialogue context by serving to build racial equity so that past and continuing sociopolitical realities can mediate the sharing of experiences and exchange of ideas inside the dialogue.
3. Norm	*Conflict negotiation*: Enable people of color to be able to share long-standing concerns about race and racism with White people, and for White people to be able to hear and heed those concerns without the expectation that a comparable round of sharing from, for example, Whites toward Blacks, will ensue.
4. Perform	*Collaborative action*: Come together and act in some meaningful way to continue to challenge on-going manifestations of oppression and discrimination relative to race and racism.

Video/Film Screenings

Another tool in building race consciousness is video/film screenings. This applies most directly to step one: *racial literacy*. Many excellent video/film resources promote racial literacy among inclusive educational leaders. One such example is the Public Broadcasting Service's (PBS) three-part documentary, *RACE: The Power of an Illusion* (2003). Episode 1 focuses on dispelling the myths associated with race as a biological construct in discussing the origin of commonly noted group traits as resulting from cultural adaptation to time and place (origins), rather than from fundamental genetic differentiation. Episode 2 examines the history of racism in science, as well as the use of race as a social and legal construct throughout US history (especially in governance) to attempt to justify social inequalities as "the natural order of things" in American life. Lastly, Episode 3 reveals how institutional racism and the evolution of "Whiteness" as a racialized category of identity have in the past, and continue today, to systematically advantage some while marginalizing others along political, economic, and social lines.

Powerful videos and films such as this provide a great way for leaders to foster their own racial literacy, as well as that of others. For instance, school leaders can host a shared viewing for school staff and aspiring leaders. Another possibility is having inclusive leaders host shared viewings of this series for their school and/or district communities. Whatever the format, viewings are most effective in building race consciousness when accompanied by skilled co-facilitated dialogue (described above). As a result, new understandings of race can emerge as a result of direct education on race content, as well as through the uniquely challenging pedagogical or process tool of race-based dialogue. It is common for both race content and dialogue to be avoided or only engaged superficially, precisely because it is hard to start and harder to sustain. For that reason, opportunities to become more deeply engaged, and to persist in the engagement, create the possibility for meaningful movement toward the creation of inclusive school communities in which racial equity and justice can develop and thrive.

Book Circles

A third tool in building race consciousness is the use of book circles. This applies most directly to *racial realism*, the second step in the progression of racial consciousness. A plethora of exceptional, hard-hitting books provide occasions for inclusive educational leaders' engagement in racial realism within their leadership spheres of influence. For example, the four books listed here as Key Books on Race and Intelligence all offer substantive opportunities to unpack the racism of the past relative to its continuing impact on the present.

KEY BOOKS ON RACE AND INTELLIGENCE

Steven Fraser (Ed.) (1995). *The Bell Curve Wars: Race, Intelligence, and the Future of America.*
Stephen Jay Gould (1996). *The Mismeasure of Man.*
Steven Selden (1999). *Inheriting Shame: The Story of Eugenics and Racism in America.*
Claude M. Steele (2011). *Whistling Vivaldi: How Stereotypes Affect Us and What We Can Do.*

Specifically, these are vehicles for engaging in racialized discourses concerning intellectual ability and educational achievement, and the implications of these discourses on school funding, curricular, and disciplinary policies. The first two books recount the history of the eugenics movement and the false "science" that attempted to provide cover for the violent actions undertaken during that movement. While school personnel are inclined to think of the kind of racism described in these books as extreme and long past, race-based dialogue provides the opportunity for participants to examine the manners in which such racism persists in common educational policies today, such as voucher programs, educational tracking, and zero-tolerance policies. The third and fourth books reveal the absurdity of race-based prejudices and provide information that can be used to counter those prejudices in a variety of school-based situations (e.g., professional development sessions, classroom teaching, staff meetings, parent-teacher conferences). Dialogue across these books affords circle participants the opportunity to develop racial realism regarding how race and racism have historically as well as currently operate in US society and schools. This can lay a foundation for a sense of agency necessary to push back against negative discourses, and push toward positive change.

In contrast, Key Books on Race and Educational Inequity situate the complex relationships between race, and educational inequity in the United States in historical contexts. In so doing, engagement with these books enables circle participants to develop greater insight into related present-day realities that can then lead them toward more robust solutions for bridging educational divides. Put differently, all four of these books again help school leaders foster racial realism.

KEY BOOKS ON RACE AND EDUCATIONAL INEQUITY

Derrick Bell (2004). *Silent Covenants: Brown v. Board of Education and the Unfulfilled Hopes for Racial Reform.*
Beth Harry & Jeanette Kilingner (2006). *Why Are So Many Minority Students in Special Education? Understanding Race and Disability in Schools.*

Jonathan Kozol (2012, 1991). *Savage Inequalities: Children in America's Schools.*

Sonya Douglass Horsford (2011). *Learning in a Burning House: Educational Inequality, Ideology, and (Dis)Integration.*

William Watkins (2001). *The White Architects of Black Education: Ideology and Power in America, 1865–1954.*

The first third, and fifth books examine the specific educational inequities that have faced, and continue to face, African American students. The second and fourth books extend this examination to other historically underrepresented groups of students, based on race, as well as on these other key dimensions of difference. In sum, circle participant dialogue on all five these books reveals the historical roots of current inequities—why things are as they are in schooling today. The second book goes one step further in suggesting very practical steps that especially classroom teachers can take to stop perpetuating these inequities (e.g., reducing or eliminating disciplinary referrals of students out of their classroom by focusing on improving their own classroom management skills). Circle participant dialogue on this book can surface additional inequity interventions that all school personnel, as well as students and their families, can undertake to move toward greater educational equity for all students, but especially those from historically underrepresented groups.

GUIDING QUESTIONS FOR REFLECTION ON BOOK CIRCLES

- Some define racial realism as acknowledging the history, pervasiveness, and salience of race and racism in US society and schools. How do *you* define it? How do you come to this definition?
- What examples of racial realism did you see in the book at focus in the circle today?
- What, if any, connections can you make between the examples of racial realism you saw in the book and your school-based role?
- What are the implications for racial realism in your work with students?

Multicultural Curriculum Transformation Seminars

A fourth strategy, multicultural curriculum transformation seminars, addresses the step of *racial reconstruction*. Recall that by racial reconstruction, we are referring to the process of ascribing new meaning to race in ways that transform existing assumptions, beliefs, and biases. Multicultural curriculum transformation engages school instructional staff in the revision of existing and development of new PreK–12 curriculum across grade levels and subject areas (Banks, 1993, 2009; Clark, 2002a; Gibson, 1976; Nieto & Bode, 2011). Because multicultural curriculum transformation's educational roots derive from various Ethnic Studies traditions, offering multicultural curriculum transformation seminars to instructional staff provides inclusive educational leaders the specific opportunity to facilitate curricular racial reconstruction—ensuring that the histories, lives, cultures, countries of origins, contributions, and works of people of color throughout human history are integrated or reintegrated into the PreK–12 curriculum in age-appropriate and topic area-specific manners (Banks, 1993).

Revisioning/development processes are primarily focused in three areas of the curriculum: (a) content (what is taught); (b) pedagogy (how it is taught); and (c) assessment (of student learning and teaching effectiveness). Such processes are primarily concerned with curricular representativeness and responsiveness, especially relative to local student communities. Generally, multiculturally transformed curricula seek to do for all students what monocultural or traditional curriculum is understood to do only or primarily for White, male, and at least middle-class students, among dominant others (e.g., speakers of English as a first language, Christians, the able-bodied) (Banks, 1993, 2009; Clark, 2002a; Gibson, 1976; Nieto & Bode, 2011). In other words, multiculturally transformed curricula address multiple dimensions of diversity.

Necessarily, multicultural curriculum transformation starts with critical review of the existing curriculum content to surface errors, inaccuracies, unacknowledged biases, and omissions in what has been codified as knowledge in every subject area relative to what is sometimes referred to as the "laundry list" of dimensions of difference most closely related to structures and relations of power, privilege, and oppression in society (e.g., race, color, ethnicity, geographic origin, immigration status, and first language; caste, socioeconomic class, and employment status; sex, gender, gender identity and expression, family configuration, and sexual orientation; physical, developmental, and psychological ability; veteran status, age, and generation; religious, spiritual, faith-based, or secular belief; physical appearance; environmental concern; and political affiliation, including the exercise of rights secured by the First Amendment of the Constitution of the United States) (Banks, 1993, 2009; Clark, 2002a; Gibson, 1976; Nieto & Bode, 2011).

Multicultural curriculum transformation seeks to replace the existing Eurocentric Canon with a multicultural one as is appropriate to each disciplinary area in order to establish the most comprehensive, and therefore truthful, record of human knowledge possible. In working to ensure that all students can "find themselves" in the curriculum in critically conscious fashion—not just as members of groups that are centered or marginalized, but groups that have both rich traditions and grave inadequacies that can only be reconciled through complex, multi-perspectival intellectual engagement. Multicultural curriculum transformation also explores the manners in which students are taught content and assessed on their learning of it (Banks, 1993, 2009; Clark, 2002a; Gibson, 1976; Nieto & Bode, 2011). Generally, the goal is to provide all students exposure to varied instructional and evaluation practices in the effort to affirm what is normative to each so that learning occurs and is understood to occur, while also challenging each to build capacity for learning and demonstrating learning in ways that go beyond the normative.

Inclusive educational leaders who understand the value of multicultural curriculum transformation dedicate ample time during the school year for instructional staff to engage in professional development seminars on this topic. They also incentivize staff participation in advanced education by publicly recognizing efforts in this regard, rewarding time spent to develop additional prowess with salary step increases, and providing opportunities for additional learning to be showcased/shared with peers.

GUIDING QUESTIONS FOR REFLECTION ON MULTICULTURAL CURRICULUM TRANSFORMATION SEMINARS

- If racial reconstruction is defined as a process of ascribing new meaning to race in ways that transform existing assumptions, beliefs, and biases, what does this mean to you?
- What examples of racial reconstruction can you pull from your experiences in the multicultural curriculum transformation seminar?

- What, if any, connections can you make between the examples of racial reconstruction that you saw come up in the seminar and your school-based role?
- What are the implications for racial reconstruction in your work with colleagues?

Parent Involvement Outreach and Programming

Finally, a fifth strategy is parent outreach and programming. This aligns with the step of *racial reconciliation*. Parent involvement initiatives have tended to focus parental development exclusively or primarily on directly impacting student educational performance (Tinkler, 2002; Zarate, 2007), such as teaching parents to regularly communicate high educational expectations to their children. Improved student performance, however, may actually come about more predictably when the individual development of parents is more central (Clark, et al., 2012). For example, emphasizing and supporting parents' own educational achievement may lead their children to finish homework assignments more reliably than does simply focusing parents on supervising their children's homework completion. This perspective challenges long-standing thinking about the relationship between parental involvement and student academic achievement—namely that student performance improves when parents are only or mostly directly focused on improving it alone. In fact, more effective approaches for building student success in schools may focus on parental participation in the democratic life of their local community, to include their child's school.

In being willing to push back against this key assumption of the so-called *American Dream* (e.g., that the next generation will benefit most from the personal sacrifices, in this case educational ones, of the current generation), parental involvement initiatives hold the promise of bringing about racial reconciliation. As described above, racial reconciliation is a process of healing the soul wounds and damage resulting from racism in society and schools. This is particularly the case when such initiatives consider the school experiences of Baby Boomer-aged parents of color. It should not surprise inclusive educational leaders to learn that for many parents—particularly those who are racially minoritized—school was an unwelcoming place. Thus re-entering schools as adults churns up many troublesome memories (Quezada et al., 2003; Quiocho & Daoud, 2006). By recasting parental involvement as civic engagement, inclusive educational leaders can join with parents to not only jettison the educational past, but to re-imagine its present and future as affirming and transformational for *all* students and their families.

To illustrate this strategy, we return to the concept of participatory democracy introduced in the discussion of dialogue. When inclusive school leaders reconceptualize parental participation as part and parcel of the democratic functioning of schools and the communities that host these schools, they are co-charting (with parents) pathways to educational equity for all students. According to Fishkin (2011), when constituents of democratic systems broadly participate in the operation of those systems, their quality of life improves. Building on Fishkin's premise, a student's educational performance may be significantly increased by his or her parents' civic involvement because of how this involvement is perceived to improve, and/or actually improves, the family's overall quality of life.

While parental outreach and programming can promote racial reconciliation, this should not imply a developmental linearity between education and social opportunity. Perhaps civic engagement fosters, or even drives, educational accomplishment. Perhaps the relationship between involvement in community life and commitment to educational advancement is more reciprocally complex. While education indeed opens doors to robust citizenship, it has not done so as quickly and predictably as expected, particularly for racially minoritized students. As a result, parent civic engagement in schools and surrounding communities may more expediently and reliably promote improved student educational outcomes than parent involvement focused only or largely on their children's performance in school. (See further Scanlan & Johnson, this volume.)

GUIDING QUESTIONS FOR REFLECTION ON PARENT INVOLVEMENT OUTREACH AND PROGRAMMING

- What is your definition of racial reconciliation and why?
- What, if any, opportunities for racial reconciliation do you see come up in your school-based role?
- What are the implications for racial reconciliation in your work with parents?

Equity Audit Questions

The final chapter of this text describes a comprehensive equity audit process. See the race section and full equity audit detailed in Chapter 10 and online (www.routledge.com/cw/theoharis). Some of the questions are intentionally challenging, drawn from the reality of educational inequity that has in the past faced, and continues today to face, students of color, as well as their parents, teachers, school administrators, and education policy makers. While these questions are not entirely new, they persist unanswered, in large measure because they are often considered unanswerable. Accordingly, we provide guidance, through specific data gathering and related analyses, for inclusive leaders interested in rising to the challenges these questions pose in seeking to, finally, answer them, and then to act in accordance with their findings to improve educational outcomes for racially minoritized students.

CONCLUSION: FROM CURIOSITY AND COMPASSION TO INCLUSION AND JUSTICE

The racial, ethnic, cultural, and linguistic diversity reflected in US K–12 schools elicits what Nieto (2010) defined as "profoundly multicultural questions" (p. 25)—uneasy questions that require educators to rethink what they have been trained to believe is impossible to change. Regrettably, the effects of such training have transformed many progressively minded, inclusive educational leaders into accountability-driven managers who have come to accept the persistent educational failure of racially minoritized student populations (Moll, Amanti, Neff, & González, 1992; Yosso, 2005). Whether acknowledged or not, once accepted, these leaders are compelled to resort to the gaze of "curiosity" in attempts to close racialized achievement gaps or the practice of "compassion" in seeking to "fix" racially minoritized students rather than addressing the structural and organizational systems of oppression and discrimination that continue to exclude, segregate, and limit the educational experiences and opportunities for certain students based on race.

In her reframing of the achievement gap as an education debt, Ladson-Billings (2006) underscored the fact that closing the gap required repaying the debt. Accordingly, we argue here that educational leaders who are inclusive around issues of race recognize the historical significance that race has played in the education of K–12 students in the United States. Indeed, a century-long history of racial exclusion in US schools holds direct implications for K–12 educational leadership today. The legacy of government-sanctioned segregation of schools for African Americans (see *Brown I and II* [*Brown v. Board of Education*, 1954, 1955], *Milliken v. Bradley*, 1974), Mexican Americans (see *San Antonio Independent School District v. Rodríguez*, 1973), Asian Americans (see *Gong Lum v. Rice*, 1927), and American Indians (see Racial Integrity Act, 1924) was not long ago and efforts to desegregate schools and school systems racially, ethnically, and socioeconomically continue to fall short of meaningful integration for a variety of reasons. Residential housing patterns, suburbanization, gentrification, and growing class divides within racial groups present not only new challenges, but perhaps opportunities to rethink and revisit our conceptualizations and understanding of racial diversity and its intersection with class, citizenship, language, geography, and opportunity.

Yet this is where intersectional analysis, despite its power, can also lead us away from solving the most persistent and pervasive aspects of racial inequality and injustice in schools. A major critique of multicultural education from the political left is the tendency for an attention to multiple dimensions of difference to result in a "laundry list" of identities that distracts and subtracts from a meaningful analysis of injustices experienced by one particular group. The future of education leadership research and practice, as contextualized by increasing diversity and intersectionality across various areas of difference, demands analyses that surface the interests of those who remain invisible in education discourse by virtue of their intersectional identities (e.g., undocumented immigrant children; lesbian, gay, bisexual, transgender, or questioning (LGBTQ) students of color; middle-class Muslim students, affluent Black and Latino students). Rather than conceptualizing these students as objects of curiosity or compassion, we can begin to utilize and further develop the tools, strategies, and dispositions that reject the notion that students of color are problems to be solved, and rather, view their engagement of racially literate and inclusive leadership practices as possible solutions.

NOTES

1   We use the term "minoritized," not minority, to reveal that there are institutionally discriminatory processes by which students of color (and, more generally, people of color) are made into minorities and then treated as "less than." This is in contrast to the use of the term minority, which has the default effect of conveying that students/people labeled as minorities are, in some inherent sense or by virtue of an objective reality, just that, minorities.
2   It should be noted that these case study examples are not intended to be "perfect" illustrations of inclusive leaders' disposition at each step in Horsford's multistep progression, rather they are provided as one among many examples of how each step might manifest.
3   These tools and strategies can also be employed to engage in critical dialogue regarding the extent to which each case study is or is not a good example of the step in the multistep progression of race consciousness it is used to illustrate, and why or why not.

REFERENCES

Alexander, M. (2012). *The new Jim Crow: Mass incarceration in the age of colorblindness*. New York: The New Press.

Anzaldúa, G. (1999). *Borderlands/la frontera: The new Mestiza* (2nd ed.). San Francisco, CA: Aunt Lute Books.

Bahena, S., Cooc, N., Curie-Rubin, R., Kuttber, P., & Ng, M. (2012). *Disrupting the school-to-prison pipeline*. Boston, MA: Harvard Education Press.

Banks, J. (1993). Multicultural education: Historical development, dimensions, and practice. *Review of Research in Education, 19*(1), 3–49.

Banks, J. (2009). *Teaching strategies for ethnic studies* (8th ed.). Boston, MA: Pearson.

Bell, D. (2004). *Silent covenants: Brown v. Board of Education and the unfulfilled hopes for racial reform*. New York: Oxford University Press.

Brown v. Board of Education, 347 U.S. 483 (1954).

Brown v. Board of Education of Topeka II, 349 U.S. 294 (1955).

Cammarota, J. (2007). A social justice approach to achievement: Guiding Latina/o students toward educational attainment with a challenging, socially relevant curriculum. *Equity & Excellence in Education, 40*(1), 87–96.

Capper, C.A., & Young, M.D. (2014). Ironies and limitations of educational leadership for social justice: A call to social justice educators. *Theory Into Practice, 53*(2), 158–164.

Center for Public Education (CPE). (2012). *The United States of education: The changing demographics of the United States and their schools*. Retrieved from http://www.centerforpubliceducation.org/You-May-Also-Be-Interested-In-landing-page-level/Organizing-a-School-YMABI/The-United-States-of-education-The-changing-demographics-of-the-United-States-and-their-schools.html

Clark, C. (2002a). Effective multicultural curriculum transformation in "advanced" mathematics and "hard" sciences. *Association of American Colleges and Universities: Diversity Digest, 6*(12), 18–19.

Clark, C. (2002b). Intergroup dialogue on campus. *Multicultural Education, 9*(4), 30–31.

Clark, C. (2005). Intergroup dialogue as pedagogy across the curriculum. *Multicultural Education, 12*(3), 51–61.

Clark, C. (2012). School-to-prison pipeline. In J.A. Banks (Ed.), *Encyclopedia of diversity in education: Vol. 4* (pp. 1894–97). Thousand Oaks, CA: Sage Publications.

Clark, C., Flores, R., Rivera, L., Biesinger, K., & Morgan, P. (2012). We make the road by walking: The family leadership initiative in Las Vegas. In A. Cohen & A. Honigsfeld (Eds.), *Breaking the mold of education for culturally and linguistically diverse students: Innovative and successful practices for 21st century schools* (pp. 85–94). New York: Rowman and Littlefield.

Crenshaw, K. (1991). Mapping the margins: Intersectionality, identity politics, and violence against women of color. *Stanford Law Review, 43*(6), 1241–99.

Crenshaw, K.W. (1995). Race, reform, and retrenchment: Transformation and legitimation in anti-discrimination law. In K. Crenshaw, N. Gotanda, G. Peller, & K. Thomas (Eds.), *Critical race theory: Key writings that formed the movement* (pp. 103–22). New York: The New Press.

Davis, A. (2003). *Are prisons obsolete?* New York: Seven Stories Press.

Delgado Bernal, D. (2002). Critical race theory, LatCrit theory and critical raced-gendered epistemologies: Recognizing students of color as holders and creators of knowledge. *Qualitative Inquiry, 8*(1), 105–26.

Delgado-Gaitán, C. (2004). *Involving Latino families in schools: Raising student achievement through home-school partnerships*. Thousand Oaks, CA: Corwin Press.

Dixson, A., & Rousseau, C. (2006). *Critical race theory in education: All God's children got a song*. New York: Routledge.

Du Bois, W.E.B. (1903). *The souls of black folk*. Chicago, IL: A.C. McClurg.

Feistritzer, E. (2011). Profile of teachers in the U.S. 2011. Washington, DC: National Center for Education Information. Retrieved from http://www.edweek.org/media/pot2011final-blog.pdf

Fishkin, J. (2011). *When the people speak*. Oxford, UK: Oxford University Press.

Fletcher, M. (2009). *The origins of the Indian Child Welfare Act (ICWA): A survey of the legislative history*. East Lansing, MI: Michigan State University College of Law: Indigenous Law & Policy Center. Retrieved from http://www.law.msu.edu/indigenous/papers/2009-04.pdf

Foster, K. (2004). Coming to terms: A discussion of John Ogbu's cultural-ecological theory of minority academic achievement. *Intercultural Education, 15*(4), 369–84.

Foucault, M. (1995). *Discipline and punish: The birth of the prison (Second Vintage Books Edition)*. New York: Knopf Doubleday Publishing Group.

Fraser, S. (Ed.). (1995). *The bell curve wars: Race, intelligence, and the future of America*. New York: Basic Books.

General Allotment Act (Dawes Act) of 1887, 24 Stat. 388, Ch. 119, 25 U.S.C. §331.

Gibson, M. (1976). Approaches to multicultural education in the United States: Some concepts and assumptions. *Council on Anthropology and Education Quarterly, 7*(4), 7–18.

Giroux, H. (2010). Dumbing down teachers: Rethinking the crisis of public education and the demise of the social state. *Review of Education, Pedagogy, and Cultural Studies*, *32*(4/5), 339–81.

Gong Lum v. Rice, 275 U.S. 78 (1927).

Gould, S.J. (1996). *The mismeasure of man.* New York: W.W. Norton & Company, Ltd.

Gurin, P., Dey E. L., Hurtado, S., & Gurin, G. (2002). Diversity and higher education: Theory and impact on educational outcomes. *Harvard Educational Review, 72*(3), 330–66.

Gurin, P., Gurin, G., Dey, E. L., & Hurtado, S. (2004). The educational value of diversity. In P. Gurin, J. Lehman, & E. Lewis (Eds.), *Defending diversity: Affirmative action at the University of Michigan* (pp. 97–188). Ann Arbor, MI: University of Michigan Press.

Gurin, P., Nagda, R., & López, G. (2004). The benefits of diversity in education for democratic citizenship. *Journal of Social Issues, 60*(1), 17–34.

Harry, B., & Klingner, J. (2006). *Why are so many minority students in special education? Understanding race and disability in schools.* New York: Teachers College Press.

Hemphill, F.C., Vanneman, A., & Rahman, T. (2011). *Achievement gaps: How Hispanic and White students in public schools perform in mathematics and reading on the National Assessment of Educational Progress* (NCES 2011–459). Washington, DC: National Center for Education Statistics, Institute of Education Sciences, U.S. Department of Education.

Hill-Collins, P. (1986). Learning from the outsider within: The sociological significance of Black feminist thought. *Social Problems, 33*(6), S14–S32.

Horsford, S. D. (2009, Summer). The case for racial literacy in educational leadership: Lessons learned from superintendent reflections on desegregation. *UCEA Review, 50*(2), 5–8.

Horsford, S. D. (2010). Mixed feelings about mixed schools: Superintendents on the complex legacy of school desegregation. *Educational Administration Quarterly, 46*(3), 287–321.

Horsford, S.D. (2011). *Learning in a burning house: Educational inequality, ideology, and (dis)integration.* New York: Teachers College Press.

Horsford, S. D. (2014). When race enters the room: Improving leadership and learning through racial literacy. *Theory Into Practice, 50*(1), 123–30.

Horsford, S.D., Sampson, C., & Forletta, F. (2013). School resegregation in the Mississippi of the West: Community counternarratives on the return to neighborhood schools in Las Vegas, Nevada, 1968–1994. *Teachers College Record, 115*(11), 1–28.

Horsford, S.D., & Tillman, L.C. (Eds.). (2014). *Intersectional identities and educational leadership of Black women in the USA.* Abingdon, UK: Routledge.

Howard, T. (2003). Culturally relevant pedagogy: Ingredients for critical teacher reflection. *Theory Into Practice, 42*(3), 195–202.

Hurtado, S. (2001). Linking diversity with educational purpose: How the diversity impacts the classroom environment and student development. In G. Orfield (Ed.), *Diversity challenged: Legal crisis and new evidence* (pp. 143–74). Cambridge, MA: Harvard Publishing Group.

Hurtado, S., Dey, E.L., Gurin, P., & Gurin, G. (2003). The college environment, diversity, and student learning. In J.S. Smart (Ed.), *Higher education: Handbook of theory and research, Volume 18* (pp. 145–89). Amsterdam: Luwer Academic Press.

Indian Child Welfare Act (ICWA) (1978). Pub. L. 95-608, 92 Stat. 3069, codified at 25 U.S.C. §§ 1901–1963.

Kim, C., Losen, D., & Hewitt, D. (2012). *The school-to-prison pipeline: Structuring legal reform.* New York: New York University Press.

Kozol, J. (2012). *Savage inequalities: Children in America's schools.* 1991; New York: Crown Publishing Group.

Ladson-Billings, G. (2006). From the achievement gap to the education debt: Understanding achievement in U.S. schools. *Educational Researcher, 35*(7), 3–12.

Ladson-Billings, G., & Tate, W. (1995). Toward a critical race theory of education. *Teachers College Record, 97*(1), 47–68.

Lawrence, III, C.R. (2005). Forbidden conversations: On race, privacy, and community (A continuing conversation with John Ely on racism and democracy). *The Yale Law Journal, 114*(6), 1353–1403.

López, G. R. (2003). The (racially neutral) politics of education: A critical race theory perspective. *Educational Administration Quarterly, 39*(1), 68–94.

Luna, N. (2008). *Clark County dropout needs assessment report: Community readiness data collection process to address Latina/Latino school dropout.* Reno, NV: University of Nevada Cooperative Extension.

Milem, J., & Hakuta, K. (2000). The benefits of racial and ethnic diversity in higher education. In D. Wilds (Ed.), *Minorities in higher education, 1999–2000: Seventeenth annual status report* (pp. 39–67). Washington, DC: American Council on Education.

Milliken v. Bradley, 418 U.S. 717 (1974).

Moll, L., Amanti, C., Neff, D., & González, N. (1992). Funds of knowledge for teaching: Using a qualitative approach to connect homes and classrooms. *Theory Into Practice, 31*(2), 132–41.

Nagda, B.A., Gurin, P., & López, G.E. (2003). Transformative pedagogy for democracy and social justice. *Race Ethnicity & Education, 6*(2), 165–191.

Nagda, B.A., Kim, C.W., & Truelove, Y. (2004). Learning about difference, learning with others, learning to transgress. *Journal of Social Issues, 60*(1), 195–214.

Nagda, B.A., & Zúñiga, X. (2003). Fostering meaningful racial engagement through intergroup dialogues. *Group Processes and Intergroup Relations, 6*(1), 111–28.

Nieto, S. (2010). *The light in their eyes: Creating multicultural learning communities* (10th anniversary ed.). New York: Teachers College Press.

Nieto, S., & Bode, P. (2011). *Affirming diversity: The sociopolitical context of multicultural education* (6th ed.). Boston, MA: Allyn & Bacon.

Nieto, S., & Rivera, M. (Eds.). (2010). *Charting a new course: Understanding the sociocultural, political, economic, and historical context of Latino/a education in the United States.* Chicago, IL: The Spencer Foundation.

Office for Civil Rights. (n.d.). Civil Rights Data Collection. Retrieved from http://ocrdata.ed.gov/

Ogbu, J. (Ed.). (2008). *Minority status, oppositional culture, and schooling.* New York: Routledge.

Orfield, G., & Eaton, S. (1996). *Dismantling desegregation: The quiet reversal of Brown v. Board of Education.* New York: The New Press.

Palos, A. (Director) (2011). *Precious knowledge* [Documentary]. United States: Dos Vatos Productions.

Parents Involved in Community Schools v. Seattle School District No. 1, et al., 551 U.S. (2007).

Plessy v. Ferguson, 163 U.S. 537 (1896).

Quezada, R., Díaz, D., & Sánchez, M. (2003, September/October). *Involving Latino parents. Leadership, 33*(1), 32–34.

Quiocho, A., & Daoud, A. (2006). Dispelling myths about Latino parent participation in schools. *The Education Forum, 70*(3), 255–67.

Racial Integrity Act, Virginia General Assembly. SB 219 (1924). Retrieved from http://www.snipview. com/q/Racial%20Integrity%20Act%20of%201924

Rorty, R. (1989). *Contingency, irony, and solidarity.* New York: Cambridge University Press.

San Antonio Independent School District v. Rodríguez, 411 U.S. 1 (1973).

Scanlan, M., & Theoharis, G. (2014). Inclusive schooling and leadership for social justice: Introduction to the special issue. *Theory Into Practice, 53*(2), 79–81.

Schoem, D., Hurtado, S., Sevig, T., Chesler, M., & Sumida, S. (Eds.). (2001). Intergroup dialogue: Democracy at work in theory and practice. In D. Schoem & S. Hurtado (Eds.), *Intergroup dialogue: Deliberative democracy in school, college, community, and workplace* (pp. 1–21). Ann Arbor, MI: University of Michigan Press.

Selden, S. (1999). *Inheriting shame: The story of eugenics and racism in America.* New York: Teachers College Press.

Steele, C. (2011). *Whistling Vivaldi: How stereotypes affect us and what we can do.* New York: W. W. Norton & Company.

Theoharis, G. (2009). *The school leaders our children deserve: Seven keys to equity, social justice, and school reform.* New York: Teachers College Record.

Theoharis, G., & Causton-Theoharis, J. N. (2008). Oppressors or emancipators: Critical dispositions for preparing inclusive school leaders. *Equity & Excellence in Education, 41*(2), 230–46.

Tinkler, B. (2002). *A review of literature on Hispanic/Latino parent involvement in K–12 education.* Washington, DC: United States Department of Education, Office of Educational Research and Improvement, Educational Resource Information Center (ERIC), Document Numbers ED 469134 and RC 023599.

Valdés, G. (2001). *Learning and not learning English: Latino students in American schools*. New York: Teachers College Press.

Vanneman, A., Hamilton, L., Baldwin Anderson, J., & Rahman, T. (2009). *Achievement gaps: How black and white students in public schools perform in mathematics and reading on the National Assessment of Educational Progress* (NCES 2009–455). Washington, DC: National Center for Education Statistics, Institute of Education Sciences, U.S. Department of Education.

Watkins, W. (2001). *The white architects of black education: Ideology and power in America, 1865–1954*. New York: Teachers College Press.

Weber, L. (2007). A conceptual framework for understanding race, class, gender, and sexuality. *Psychology of Women Quarterly, 22*(1), 13–32.

Wells, A. S., Holme, J. J., Revilla, A. T., & Atanda, A. K. (2009). *Both sides now: The story of school desegregation's graduates*. Los Angeles, CA: University of California Press.

White House (2014). *My brother's keeper*. Retrieved from http://www.whitehouse.gov/my-brothers-keeper

Wilson, C. M., & Horsford, S. D. (Eds.). (2013). *Advancing equity and achievement in America's diverse schools: Inclusive theories, policies, and practices*. New York: Routledge.

Winn, M. (2011). *Girl time: Literacy, justice, and the school-to-prison pipeline*. New York: Teachers College Press.

Wortham, S., & Contreras, M. (2002). Struggling toward culturally relevant pedagogy in the Latino/a diaspora. *Journal of Latinos in Education, 1*(2), 133–44.

Yosso, T. (2005). Whose culture has capital? A critical race theory discussion of community cultural wealth. *Race, Ethnicity and Education, 8*(1), 69–91.

Zambrana, R., & Zoppi, I. (2002). Latina students: Translating cultural wealth into social capital to improve academic success. *Journal of Ethnic & Cultural Diversity in Social Work: Innovations in Theory, Research & Practice, 11*(1/2), 33–53.

Zarate, M. (2007). *Understanding Latino parental involvement in education: Perceptions, expectations, and recommendations*. Los Angeles, CA: Tomás Rivera Policy Institute, University of Southern California.

Zinn, M., & Thornton Dill, B. (1996). Theorizing difference from multiracial feminism. *Feminist Studies 22*(2), 321–31.

CHAPTER 5

Inclusive Leadership and English Learners

Isabel Kelsey, Carmen Campuzano, and Francesca López

Although there are currently more than 4.7 million English Learners (ELs) in the United States (National Center for Education Statistics [NCES], 2014), it has been a nation of cultural and linguistic diversity since it emerged as a country (Mondale & Patton, 2001).[1] In spite of the long history of cultural and linguistic diversity in the United States (Crawford, 2004), a hegemonic curriculum (Connell, 1998) has dominated instructional practices, marginalizing students who are not reflected in the curriculum (Capper & Frattura, 2009; Frattura & Capper, 2007; Theoharis 2009, Scanlan & López, 2013). In consideration of the rapidly growing population of culturally and linguistically diverse students in the United States that is likely to be a salient consideration for most, if not all, elementary and secondary school leaders, this chapter focuses on the tenets of inclusive leadership for ELs. Despite our explicit focus on ELs, this chapter is meant to be applied in the larger inclusive landscape reflected in the other chapters in this book.

We begin this chapter by detailing the current context of schools, briefly explaining the hegemonic policies and practices that have contributed to the marginalization of ELs in schools. We then summarize the research literature that offers evidence favoring inclusive views of ELs. Finally, we detail the tenets of inclusive leadership for ELs using Ylimaki's (2011, 2012, 2014) framework for critical curriculum leadership. We apply this framework to case studies of two actual school leaders in otherwise highly restrictive contexts, which illustrate that inclusive leadership for ELs can occur regardless of setting.

PART 1: THE CURRENT CONTEXT OF ENGLISH LEARNERS IN SCHOOLS

Over four decades ago the Bilingual Education Act (1968) was passed, promoting innovative pedagogical practices for ELs. Yet many of today's leaders find themselves unprepared to meet the needs of the growing sector of ELs (Boscardin, 2005; Capper & Frattura, 2009; Gay,

2010; Ylimaki, 2014). In part, this is due to the proliferation of the hegemonic curriculum that is discernable by its

> . . . abstract division of knowledge into subjects, a hierarchy of subjects (with classics, now mathematics, at the top); a hierarchical ordering of knowledge within each subject (fine-grained distinction between elementary and advanced material); a teacher-centered classroom-based pedagogy; an individualized learning process; formal competitive assessment (the "exam").
>
> (Connell, 1998, p. 84)

Progressive policies toward ELs that spanned a few decades in the wake of the Bilingual Education Act were replaced with more restrictive policies, reflected most recently with the No Child Left Behind Act (NCLB, 2001) and Race to the Top (US Department of Education, 2009).

A rapidly increasing demographic shift is but one of the challenges that leaders face to provide an equitable and high-quality education for ELs (Dantley & Tillman, 2006; Theoharis, 2007; Theoharis, 2009, Ylimaki, 2011, 2012, 2014). Evidence accumulated through educational leadership research demonstrates that school leaders are *the* primary agents for school improvement. In part, successful school leaders foster organizational growth by having a clear mission, setting directions, providing professional development, and restructuring and managing the instructional program (Hallinger, 2005; Hallinger & Murphy, 1985; Leithwood, Jantzi, & Steinbach 1999; Leithwood & Riehl, 2005; Purkey & Smith, 1983). Yet to restructure schools for the new demographics reflected in schools, school leaders must be *curriculum* leaders, bringing an understanding of critical curriculum theory and cultural-political awareness (Ylimaki, 2011, 2012, 2014). Traditional instructional leadership studies "do not provide contextualized understanding (macro or micro) of curriculum leadership" (Ylimaki, 2011, p. 4). This chapter attempts to address this need.

Meeting the Needs of ELs in the US

There is a great deal of variability in ways schools meet the needs of ELs today (Gándara, Rumberger, Maxwell-Jolly, & Callahan, 2003; Ovando, 2003), due in part to the shifting policies over the past several decades. The Bilingual Education Act of 1968 was the first legislation in our recent history that focused on the rights of ELs. Although the law was not mandatory and did not prescribe *how* ELs' needs should be met by schools, it did encourage support via funding for educational resources and teacher training. In 1974, however, the Supreme Court in *Lau v. Nichols* (1974) decided that the lack of language accommodations for students with limited English constituted a violation of the 1964 Civil Rights Act. Remedies to violations were codified as the Equal Educational Opportunity Act (EEOA), which prohibits segregation of students based on race and national origin and mandates that schools and districts take actions to address linguistic barriers. Shortly after this Supreme Court decision, the *Lau Remedies* (Padilla, Fairchild, & Valdez, 1990) outlined guidelines for the use of bilingual methods in the classroom (Crawford & Krashen, 2007). Although the 1974 amendment to the Bilingual Education Act explicitly mentioned bilingual education, successive reauthorizations of the law between 1978 and 1988 have moved from supporting bilingual education strategies exclusively to including other strategies (see Gándara & Rumberger, 2009, p. 765; Ramirez, Yuen, Ramey, & Pasta, 1991).

After the withdrawal of the *Lau Remedies* by US Education Secretary Bell during the Reagan administration, language views began to shift toward a more restrictive stance. Several states witnessed a rescinding of bilingual policies (e.g., Arizona, California, and Massachusetts), with many more implementing a more forceful focus on the reclassification of ELs and their removal from bilingual programs after the passing of NCLB (2001). This, in turn, resulted in the elimination of many bilingual programs from public schools across the United States (López & McEneaney, 2012). Even teachers who remained in bilingual programs were "powerfully pressed into teaching only through English, fearful of parents, managers and their own perceived failure" (Baker, 2006, p. 199). Current educational policies like the Race to the Top competition, which granted $4.35 billion to states to spur innovation and reform, continue to abrogate the effectiveness of bilingual education. For instance, nearly three in four ELs live in the states that were not awarded funds, and some of the awardees—such as Massachusetts—have particularly problematic track records in terms of providing these students equitable opportunities to learn (Lyons, 2014).

The changing views toward non-English languages in schools can be understood using Ruiz's (1984) language orientations: language as a problem, language as a right, and language as a resource. School leaders who blindly adhere to policies (e.g., Race to the Top) without a critical examination of their consequences tend to view language as a *problem* (Brisk, 2006). This perception of language as a problem is reflected in views that home languages other than English are simply barriers to be overcome as ELs learn English. It is fueled by the erroneous belief that bilingual education prevents the assimilation of ELs into American culture, which jeopardizes national identity (Ylimaki, 2014). Socially just leaders who view students' home language as a *resource* (Ruiz, 1984), in contrast, promote pedagogical strategies that support ELs' native language in the class and school and view EL students' native languages as assets to peers. Indeed, empirical research tends to favor inclusive methods for both English acquisition and academic achievement of ELs (see Scanlan & López, 2014)—underscoring the importance of school leaders' understanding of both evidence-based practices and viewing ELs in ways that promote inclusion.

What Do English Learners Have to Say? Voices of the Community

In the previous section, we describe socially just leaders as those who view language as a resource and advocate for ELs amidst a repressive educational policy that attempts to remediate language differences by imposing hegemonic policies that omit the voices of students most deleteriously affected. In the following vignette, we describe some of Josefa's experiences. Josefa, a Latina fifth-grade EL student, reflects the epitome of many EL students living in poverty. Her educational experiences are aggravated because of the many adversities she has faced since an early age.

By the time Josefa was in fifth grade, she had attended 12 different schools and crossed different district borders. Josefa had also been identified as learning disabled in kindergarten. These two distinct labels had forged Josefa's identity, both in terms of her self-perception and how others viewed her. In addition to these labels, Josefa had other less salient dimensions of diversity: she came from a low socioeconomic background and her parents spoke a limited amount of English. As a female, she faced cultural and social barriers.

Educators placed Josefa in an English Learner Development (ELD) class and she received pullout services for speech, special education, and at-risk intervention classes. Despite the intentions of improving academic outcomes with the pullout programs, the multiple services she received resulted in her being continuously pulled out throughout the day, interrupting routines and reintroducing her to her classroom mid-lesson. Initially, she expressed her dislike by frowning or letting out a big sigh but eventually began expressing her frustration at missing science or physical education by stating, "I miss all the fun stuff." Once, when she asked to leave the classroom to attend yet another pullout program, she shouted across the room, "I don't want to go!" Josefa's experiences, like those of many other ELs, involve multiple factors that impede her integration in the classroom. The constant pullout and remedial programs fragment students' educational experiences, leaving them with a sense of social ostracization.

Many students placed in designated ELD classrooms relate to Josefa's experiences. They dislike being pulled out and having the label "English Learner." When students are cognizant that they have been separated from their peers because they have not passed the state's language test requirement, they often feel a passive abandonment of their fate in the school and society. For example, three of Josefa's classmates, Alex, Yadira, and Miguel, always asked why they were in the ELD class and what they had to do to "get out and be with their friends." In fact, Yadira once stated that the girls in the "regular class" suggested that she was placed in an ELD class because she was not as smart. Clearly, the perceptions of pullout by students who are pulled out of the classroom and by their peers who remain in the classroom can have marked effects on ELs' identities, suggesting to them that they do not belong as members of their classroom, but as individuals who must be pulled in multiple directions to fit in.

Arizona is a context that is laden with policies that are exclusionary, not inclusive. What began as the elimination of bilingual programs with Proposition 203 has most recently evolved into a four-hour English language development block that explicitly segregates ELs on the basis of their English proficiency. Many EL students in these blocks seem to believe that they are not capable of academically performing commensurately with their peers, and suffer from a sense of futility. It is notable that Arizona leads the nation in the proportion of Latino youth who drop out of high school (National Center for Education Statistics [NCES], 2013). Among them, close to 30% of Latino youth fail to complete high school within four years (NCES, 2013). When Latino youth are ELs, the dropout rate soars to 75% (US Department of Education, 2012).

Would Josefa's educational experience have been different if she had not been labeled learning disabled and EL at such an early age and educated in segregated classrooms? What would her schooling experiences have been like if the school leaders had taken an inclusive perspective for all students? What can school leaders in other states learn from critically reflecting on Josefa's experiences in Arizona? We describe socially just school leaders in a subsequent section of this chapter, but first turn to some of the challenges that may have contributed to Josefa's experiences.

PART 2: WHAT WE KNOW ABOUT ENGLISH LEARNERS: THE LITERATURE

Social justice leadership theory attempts to reverse the historical trend of marginalization by providing leaders with the necessary "dispositions and analytical tools to advocate for a comprehensive curriculum beyond dominant groups' values about knowledge" (Ylimaki, 2014, p. 5). Indeed, the hegemonic curriculum reflects the dominant groups' values about knowledge, and is in part the reason ELs are excluded from the curriculum. According to Apple (2000), the dominant group includes neoliberals whose self-interests in the economy and the markets connected to it drive their pursuit to a *back-to-basics curriculum*. With their collective expertise in accountability, efficiency, and management, the dominant group has "succeeded in pushing a large portion of the discussions, rhetoric, and policies in education in particular directions" (p. xxv)—which exclude ELs. For example, one strategy is the dominant group's use of the rhetoric of *common sense* to perpetuate a belief that US public schools are failing—particularly in the areas of mathematics and science. This notion of failure suggests an absence of rigor, which promulgates and prioritizes efforts that are results-driven, yet focus on narrow and dubious accountability measures (Moss, Pullin, Gee, Haertel, & Young, 2008). This focus is notably *not* about providing opportunities to learn to traditionally marginalized students, including ELs.

In contrast to dominant groups' values about education ("results-driven"), leaders who promote a socially just school climate focus on inclusiveness, equity, and diversity (Scanlan, 2012; Theoharis, 2009; Tillman & Scheurich, 2013) that require "action and advocacy" (Ylimaki, 2014, p. 4) through building capacity. Thus, rather than being critical of students' achievements in and of themselves, a socially just leader is critical of the inequities that society has placed on marginalized students. In response, such a leader strives to create an inclusive, culturally responsive curriculum. Capper and Frattura (2009) capture this sentiment in their assertion that, "To lead for social justice, advocating for students who struggle in school must be paired with a core belief in heterogeneous learning environments" (p. 42). A heterogeneous learning environment for ELs in particular "involves valuing students learning English and positioning them and their families, language, and cultures as central, integral aspects of the school community" (Theoharis, 2011, p. 648).

Socially just school leadership often must resist the hegemonic curriculum that is reinforced in particular political contexts. For instance, since 2006, Arizona policy has expressly required the segregation of ELs given its self-appointed status as an "English first" state. The Structured English Immersion (SEI) model used in Arizona requires that ELs are grouped homogenously to the extent possible based on English proficiency, and that they receive explicit English instruction in four-hour blocks (Arizona Department of Education, 2008). Thus, English learners are segregated from students with different English proficiency levels as well as from academic content that is covered while they attend the four-hour block of English instruction.

Socially just leaders promote inclusive practices that are informed by research (Montecel & Cortez, 2002) and make a stance against policies based on "common sense" and the rhetoric of cultural politics. In other words, socially just leaders implement a culturally relevant curriculum in spite of considerable pressure toward a hegemonic curriculum. In addition, these school leaders create school communities that incorporate multiple dimensions of diversity. Central to the development of such schools is *curriculum leadership*.

The curriculum leadership framework (Ylimaki, 2011, 2012, 2014) addresses the complexities of 21st-century leadership. It is grounded in both traditional instructional leadership theory (Hallinger & Murphy, 1985; Marks & Printy, 2003) and critical curriculum theories (Dewey, 2008; Freire, 2000; Pinar, 2012). In traditional educational administration, the principal is characterized by a set of characteristics and behaviors that are necessary for instructional leadership (Hallinger, 2005), and this leadership may be distributed with other staff across the school (Spillane, Diamond, & Jita, 2003). Curriculum leadership combines this traditional framework with critical curriculum theory. Critical theorists like Dewey (Foster, 1986) believed that the aim of education was democracy toward a socially just society. While instructional leadership emphasizes pedagogical and instructional practices, curriculum leadership "extends beyond teaching practice to the sociocultural and political aspects of educational content decisions: what is taught, to whom, and by whom" (Ylimaki, 2012, p. 305). In the sections that follow, we elaborate on how a curriculum leadership framework provides a useful lens to unpacking the research literature regarding inclusively meeting the educational needs of ELs and for leadership practice toward these ends.

Inclusive, Culturally Responsive Curriculum and Instruction

As the number of ELs continues to grow, schools need to improve in their capacity to provide grade-level content instruction and inclusive education to linguistically diverse students. Approximately 70% of ELs speak Spanish as a first language (Fry, 2007). This significant language shift has impacted school leaders who must ensure that ELs have equitable opportunities to learn. Toward this end, schools must develop high-quality and culturally responsive curriculum and instruction that supports learning English through content knowledge and the use of diverse strategies (Brisk, 2006). This is best accomplished in a bilingual and biliterate school climate (Crawford, 2004; Ovando & Collier, 1998).

Exemplary school leaders are the primary agents in meeting the needs of students who are culturally and linguistically diverse (CLD) with community support (Scanlan & López, 2013; Theoharis, 2011; Ylimaki, 2011). These leaders view language as a resource (Ruiz, 1984), are supportive of bilingualism, and regard the education of students who are CLD as additive because the most effective education uses a student's home language for instruction and as a basis for learning English. Bilingual education and dual language education are supportive of ELs' English proficiency and maintaining their home language (Baker, 2006). These educational practices support and require inclusive classrooms. Because Spanish and English languages are equally valued, they also provide English-speaking and Spanish-speaking role models among the students and teachers (Brisk, 2006).

Contrary to dual-language and bilingual education, other practices focus only on the acquisition of English. Ylimaki (2014) asserts, "Neo-nationalist groups are also increasingly vocal about the need to assimilate immigrant students to help them quickly acquire English" (p. 32). In other words, the rhetoric of "common sense" has infiltrated schools and the general public in the belief that English is the only way of instruction for EL students. Education practices that focus on English acquisition and purposely do not further develop a student's home language that is other than English include English as a Second Language (ESL) and Sheltered Instruction. Educators often implement these practices when a variety of languages other than English are spoken in the school, when just a few students speak a language other than English in the school, or when schools lack resources for bilingual or dual-language education. ESL, however, provides only "the bare essentials of bilingual education" (Crawford, 2004, p. 33). Most ESL instruction is oral, leveled by proficiency, and requires students to be pulled out. English instruction is often in small groups for a period of approximately 30 to 45 minutes daily.

Other schools rely on Sheltered English[2] instruction, providing content-based instruction supporting the acquisition of English via content (e.g., science). With Sheltered English instruction, EL students are grouped apart from their non-EL peers and expected to make the transition into mainstream classrooms within one to five years (Christian, 2006). Both ESL and Sheltered English approaches are subtractive because the student learns English at the risk of losing his/her home language. These practices attempt to "fix" the language "problem" and have been developed in response to recent cultural political shifts that emphasize the rapid acquisition of English.

In scenarios where bilingual education is not possible in schools because of the variety of languages spoken other than English, additive practices are the most effective. For example, bilingual education that continues over many years can support the acquisition of English while still maintaining a student's home language. De Jong (2006) suggests five principles should undergird the effective education of students who are CLD: (1) enrichment that builds on students' language and cultural background; (2) allocation of resources toward realistic "linguistic, cultural, and academic goals"; (3) assurance that personnel use instructional strategies that support "content, language, and literacy development"; (4) use of fair and continuous assessment that sets goals that meet student "linguistic, cultural and academic goals"; and (5) development of a strong school-home community relationship (p. 91). In sum, the curriculum leadership framework guides socially just leaders to ensure that an assets-based, additive, language-as-resource (Ruiz, 1984) philosophy undergirds home and English-language acquisition (see further, Scanlan & López, 2014).

In turn, instruction that fosters home language and English by nature reflects culturally responsive instruction. A culturally responsive classroom environment is one where curriculum is relevant to ELs and other students of diversity. A relevant curriculum teaches through a multicultural lens acknowledging diversity and language needs. It requires joint planning from the homeroom teacher, EL instructor, and other resource personnel to address the curriculum and cultural needs of students throughout the school year. Implementing culturally responsive practices is indispensable to creating an inclusive environment for ELs (Gay, 2010; Tillman & Scheurich, 2013; Theoharis, 2007; Ylimaki, 2014). However, many school leaders find this practice to be the most challenging.

Academic Rigor via Funds of Knowledge

Principals must ensure that the curriculum and instruction for CLD students are defined by high expectations and rigor. That is, ELs need to be "taught through the use of challenging material that does not get 'watered down' merely because students are not fluent in the language of instruction" (Gersten & Baker, 2000, p. 461). In particular, the principal builds a culture in which teachers—individually and collaboratively—ensure that ELs do not receive subpar materials and a less rigorous curriculum than their non-EL peers (Brisk, 2006).

Rigor is a popular term used since NCLB (2001) to refer to a curricular policy that is composed of pacing calendars and high test taking. The curriculum leadership framework broadens this perspective on academic rigor using a Funds of Knowledge lens to analyze how students who are CLD can access a rigorous curriculum and instruction. This framework directs school leaders to consider students' background knowledge and experiences to develop curriculum that is culturally responsive. A rigorous curriculum that is responsive to students' cultural backgrounds facilitates access to this curriculum for students with CLD.

Throughout US educational history, the cultural integration of students has been addressed by enacting desegregation laws. However, as demographic shifts increase and "minority" students become the numerical majority, desegregation laws become outdated and ineffective in serving students who are culturally and linguistically diverse. For example, magnet schools and specialized "pullout" services were created to comply with desegregation orders to provide an equitable education to ELs and marginalized students (by creating schools that would be appealing to non-minority students, thus assisting the school to attain a racial/ethnic balance). When districts become majority-minority, however, compliance becomes increasingly unattainable. For example, in one large, Latino-majority district, magnet schools that were originally under desegregation orders to comply with race inequalities of Latino students are now at risk of losing their magnet status or closing because the ratio of non-Latino students has not been met.

Accountability

As a result of NCLB (2001), accountability and assessment pressures have greatly impacted US schools. In this context, curriculum leadership requires leaders to be literate in assessment implementation and analysis of results and rely on this information to create a culturally responsive curriculum.

To assist this analysis, equity audits are key tools of inclusive and socially just school practices (Ylimaki, 2014). Unfortunately, in recent "results-driven" decisions, leaders collapse beneath the neoliberal pressures of accountability and high-stakes testing, without analyzing assessments through a culturally responsive lens. Thus equity audits are often non-existent. A traditional curriculum emphasizing fact memorization, drill and skills, and textbooks continues to exist in EL-majority schools. School leaders who are not well informed about bilingual and additive models are easily influenced by the "common sense" rhetoric that such a traditional curriculum provides "rigor and relevance," failing to see how this limits students' opportunities to learn. Instead, a socially just curriculum is needed.

All too often schools and districts impose a "back to basics" curriculum, and in some cases dismantle existing culturally responsive programs, in effect converting the school into a hegemonic institution. This is typical of turnaround models where failing schools are transformed to charter schools mostly affecting poor Black or Latino students with the pretext that students are failing specifically in math and science. In the case of ELs, we have seen bilingual programs that originally supported a student's language and culture eliminated without community or faculty consent. Other examples include the dismantling of an authentic balanced literacy resource book room. More generally speaking, ELs' instruction is homogenized and not supported with the practices that were created when SEI replaced bilingual education. Therefore, there is a need for neo-progressive leaders to enact culturally responsive practices that are inclusive for student learning, family, and community.

The New Instructional Leader Beyond 21st-Century Practices

As demographic shifts continue to increase, amplifying the complexities of schooling, a social justice school leader draws upon his/her beliefs and understanding of critical and traditional theory to promote an inclusive and equitable high-quality education. Thus, a social just leader uses discourse as an analytical tool to work through unfair accountability and assessment policies that negatively affect ELs and marginalized students.

Such a leader cultivates a neo-progressive education movement and influences curriculum content, classroom practices, and communities. In the following section, we provide examples of two successful bilingual schools that are inclusive to ELs by providing each student the right to an authentic sense of belonging (Theoharis & O'Toole, 2011, p. 649). More specifically, the principals have resisted the "common sense" rhetoric of policy and cultural politics. Principals Carla Cruz and Regina Castillo are critical leaders who have fought against unjust policies and have created culturally responsive schools that are inclusive to EL students and span across dimensions of diversity.

PART 3: INCLUSIVE LEADERSHIP AROUND ENGLISH LEARNERS IN K–12 SCHOOLS

This section begins with case study examples of two schools. We then describe the process that leaders use in moving their schools to become more inclusive. Bilingual Elementary and Hope Academy[3] were selected because their principals exemplify Ylimaki's (2014) socially just framework for school leaders as curriculum leaders.

Case Studies

Bilingual Elementary and Hope Academy are located in the same Arizona school district. They are both urban and each school has implemented a bilingual program that is unique to its community's needs. As a result of district and state policies, schools in Arizona are provided additional resource support for ELs. Resource personnel are responsible for maintaining documentation and facilitating testing for language proficiency.

A description of the school is outlined to understand each school's inclusive EL bilingual model. Each school scenario presents two different leadership styles and their effort to promote and sustain a bilingual model and service ELs and their community. Indeed, each leader approached her school's needs differently, dependent on demographic shifts in the school population and community, as well as the socioeconomics of the students. For both schools, we illustrate the restructuring effort led by the principal and the faculty, which includes details about both the process and challenges.

Bilingual Elementary

Bilingual Elementary (BE), a K–5 school, is centrally located in a historic neighborhood and is one of the oldest schools in the city. The school is also a *magnet school*[4] focused on *dual-language immersion* in Spanish with English as the additive language. The majority of close to 350 students have enrolled from other parts of the district, whereas only about 25% live in the neighborhood. The school has traditionally served students who are most often Latino (approximately 70%), although many identify as having a mixed ethnicity. The mission at BE is to develop full bilingualism and biliteracy within a culturally responsive curriculum, which reflects the demographics of the school (as well as the district). Under the leadership of the principal as well as with support from teachers, parents, the local community, and the school district, BE continues to sustain its bilingual model despite policies that have restricted the use of students' non-English language in instruction via Proposition 203 (2001; Arizona Revised Statutes, 2000). The school has also been lauded for high success rates on achievement tests, despite using a curriculum that is distinct from that typically promulgated by the state.

The dual-language bilingual program at BE reflects a Spanish immersion model and includes as a key component the EXITO (SUCCESS) Spanish reading/language arts block as part of its core curriculum. EXITO is a multi-grade level Spanish literacy exchange program that was developed by a university researcher and BE teacher (Smith & Arnot-Hopffer, 1998). The exchange takes place three times a week for a 75-minute block. It is a non-scripted program and teachers use their pedagogical knowledge and strategies to implement various theme units that align with the language needs of the students and language arts state standards (Smith & Arnot-Hopffer, 1998).

BE is currently the only dual-language bilingual model in the district that implements a full Spanish immersion program in kindergarten and first grade and continues to adhere to its mission of developing bilingualism and biliteracy while complying with state policies and high-stakes testing. Since the BE model was first implemented, many political, demographic, and personnel factors have changed and added pressures to the implementation of existing practices. After NCLB (2001) and Proposition 203 (2001; Arizona Revised Statutes, 2000) in Arizona, additional documentation was required for schools that used non-English language in instruction. Schools were required to identify and assess EL students, and document parental waivers for EL students' participation in a program that used non-English language in instruction. The school district's new superintendent has given support to replicate the immersion model in grades K–2 in ten dual-language schools for the upcoming school year.

Although the state of Arizona requires an SEI endorsement to teach ELs, the district requires a bilingual endorsement to teach in a dual-language bilingual classroom. Although BE families are culturally, linguistically, and socioeconomically diverse, the overwhelming majority of students have Mexican American heritage and many are multi-racial families. To many BE parents, regaining Spanish is the reason they selected the school. As Garcia (2012) points out, the parents are taking a *recursive action* because

> In cases when bilingualism is developed after the language practices of a community have been suppressed, the development of the community's mother tongue is not a simple addition that starts from a monolingual point. Therefore, bilingualism is not simply additive, but recursive.
>
> (p. 52)

Parents of children enrolled at BE see the value and benefit of regaining bilingualism and becoming bicultural (Smith & Arnot-Hopffner, 1998). As such, it should come as no surprise that at BE, parent involvement is high (Peña, 1998). They are active not only in their child's education, but also participate in school events, the Parent-Teacher Association (PTA), Site Council, and numerous fundraisers. Many active parents also represent the minority population of White families, who are very invested in the BE program. The principal, teachers, and parents work together for a common good, which promotes social justice and is inclusive of diverse family units who bond together to celebrate language and cultural diversity.

As proposed by Furman (2004), the BE community is the avenue of social justice for educational administration practices. For example, *Noche de Aguilitas* (Night of the Little Eagles), also known as the Fall Carnival, is the school's biggest and most important fundraiser. This event is planned a year ahead of time by the PTA. This active group is headed by parents, faculty, staff, and community members and receives full support and collaboration from the principal, who does not miss a meeting. *Noche de Aguilitas* is an evening-long mariachi concert, along with booths, food, and auctions. This event is possible due to the efforts of a community that works together as an avenue of social justice. Funding from this event supports the school in bringing in bilingual authors, artists, and musical performances otherwise not accessible to this community of children. Another example of BE's community includes the participation of parents, teachers, community members, and university students in an effort to revive the school's community garden, which now plays a major role inside the classroom as part of a socially just curriculum that includes ecology lessons and experiences, which teach children to be responsible stewards of our planet. The garden committee designates one Saturday a month for clean-up, planting, harvesting, or just enjoying a day in the garden, which was recently renamed to honor a civil rights leader who frequently visits BE. On other occasions, celebrations are held in the evenings. Pizza is baked in the garden's brick oven and the community pitches in with pizza toppings, beverages, and sides. In essence, at BE, the school leader has fostered a *family* within and around the school.

In addition to its language focus, BE has curricular attractions that make it unique—particularly given the rescinding of subjects since NCLB (2001). The *especialistas* (specialists) provide music, art, and physical education in which Spanish is the language of instruction, giving children opportunities for authentic language experiences outside the academically rigorous classrooms. Its talented and well-known mariachi band not only plays locally, but nationally and internationally. Currently 77 children ranging from grades K–5 are part of the very popular mariachi, which relies completely on an equally large number of active parents who volunteer countless hours of their time to transport, feed, dress, and applaud the children's talented performances. BE's principal focuses her full support to recruit funding and district support for this activity, which she considers a key to children's academic success. She points out that the mariachi children from BE continue this lifelong skill and become integrated into the middle and high school mariachi groups in the district and ultimately become part of the graduation statistics for Hispanic students.

For ten years, the school has offered Mariachi Summer Camp, which opens up the BE campus to the entire community to participate in learning and continuing the beautiful cultural tradition of mariachi music. Other after-school extra-curricular activities include folklorico dancing, gardening, hip-hop, embroidery, and sports, among other activities. The curricular attractions provide an inclusive space not only for ELs, but also for students with special needs. These diverse focal areas underscore the way in which BE conceptualizes children's needs at multifaceted rather than solely test-score based.

Although BE's unique bilingual model has much appeal, the historical school building limits student capacity. Attempts to move this unique bilingual program away from the current neighborhood are not supported by the principal, who strongly believes the bilingual-bicultural focus must be rooted in an authentic bilingual-bicultural site and in an authentic historical neighborhood, which is at the root of a socially just curriculum. There are more than 60 students on the waiting list at any given time. Typically there have been two classrooms per grade level but additional classrooms have been added to specific grades to accommodate enrollment surplus and as the principal moves and maneuvers to protect the program and avoid teacher reduction and district pressures to close down small school sites.

Although BE has traditionally served Latino children, a desegregation court order from 1978 requires less than 70% Latino enrollment for the magnet program to continue, despite the fact the district is approaching 70% Latino students overall. As a consequence, the school could lose its magnet status and financial support. Nevertheless, as a firm advocate of bilingual education, the principal has demonstrated her commitment in maintaining ELs' first language by actively participating in the district's social-political framework and firmly advocating for ELs and for equity in a climate of school "standardization."

In an effort to maintain and strengthen its dual-language model, a restructuring effort to strengthen the model and the school-wide program is taking place through professional development headed by the principal and the magnet committee, as well as teachers and paraprofessionals. The purpose is to revisit the school's goals, mission, philosophy, and student outcomes. This underscores the capacity-building approach of school leadership at BE (Day, 2009).

To further initiate dialog and discussion about the school's current bilingual status, a survey was given to faculty to have a clear understanding of the model's language fidelity used in the classroom and building. In addition, problems, questions, and teacher frustrations were addressed in the initial professional development. Further goals are to revisit the dual-language model and review the current plan to strengthen it. This year the school will gain a magnet coordinator to strengthen its curriculum focus and redouble its recruiting in an effort to attract White families to BE and meet the integration requirements under the desegregation court orders.

In short, BE maintains and continues to strengthen the bilingual program and culturally responsive curriculum. Under the state's new school grading system, the school has made academic gains from a C to a B status and the faculty continues to set new academic goals to achieve an A letter grade, without compromising its mission to create bilingual-biliterate students. District statistics demonstrate that BE fifth-graders exceed the district averages in reading and outscore other English-only programs. Recent "Move on When Reading" (MOWR) legislation in Arizona has added yet another obstacle in protecting language usage in the classroom. According to this law, every third-grader will be expected to meet or approach reading goals on the state standardized achievement test, Arizona's Instrument to Measure Standards (AIMS), or face possible retention (Arizona Department of Education, 2014). The 2013–2014 results on the AIMS saw every eligible third-grader meet this goal and not a single BE third-grade student was retained. Long-range district statistics also attest to these long-term gains as former BE students continue to outperform other eighth-graders in reading.

Hope Academy K–8

Hope Academy is located in the same District as BE, but it is located in a different part of the city that reflects distinctly different demographics. With a population of 60% Native American and 35% Latino, Hope Academy has the largest Native American percentage in the district. ELs make up a majority of the students in which Spanish or an indigenous language or both are part of the home language. As such, Hope Academy has a trilingual community.

Hope Academy has faced similar political pressures as BE, but differs greatly because the school's underperforming status has been exacerbated by marginalization that was created by previous administrators (Dugan, Ylimaki, & Bennett, 2012). Namely, the community was pushed away and not allowed to take part in the school's decision-making. Ultimately, students and parents were divided by race (Scanlan & Palmer, 2009).

Not surprisingly, when Principal Regina Castillo first entered Hope Academy she faced mistrust by the community. She also had a new faculty and only one early childhood teacher remained (Dugan et al., 2012). Nevertheless, she had a strong belief that community and school relationships were important to set the foundation and direction.

Principal Regina Castillo was an advocate and believed that "schools should be part of the community" (as cited in Dugan et al., 2012, p. 57). Therefore, she began to gain the trust of the community by visiting their homes and listening to parent concerns. By doing this, Castillo used the Funds of Knowledge paradigm (Gonzalez, Moll, & Amanti, 2005) drawing on parents' culture as a strength to bring the community and school together. With this approach, many of the residents soon felt that their needs were being heard and, as a result, began to participate in school activities.

Over the following months, Hope Academy started resembling the culturally and linguistically diverse community it represented. Native American and Mexican artifacts decorated the school building. These cultural artifacts brought pride to the community. Most importantly, however, an after-school bilingual program was implemented. It valued the Native American home language that many of the parents and tribe elders wished to revive. In addition, Hope Academy provided after-school English classes for parents. One parent expressed his gratitude by stating,

> I just want to thank everyone for allowing me an opportunity to learn English three times a week. This class has helped me a lot and my son sees the value of school. I have become a role model for him. He sees me in a different way than before. It has helped me to help him with homework and we spend time learning from each other. For this I thank you.

(as cited in Dugan et al., 2012, p. 61)

This sentiment is indicative of a shift toward curriculum leadership and the call for "action and advocacy" (Ylimaki, 2014). In other words, Castillo believed that "building bridges" would bring the community together. She supported parents' requests to bring a Yaqui bilingual program and students' Funds of Knowledge into the school (Gonzalez et al., 2005).

To conclude, Castillo is known as a "turnaround" principal because she turned around Hope Academy from an "underperforming" to a "performing plus" school. Moreover, Castillo engaged and included students and families alike that had been traditionally marginalized. She did this by establishing a real connection to the community so that the community could be found in the school, and the school in the community. Castillo built EL-inclusive practices for Native American students and Latino students. She fostered a culturally responsive curriculum by using students' backgrounds and language and worked through multiple dimensions of diversity (Dugan et al., 2012).

GUIDING QUESTIONS

The principals of Bilingual Elementary and Hope Academy faced multiple dilemmas.
- What were their challenges? How were they the same or different?
- What strategies did they use to make a stance against unfair policy?
- How was their belief in social justice and inclusion the catalyst for their successful leadership?
- Reflect on your belief system. How is it similar to or different from the principals in the cases in your quest for leading in socially just ways?

LEADERSHIP QUESTIONS

- What is the policy regarding ELs in your district or state, and how can you leverage it to create an inclusive and culturally responsive curriculum?
- How are students who are CLD in your school currently being served? To what extent is their education inclusive, culturally responsive, and draws from their funds of knowledge?
- How can leadership bridge the realities ELs face between school and home?

Supporting Leadership Around ELs: Inclusive School Reform

This section of the chapter builds on the two case studies to identify leadership strategies for creating inclusive schools for EL students. It synthesizes research into practice, providing suggestions on how leaders can create and maintain inclusive practices. The two leaders described in this chapter used similar strategies that considered their student populations (i.e., demographic shifts), the unique curriculum that needed to be incorporated, and considerations of social and cultural perspectives all in the context of imposed accountability. As curriculum leaders, they: (1) incorporated professional development that addressed building professional learning communities; (2) analyzed discourse of common sense" around ELs and diversity; and (3) strengthened the culturally responsive curriculum by creating inclusive practices.

Professional Development

The curriculum leadership framework focuses on fostering a school climate that promotes the ongoing learning and development of teachers in their pedagogical practices (Drago-Severson, 2012, Marks & Printy 2003). As such, success for students who are CLD must be anchored in professional development to develop staff capacity in culturally relevant instruction and inclusive practices. Professional development must be driven by the school's mission and facilitated by professional learning communities in the school. Curriculum leaders rely on PD to:

- Examine strategies that did not work and identify the reasons underlying the lack of success.
- Identify the strategies that *were* successful at grade-level Professional Learning Communities (PLCs) and as a whole school community.
- Examine service delivery that removes ELs from general education and re-deploy human resources to provide inclusive service delivery. Re-visit this each year.
- Collaborate to align PLC goals with the school's mission.
- Set new goals for the school year to avoid fragmentation and build a school culture that embraces diversity and creates a safe place for learning.
- Design a visual outline of the goals and process for the whole school year. Evaluate past goals and foresee the setbacks and brainstorm how PLCs can work through them.

Successful Professional Development Must Be Driven by the School's Mission

Central to inclusive schools, the school mission reflects the goals and culture of the school, facilitating a common ground among all members of the community. As such, school leaders must revisit the school's mission at the beginning of the school year, reflect on what it represents, and revise as necessary. Questions that can guide the discussion about the school mission as related to professional development include:

- What does the school mission represent?
- To what extent does it reflect the ideology of the school and community?
- How does it reflect inclusive and culturally responsive practices?
- To what extent do staff and community members support and are fully committed to the school's mission?

PLCs should then facilitate professional development. Unlike in the literature on PLCs, PLCs in this context are specifically aimed toward inclusive, social justice ends. To that end, in inclusive schools for students who are CLD, school leaders rely on these strategies to ensure PLCs reflect the school mission and facilitate effective professional development:

- Rotate the PLC coordinator so that everyone has a voice.
- Include all staff and other resource personnel.
- Create blocks of times outside of instruction where planning time is protected, including a weekly schedule to safeguard PLC times.
- Meet regularly and have the agenda ready to discuss pertinent issues.
- Continuously discuss if inclusiveness is being practiced at the school site: In what ways? How can it be improved?
- Strategically rotate faculty and staff to share ideas about what other PLCs are doing to achieve the school's mission.

- Periodically rearrange PLCs by multi-grade levels to provide opportunities for vertical planning and seeking new ideas. The designated coordinator then reports meeting discussions in the next professional development session.
- Review the education of students who are CLD with the goal of refining and creating more inclusive services. Often this results in creating collaborative and co-teaching teams between bilingual and ESL-certified teachers and general education teachers. For ideas and strategies, see Honigsfeld and Dove (2010).

Analyzing Discourse of "Common Sense" Around ELs and Diversity

In Arizona, the dismantling of bilingual education with Proposition 203 and the waves of massive deportations with HB 1070 have contributed to a negative message about non-English language and immigration that has directly affected ELs and marginalized students. By analyzing the discourse of "common sense" that surrounded these and other policies, faculty, staff, and the community can discuss the underlining problems rooted in policies that affect the community. By using discourse as an analytical tool, school leaders, faculty, and staff can become well-informed and differentiate between facts and assumptions rooted in discrimination.

Taking a stance against "common sense" requires understanding the various sides of an issue. Just as each individual holds a belief system, schools should construct a collective belief system about inclusiveness and culturally relevant practices at their site. School staffs can redesign service delivery to seek to incorporate inclusive service delivery and inclusive practices. Inclusiveness is not only about taking a stance, but also building a foundation and cultivating inclusiveness so that future generations can live in a true democracy.

Strengthening the Culturally Responsive Curriculum by Creating Inclusive Practices

A school's curriculum should transcend state and federal requirements by aligning standards to the schools mission, thus reflecting the school's stance against a rhetoric of "common sense." The curriculum should infuse what Banks (1993) refers to as *content integration*, which reflects decisions about "what information should be included in the curriculum, how it should be integrated into the existing curriculum, and its location within the curriculum" (p. 8). The culturally responsive curriculum cannot be isolated in separate EL classrooms or in general education classrooms from which EL students are removed. This expansive curriculum requires inclusive service delivery in order to meet the broader aims of a socially just school for ELs.

The process of developing a curriculum involves meaningful dialogue and careful planning by PLCs, students, and the community. For example, Principal Regina Castillo worked endlessly to build community with a new staff and further reached out to the Native American Community. Through her efforts, Hope Academy created an inclusive environment and practiced culturally responsive curriculum. The curriculum was infused with the language, artwork, and culture of the students represented in the school.

CONCLUSION

As cultural and linguistic diversity shifts continue to increase in US schools, principals, teachers, and community leaders need the knowledge, skills, dispositions, and analytical tools to disrupt cultural and political rhetoric that public schools are failing. Today's leaders must have the knowledge of traditional educational leadership theory and critical theory to act as social just leaders to foster a critical curriculum that is inclusive to historically marginalized students. Although progressive leaders continue to resist hegemonic alliances and advance in their pursuit for equitable and high-quality education, there continues to be a limited number of social justice leaders and their lived experiences. Research therefore needs to seek out and widen the perspective of social justice leaders like those we describe in Bilingual Elementary and Hope Academy. These two principals provided characteristics that distinguish social justice leaders in the complexities of 21st-century schools.

As complexities like demographic shifts, curriculum, social cultural perspectives, and accountability pressures continue to be part of the US school system, Ylimaki (2014) proposes that a leader's belief system and capacity to influence faculty and the community can create a positive school climate and a difference in the lives of marginalized students. Exemplary principals like these are aware of policy and cultural political rhetoric and influence others to make a stance for social justice and value diversity. Moreover, they reflect the community that they serve.

NOTES

1   In this chapter, we use the label "ELs" to refer to culturally and linguistically diverse students. We acknowledge that all labels, including this one, are limited and limiting. As Palmer (2013) states, "so often the labels placed on us in schools serve to delimit the types of opportunities for which we are considered eligible" (p. 271). In the context of this chapter, we choose to refer to students whose mother tongues are not English as ELs to be congruent with the standard reporting labels with which school leaders must work. As will be clear, we focus this chapter on the importance of learning English while also seeing these home languages as important resources and assets.
2   Sheltered English is also used in some bilingual models (see Krashen, 1991).
3   All names are pseudonyms.
4   As part of a desegregation order stemming out of a lawsuit in the 1970s, magnet schools were established to encourage integration. Magnet schools receive additional funding and are monitored for compliance.

REFERENCES

Apple, M. W. (2000). *Official knowledge: Democratic education in a conservative age*. New York: Routledge.
Arizona Department of Education (ADE). (2008). *Structured English immersion EDL models*. Retrieved from http://www.azed.gov/wp-content/uploads/PDF/SEIModels05-14-08.pdf
Arizona Department of Education (ADE). (2014). Move on when reading. Retrieved from http://www.azed.gov/mowr/
Arizona Revised Statutes §15-751 (2000).
Baker, C. (2006). *Foundations of bilingual education and bilingualism*. Tonawanda, NY: Multilingual Matters Ltd.
Banks, J. A. (1993). Multicultural education: Historical development, dimensions, and practice. *Review of Research in Education, 19*, 3–49.
Bilingual Education Act of 1968, Pub. L. 90-247, 81 Stat. 816.
Boscardin, M. L. (2005). The administrative role in transforming secondary schools to support inclusive evidence-based practices. *American Secondary Education, 33*(3), 21–32.
Brisk, M. E. (2006). *Bilingual education: From compensatory to quality schooling*. Mahwah, NJ: Erlbaum.
Capper, C. A., & Frattura, E. M. (2009). *Meeting the needs of students of all abilities*. Thousand Oaks, CA: Corwin Press.

Christian, D. (2006). What kinds of programs are available for English language learners? In E. Hama-yan & R. Freeman (Eds.), *English language learners at school* (pp. 91–92). Philadelphia, PA: Caslon.

Civil Rights Act of 1964, Pub.L. 88-352, 78 Stat. 241 (1964).

Connell, R.W. (1998). Social change and curriculum features. *Change: Transformations in Education, 1,* 84–90.

Crawford, J. (2004). *Educating English learners.* Los Angeles, CA: Bilingual Educational Services.

Crawford, J., & Krashen, S. (2007). *English learners in American classrooms: 101 questions, 101 answers.* New York: Scholastic.

Dantley, M., & Tillman, L. C. (2006). Social justice and moral transformative leadership. In C. Marshall & M. Oliva (Eds.), *Leadership for social justice. Making revolutions in education* (pp. 16–30). Boston, MA: Pearson.

Day, C. (2009). Building and sustaining successful principalship in England: The importance of trust. *Journal of Educational Administration, 47*(6), 719–730.

De Jong, E. (2006). How do you decide what kind of program for English language learners is appro-priate for your school? In E. Hamayan & R. Freeman (Eds.), *English language learners at school* (pp. 91–92). Philadelphia, PA: Caslon, Inc.

Dewey, J. (2008). *Democracy and education.* Chicago, IL: Seven Treasures.

Drago-Severson, E. (2012). New opportunities for principal leadership: Shaping school climates for enhanced teacher development. *Teachers College Record, 114*(3), 1–44.

Dugan, T., Ylimaki, R., & Bennett, J. V. (2012). Funds of knowledge and culturally responsive leader-ship: Transforming a failing school in a postcolonial border context. *Journal of Cases in Education Leadership, 15*(3), 56–65.

Foster, W. (1986). *Paradigms and promises.* Buffalo, NY: Prometheus Books.

Frattura, E. M., & Capper, C. A. (2007). *Leading for social justice: Transforming schools for all learners.* Thou-sand Oaks, CA: Corwin Press.

Freire, P. (2000). *Pedagogy of the oppressed.* New York: The Continuum Publishing Group.

Fry, R. (2007). *How far behind in math and reading are English language learners?* Retrieved from http://www.pewhispanic.org/2007/06/06/how-far-behind-in-math-and-reading-are-english-language-learners/

Furman, G. (2004). The ethic of community. *Journal of Educational Administration, 42*(2), 215–235.

Gándara, P., & Rumberger, R. (2009). Immigration, language, and education: How does language policy structure opportunity? *Teachers College Record, 111,* 750–782.

Gándara, P., Rumberger, R., Maxwell-Jolly, J., & Callahan, R. (2003). English learners in California schools: Unequal resources, unequal outcomes. *Education Policy Analysis Archives, 11.* Retrieved from http://epaa.asu.edu/epaa/v11n36/

Garcia, O. (2012). *Bilingual education in the 21st century: A global perspective.* Hong Kong / Singapore: Fabulous Printer.

Gay, G. (2010). *Culturally responsive teaching: Theory, research, and practice.* New York: Teachers College Press.

Gersten, R., & Baker, S. (2000). What we know about effective instructional practices for English language learners. *Exceptional Children, 66,* 454–470.

González N., Moll, L., & Amanti, C. (2005). *Funds of knowledge: Theorizing practices in households, com-munities, and classrooms.* Mahwah, NJ: Lawrence Erlbaum Associates.

Hallinger, P. (2005). Instructional leadership and the school principal: A passing fancy that refuses to fade away. *Leadership and Policy in Schools, 4*(3), 221–239.

Hallinger, P., & Murphy, J. (1985). The social context of effective schools. *American Journal of Educa-tion, 94*(3), 328–355.

Honigsfeld, A., & Dove, M. G. (2010). *Collaboration and co-teaching: Strategies for English learners.* Thou-sand Oaks, CA: Corwin Press.

Lau v. Nichols, 414 U.S. 563 (1974).

Leithwood, K., Jantzi, D., & Steinbach, R. (1999). *Changing leadership for changing time.* Florence, KY: Taylor & Francis.

Leithwood, K., & Riehl, C. (2005). What we know about successful school leadership. In W. Firestone & C. Riehl (Eds.), *Directions for research on educational leadership* (pp. 22–47). New York: Teachers College Press.

López, F., & McEneaney, E. (2012). State implementation language acquisition policies and reading achievement among Hispanic students. *Educational Policy, 26*, 418–464.

Lyons, J. (2014). Opportunity lost: The promise of equal and effective education for emerging bilingual students in the Obama administration. University of Colorado, Boulder, School of Education: Bueno National Policy Center for Bilingual and Multicultural Education. Retrieved from http://nmabe.net/wp-content/uploads/2014/01/Final-Policy-Review-of-U.S.-Dept-of-Ed-2014.pdf

Marks, H., & Printy, S. (2003). Principal leadership and school performance: An integration of transformation and instructional leadership. *Educational Administration Quarterly, 4*, 293–331.

Mondale, S., & Patton, S. (2001). *School: The story of American public education.* Boston, MA: Beacon Press.

Montecel, M. R., & Cortez, J. D. (2002). Successful bilingual education programs: Development and the dissemination of criteria to identify promising and exemplary practices in bilingual education at the national level. *Bilingual Research Journal, 26*, 1–21.

Moss, P. A., Pullin, D. C., Gee, J. P., Haertel, E. H., & Young, L. J. (2008). *Assessment, equity, and opportunity to learn.* New York: Cambridge University Press.

National Center for Education Statistics (NCES). (2013). Public school graduates and dropouts from the Common Core of Data: School year 2009–2010. U.S. Department of Education, NCES 2013-309rev. Retrieved from http://nces.ed.gov/pubs2013/2013309rev.pdf

National Center for Education Statistics (NCES). (2014). *English language learners.* Retrieved from http://nces.ed.gov/fastfacts/display.asp?id=96

No Child Left Behind (NCLB) Act of 2001, Pub. L. No. 107-110, § 115, Stat. 1425 (2002).

Ovando, C. (2003). Bilingual education in the United States: Historical development and current issues. *Bilingual Research Journal, 27*, 1–25.

Ovando, C., & Collier, V. (1998). *Bilingual and ESL classroom: Teaching multicultural contexts.* Boston, MA: McGraw-Hill.

Padilla, A. M., Fairchild, H. H., & Valdadez, C. M. (1990). *Bilingual education: Issues and strategies.* New York: Sage.

Palmer, D. (2013). Teacher agency in bilingual spaces: A fresh look at preparing teachers to educate Latina/o bilingual children. *Review of Research in Education, 37*, 269–297.

Peña, R. A. (1998). A case study of parental involvement in a conversation from transitional to dual language instruction. *Bilingual Education Journal, 22*(2–4), 237–259.

Pinar, W. (2012). *What is Curriculm Theory?* New York, NY: Taylor & Francis.

Purkey, S., & Smith, M. (1983). Effective schools: A review. *The Elementary School Journal, 83*(4), 427–452.

Ramirez, J. D., Yuen, S. D., Ramey, D. R., & Pasta, D. J. (1991). Longitudinal study of structured English immersion strategy, early-exit and late-exit transitional bilingual education programs for language-minority children, final report. Retrieved from http://eric.ed.gov/?id=ED330216

Ruiz, R. (1984). Orientation in language. *NABE Journal, 8*(2), 15–34.

Scanlan, M. (2012). A learning architecture: How school leaders can design for learning social justice. *Educational Administration Quarterly, 49*(2), 348–391.

Scanlan, M., & López, F. (2013). Leadership promoting equity and excellence for bilingual students. In L. C. Tillman & J. J. Scheurich (Eds.), *Handbook of research on educational leadership for equity and diversity* (pp. 380–403). New York: Routledge.

Scanlan, M., & López, F. A. (2014). *Leadership for culturally and linguistically responsive schools.* New York: Routledge.

Scanlan, M., & Palmer, D. (2009). Race, power, and (in)equity within two-way immersion settings. *Urban Review, 41*, 391–415.

Smith, P. H., & Arnot-Hopffer, E. (1998). Exito bilingue: Promoting Spanish literacy in a dual language immersion program. *Bilingual Research Journal, 22*(2–4), 261–277.

Spillane, J. P., Diamond, J. B., & Jita, L. (2003). Leading instruction: The distribution of leadership for instruction. *Journal of Curriculum Studies, 35*(5), 533–543.

Theoharis, G. (2007). Social justice educational leaders and resistance: Toward a theory of social justice leadership. *Educational Administration Quarterly, 43*(2), 221–258.

Theoharis, G. (2009). *The school leaders our children deserve: Seven keys to equity, social justice and school reform.* New York: Teachers College Press.

Theoharis, G. (2011). Creating a climate of belonging in socially just schools. In S. Auerbach (Ed.), *School leadership for authentic family and community partnerships: Research perspectives for transforming practice* (pp. xiii–xv). New York: Routledge.

Theoharis, G., & O'Toole, J. (2011). Leading inclusive ELL social justice leadership for English language learners. *Educational Administration Quarterly, 47*(4), 646–688.

Tillman, L. C., & Scheurich, J. J. (2013). *Handbook of research on educational leadership*. New York: Routledge.

US Department of Education (2009). *Race to the Top Program executive summary*. Retrieved from http://www2.ed.gov/programs/racetothetop/executive-summary.pdf

US Department of Education (2012). *Ed Data Express: Data about elementary and secondary schools in the US*. Retrieved at http://eddataexpress.ed.gov/

Ylimaki, R. (2011). *Critical curriculum leadership: A framework for progressive education*. New York: Routledge.

Ylimaki, R. (2012). Curriculum leadership in a conservative era. *Educational Administration Quarterly, 48*(2), 304–346.

Ylimaki, R. (2014). *The new instructional leadership: ISSLC standard two*. New York: Routledge.

CHAPTER 6

Inclusive Leadership and Lesbian, Gay, Bisexual, Transgendered, and Questioning Students

Frank Hernandez and Don Fraynd

PART 1: THE CURRENT CONTEXTS FOR LESBIAN, GAY, BISEXUAL, TRANSGENDERED, AND QUESTIONING STUDENTS IN SCHOOLS

In 2008 a 15-year-old eighth-grade student named Lawrence King was sitting in a school computer lab when another student, Brandon McInerney, walked into the lab with a gun and shot Lawrence in the head. According to reports (Catchart, 2008), Lawrence had publicly announced that he was gay and had begun wearing mascara, lipstick, and his favorite high-heeled boots to school. In 2000, Damilola Taylor, a 10-year-old, was stabbed to death. According to Damilola's parents, Damilola had recently and tearfully told them that other boys had been calling him "gay." People with first-hand knowledge have suggested that Damilola was probably not gay at all, but very smart, somewhat feminine, and not active in sports (Hopkins, 2000). Within a two-year time period, eight students committed suicide in the Anoka-Hennepin School District in Minnesota. At least four of the students were gay or bisexual and had struggled with being harassed (Eckholm, 2011).

We share these stories to emphasize that in K–12 schools, issues related to being—or being perceived as—lesbian, gay, bisexual, transgender, or questioning (LGBTQ) are vitally important. We have also set out to discuss the role that school leaders can play in protecting students like Lawrence King and Damilola Taylor; that is, in promoting innovative and entrepreneurial leadership supportive of safe learning environments that are inclusive and that protect children from harassment and crimes related to LGBTQ affiliation.

It is important to note that far too often, LGBTQ and perceived-LGBTQ students are portrayed as perpetual victims of violent acts. Namely, LGBTQ and perceived-LGBTQ adolescents are constructed as weak, suicidal, and susceptible to drugs and alcohol, and this construction is based on these adolescents' treatment at the hands of others (Rasmussen, Rofes, & Talburt, 2004). Our intention in this chapter is to convey a very different message. Even though LGBTQ and perceived-LGBTQ students continue to experience high levels of harassment, we seek to shift the discourse about LGBTQ and perceived-LGBTQ students away from a pathological-victimization mindset to one that highlights the ways in which these students have supported themselves by creating positive networks and by demanding from their schools a modicum of support in a safe environment (see Blackburn, 2004). Educators in general, and school leaders in particular, should no longer identify LGBTQ and perceived-LGBTQ youth through the lens of victimization and homophobia; rather, an effort should be made to identify them as courageous and change agents who are willing to stand up to the challenges that they face in a society that assumes many hetero-sexual and gender roles for them. In this chapter we highlight programs being implemented across the country that are helping to strengthen the voices of LGBTQ and perceived-LGBTQ youths—youths who, in fact, are playing a leading role in these efforts.

Moreover, care must be taken to remember that many LGBTQ students do not just face harassment because of their sexual orientation. Many of these students may face harassment in different ways, and from different people, because of their membership in another minority group that intersects with their sexual identity. In order for these youth to continue to be courageous change agents, they must have school leaders who are commit-ted to creating environments that are safe and inclusive of students across these multiple dimensions of diversity.

Speaking From Experience

As the two authors of this chapter, we (Frank and Don) are uniquely positioned to provide insights into the lives of LGBTQ students because we are gay ourselves, we have worked as school leaders in K–12 schools, and we have seen the results of environments that are not inclusive of LGBTQ students. We are able to bring personal stories with us to the university and K–12 classrooms that reflect the ways in which principals are trained and the ways in which schools are run. Professionally, we have witnessed, first hand, the harm that non-inclusive schools can do to LGBTQ and perceived-LGBTQ students. Frank has worked as a principal, as a professor in principal-preparation programs, and now as a dean for a col-lege of education. He has focused his attention on training aspiring school leaders to create inclusive and safe communities in schools. Don has focused his attention on implementing inclusive and safe school communities within K–12 schools. As a former principal, later a district administrator in one of this country's largest school districts, and currently lead-ing his own start-up education company, Don has worked to develop a climate where all students can succeed.

Because of our experiences with LGBTQ issues, both personally and professionally, we are able to talk about the current state of LGBTQ and perceived-LGBTQ students, schools, and leadership training. For example, the massive school district where Don worked has had a general non-discrimination policy inclusive of lesbians and gays since 2005 and of gender-identity issues since 2008. However, according to the Gay, Lesbian, & Straight Edu-cation Network (GLSEN) (2012), only 7% of the students they sampled attended a school with a comprehensive anti-harassment policy, only 17% were taught positive representa-tions of LGBTQ people, and only 51% could search for information pertaining to LGBTQ support online. The lived reality for LGBTQ and perceived-LGBTQ individuals in the district's population of 400,000+ students and of 46,000 employees has varied widely. Only 40 of the 700+ schools (5.7%) as of 2012 (the last year that Don worked in this district) have active Gay-Straight Alliances. Only one person in this district handles the district policy's complaint process, and she handles it for *all* forms of discrimination, including discrimination pertaining to gender, race, age, and ability. Moreover, she does that work on top of duties outside the scope of the policy.

During his career in the district, Don supervised more than 50 schools, visited approximately 50 more, and collaborated with the majority of the school system's principals in various settings. Anecdotally, Don has noted that most principals are unable to discuss LGBTQ issues openly, let alone provide proactive support for LGBTQ students and staff. The exception is in the small number of high-performing and racially and socioeconomically integrated selective enrollment and magnet schools. As a result, the vast majority of students in this school system have been left isolated despite the presence of several high-level openly gay district administrators (like Don), several exemplary Gay-Straight Alliances (located at the district's top-performing schools), and relatively advanced policy conditions.

According to Frank, the school district overseeing the high school he attended from 1980 to 1982 had no anti-bullying policies. The repeated harassment that he experienced from certain individuals in school was so overwhelming at the time that he considered quitting school altogether. When he reported the harassment to a school counselor, it was met with confusion about what to do, but also with the mentality that "boys will be boys" and that the brunt of the responsibility fell on Frank to "suck it up" and "roll with the punches" of high school. Ultimately, Frank transferred to a different high school and had a much more positive experience at the new school. Even though Frank's new high school was part of the same district as the high school he first attended, his school principal, assistant principal, and teachers seemed to be much more concerned about the climate of the school and were adamant about creating a safe environment for all students. Frank does not recall hearing his school administrators talk about LGBTQ issues; however, bullying of any type would not be tolerated. Frank went on to succeed academically and excelled in sports during his high school years.

Reflecting on his own high school experiences, Don can now see that he was in denial about his sexuality, never allowing himself to consider what it would mean to be gay. He attended an all-boys Catholic school that reinforced standard male gender roles in some ways, but then also created a space where traditional straight male machismo was not as intense because there was no female audience. In this way, Don could effectively hide his sexuality, as no one ever expected him or his peers to show off their girlfriends. His way of coping in his early high school years was to remain as quiet and as inconspicuous as possible.

Frank recalls that, as a gay youth, he would feel like the only male in the world attracted to other males. This isolation and loneliness at times would lead him to perceive the entire school as hating him; in turn, thoughts of suicide would take hold in his mind. This inner turmoil compelled him to hide hugely important aspects of his own existence from others during these formative years. Thoughts of suicide are not uncommon among LGBTQ and perceived-LGBTQ youth. In the past three years, the issue of suicide among such youths has gained national media attention. In his recent study, Hatzenbuehler (2011) found that gay, lesbian, and bisexual youth were 20% more likely to attempt suicide than their straight counterparts, particularly in unsupportive environments. Other studies (see O'Donnell, Meyer, & Schwartz, 2011) found that among ethnic-minority youth who identify or are perceived as lesbian, gay, or bisexual, the risk of suicide attempts is greater than among Whites who identify or are perceived as such (more about students of color that identify as LGBTQ later in this chapter).

Somewhat different from Frank, Don would practice secrecy and denial by establishing relationships with his male peers and by thriving on support from mentors. Indeed, he would avoid confronting his own concealed turmoil through over-involvement in co-curricular activities that would leave him in a state of perpetual exhaustion. On very rare occasions such as homecoming and prom, when he felt compelled to show evidence of relationships with girls, he would take along a female friend and pretend that they were dating. The dangers of this course of action were psychological as well as physical, in that he developed a pattern of over-work and remained isolated romantically and emotionally until the age of 29, when he prepared to enroll in graduate school.

Don recalls that, as he was preparing to leave for graduate school, he had a very jolting and painful conversation with a former student, Jim: "As I was visiting with former students and their parents at my going-away party, Jim came up to me and said, 'I wish I would have known you were gay when you were my teacher because then I wouldn't have felt so alone.'" Don recognized how his inability to come out as an adult educator had directly and negatively affected LGBTQ students. However, as Don's recent experience as an openly gay district-level administrator illustrates, even when LGBTQ leaders and courageous young people come out, the process by which one comes to terms with one's sexual orientation often remains difficult at best and wrenching at worst. Jim's experience of coming out is not an exception. The difficulty of coming to terms with one's sexual orientation is found throughout the literature.

To set the context for this discussion of potential changes in leadership practices for LGBTQ and perceived-LGBTQ youth, we turn to a comprehensive literature review that examines terms most often used when discussing LGBTQ issues, what we know about bullying and harassment of LGBTQ and perceived-LGBTQ youth, and defining social-justice leadership. To aid school leaders who want to create inclusive environments, the section ends with a thorough examination of LGBTQ identity-development models.

PART 2: WHAT WE KNOW ABOUT LGBTQ STUDENTS AND PERCEIVED-LGBTQ STUDENTS: THE LITERATURE

Defining the Terms

We believe it would be helpful to clarify general terms related to sexual orientation and terms that will be used throughout this chapter. For example, school leaders often conflate terms such as "sexual orientation," "gender identity," and "sexual identity" with one another. Though *sexual identity* and *sexual orientation* are closely related, they are distinguishable from each other, and from *gender identity*. While *identity* refers to the individual and subjective perception of one's self, *orientation* refers to the objective definition of sexual attraction. Conversely, *gender identity* refers to an individual's subjective experience of his/her gender; that is, the individual's perception of the social category and/or role he or she fulfills or subscribes to (i.e., feminine, masculine, other, etc.).

Another regularly used term is "sexual minority," which refers to an individual whose identity or orientation differs from that of the majority. It is important to clarify that the term "sex" connotes one's biological sex as determined by chromosomes and sexual organs. "Gender identity" refers to an individual's identification with male-associated roles or female-associated roles. According to Lugg (2003), "Gender is an ongoing, lifelong series of evolving performances. Sex is chromosomal" (p. 98). In some cases, there are individuals who believe that their sex and their gender identity do not match. These individuals are generally referred to as "transgender" and may present themselves (by means of behavior, dress, and language) in ways associated with the opposite sex, all in order to reflect the individuals' perception of their true gender. "Transsexual" is a term that refers to individuals who have had sex-reassignment surgery. Finally, "questioning" refers, as one might guess, to a person questioning his or her sexual orientation or gender identity (for a thorough review of these terms, see Lugg, 2003).

According to Catchings (2009) and GLSEN (2008), most researchers agree that the most commonly used terms referring to sexual orientation are as follows:

- *Heterosexual*: an individual whose primary attraction is to people of the opposite sex.
- *Homosexual*: an individual whose primary attraction is to people of the same sex.
- *Bisexual*: an individual who is attracted to both males and females.
- *Heteronormative*: a worldview that promotes heterosexuality as being the normal or preferred sexual orientation.

Intersectionality

When discussing ways to combat normativity, prejudice, and harassment, it is important to consider that forms of oppression do not operate independently. As is discussed throughout this book, many forms of diversity and discrimination are intertwined with others, and intersect within the various areas of race, ethnic, socioeconomic, and religious identities. The study of how different systems of discrimination interact and influence one another is called intersectionality (McCall, 2005; Knudsen, 2006). This concept was first defined academically in the 1980s (Crenshaw, 1989), but it has been subject to discourse since the early 1900s when women's rights and feminism began gaining traction.

It may be easy to consider a specific form of oppression or discrimination as operating in a vacuum. For example, when considering the victimization of LGBTQ youth, many leaders and administrators may simply see them as LGBTQ youth and ignore their membership in other minorities. However, personal identity is fluid and multi-faceted, and developing this sense of identity is a complex and varied process. Similarly, a student's experience is not accurately described simply as being gay *and* as being a religious minority—these experiences intersect, intertwine, and influence each other. When categorizing students by minority membership, one runs the risk of stereotyping and having reductionist attitudes toward solutions.

At the intersection of race and sexual orientation, for example, individuals may attribute their victimization to a single category, to a different category, or to many categories at once, which, in turn, shapes their perception of the experience. Further, the experience of intersectional harassment is not additive. That is, there is no evidence showing that individuals actively separate their experiences of discrimination or harassment (Pastrana Jr., 2006; Anderson & McCormack, 2010; Meyer, 2010, 2012), but rather that they see it as a cohesive experience and choose which battles to fight (Daley, Solomon, Newman, & Mishna, 2008).

Harassment of LGBTQ and Perceived-LGBTQ Youth Relative to Social Justice Leadership

The field of school leadership preparation has recently made a concerted effort to embed social-justice issues in the preparation of aspiring principals (Cambron-McCabe & McCarthy, 2005; Dantley & Tillman, 2006; DeMatthews, 2014; Goldring & Greenfield, 2002; Grogan & Andrews, 2002; Pounder, Reitzug, & Young, 2002; Scheurich & Skrla, 2003; Theoharis, 2007, 2008, 2009). Other authors have suggested pedagogical practices that schools' faculty could implement in educational administration programs to help cultivate leaders appreciative of social justice (Adams, Bell, & Griffin, 1997; Brown, 2004; Hafner, 2005; McKenzie et al., 2008; Nagda, Gurin, & Lopez, 2003; Pounder et al., 2002). Theoharis (2007) has argued that social justice principals "make issues of race, class, gender, disability, sexual orientation, and other historically and currently marginalizing conditions in the United States central to their advocacy, leadership practice, and vision" (p. 223). Much of this effort has focused on the academic achievement of students who are low income, English-language learners, or students of color. Very little attention has been paid to students who identify as or are perceived as LGBTQ.

According to reports, school-based homophobic bullying is pervasive (Predrag, 2003) and often goes unchecked. It is well documented that LGBTQ and perceived-LGBTQ students are regularly bullied and harassed in schools (Baker, 2002; Birkett, Espelage, & Koenig, 2009; Blumenfeld, 2000; Espelage, Aragon, Berkett, & Koenig, 2008; Frankfurt, 2000; Goodenow, Szalacha, & Westhernier, 2006; Human Rights Watch, 2001). Birkett at al. (2009) reported that more than 7,000 lesbian, gay, bisexual, and questioning middle school students were more likely to experience high levels of bullying, homophobic victimization, and various negative outcomes than heterosexual youth. In the face of this evidence, school leaders generally have underestimated the frequency of this type of harassment. According to the report *The Principal's Perspective: School Safety, Bullying, and Harassment* (Markow & Dancewicz, 2008), most principals reported that students had been suffering harassment targeting their gender expression in school, yet few school leaders believed that this harassment was a frequent occurrence (only 12% characterized the frequency as "very often" and 9% as "often"). In comparison, *students* reported that they had suffered harassment regarding their gender expression at much higher rates (90% of LGBTQ students characterized the frequency of this harassment as "very often" and 62% of non-LGBTQ students characterized it as "very often").

According to this same report (Markow & Dancewicz, 2008), 96% of principals reported having anti-bullying policies in their districts; however, only 46% reported having anti-bullying policies relative to sexual orientation, and even fewer (39%) reported having anti-bullying policies related to gender identity. According to Macgillivray (2009), anti-discrimination policies in some districts use "blanket statements" such as "all students" instead of "enumerating sexual orientation and gender identity/expression" (p. 33). While anti-bullying laws and policies are in effect in all except nine states, this protection does not often extend to sexual diversity or is not enforced as such. Further, federal civil rights laws do not extend to bullying or harassment concerning sexual identity or orientation (GLSEN, 2008; Macgillivray, 2009; US Department of Education, 2012). Therefore, the decision on how to actively combat this behavior and advocate for students is largely perceived as an individual endeavor, reliant upon Gay-Straight Alliances and teacher involvement (Swearer Napolitano, 2011). Short (2007) argues that even among school districts equipped with anti-bullying policies, these policies are often "undermined by a lack of administrative will to do so" (p. 38). Still others (Ian, 2004; Macgillivray, 2009; Rienzo, Button, Jiunne-jye, & Ying, 2006) have recognized that while schools are expected to address the needs of their LGBTQ students, doing so is a politically sensitive undertaking that is often drawn out and challenged by conservative parents and families.

The findings are even more egregious for bullying directed at students who identify as transgender. Again, GLSEN (2008) and Greytak, Kosciw, and Diaz (2009) found that transgender youth reported higher levels of harassment and victimization than their non-transgender gay, lesbian, and bisexual peers. According to the GLSEN report, nine out of ten surveyed transgender youth had experienced verbal harassment at school; more than half had experienced physical harassment; and over 25% had reported physical assaults, all based on their sexual identity and gender identity. The same report found that one out of four LGBTQ students skipped school in the past month because they were simply too afraid to go.

Bullying and harassment rates have been shown to increase dramatically when students enter middle school (Pellegrini, 2002), coincidentally at a time when students are beginning

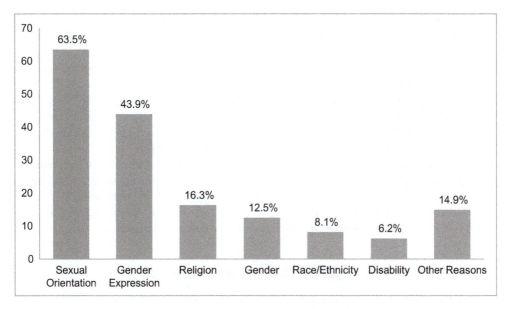

Figure 6.1 Percentage of Students Who Felt Unsafe at School (Kosciw et al., 2012)

to question the expression of their gender identity, or express it in new ways (Friedrichs, 2014). Sexual orientation was found to be one of the most common reasons students were bullied, second only to physical appearance (DeVoe & Kaffenberger, 2005). While students may be victimized for other reasons, including race/ethnicity, gender, disability, or religious orientation, these rates are much lower (DeVoe & Kaffenberger, 2005; Kosciw et al., 2012; see Figure 6.1). However, they may intersect with harassment because of sexual orientation. Students who were questioning their sexual orientation report higher harassment rates and more negative outcomes than heterosexual students (Birkett et al., 2009; Kosciw et al., 2012). Common themes emerging in research on intersectionality highlight the subjective severity of the harassment according to different factors such as race (Pastrana, 2006; Anderson & McCormack, 2010) and social status (Meyer, 2010), and that people often report a tendency to "pick their battles" (Daley et al., 2008). However, some things left for consideration are that students may victimize other members of their own groups, and that effects of harassment, bullying, and name-calling, whether verbal or physical, are severe and long-lasting.

The Effects of Name-Calling

Other research has found that the effects of sexually degrading name-calling on male students may differ in unique ways from the corresponding effects on female students (Capper, Schulte, & McKinney, 2009; Espelage, Aragon, Birkett, & Koenig, 2008; Swearer, Turner, Givens, & Pollack, 2008). Capper et al. (2009) found that male high school students who experienced sexually degrading name-calling would exhibit more anger, combativeness, and physical ailments than otherwise would be the case. Similarly, Swearer et al. (2008) found that boys who were called "gay" experienced "higher anxiety and depression, and displayed a more external locus of control than boys who were bullied for other reasons" (p. 170). These boys also experienced more verbal and physical bullying than boys who were bullied for other reasons.

This violence against LGBTQ and perceived-LGBTQ adolescents has taken its toll and has contributed to high levels of suicide attempts and actual suicides in this population. According to Gibson (1989), gay and lesbian youth are two to three times more likely to attempt suicide than their straight counterparts. Gay and lesbian youth who are raised in unsupportive families often experience rejection, isolation, and high levels of stress, and are frequently victims of physical and emotional abuse. Terms such as "faggot," "dyke," and "sissy" are examples of the verbal abuse that many youth face during their adolescent years. Some researchers have suggested that gay and lesbian youth may compose up to 30% of completed youth suicides annually (Gibson, 1989; Kourany, 1987).

Clearly, there is a need for school leaders to create spaces where all students feel safe and are free from victimization experiences. However, very little has been written about this issue in the leadership research. To begin meaningful work in creating inclusive environments, it is important for school leaders to understand the identity development of LGBTQ youth and how it compares and contrasts to the sexual majority.

LGBTQ Identity-Development Theories and Research

School leaders must be knowledgeable about the developmental experiences of the gay and lesbian students who attend their schools. When principals and other school leaders understand the research on LGBTQ youth identity development, it becomes easier to empathize and then to take appropriate action to build cultures and implement programs that can help create an inclusive environment that nurtures healthy development.

According to Evans and D'Augelli (1996), students begin to explore their sexual identities during college since college is often where people typically come to terms with much of their identity. However, in recent years, more and more students have been coming out with their sexual identity in middle and high school (Friedrichs, 2014).

While a number of sexual orientation models have been used and developed over time, Cass' model (1979, 1984) has been used more widely and has endured since the 1970s. (While we focus primarily on Cass' model, there are other models as well that should be reviewed and analyzed [for a review, see D'Augelli, 1994].) Cass' model is composed of six stages of identity that gay or lesbian people go through as they become aware and accept their own sexual identity (see Figure 6.2). Stage One is called *Identity Confusion*, which is often characterized by denying homosexual feelings and avoiding addressing topics related to sexual identity. Stage Two is known as *Identity Comparison* and is described as having feelings of alienation if the individual accepts his or her sexual identity. That is, while an individual may accept his sexual identity, in this stage he may continue to act "straight" in order to maintain a heterosexual identity. Stage Three, called *Identity Tolerance*, is when individuals begin to seek out other gays or lesbians. This counters the feelings of isolation and allows individuals to begin to develop a positive self-image. However, individuals in this stage have not come to terms with integrating both their public and private image as gay or lesbian.

Stage Four, *Identity Acceptance*, is characterized by disclosing their sexual identity to others, often just a small group of trusted friends. An individual in this stage begins to merge public and personal and begins to accept himself or herself as gay or lesbian. The coming out process begins in this stage. Stage Five, called *Identity Pride,* is when an individual becomes connected in the gay culture and may problematize straight people and values. An individual in this stage finds his or her support system with other gays or lesbians and becomes less reliant on the heterosexual community. Finally, Stage Six is called *Identity Synthesis.* This is associated with individuals who have fully accepted themselves and see their sexual identity as *one aspect* of their identity. In other words, their identity is integrated

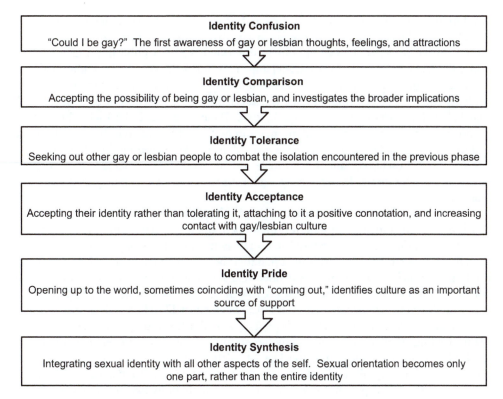

Figure 6.2 Cass' Identity Model

with all aspects themselves. Knowledge of these LGBTQ identity-development theories—of which Cass' model provides an excellent example—can help school leaders understand how individuals in their school community think about and develop their sexual identity.

PART 3: INCLUSIVE LEADERSHIP AROUND LGBTQ ISSUES IN K–12 SCHOOLS

Creating Environments That Support LGBTQ and Perceived-LGBTQ Students

In the first two sections we have discussed the context and literature regarding creating inclusive environments for LGBTQ and perceived-LGBTQ students. However, in order to be effective, leaders must understand the ways in which they can create inclusive environments. The challenge here is to create awareness, promote safety, and reduce stigma without resorting to reductionism or stereotyping. In this third section we describe specific strategies for doing this. We also outline several excellent resources that can be consulted when implementing policies or professional development plans.

Leadership for Social Justice

Despite the bullying that is visited upon LGBTQ and perceived-LGBTQ students, and despite the comprehensive research that has been conducted on the topic of sexual-identity development, very little published research in the field of educational leadership has explicitly addressed the role that school leaders, particularly principals, can play in creating safe schools for all students. The exceptions to this rule have been published and assembled under the category of social-justice leadership. This literature has called for administrators to strive for equity in their districts and buildings regarding marginalized sexual-minority students and staff (Cambron-McCabe & McCarthy, 2005; Koschoreck & Tooms, 2009; Marshall & Oliva, 2006; McKenzie et al., 2008; Pounder et al., 2002; Riehl, 2000). One promising endeavor that has created momentum in this call for action is the recently edited volume titled *Sexuality Matters: Paradigms and Policies for Educational Leaders* (Koschoreck & Tooms, 2009). Koschoreck and Tooms make a deliberate effort to merge both sexual orientation and educational leadership by exploring issues related to policy, pedagogy, and identity.

While some pre-service administrators might already feel compelled to act equitably on behalf of all their students and staff, it is incumbent upon preparation programs to prepare them to do so. One promising educational strategy from the pedagogy of social justice has been to ask students to reflect critically upon their beliefs about equity and elements of cultural identity such as race, ethnicity, gender, sexual orientation, and socioeconomic status (Brown, 2004; Hafner, 2005; Hernandez & Marshall, 2009; McKenzie et al., 2008).

To address the experiences that LGBTQ and perceived-LGBTQ students are having in K–12 schools, interested parties have developed several national programs that include No Name-Calling Week, anti-bullying activities starting as early as at the elementary-school level, Gay-Straight Alliances, and the Day of Silence, in which students protest harassment by refusing to speak at school. Despite these efforts, LGBTQ and perceived-LGBTQ students continue to experience high levels of harassment, bullying, and violence. Administrators must be prepared to be proactive and organized in their approaches to creating environments that are supportive for LGBTQ students.

Given this context of social justice leadership, we now turn to describing important strategies administrators can use to be proactive in creating inclusive and supportive environments for LGBTQ students. We focus on four strategies: countering heteronormativity, creating rituals and activities, implementing equity audits, and becoming aware of policies, laws, and the community. While we primarily apply these strategies to LGBTQ and perceived-LGBTQ students, we also show how the strategies link to other dimensions of diversity as well.

Countering Heteronormative Perspectives

School leaders should make efforts to counter the heteronormative perspectives that often permeate schools and school districts and have profound psychosocial effects. School leaders should constantly refrain from presumptuously identifying all students as heterosexual and should collaboratively combat any school culture where support for straight students translates into marginalization of LGBTQ and perceived-LGBTQ students. Other normative expectations may also intersect with heteronormativity, such as assuming that all students are Christian. Further, some attempts to counteract normalization focus on one aspect and ignore another, such as *not* assuming that students live with two parents, but still assuming that they have a Mom and Dad. Queer theory can help educators in these efforts by discussing the burden that normalizing structures (structures where everyone is presumed to be straight) place on "queer" persons—the burden to come "out"; if no such coming out takes place, school activities and events often operate on the presumption that the student body is fundamentally straight. When this perspective is taken, LGBTQ and perceived-LGBTQ students are then identified as the other, which most often results in feelings of isolation.

School leaders can counter the heteronormative perspectives by creating (and insisting upon) opportunities for faculty, staff, and students to learn about related issues and to dialogue with LGBTQ and perceived-LGBTQ individuals using panel discussions or other formats. Also, school leaders can help these youth feel included in their surroundings by encouraging faculty, staff, and students either to reference personal affiliations with LGBTQ individuals or to make neutral references regarding sexual orientation. References like these can weaken heteronormative forces. A good example of a neutral reference could come from school coaches who train themselves to ask a prom-bound male athlete, "Are you taking someone to the prom?" rather than, "Are you taking your girlfriend to the prom?" LGBTQ youth are highly attuned to such subtle signals around them, and the more often school leaders insist upon inclusion across conversational settings, the more likely youth will be to feel relieved that it is OK to be LGBTQ.

Additional Resources for Professional Development

Countering normalizing behaviors and expectations is a daunting task but should be a district-wide effort, extending past the administrative level. Likewise, preparing teachers to be effective and equitable educators begins pre-service, and should continue throughout their tenure. There are many ways to begin organizing training and awareness efforts, including community involvement, training and workshops for parents and educators, and administrator events to discuss legal concerns and best practices (Chasnoff, Cohen, Yacker, & McCarthy, 2008). There are also a variety of materials available to assist in these efforts such as workbooks and videos, training and seminar materials, questionnaires to assess the climate of the school, and other diagnostic tools and activities for use in classrooms (Teaching Tolerance, 2014). Finally, there are several organizations and communities that support LGBTQ activism and awareness and assist in opening local student or community chapters to promote events and activities (see *Additional Resources* on the companion webpage, www.routledge.com/cw/theoharis).

GUIDING QUESTIONS

- How do you see heteronormative perspectives in your school context? How can you sensitize yourself and your colleagues to notice these perspectives?
- What are some tangible ways that you can interrupt and counter these heteronormative perspectives? What are some resources that can support you in this work?

Creation of LGBTQ-Supportive Rituals, Celebrations, and Activities

A second strategy for school leaders to support LGBTQ and perceived-LGBTQ students in K–12 schools is to institute rituals, celebrations, and activities designed to affirm LGBTQ youth. For example, leaders can participate in national programs developed to counter the negative experiences that these students have and to shed light on the issue in schools. Programs include the aforementioned No Name-Calling Week, Day of Silence protests, and Gay-Straight Alliances. The No Name-Calling Week is an annual weeklong event that focuses on ending name-calling of all kinds. The hope is that this program can provide schools with the tools and inspiration necessary for successfully launching an on-going dialogue about ways to eliminate bullying in communities. For many school leaders, this type of activity could mark the start of creating a positive environment for LGBTQ and perceived-LGBTQ students. However, these activities are not exempt from their criticism and are most effective when they are part of larger on-going efforts to reduce the possibility of marginalizing them into one-time events (Griffin & Ouellett, 2002).

A Gay-Straight Alliance (GSA) is a student-initiated and student-run club whose primary goal is to provide a supportive and safe school community in which LGBTQ youth and their allies can work together to create a school-wide community free of discrimination and harassment. Lee (2002) has cited evidence that GSAs have tangible positive effects on LGBTQ students by providing them with both a forum to discuss issues and a community of students who have had similar experiences or who have positive things to say about LGBTQ individuals and communities. In her two-year study, Lee found that the benefits of belonging to a GSA included improved academic performance; stronger relationships at school, in families, and within society; elevated comfort levels with sexual orientation; a strengthened sense of physical safety; and an enhanced sense of belonging to one's school community.

Sponsored by GLSEN, Day of Silence events bring attention to the experiences of LGBTQ youth and, more generally, to issues surrounding gender and sexuality. Chiefly, students in middle school through college participate in a day of silence to encourage their schools to address the challenges that are faced by LGBTQ youth and others every day. Students protest harassment directed at LGBTQ and perceived-LGBTQ students by refusing to speak at school on the selected day. There should be no surprise that, despite these efforts, LGBTQ and perceived-LGBTQ students continue to experience high levels of harassment and other forms of violence.

Clearly, this strategy of creating rituals, celebrations, and activities affirming LGBTQ and perceived-LGBTQ students is closely related to affirming other dimensions of diversity. As the chapters throughout this book emphasize, all students—particularly those who have been traditionally marginalized—need to see themselves as welcomed, valued members of the school community.

GUIDING QUESTIONS

- What is the role of ritual and celebration in your school context? Are these prominent?
- What are some initial steps you can take to utilize ritual and celebration to affirm the identities of all members of your school community, explicitly including LGBTQ members (including students, teachers, staff, administrators, and families)?

Implementation of a School-Wide Equity Audit Regarding LGBTQ Matters

A third helpful strategy in diminishing this violence is to assess the current equity conditions in a particular school environment. As a professor in a program that prepares future school leaders, Frank has found that equity audits (Scheurich & Skrla, 2003) regarding sexual orientation are very beneficial to students for two reasons. First, while participating in these audits, future leaders must talk with other school personnel about data related to sexual orientation. These conversations alone, in most cases that Frank has observed in his classes, constitute a major departure from traditional patterns of behavior and thinking. That is, most interlocutors participating in an audit are unaccustomed to the sensitive, oftentimes embarrassing, and unavoidably controversial nature of the discussed topic: sexual orientation. Second, whereas schools typically collect data concerning student achievement, this activity provides an opportunity for data collection related to school-wide sexual orientation, and most often brings to light glaring gaps in data related to sexual orientation. Operating in their own school or another school, participating students collect student data from peers and educators who answer the equity audit questions. The final chapter of this text describes a comprehensive equity audit process. See the sexuality section and full equity audit detailed in Chapter 10 and online (www.routledge.com/cw/theoharis).

Once the data are collected, the students prepare a one-page analysis of the data. That is, the students try to explain the significance of the data, while examining where major gaps appear in the data and how a school leader can address these gaps. For example, one principal who was conducting an equity audit about sexual orientation at his elementary school found that the library had a collection of 2,000 books; however, when he inquired into books pertaining to sexual orientation (e.g., picture books that address same-sex families), he found that the library was in possession of only one. As a result, he was able to include this dearth of literature on his list of problems to be resolved in the coming school year. Beyond the tangible findings of an equity audit, it can be helpful in assessing the policy landscape of districts. (Guiding questions for this section are found in the sexuality section and full equity audit detailed in Chapter 10 and online at www.routledge.com/cw/theoharis.)

District Policies and Community Involvement

The fourth strategy that school leaders can use to create inclusive school communities requires school leaders to be knowledgeable about district policies and to advocate on behalf of LGBTQ and perceived-LGBTQ individuals. Policies should ensure that schools offer *all* students a process whereby they can quickly and confidentially report bullying. Safe zones, or areas of a school where students can freely express themselves, constitute another example of how schools can support LGBTQ and perceived-LGBTQ students. District policies, such as inclusion, expression, and bullying policies, as well as state and federal laws, such as those regarding marriage equality and anti-discrimination, can also bolster such support. Allies in the community—support groups, advocacy groups, and the like—are critical in this effort. For example, when Don served as a principal, he helped the co-sponsors of his Gay-Straight Alliance bring in a local queer-theater group to perform for the whole student body and he ensured that local LGBTQ mental-health groups and recreational organizations attended school–community partnership fairs. (For further discussion of engaging community allies, see Scanlan & Johnson, this volume.)

GUIDING QUESTIONS

- What are some practical steps you can take to raise your own awareness of district policies regarding LGBTQ and perceived-LGBTQ individuals?
- Who are some allies in the community that can support you, in your leadership role, in strengthening inclusive structures for LGBTQ and perceived-LGBTQ individuals in your school?

Case Studies

Beyond these four tangible strategies, it is instructive to share examples of school leaders who have made a difference for LGBTQ and perceived-LGBTQ students. Toward this end, we offer the following two mini-case studies.

A Popular Principal Decides to Become an Ally for a Transgender Student

Patrice Jenkins had her hands full as she took over as principal of one of Chicago's lowest performing and most violent high schools. Hired as part of the district's school-turnaround efforts, she was expected to stabilize the school culture and radically change the learning environment. Her school had a 40% attendance rate, the top number of serious misconduct incidents of all high schools in the city, and only 3% of students meeting state standards. As Principal Jenkins and members of the district turnaround team worked tirelessly on climate, she came to know her student body well and she was known to be quite firm but loving. In fact, Jenkins quickly became highly regarded and beloved by her students, all part of her strategy to make meaningful change in the school.

A few months after her arrival she met a sophomore named Tyrone who gradually started wearing makeup and clothing more traditionally associated with girls. Other students, many of whom had known Tyrone since elementary school, did not know what to make of the changes in Tyrone's appearance and he started to get teased with growing intensity. He started to cut class and was found by Jenkins in a stairwell smoking. She used this opportunity to build a relationship of support with Tyrone. "I was brought up in a very conservative church-going family and we have always been taught that being gay is a sin. I was totally ignorant about what to do in this situation. But I knew I had this beautiful young person in front of me who was going through a tough time," Jenkins recalls, "and so I knew I had to come to you, boss, to get educated and figure out how to best support Tyrone!" The "boss" in question here was Don, this chapter's co-author, who at the time was working as a district administrator.

Don helped Jenkins learn more about LGBTQ terminology and about some of the research on LGBTQ social-emotional development. Jenkins also talked to principals from other schools who had recently witnessed the establishment of GSAs. Concurrently, she became an active advocate for and with Tyrone. She made sure other students knew that she was friends with Tyrone by talking with Tyrone in the hallways, giving Tyrone high-fives in the lunchroom, and introducing Tyrone to other students that she knew were kind. She used her relational influence with the student body to become an active ally for Tyrone. "But I know that I can't always be around and be his mother, so we've had several talks about how to handle bullying. It isn't going to be an easy road for Tyrone, but I hope I can help and engage our student body to help him . . . or her, I should say." Using direct influence with students in just a few small ways, a principal focused on social justice can help ensure a safe environment for LGBTQ and perceived-LGBTQ students. Another way is to be a voice among peers, as the next vignette illustrates.

Speaking Up for the Voiceless Among Peers

Principal Carl Parker had been on the job for two years and was just starting to become comfortable among the other 40 principals in his area. He had been hired from outside the school system, and most of his colleagues had gotten to know each other over the course of decades working within the district. Because of this, his colleagues were just beginning to accept him and Carl was grateful. This dynamic, however, made it very difficult for Carl to figure out what to do when faced with a moral dilemma.

Shortly after reading a story in a neighborhood newspaper about students at a nearby school wanting to start a GSA, Carl heard their principal talking to colleagues at the next area meeting. "I heard her talking about how there would be no club in her school that encouraged deviant behavior. I was petrified," Carl recalled. "As I walked by her table, I felt like I was in middle school again and I could feel a lump form in my throat." Carl had spent so much time trying to fit in with his colleagues that he didn't want to do anything to jeopardize that. Yet he has strong beliefs about equity for all students and had learned a great deal about leadership for social justice in his graduate program. "I knew that I needed to find a way to talk with her, but I didn't know if I could."

After a few days of deliberation, Carl decided to call his colleague. "She had such a strong personality that I thought that she was going to give me a piece of her mind, so I was very careful in my approach." He calmly explained that he had read the article in the paper and that he had heard her talking about how to respond to it at the area meeting. Carl told her that he knew a little bit about how these situations unfold because a colleague of his had faced a similar situation in another district. He explained the law that requires schools to allow GSAs if other school activities exist in the school. "She didn't know anything about the legalities and was actually very grateful because she felt that I was looking to keep her out of trouble, but I didn't want that to be her only takeaway." After Carl opened her mind using the legal argument, he also said that he had known several students who were LGBTQ and shared a couple stories about their journey. His colleague paused and asked more questions. "It was clear that she was not a bad person—she just had no experience with LGBTQ issues or people." Carl's colleague went on to allow the GSA and took the time to listen to the students. "She even called me a couple months later to thank me again. I think it got her thinking."

CONCLUSION

School leaders have a tremendous amount of influence over the culture and climate of their districts and schools. If schools are to become truly inclusive, leaders at the school, district, state, and federal levels must examine the experiences of students who are LGBTQ and those perceived to be LGBTQ, and take appropriate action to ensure the protection and care of these individuals. Policies are important tools in this effort, but policies are not enough. Leaders must also take proactive steps such as countering hetero-normativity and other normalizing assumptions, being a voice among peers, being aware of district policies and community alliances, and considering intersecting perspectives. Further, socially just school leaders must be proactive in providing professional development for staff and instituting rituals, celebrations, and other activities that support LGBTQ and perceived-LGBTQ people. Most of all, school leaders need the skills and tools to take courageous action. Clearly, this chapter does not present an exhaustive list of strategies that can help school leaders create inclusiveness for LGBTQ and perceived-LGBTQ students in school settings. Nevertheless, the remarks and proposals herein represent a positive step forward, and can strengthen the current and future efforts needed in this direction.

REFERENCES

Adams, M., Bell, L. A., & Griffin, P. (1997). *Teaching for diversity and social justice: A sourcebook*. New York: Routledge.

Anderson, E., & McCormack, M. (2010). Intersectionality, critical race theory, and American sporting oppression: Examining Black and gay male athletes. *Journal of Homosexuality*, *57*(8), 949–967.

Baker, Jean M. (2002). *How homophobia hurts children: Nurturing diversity at home, at school, and in the community*. Binghamton, NY: Harrington Park Press. Retrieved from ERIC database. (ED479960).

Birkett, M., Espelage, D. L., & Koenig, B. (2009). LGB and questioning students in schools: The moderating effects of homophobic bullying and school climate on negative outcomes. *Journal of Youth and Adolescence*, *38*(7), 989–1000.

Blackburn, M. V. (2004). Understanding agency beyond school sanctioned activities. *Theory Into Practice 43*(2), 102–110.

Blumenfeld, D. E. (2000). How homophobia hurts everyone. In M. Adams (Ed.), *Readings for diversity and social justice* (pp. 267–275). New York: Routledge.

Brown, K. M. (2004). Leadership for social justice and equity: Weaving a transformative framework and pedagogy. *Educational Administration Quarterly, 40*(1), 77–108.

Cambron-McCabe, N., & McCarthy, M. M. (2005). Educating school leaders for social justice. *Educational Policy*, *19*(1), 201–222.

Capper, C. A., Schulte, K., & McKinney, S. A. (2009). Why school principals must stop all teasing, harassment, and bullying in schools and how they can do so. In J. Koschoreck & M. Tooms (Eds.), *Sexuality matters: Paradigms and policies for educational leaders* (pp. 118–140). Plymouth, UK: Rowman & Littlefield Education.

Cass, V. C. (1979). Homosexuality identity formation: A theoretical model. *Journal of Homosexuality*, *4*(3), 219–235.

Cass, V. C. (1984). Homosexual identity formation: Testing a theoretical model. *Journal of Sex Research*, *20*(2), 143–167.

Catchart, R. (2008, February 23). Boy's killing, labeled a hate crime, stuns a town. *New York Times*.

Catchings, B. (2009). *Bi-homo-hetero-trans-sexual: Epistemological and ontological functions of identity categorization*. Paper presented at the NCA Annual Convention, Chicago, IL.

Chasnoff, D., Cohen, H. S., Yacker, F., & McCarthy, S. (2008) *It's elementary: Talking about gay issues in school*. In *A guide for community organizing, professional development and K-8 curriculum*. Retrieved from http://groundspark.org/download/IE_Guide_08_Final.pdf

Crenshaw, K. (1989). Demarginalizing the intersection of race and sex: A Black feminist critique of antidiscrimination doctrine, feminist theory and antiracist politics. *University of Chicago Legal Forum, 140*, 139–167.

Daley, A., Solomon, S., Newman, P. A., & Mishna, F. (2008). Traversing the margins: Intersectionalities in the bullying of lesbian, gay, bisexual and transgender youth. *Journal of Gay & Lesbian Social Services*, *19*(3–4), 9–29.

Dantley, M. E., & Tillman, L. C. (2006). Social justice and moral transformative leadership. In K. Marshall & M. Olivia (Eds.), *Leadership for social justice: Making revolutions in education* (pp. 16–30). New York: Pearson.

D'Augelli, A. R. (1994). Identity development and sexual orientation: Toward a model of lesbian, gay, and bisexual development. In E. J. Trickett, R. J. Watts, & D. Birman (Eds.), *Human diversity: Perspectives on people in context* (pp. 312–333). The Jossey-Bass Social and Behavioral Science Series. San Francisco, CA: Jossey-Bass.

DeMatthews, D. (2014). Deconstructing systems of segregation leadership challenges in an urban school. *Journal of Cases in Educational Leadership*, *17*(1), 17–31.

DeVoe, J. F., & Kaffenberger, S. (2005). *Student reports of bullying: Results from the 2001 School Crime Supplement to the National Crime Victimization Survey*. Washington, DC: US Department of Education.

Eckholm, E. (2011, September 13). Eight suicides in two years at Anoka-Hennepin School District. *The New York Times*. Retrieved from http://www.nytimes.com/2011/09/13/us/13bullysidebar.html?_r=0

Espelage, D. L., Aragon, S. R., Birkett, M., & Koenig, B. W. (2008). Homophobic teasing, psychological outcomes, and sexual orientation among high school students: What influence do parents and schools have? *School Psychology Review*, *37*(2), 202–216.

Evans, N. J., & D'Augelli, A. R. (1996). Lesbians, gay men, and bisexual people in college. In R. C. Savin-Williams & K. M. Cohen (Eds.), *The lives of lesbians, gays, and bisexuals: Children to adults* (pp. 201–226). Orlando, FL: Harcourt Brace.

Frankfurt, K. (2000). A place for everyone. *Principal Leadership, 1*, 64–67.

Fratura, E. M., & Capper, C. A. (2007). *Leadership for social justice in practice: Integrated comprehensive services for all learners*. Thousand Oaks, CA: Corwin Press.

Friedrichs, E. (2014). *Coming out gay in middle school: Younger and younger kids and teens are telling their peers they are GLBT*. Retrieved from http://gayteens.about.com/od/experiences/a/Coming-Out-In-Middle-School.htm

Gay, Lesbian & Straight Education Network (GLSEN). (2008, May). *The principal's perspective: School safety, bullying and harassment*. Washington, DC: Author.

Gay, Lesbian & Straight Education Network (GLSEN). (2012). *The 2011 national school climate survey: Executive summary*, 2106-1. Retrieved from http://www.glsen.org

Gibson, P. (1989). Gay male and lesbian youth suicide. In M. R. Feinleib (Ed.), *Report of the Secretary's Task Force on Youth Suicide: Vol. 3. Preventions and interventions in youth suicide* (pp. 110–142). Washington, DC: US Department of Health and Human Services.

Goldring, E., & Greenfield, W. (2002). Understanding the evolving concept of leadership to education: Roles, expectations, and dilemmas. *Yearbook of the National Society for the Study of Education*, *101*(1), 1–19.

Goodenow, C., Szalacha, L., & Westheimer, K. (2006). School support groups, other school factors, and the safety of sexual minority adolescents. *Psychology in the Schools*, *43*(5), 573–589.

Greytak, E. A., Kosciw, J. G., & Diaz, E. M. (2009). *Harsh realities: The experiences of transgender youth in our nation's schools*. New York: GLSEN.

Griffin, P., & Ouellett, M. L. (2002). Going beyond gay-straight alliances to make schools safe for lesbian, gay, bisexual, and transgender students. *The Policy Journal of the Institute for Gay and Lesbian Strategic Studies*, *6*(1), 2–8.

Grogan, M., & Andrews, R. (2002). Defining preparation and professional development for the future. *Educational Administration Quarterly*, *38*(2), 233–256.

Hafner, M. (2005). *Preparing school leaders to ensure equity and work toward social justice: An exploratory study of leadership dispositions*. Paper presented at the American Educational Research Association, Montreal, Canada.

Hatzenbuehler, M. (2011). The social environment and suicide attempts in lesbian, gay, and bisexual youth. *Pediatrics, 127*(5), 896–903.

Hernandez, F., & Marshall, J. (2009). "Where I came from, where I am now and where I'd like to be": Aspiring administrators reflect on Equity, diversity and social justice. *Journal of School Leadership, 19*(3), 299–333.

Hopkins, N. (2000, November 29). Death of a schoolboy: He came for a better life. He was killed on the streets. *The Guardian*. Retrieved from http://www.theguardian.com/uk/2000/nov/29/ukcrime. nickhopkins

Human Rights Watch (2001). *Hatred in the hallways: Violence and discrimination against lesbian, gay, bisexual, and transgender students in U.S. schools*. New York: Author.

Ian, K. M. (2004). Gay rights and school policy: A case study in community factors that facilitate or impede educational change. *International Journal of Qualitative Studies in Education*, *17*(3), 347–370.

Knudsen, S. V. (2006). Intersectionality–a theoretical inspiration in the analysis of minority cultures and identities in textbooks. *Caught in the Web or Lost in the Textbook*, *53*, 61–76.

Koschoreck, J. W. & Tooms, A. K. (Eds.). (2009). *Sexuality matters: Paradigms and policies for educational leaders*. Lanham, MD: R&L Education.

Kosciw, J. G., Greytak, E. A., Bartkiewicz, M. J., Boesen, M. J., & Palmer, N. A. (2012). *The 2011 National School Climate Survey: The experiences of lesbian, gay, bisexual and transgender youth in our nation's schools*. New York: GLSEN.

Kourany, R. F. (1987). Suicide among homosexual adolescents. *Journal of Homosexuality, 13*(4), 111–117.

Lee, C. (2002). The impact of belonging to a high school gay/straight alliance. *The High School Journal, 85*(3), 13–26.

Lugg, C. A. (2003). Our straitlaced administrators: The law, lesbian, gay, bisexual, and transgendered educational administrators, and the assimilationist imperative. *Journal of School Leadership, 13*(1), 51–85.

Macgillivray, I. (2009). Gay straight alliances and other student clubs. In W. Koschoreck & A. Tooms (Eds.), *Sexuality matters: Paradigms and policies for educational leaders*. New York: Rowman & Littlefield.

Markow, D., & Dancewicz, J. (2008). *The principal's perspective: School safety, bullying, and harassment: A survey of public school principals*. New York: GLSEN.

Marshall, C., & Oliva, M. (2006). Building the capacities of social justice leaders. *Leadership for social justice: Making revolutions in education*, 1–15.

McCall, L. (2005). The complexity of intersectionality. *Signs, 30*(3), 1771–1800.

McKenzie, K. B., Christman, D. E., Hernandez, F., Fierro, E., Capper, C. A., Dantley, M., Scheurich, J. J. (2008). From the field: A proposal for educating leaders for social justice. *Educational Administration Quarterly, 44*, 111–138.

Meyer, D. (2010). Evaluating the severity of hate-motivated violence: Intersectional differences among LGBT hate crime victims. *Sociology, 44*(5), 980–995.

Meyer, D. (2012). An intersectional analysis of lesbian, gay, bisexual, and transgender (LGBT) people's evaluations of anti-queer violence. *Gender & Society, 26*(6), 849–873.

Nagda, B. R. A., Gurin, P., & Lopez, G. E. (2003). Transformative pedagogy for democracy and social justice. *Race, Ethnicity and Education, 6*(2), 165–191.

O'Donnell, S., Meyer, I., & Schwartz, S. (2011). Increased risk of suicide attempts among Black and Latino lesbians, gay men, and bisexuals. *American Journal of Public Health, 101*(6), 1055–1059.

Pastrana Jr., A. (2006). The intersectional imagination: What do lesbian and gay leaders of color have to do with it?. *Race, Gender & Class, 13*(3–4), 218–238.

Pellegrini, A. D. (2002). Bullying, victimization, and sexual harassment during the transition to middle school. *Educational Psychologist, 37*, 151–163.

Pounder, D., Reitzug, U. C., & Young, M. (2002). Preparing school leaders for school improvement, social justice, and community. In J. Murphy (Ed.), *The educational leadership challenge: Redefining leadership for the 21st century* (pp. 261–288). Chicago, IL: The University of Chicago Press.

Predrag, S. (2003). Study finds homophobic bullying in schools is widespread. *Lesbian News, 28*(6), 15.

Rasmussen, M. L., Rofes, E., & Talburt, S. (Eds.) (2004). *Youth and sexualities: Pleasure, subversion, and insubordination in and out of schools*. New York: Palgrave Macmillan.

Riehl, C. J. (2000). The principal's role in creating inclusive schools for diverse students: A review of normative, empirical, and critical literature on the practice of educational administration. *Review of Educational Research, 70*(1), 55–81.

Rienzo, B. A., Button, J. W., Jiunn-jye S., & Ying, L. (2006). The politics of sexual orientation issues in American schools. *Journal of School Health, 76*(3), 93–97.

Scheurich, J. J., & Skrla, L. (2003). *Leadership for equity and excellence: Creating high-achievement classrooms, schools, and districts*. Thousand Oaks, CA: Corwin Press.

Short, L. (2007). Lesbian mothers living well in the context of heterosexism and discrimination: Resources, strategies, and legislative change. *Feminism & Psychology, 13*, 106–126.

Swearer, S. M., Turner, R. K., Givens, J. E., & Pollack, W. S. (2008). "You're so gay!": Do different forms of bullying matter for adolescent males? *School Psychology Review, 37*(2), 160–173.

Swearer Napolitano, S. M. (2011). Risk Factors for and Outcomes of Bullying and Victimization (white paper; Educational Psychology Papers and Publications, Paper 132). Retrieved from http://digitalcommons.unl.edu/edpsychpapers/132/

Teaching Tolerance (2014). Retrieved from http://www.tolerance.org

Theoharis, G. (2007). Social justice educational leaders and resistance: Toward a theory of social justice leadership. *Educational Administration Quarterly, 43*(2), 221–258.

Theoharis, G. (2008). Woven in deeply: Identity and leadership of urban social justice principals. *Education and Urban Society, 41*(1), 3–25.

Theoharis, G. (2009). *The school leaders our children deserve: Seven keys to equity, social justice, and school reform*. New York: Teachers College Press.

US Department of Education (2012). Retrieved from http://www.stopbullying.gov

CHAPTER 7

Inclusive Leadership and Gender

Margaret Grogan and Shamini Dias

The history of gender stratification in education in the United States has, ironically, been intertwined with its founding ideas of freedom and equality for all. The dream of a new nation liberated from England's corrupt monarchy was based on Enlightenment aspirations rooted in education that shaped men and women to be virtuous citizens. However, women played the supporting cast within narrow social and intellectual spheres. Benjamin Rush, an 18th century education reformer, supported women's education by arguing that the new republic demanded women who were "qualified to a certain degree, by a peculiar and suitable education, to concur in instructing their sons" (Rush, 1787, p. 6) and who could "be an agreeable companion to a sensible man" (Rush, 1787, p. 9). History shows an abundance of such discourse delineating different educational spheres for men and women (Cott, 1997; Kerber, 1980). Even when women such as Catherine Beecher, Emma Willard, and Mary Lyon established women's academies, their fundamental aim was to prepare women for their social and moral roles as wives and mothers (Riordan, 1990).

Women's broader educational access from the late 19th century was also uneven. According to Perkins (1997), the push for women's college education came through the establishment of the Seven Sisters colleges—Mount Holyoke, Vassar, Wellesley, Smith, Radcliffe, Bryn Mawr, and Barnard—which offered high-quality, rigorous education to women. However, these elite, private institutions catered almost exclusively to wealthy or middle-class white women. In a nation with a slave history and where racial segregation was a norm, African American women had far narrower access. Clearly, gender inequities are exacerbated when intersected by race. Full access to education for ethnic minorities, and specifically for women of color, only became a reality with the 1954 *Brown v. Board of Education* Supreme Court ruling that declared all segregated schools to be unconstitutional.

The last quarter of the 20th century saw serious efforts to address gender and race inequities in education. And yet, we cannot seem to address the historical gender imbalance. In spite of legal measures, gender inequities for women are increasingly complicated by the intersection of other factors such as race, poverty, ability, sexuality, religion, and social segregation. Legal measures cannot mitigate complex and historically rooted assumptions about gender that persist in myriad social narratives and actions around us. More powerful than overt actions, parents, teachers, counselors, leaders, and the children themselves embody and enact these narratives unconsciously in their choices and responses to each other.

This is not merely a "girl" issue; stereotypical perceptions of boys and girls negatively impact everyone. Stereotypes that marginalize girls also limit boys in the ways they perceive and respond to girls. Similarly, masculine stereotypes that limit boys create perceptions that negatively affect how girls interact with boys, and how boys interact with boys. All genders, and especially transgendered individuals, are losers in this polarizing process where each gender becomes an "other." This also plays out in the way adults interact with students in school contexts. Therefore, while legal measures are necessary, they are not sufficient to redress gender inequities. To realize the founding ideals of freedom and equality in terms of inclusivity and the social justice we seek for students today, school leaders must work holistically against inequities in their communities by helping teachers, parents, and students build actions rooted in awareness of our own unconscious assumptions and responses to gender.

While gender issues affect the educational trajectories of all genders, this chapter focuses primarily on the continuing (and often invisible) inequities for girls as a way to create a sharp and contained focus. We maintain that reflection and action to address these historical inequities against girls are at the heart of creating gender equity overall. By surfacing this issue and changing the discourse around gender, school leaders can help their communities move forward in addressing the complex intersections that affect *all* genders. In researching the current context for girls in US K–12 schools, we report voices of the community, synthesize the literature on what we know about the marginalizing effects of gender on education, and offer a general approach for social justice leaders to create gender-inclusive environments. There are still major concerns about how schools deal with issues affecting girls, including pregnancy, sexual harassment, course-taking patterns, and career preparation. We attend to all, but in certain places, we focus on gender in the context of mathematics education as this is a well-documented area that foregrounds exclusionary discourses and limiting institutional processes. This focus helps social justice leaders detect and critique persistent gender-based perspectives that shape how educators interact with and deeply affect our students' educational, and thus, life trajectories.

PART 1: THE CURRENT CONTEXT OF GENDER IN SCHOOLS

The passing of Title IX in 1972 and the Women's Educational Equity Act (WEEA) of 1974 and accompanying social changes have improved educational opportunities for women. Particularly well documented are improved performances by girls in the science, technology, engineering, and math (STEM) areas (Hyde & Mertz, 2009). In the early 1980s, only one in 13 girls in seventh and eighth grade scored in the top percentile in SAT math tests. By 2010, this had increased to one in three girls. More women receive doctorates across all STEM fields, rising from 11% in 1972 to 40% by 2006 (National Coalition for Women and Girls in Education, 2014). More high school girls now take upper-level math and science courses required for math and science majors in college. Hyde and Mertz (2009) compared meta-analyses done using No Child Left Behind test scores and also conducted their own analyses using National Assessment of Educational Progress test scores. Their results showed that "U.S. girls have now reached parity with boys, even in high school, and even for measures requiring complex problem solving" (p. 8802). At the college level, women earn more than half the bachelor's degrees in biological and social sciences.

However, a closer look reveals that gender inequities persist in significant and long-reaching ways. Girls show a declining enrollment and achievement pattern in math-related classes over time. While in middle school grades, more girls (20%) take Algebra I compared to boys (18%); by high school, fewer girls enroll in physics (46%) and calculus (49%) than boys (54% and 51%, respectively) (US Department of Education, 2012). Similarly, fewer girls took computer science and engineering, and although girls accounted for 56% of Advanced Placement (AP) course-takers, only 19% took AP Computer Science in 2012 (Ashcraft, Eger, & Friend, 2012). While more girls than boys are enrolled in AP classes overall, boys consistently outnumbered girls in AP mathematics. Boys also passed AP tests at higher rates than girls (60% vs. 55%) (US Department of Education, 2012).

Women are still underrepresented in physics, engineering, and computer science. In the US Department of Education's 2012 report, while many college women took STEM courses, fewer compared to men received STEM degrees. In addition, of those women who received STEM degrees, many focused on physical and life sciences (57% compared to 31% of men), while men were more predominant in engineering (48% compared to 24% of women). Only 25% of PhDs in physical sciences were given to women. In engineering, only 18% of bachelor's degrees, 21% of master's degrees, and 12% of PhDs went to women. In computer science, women's representation in enrollment has actually been declining from 22% in the late 1980s to 18% in 2009. AAUW reports that in 2008 "women comprise 24.8 percent of computer and mathematical professionals, down from 27 percent in 2006" (AAUW, 2010, p. 1). In addition, despite these early efforts to diversify girls' career preparation, women are still concentrated in traditionally feminized fields in career and technical education (CTE) as well. Even in secondary schools, girls are underrepresented in programs funded by the Perkins Act leading to high-paying occupations such as manufacturing, architecture and construction, transportation, and distribution and logistics (National Coalition for Women and Girls in Education, 2012). Given that computer science and engineering degrees lead to some of the best-paid careers but have the lowest representation of women, we see how women's under-representation in these domains underscores and perpetuates gender inequities that were likely to have been reinforced in school.

To what extent are these trends a product of social and educational barriers for women, particularly women of color? To what extent do schools, in mirroring and focusing broader social gender assumptions and biases, "gender" students' perspectives about intelligence and aptitude? Research has refuted biological determinism and overt discrimination as barriers to women (Fine, 2010). Sadker and Sadker (1994) showed that within the same educational settings, girls receive a different education, especially in the shaping of agency and self-efficacy that influence their educational choices and performance levels in mathematics. Ceci and Williams (2011) showed that the under-representation of women in STEM fields is "due primarily to factors surrounding family formation and childrearing, gendered expectations, lifestyle choices, and career preferences—some originating before or during adolescence" (p. 5). Given the positive changes in women's academic access and achievement over the past half century, we wondered how gendered were the school experiences of young women in our Southern California community. Not surprisingly, we heard many stories of limiting and/or damaging experiences in math and science, which we summarize below. Examining these sociocultural processes might reveal useful patterns that can inform how school leaders lead initiatives to counter gendering processes that negatively shape girls' academic aspirations.

Voices of the Community

To lend authenticity and recency to our work on this chapter, we spoke to a variety of community members including educators (e.g., teachers and administrators) as well as individuals who had no connection to PreK–12 schools. We talked with several young women and a few men between the ages of 25 and 40 in a small, academic town outside of a major metropolitan area in Southern California. We asked them what gendered school experiences they recalled. Gendered narratives and cultural stereotypes showed up particularly clearly in certain subject areas such as math and art. The issues that emerged did not pertain only to gender, but rather seemed to polarize gender, race, and class.

In these conversations, math was perceived to be a masculine (and specifically white) domain. For instance, M.H., a PhD candidate in education, majored in math and engineering as an undergraduate. She reported a clear and exclusionary math culture. As a woman and a Latina, she has encountered people who are surprised at finding out that she has a math degree or is good at math. How she looks seems to be at odds with people's expectations of math degree holders. She frequently hears women articulate gender stereotypical statements such as, "Math is not for me" or "I hate math." She also noted that all her math teachers through high school and college were white male teachers. While she developed the persistence to seek help when needed, she felt that it might have been hard for girls of color to approach teachers with questions or, worse, to be noticed negatively by teachers. We also see this in T.G.'s story of being the only African American student in a summer Algebra class. "I was fine through Chapter 5, but I found Chapter 6 hard. I said, 'I don't get it' or 'This is hard,' but in the end I did it. But the teacher told me on the last day that I was the worst student she'd ever had. My best friend took the class with me and she's White Latina, and she said the same things I did, but the teacher just singled me out."

Another person we talked to, W.P., spoke at a 2012 TEDx event. She is a math major and plans on pursuing a career in math, but shared her anger over math education:

> I feel personally betrayed. . . . I was never told until college what it meant to be good at math. Since I was in preschool, I was told I was good at math because I exhibited a particular set of traits—speed and accuracy. I memorized things quickly, I computed things quickly, I applied things quickly and I turned in quizzes and tests quickly. I got the high scores—that's what my peers and teachers admired me for. . . . In college I discovered math is a lot harder . . . math is not about computation, it's about problem solving. I started struggling, not succeeding. . . . I quickly became convinced that I am not good at math, because I am not fast anymore, I'm not accurate anymore; maybe this isn't for me. And I'm angry because that convinced me almost to abandon mathematics, something that I loved so dearly. And I am sure that it convinces millions of people around this country every year not to pursue mathematics.

These voices of the community reveal a male-centered math culture underscored by issues of race. The narratives suggest that the (unconscious) discourse around math is narrowly delimited and works not just against girls, but also against boys. We see similar narratives in the very different context of art. For many years, P.Y., an African American undergraduate, suppressed his strong interest in art. "Art was like a soft option, something girls were good at, or the girly boys who wrote poetry. Unless of course I did sculpture with metal and concrete." Race complicated this because "only rich, white students really got into the types of art and theatre that teachers liked. Black kids maybe did street art but we weren't Banksy[1] so our stuff was seen as graffiti and gang related." For H.A., a female student majoring in English, the fine arts were for "the rich, white kids who felt comfortable going to museums and places" and "definitely not for guys—unless you were white." H.A.'s brother was a football player who played down his interest in literature.

Another perspective that emerged in these community voices is how parents perpetuate gendered discourses. G.A. spoke of her children's college experiences. Her daughter found computer science "too demanding" and changed her focus to something "better for women," while she encouraged her son to persist in challenging courses. S. E. recalls an incident when she was 7 years old. Her aunt brought some friends to visit with her parents, and there was a boy her age or a little younger. Seeing how shy and scared he was, and being shy herself, she plucked up the courage to ask if she should show him her toys. She remembers being mortified when her aunt laughed and very loudly remarked, "Don't be silly! Boys don't play with girls' toys!"

Finally, providing a curious epilogue to our revealing anecdotes, one of us witnessed this exchange at the checkout counter of a local supermarket. The female cashier had trouble recalling the item code for a product. The male cashier at the other counter called it out and she shook her head and remarked how good he was at math, while she just did not get it. She clearly equated a good memory with mathematical ability, and went on to describe how her daughter in community college switched from accounting to a "less demanding" course because she too didn't have a "head for numbers."

Listening to the Voices in the Community

Listening to these community voices provides a practical example for how school leaders can begin to detect and critique the persistent gender-based perspectives in their school contexts. These voices show how commonplace it is for social and educational discourse to be gendered; certain subject areas and ways of behaving are for boys, and others for girls. Often, teachers, parents, and children do not realize how gendered their perceptions and beliefs are, nor how this can significantly affect choices, actions, and ultimately life outcomes. As the vignettes about math and art illustrate, girls and boys received gendered and racialized messages about how intelligence, creativity, and academic aptitude were demonstrated in school. Early on, the emphasis was on turning in homework, performing well on tests of recall, and paying attention to the teacher. For girls, as they got older, the capacity for complex problem-solving associated with perseverance and struggling appears not to have been taught. That some boys (and some girls) acquire these capabilities may have little to do with what is rewarded in the classroom, but ultimately serves well those who do learn to grapple with problems. The anecdotes help us to appreciate that while classroom behaviors that many girls adopt may earn good grades, these behaviors may not have lasting academic benefits.

In contrast to these anecdotes, when we spoke to school leaders, we were surprised by the lack of attention (and interest) in girls' issues. We learned that gender (meaning girl) issues were presumed to no longer be a problem. When we spoke with school leaders, conversations invariably began with their assertion that "girls in this school are doing fine, it's the boys we are worried about." Upon probing those beliefs, though, we learned that only in rare circumstances were test scores or other achievement data actually disaggregated by gender, and even more rarely were they disaggregated by race/ethnicity, socioeconomic status, and gender. When principals said the girls were doing fine, they meant their grades were good and they behaved well. Consequently, principals and teachers are often unlikely, in fact, to know how Latinas are faring, or how African American boys versus Latino[2] boys are doing. What they can tell you quickly is that African American girls are more likely to be suspended than other girls, but behavior-wise, boys are the most problematic. One commented, "The teachers complain loudly if they have a class with more boys than girls." At another school, the principal talked of spending most of her time "dealing with fragile, White, middle-class boys having continual emotional outbursts."

And even though principals often disaggregated data on students with special needs, they didn't look at the intersections of race/ethnicity or gender of students in special education. Thus, very few seemed aware of the potential disproportionate number of African

American boys placed in special education because of behavior issues (Noguera, 2008). Similarly, a high school assistant principal told us that they did not keep data on the numbers of girls signing up for higher-level math courses or science electives. Few leaders expressed interest in tracking grades and/or course selection or completion by gender and/or race/ethnicity. Whereas all principals agreed that such data could be generated, they believed obviously there was no demand for these data to be gathered, presented, or discussed. Since many of our local schools are majority Latino, leaders did comment that stereotypical female and male roles were still assumed in their diverse communities, complicating Latinas' options for attending four-year colleges after high school. Many Latinas from low-income families are expected to stay home to help raise younger children and support their mothers although they can attend the local community college part-time. We heard compassion from principals for the circumstances with which their students were dealing but we did not hear any attempts to *change the discourse*.

Equally troubling were the leaders' admissions that nobody was talking about sexual harassment. Lesbian, gay, bisexual, transgender, or questioning (LGBTQ) students (and those perceived to be) were often mentioned as targets of bullying, but there were no conversations about bullying or other discriminating behaviors targeted at female stereotypes. Are school leaders everywhere as complacent about accepting the status quo regarding gender issues? The following literature review clearly indicates good reasons to problematize such attitudes if that is the case.

PART 2: WHAT WE KNOW ABOUT GENDER: THE LITERATURE

Most scholars today believe individuals are socialized into being girls and then women, boys and then men. However, the predominant theories explain that acquiring gender is not a passive experience. Individuals are active learners of how to do gender and their learning is embedded in the contexts of ethnicity, race, culture, class, religion, socioeconomic status, historical period, etc. West and Fenstermaker (1993) argue that gender is "an emergent feature of social situations that is both an outcome and a rationale for the most fundamental division of society" (p. 151). Gender is thought of as a social identity. It is not simply an individual attribute, but is produced through interactions with others. "Being a man or woman . . . is not a pre-determined state. It is a *becoming*, a condition actively under construction" (Connell, 2009, p. 5, emphasis in original).

Needless to say, schools provide a large part of the environments within which this process takes place, but principals and other school leaders pay little attention to the ways in which the organization contributes to the process. Ethnographers using feminist lenses explain how schools are fundamental sites in the production, reproduction, and struggle against gender inequality (Foley, Levinson, & Hurtig, 2000). Teachers, clerical staff, custodians, bus drivers, administrators, and especially the students themselves make comments, offer criticism, and act as role models on a daily basis. Children bring knowledge of gender to school at the earliest ages from home, television, shopping, reading, and playing games. They are "born into a world in which gender is continually emphasized through conventions of dress, appearance, language, color, segregation, and symbols. Everything around the child indicates that whether one is male or female is a matter of great importance" (Fine, 2010, p. 227).

Moreover, children soon learn which gender is more highly valued. Stereotypes abound in fairy tales, children's literature, toys, and games where males are heroes and females are rescued. Analyses of children's books, including those winning the prestigious Caldecott Medal, find that males have title roles nearly twice as often as females and they appear much more often in pictures (Fine, 2010). When attempts are made to create non-stereotypical characters, females inevitably take on male characteristics. As Fine remarks of current literature, "it is easier to find an adventurous girl than a sissy boy" (p. 221). When boys are told not to act like girls, children learn that to be a girl is not a good thing. Even when young children learn to push against norms and to experiment with different ways to do gender, the hierarchy remains intact. Though resistance to norms grows as children mature, the notion of difference between genders is much more often reinforced than similarity between them. Because gender is considered a status characteristic in most societies, females are seen as less than or subordinate to males (Ridgeway, 1993). Stereotypic and traditional notions of privileged masculinity are perpetuated through social processes of family life, play choices, pop culture, and the media. In addition to the more obvious negative impact on girls, this also affects boys who embrace the stereotypes and reinforce them in their perceptions and actions toward girls and boys who opt for different kinds of masculinities or femininities.

Whether conscious of their influence or not, educators have known for a long time that perceptions of gender shape the way students experience schools PreK–12. The most compelling empirical evidence of what was going on in classrooms was offered by Sadker and Sadker (1994). Their book, provocatively titled *Failing at Fairness: How Our Schools Cheat Girls*, documents narratives of girls' experiences contrasted to boys' in elementary and secondary schools across the country. Fifteen years later, the book was updated and re-published as *Still Failing at Fairness: How Gender Bias Cheats Girls and Boys in School and What We Can Do About It* (Sadker, Sadker, & Zittleman, 2009). While some positive changes in girls' experiences of school were documented during those 15 years, the conclusion the authors reached in 2009 was not very encouraging. Most important was the expanded lens they used that showed both boys and girls suffered from gender bias and stereotypes that profoundly affected their lives in schools. In addition, they realized that the dimensions of race, ethnicity, and poverty allowed for a much more nuanced understanding of how schooling determines not only the ways students view themselves and their capabilities, but also what chances they have of getting postsecondary education and/or well-paying jobs. This scholarship highlights the following five gender issues: (1) legislation such as Title IX (1972), WEEA (1974), and the Civil Rights Act of 1978; (2) classroom pedagogies, course content, and curriculum materials reinforcing gender stereotypes; (3) academic performance, gendered career preparation, and encouragement; (4) sexual harassment in schools; and (5) pregnancy and parenting. We address each of these areas in the following sections through the lens of intersectionality of gender with the multiple dimensions of diversity and identity addressed throughout this book.

In the following sub-sections, we review the most recent literature on these issues to establish the context within which girls are receiving an education in the elementary and secondary grades. While our focus is on girls, we also comment on how girls and boys are shortchanged by biases and stereotypes in an effort to draw attention to the heavily gendered notions that still ground schooling in the early 21st century. This literature will help school leaders be well informed and conscious of what insights law, policy, and research provide them. Unfortunately, our research indicates that gender inequities remain on the forefront of social justice issues to be addressed by courageous leaders all across this country.

Legislation

The 1972 passing of the Title IX law aimed to outlaw sexual discrimination in schools. Sex bias was prohibited in all school activities and services, including athletics, admissions, counseling, medical services, financial aid, and the handling of students (Sadker & Sadker, 1994). Violating Title IX meant a loss of federal funds. As the authors point out, "There was now a legal weapon to fight schools that refused to treat girls fairly" (p. 36). However, while we can celebrate many positive outcomes of Title IX in the PreK–12 arena, such as more opportunities for girls to compete in athletics and more access to higher-level math and the life sciences, Title IX's potential was never fully realized. Sadker et al. (2009) argue that "Decades after Title IX was passed, despite the fact that most districts were to one degree or another violating the law, it was difficult to find even a single school district that was actually fined for such violations" (Chapter 2, Section 9, para. 5). This suggests that schools do not take the threat of violating Title IX seriously. In addition, we note that the purpose of the legislation has been largely forgotten amidst a backlash against what is seen as an entitlement program for girls (Sadker et al., 2009).

Title IX benefits both girls and boys in schools by ensuring equality in education. Everyone benefits from equal access to programs and a supportive atmosphere. "By prohibiting hostile, threatening and discriminatory behavior, Title IX protects the rights of all students to learn in a healthy environment" (NCWGE, 2012, p. 1). However, as many scholars and organizations point out, what is missing is the monitoring of programs and activities in schools. If there are still Title IX coordinators in districts or at the state level, their work is not well known. Both AAUW and NCWGE emphasize the urgency of appointing coordinators at the local and state level, highlighting them on websites, and ensuring their work is coordinated across programs and amongst federal, state, and local agents. Klein (2008) published a study of information about Title IX (or the lack thereof) found on state education agency (SEA) websites. With few exceptions, she found them extremely limited and largely unhelpful.

The other two pieces of legislation most related to gender equity in education, Women's Educational Equity Act (WEEA) in 1974 and the expanded Civil Rights Act (1978), have also dropped off the radar screen. WEEA was passed to help fund educational materials and training to address sex bias and help schools meet the terms of Title IX, but the resource center created to support the legislation has been defunded. In addition, the Civil Rights Act was expanded to include sex equity work with the creation of ten equity assistance centers. While the centers do provide resources and training on the broad issues of educational equity, funding, specifically targeting sex equity, has virtually disappeared (Sadker et al., 2009).

Classroom Pedagogies, Course Content, and Curriculum Materials

Since at least the mid-1980s, research on teacher and student interactions in classrooms has revealed various kinds of gender bias. Sadker & Sadker (1994) painstakingly documented how most teachers praised girls for social and behavioral skills like turning in neat, tidy work, but challenged boys to think more critically. Boys also received the lion's share of teachers' attention in the classroom, although often for misbehavior. Ten years later, a meta-analysis confirmed those findings (Jones & Dindia, 2004). In addition, in a study using K–8 national longitudinal data of 7,075 students, Robinson and Lubienski (2011) found that teachers consistently rated girls higher than boys in both math and reading, even when cognitive assessments indicated otherwise.

More troubling patterns emerged when the data were disaggregated by race, class, and gender. African American students, in particular, were punished more harshly for the same infractions (Sadker et al., 2009). In a predominantly minority school, Morris (2007) found that African American high school girls were shut down in class for being too outspoken and "unladylike." Teachers' and other school personnel's stereotypical notions of femininity were seen as having a negative effect on these girls' academic performance. In an extensive study of high school classrooms, Wortham (2004) found that students' social identity strongly influenced what they learned and how they learned. Teachers' and other students' characterization of students as well as their own sense of race, class, and masculinity or femininity were intertwined in the process. The pernicious effects of classroom discourse within which gender, race, and class combine to situate students as "unpromising boys," "quiet Asians," "overachieving girls," or "loud Black girls" is detrimental in terms of limiting students' aspirations as well as in curtailing what they are able to learn. Excellent examples are given in a comprehensive review of the literature that discusses the social production of adolescent risk and promising new approaches to literacy (Vasudevan & Campano, 2009).

As is discussed in the chapters throughout this book, the extent to which students see themselves in the curriculum—and what images of themselves they see there—shapes the learning process powerfully. Gender roles are clearly taught through many components of the curriculum in addition to the stories, plays, and visual images that students study. Schools become incubators for gender sense-making as students interact with peers, staff, teachers, course materials, and popular culture inside and outside the classroom. Vasudevan and Campano (2009) show how learning is clearly framed by ". . . the gender oppression that both boys and girls experience when they do not conform to school expectations and the ways that these gender identities are complicated by racial and class ascriptions" (p. 322). Not only is this a complex process that takes shape in local and diverse ways, but its features are hard to detect. For the most part, teachers believe they attend only to the subject matter and the tests they are preparing the students to take. Believing themselves neutral or sensitive to gender and, to a more or lesser extent, race, ethnicity, sexual orientation, and socioeconomic status, teachers miss how much learning and teaching takes place in fully gendered ways (Sadker et al., 2009; Morris, 2007, 2012; Wortham, 2004).

Academic Performance, Gendered Career Preparation, and Encouragement

In very general terms, boys and girls are both performing better academically today than ever before (Corbett, Hill, & St. Rose, 2008). Much attention has been paid to school grades, standardized test scores, college entrance exams, and other measures of academic achievement to determine whether gender influences academic performance. Diprete and Buchmann (2013) report that ". . . there has been a high degree of stability in the gender gap in academic performance over many decades with girls outperforming boys in one central measure: course grades" (p. 10). Also well documented are the facts that women are graduating from high school and college at higher rates than men (Corbett et al., 2008; DiPrete & Buchmann, 2013). Unfortunately, a reactionary public has leapt on these trends to frame a "boy-crisis" or "gender war" (Datnow & Hubbard, 2002; Hoff Summers, 2000; Sadker et al., 2009; Sax, 2007). Much hyperbole has been aimed at the so-called "feminization of schools" or of the curriculum. Sax (2007) argues that boys are underperforming academically because they are turned off school. He suggests it is a male thing. "For many boys, not caring about anything has become the mark of true guydom" (p. 7). Suggestions are made that paying attention to girls as a result of Title IX actually harms boys.

A close look at the data reveals a more complex picture. When looking at gender, some boys, indeed, as well as some girls are in dire need of effective learning interventions if they are to reap the benefits of a good education. Considering other dimensions of diversity reveals other concerns. Corbett et al. (2008) found that family income level, and race/ethnicity accounted for much more variance in academic performance than gender:

[G]irls often have outperformed boys within each racial/ethnic group on the NAEP reading test. When broken down by race/ethnicity, however, this gender gap is found to be most consistent among white students, less so among African American students, and least among Hispanic students. Similarly, boys overall have outperformed girls on both the math and verbal portions of the SAT. Disaggregated by family income level, however, the male advantage on the verbal portion of the SAT is consistently seen only among students from low-income families. (p. 3).

Indeed, the most troubling gaps in math and reading remain with African American and Hispanic girls scoring more closely to boys in the same racial/ethnic group than to White girls or boys. Math test scores show that girls perform just as well as boys. However, on tests like the SAT, where there is a larger proportion of females than males taking the test, results often slightly favor the more selective sample of boys (DiPrete & Buchmann, 2013). The importance of the SAT and ACT is that they are the gatekeepers for college entrance and for career aspirations. If there are no gender differences in test performance, the absence of women from STEM majors can only be attributed to lack of encouragement and/or hostile classroom experiences in high school and college.

Not surprisingly, this on-going fear of gender inequality continues to spark interest in single-sex schools—for girls and boys. However, there is very little evidence that single-sex institutions or classrooms are more gender-equitable than their co-educational counterparts (Arms, 2007). After research in the late '80s and early '90s showed girls had been short-changed by narrow curricular offerings and competition with boys in the STEM subjects, there was some hope that girls could be offered more equitable opportunities in single-sex classrooms and/or schools. Then, when girls' test scores began trending upward and men's attendance and perseverance at college began to fall behind, the question of separating boys to remove them from distraction became salient. Datnow and Hubbard (2002) produced a comprehensive volume looking at a range of perspectives on both single-sex and co-educational schools. There appeared to be no consensus of opinion regarding the overall benefits to girls or boys of one or the other approach to education, although particular accounts claimed to serve the needs of the population for whom they were designed. But Datnow and Hubbard (2002) point out the undermining effects of the larger social milieu: ". . . even when schools, universities, or particular individuals in these settings attempted to create gender equitable environments in which young women and men could thrive, these efforts often conflict with societal beliefs in some communities regarding more traditional roles for men and women" (p. 8). Cultural stereotypes for girls and boys trumped gender equality practices in the schools. More recently, DiPrete and Buchmann (2013) report that research evidence confirms ". . . both boys and girls appear to benefit from classrooms that have higher proportions of female students" (p. 178). In addition, to address gender equity for boys, DiPrete and Buchmann (2013) also strongly recommend greater emphasis on academics. In their research, higher academic standards as opposed to less-rigorous ones appear to promote higher achievement among boys. Interestingly though, a study of AP courses found that in *contrast* to boys ". . . girls thrive in a more rigorous context, and they falter in a less rigorous context" (Moller, Stearns, Southworth, & Potochnick, 2013, p. 865). Low academic standards obviously benefit nobody. Instead of considering co-educational classrooms as one of the sources of gender inequities, perhaps the relationship between gender, rigor, and engagement needs greater attention.

Sexual Harassment

Like girls' experiences in schools generally, the literature suggests that issues of sexual harassment have retreated into the background in recent times. Issues include broad gender-based harassment that shapes perceptions of acceptable ways of being for boys and girls. For example, a girl being made to feel inadequate because she likes welding and carpentry is seen as a nerd—she cannot be part of the pretty and popular crowd—or a girl having to hide her preference for computer games and coding in order to be accepted, or a boy marginalized because he likes to write poetry. This kind of labeling and resulting exclusion from mainstream social life in middle and high school can be very distressing. The gender stereotypes and expected gender-based traits and behaviors have a very strong influence on students, their choices, and how they learn.

Paludi, Martin, and Paludi (2007) bemoaned this trend, fearing that just as gender inequality was once hidden from view prior to Title IX, it was in danger of being eclipsed again—this time by the more encompassing term "bullying." But a large proportion of bullying is sexually targeted and, unless identified as such, interventions and prevention strategies are not likely to be effective. "More than half of girls and 40 percent of boys in grades 7 through 12 reported being sexually harassed during the 2010–2011 school year. Among lesbian, gay, bisexual, and transgender students, harassment is even more extensive; 85% say they have been verbally harassed and 19% report physical assault" (NCWGE, 2012, p. 38). Unfortunately, even though most schools have anti-bullying and anti-sexual harassment policies in force, evidence suggests that from elementary grades on up, students are constantly exposed to demeaning experiences (see further Hernandez & Fraynd, this volume). According to this 2010 survey, almost half of all teachers reported hearing their students make sexist remarks. And, despite its widespread occurrence, note must be taken of the fact that significantly more girls (56%) than boys (40%) report sexual harassment (NCWGE, 2012, p. 40). Moreover, research suggests that boys are more likely than girls to harass others (Paludi et al., 2007).

Needless to say, these recurring hostilities have a profoundly negative effect on the academic performance of all those targeted, but responses differ according to socio-economic status, gender, and race/ethnicity. Girls reported harassment as more frightening than boys did and more often reported a desire to quit school (Paludi et al., 2007). Students from moderate- or low-income homes reported more negative effects than their wealthier counterparts (Hill & Kearl, 2011). Paludi et al. (2007) noted that intersections between gender and race/ethnicity as well as between gender and ability/disability can exacerbate the situation, particularly if such women find themselves in the minority. In college, women of color are more vulnerable to sexual harassment from their professors, especially if viewed as sexually mysterious. Although the sample sizes were small, Hill and Kearl (2011) found differences between White students and students of color's reactions to sexual harassment. Hispanic students were more likely to remain home and African American students were more likely to stop an activity or sport, misbehave, or have difficulty studying.

Pregnancy and Parenting

Girls who become pregnant are often discriminated against in schools. They are encouraged to attend alternative schools or programs that often do not have the same range of courses or ones taught at the same level as the regular school, and/or they are subject to severe attendance policies that make it difficult, if not impossible, to continue their education (NCWGE, 2012). Thirty percent of the 305,000 teenage girls who gave birth in 2012 say they quit school because of parenthood (Hansen, 2014). When pregnant teens drop out of school, they are likely to deal with economic insecurity for the rest of their lives (Mangel, 2010). If they had received more support from the adults in their schools, these girls report that they would have stayed in school. Numbers show that students from low-income neighborhoods are more likely to have or father a baby in their teens and the rates for African American students and Hispanic students are higher than for White students (Office of Adolescent Health, 2014). While statistics indicate that teen pregnancies are declining in all populations, the recent figures confirm an on-going, serious problem.

Many people—including school leaders—are unaware that Title IX forbids discrimination against pregnant and parenting students. Under the law's regulations, schools are required to ". . . give all students who *might be*, *are*, or *have been* pregnant (whether currently parenting or not) equal access to school programs and extracurricular activities" (NCWGE, 2012, p. 56, emphasis in original). Regulations also govern attendance, pregnancy-related absences, opportunities for makeup work, tutoring, and participation in activities after school. Participation in programs separate from the regular ones must be voluntary. NCWGE recommends action to raise awareness of the provisions of this law as well as all steps that can be taken to keep teen parents in school. Girls need targeted support to finish their education, and boys need support and encouragement to remain engaged in the lives of their children.

Obviously, all teen parents are very vulnerable, but when pregnant girls disappear from school either because of harassment, shame, and/or pregnancy-related health issues, they become invisible. In terms of equality of educational opportunity within the regular high school, this remains an under-monitored and at times completely neglected issue.

In sum, confronting gender stratification requires understanding the complex ways in which this is manifest. Toward this end, in this section we have reviewed literature across the five areas of legislation; classroom pedagogies, course content, and curriculum materials reinforcing gender stereotypes; academic performance, gendered career preparation, and encouragement; sexual harassment in schools; and pregnancy and parenting. We now turn to describe strategies for inclusive leadership to confront and eliminate this stratification.

PART 3: INCLUSIVE LEADERSHIP AROUND GENDER IN K–12 SCHOOLS

The No Child Left Behind Act (NCLB) of 2001 places enormous pressure on teachers and school leaders to raise test scores. More than ever before, schools are defined by state-mandated measures of student achievement disaggregated by race, socioeconomic status, English-language proficiency, and participation in special education because all these social markers, and the intersections between them, have been found to marginalize students. For reasons detailed above, gender must be included in this list. Scholars of educational leadership have developed a considerable research base that investigates the value of leading for social justice to address the damage of marginalization (among others, see authors in this volume as well as Bogotch, 2002; Frattura & Capper, 2007; Furman, 2012; Scanlan & Lopez, 2012; Shields, 2011; Theoharis, 2007).

Leading for social justice means paying attention to the social, economic, and political structures that position individuals in our communities, and intervening to disrupt usual school practices to improve the educational experiences of students in our schools. Social justice leadership is thus demonstrated by principals and others who use their positional power to collaboratively design rigorous, engaging academic environments within which all students flourish. The notion of inclusivity, well established in the special education discourse, has been expanded to embrace all students who have not benefited from school policies and practices that are tailored to preserve mostly White, middle-class interests. Theoharis and O'Toole (2011) define inclusive education as "providing each student the right to an authentic sense of belonging to a school classroom community where difference is expected and valued" (p. 649). Accordingly, principals who lead inclusively operate from an equity-oriented perspective. Along with the values of excellence and equality that have undergirded US education for the past half century, a commitment to equity is fundamentally necessary to combat injustice in schools.

This section will flesh out what leading inclusively from an equity-oriented perspective looks like around issues of gender in PreK–12 schools. We begin with a brief discussion of how to move from awareness of the research literature to acting in response to this literature. We then present a case study to illustrate such action. We conclude by identifying three strategies illustrated in the case study, discussing implications for school leadership practices.

From Awareness to Action

Disillusioned with the various liberal approaches to school reform, many years ago Catherine Marshall (1993) advocated for a "new" politics of race and gender that would help guide educational leaders' decision-making. Unfortunately, what we've learned since then is that it is not enough to merely draw attention to the marginalizing forces of race, gender, LGBTQ status, poverty, ability, and religion. Instead, deliberate interventions in school practices and targeted efforts to change perspectives are required. Continuing racism, sexism, homophobia and other forms of blatant discrimination in schools illustrate that educational institutions serve to create and reinforce the unequal social relations that limit many students (Grogan, 1999). It is this recognition that may help energize school leaders to build the necessary capacity in their schools to take sustainable action (Furman, 2012).

Our review of the literature reveals that even protections that have been hard fought and long in place are being disregarded. For example, under Title IX, there are required procedures for dealing with sexual harassment in schools as well as in the workplace. Guidelines from the Office for Civil Rights in 2011 make clear the procedures to be followed. But as mentioned earlier, one of the key components for monitoring the situation under this act appears to be missing from many institutions: an active and visible Title IX coordinator whose presence is known and respected throughout the institution. NCWGE (2012) recommends that coordinators have greater presence in schools; that all institutions have clear, enforceable policies against sexual harassment that offer protection to students after harassment has occurred; and that students be protected against harassment based on perceived or actual LGBTQ status. Schools must work with families and provide close follow-up after harassment has been reported. To work toward a harassment-free climate in schools, it is recommended that all members of the school community should talk openly about attitudes and behaviors that facilitate or prevent progress (p. 44).

Unhappily, we discovered that gender issues are generally neglected in local schools. This is particularly problematic because inequities continue to be perpetuated through largely unconscious cultural mores and narratives. Gender inequities are deeply rooted in historical, philosophical, and cultural narratives of gender so that we are, ourselves, articulations of gender-based narratives. We all have a blind spot to the subtle ways in which sociocultural narratives habituate us to perceive and respond to our world in gendered ways. This partly explains the gap in explicit professional development for teachers or school-based initiatives that address gender-equity issues in teaching and learning. Ellen Langer (Langer, 1997; Langer & Moldoveanu, 2000) describes mindfulness or intentional action as the countering force to habituated or mindless reactions. If we are indeed so habituated to gendered perceptions, then as educators we must develop critical self-awareness as well as intentional ways of thinking, responding, and acting if we are to change the narratives for our students.

GUIDING QUESTIONS

- How does a principal go about raising awareness about negative gender narratives that permeate the larger social contexts surrounding education, and which daily enter into and shape teaching-learning contexts?
- What can she or he do to help teachers and families counter negative narratives and offer alternatives that empower girls and boys alike?

A Case Study of Professional Development: Gender as a Sustained Theme

The following case study is built from our interactions with several principals who were atypically interested in building capacity among their communities to address gender inequities.

Context

The context consists of a large, urban high school (grades 9–12) in a poor neighborhood, where the majority of students qualify for free and reduced-price lunch and are racially minoritized (see Horsford & Clark, this volume), mostly African American and Hispanic. The principal, Dr. Q, has been leading the school for three years and has spent her time on the ground in classrooms and the community, speaking with parents, teachers, counselors, school staff, and students to understand the needs, opportunities, and challenges in her school.

Issues

Among Dr. Q's many initiatives with her community is the effort to address gender inequities in school, specifically in helping girls succeed in STEM subjects, but also in helping boys aim for careers that suit their interests and abilities.

> Not every girl wants to be an engineer or astronaut. And not every boy wants to dance. But, that should be as a result of a true choice rather than because somewhere along the way we've created a mindset that makes them feel that as men or women they do not have the ability for these careers, or that because they would be less 'womanly' or 'manly' if they made these choices.

Dr. Q is aware that in addition to subject interest and career choice, there are other gender issues intertwined with issues of race and poverty that challenge her school. As with most urban schools of this type, her community deals with myriad problems daily, ranging from bullying, LGBTQ advocacy and safety, teen pregnancy, absenteeism, and dropping out, to misbehavior and gang-related violence. Dr. Q is clear that many of these learning and behavioral issues intersect and are rooted in deep-seated gender perceptions, stereotypes, and habits of speech and action. By focusing on gender in teaching and learning, she hopes to help students develop healthier and more productive narratives allowing them to overcome some of these challenges.

Her approach is to use professional development for her staff as a staging ground from which to develop school culture transformation. The strategies for this approach are based on principles of experiential learning (Curran & Murray, 2008; Miettinen, 2000) that place direct and sustained experience at the center of developing knowledge and habits. Experiential learning also supports reflection and conversation that helps to build awareness so that we become more aware of habituated or unconscious impulses.

Dr. Q takes to heart the Quality Professional Learning Standards that were adopted by the California Department of Education in December 2013.[3] These standards were derived from the realization that traditional professional development had been poorly designed and delivered. Piecemeal professional development has traditionally stymied deep transformations in teaching and learning. To avoid this, Dr. Q, together with key members of her faculty and staff, committed to making gender equity a five-year theme for their school. This longer time frame also allows her to lead the school to more systematically address a cluster of different gender issues each year, such as gendered career choices, sexual harassment and bullying, and teenage pregnancy and parenting.

To begin the process, she first broached the idea with key members of her leadership staff so that they would be strong advocates of the idea. Then, she presented it to her teachers, counselors, and staff, making it clear that this would be a long-term effort that they would work on together in small and incremental ways. As a core theme over a sustained time period, she hopes that attention, conversations, and actions will cohere across the many related challenges the school seeks to address as a community.

Lessons for Leaders

Considering Dr. Q's experience pursuing gender equity, several lessons for inclusive leadership emerge. We focus on three: using data to guide reflection and action, reflecting as a community, and involving students. We address each in turn, showing how they interconnect.

Data-Driven Reflection and Action: The Power of Infographics[4]

Dr. Q believes in using data as persuasive evidence of the importance of gender equity in teaching and learning, as well as a resource for the community. Infographics visualize key data to present the big picture of various situations. Dr. Q uses infographics on gender equity trends in education as a way to present important data in ways that make sense, do not take very much time, sustain a focus on the data, and have high impact. In addition to enrolling her technology-savvy teachers and computer club students to help translate information and data into simple visuals, Dr. Q also uses downloadable infographics from relevant websites (see the companion website for resource list and for examples). See the companion website for examples of these infographics (www.routledge.com/cw/theoharis).

At meetings, the strong visual presentations help her staff quickly understand research trends without feeling overwhelmed by long research reports and spreadsheets. Also, these compelling infographics can be printed and put up in teachers' common rooms and offices as a constant reminder of a key issue the school as a whole seeks to address. Infographics are also useful resources for teachers as they develop greater awareness about gender-equity issues and feel confident about broaching them with parents and students. Furthermore, by placing these infographics on a special theme page on the school's website, the school sends a signal to its community on the importance of this issue. These infographics serve as key resources for the process of community reflection, which we describe next.

GUIDING QUESTIONS

- What tools do you currently use to display data?
- What advantages do you perceive in using infographics to show data about gender equity?
- How can tools like infographics help teachers, parents, and community members recognize intersectionality amongst multiple dimensions of diversity?

Reflective Practice With the Community

Because gendered perceptions are deep-seated and often unconscious, Dr. Q started a process of reflective practice with her teachers. One in-service day per semester is designated a Theme Focus day that is attended by teachers, counselors, as well as school staff. This session is used to focus on gender-equity issues in school. Intersections of other dimensions of diversity—such as race, class, and ability—are noted as well.

The Theme Focus day is split into two sections. In the first section Dr. Q and some of the teachers, counselors, and staff present the latest data, short articles, or extracts from articles; YouTube videos that focus on gender equity in schools and colleges; and websites of organizations working to address this issue. This is also when infographics are introduced. The aim is to help the community develop a sense of the issue in its wider contexts, and also of the resources and actions being taken to address it. These items are put into a commonly accessible online space so that they are available and are developed through the year.

In the second section, teachers, counselors, and staff work in groups to discuss gender issues as observed and experienced in their own school community, again with considerations of intersectionality. Through a critical reflective process, they surface actions and verbalizations in the school community that contribute to positive and negative gender experiences in teaching and learning processes. Over time, the hope is that as a result of their attention and actions, they will surface more positive than negative experiences that they can celebrate in their community. This reflection ends with each person making an entry in a special journal they have each received for this purpose. As a follow-up through the semester, they use a set of self-observation and reflection questions at designated times and make further entries in their journal. They are asked to share some of these with their colleagues in a non-public wiki space. These reflections, augmented by a school environment of visuals/infographics and actions or mini-programs (described below), form the basis for discussion at the next Theme Focus day. This reflective practice helps all members of the community in developing a critical awareness of their own gendered discourse and actions, which is the first step toward positive change.

Involving Students as Part of the Solution

Empowering students (and, by extension, their families) to shift their own narratives of gender is critical in helping teachers and school staff to develop more aware and intentional narratives themselves. In the last part of each Theme Focus day, teachers, counselors, and staff work together to plan specific initiatives for the semester that involve students both as creators/implementers and as recipients or audience. Being mindful of the scarcity of resources and time, they focus efforts on creating small but significant tactics, although at times they have also launched larger-scale projects and programs. The following principles guide this work:

1. **Interdepartment Collaboration.** Planning mini-projects involving multiple subject areas, or where teachers work with administrative staff and/or parents, helps spread the load. At the same time, engaging different stakeholders in conversation supports reflective practice at a school-wide level and is more effective in transforming the school's educational culture.
2. **Experiential Tactics or Projects.** The more any project or tactic is rooted in the children's real-world experience, the more powerful its transformative power. Children are more likely to have authentic conversations and reflections.
3. **Student-Centered Projects.** Students engage more deeply when they participate through opportunities to propose ideas and be involved in the project design. When given such agency, they are more likely to passionately and deeply embrace the cause of gender equity, taking it into their own lives and communities.
4. **Community Inclusion and Engagement.** Projects have stronger transformative power in the lives of students if the voices and actions of their families are also engaged. There is deeper relevance and authenticity when relevant community members are included and invited to interact with students, staff, and teachers.
5. **Documentation.** It is important to document the activities to present them back to the community as a way of engaging reflection and deeper learning. Documenting also helps track data on the school's progress in addressing inequities over time, which, again, helps develop awareness.

Below, we briefly describe several examples of tactics and programs that Dr. Q and colleagues have used.

- Teachers from different departments (Art, History, English, Math, Technology) created a project in which students from different grade levels researched gender narratives (written and visual) over time and created a poster and multimedia exhibition. In doing the project, the teachers ensured that many subject standards were met. The project offered experiential learning to many students, as well as created a significant buzz in raising awareness for the entire community including families. A survey was done before and after the project that showed a shift in attitude among the students, teachers, and families.

- Staff and counselors ran a Twitter project, #Whynot?, over a four-week period where students were invited to post tweets that completed the prompt "Why can't a boy . . .?" or "Why can't a girl . . .?" The discussion was live and available to the school community.

- The school counselors and some teachers ran lunchtime focus groups where students were invited to eat lunch together with a counselor or teacher to discuss gender issues in the classroom and how they could respond positively.

- School counselors worked with students to research and create posters and palm cards of women, especially women of color, in STEM careers that were placed in classrooms, hallways, restrooms, and the cafeteria. Students worked to find local businesses to help fund the projects' printing costs.

- To help students and themselves become more acutely aware of unconscious gender issues, many teachers ran a *5 Minutes for 5 Weeks* project where they used the first five minutes of each of their classes to have a snap discussion with the question, "What gender issue did you notice today?" Students could raise any gender/race perspective (positive or negative) that they observed in school as well as in the wider community, from bullying and sexual harassment to teen pregnancy issues or stereotypic remarks.

- Math and technology teachers ran a web-based project where students found and presented an annotated list of websites showcasing women in STEM, past and present.

- The school invited successful women (particularly focusing on Latinas, African American, Asian American, and Pacific Islander women) in STEM from the local community to give lunchtime talks in an informal setting that also allowed students to mingle with these women and ask questions.

- Some teachers worked with students to interview their mothers and other female relatives in a project called *If I Could Have Dreamt It. . .* on career choices they feel young female students today could aspire to, especially students of color. The English and Drama teachers worked with students to use material from these interviews to create an Open Mic session in English and Spanish to which families and the wider community were invited. Students were invited to respond to the narratives from the Open Mic event and post creative responses on the Open Mic blog. The teachers and students plan to run a parallel project focused on boys to surface and address career stereotypes they come up against.

- The teachers developed a classroom observation tool that included items on gendering discourse and actions. Dr. Q used this in visiting classrooms to observe teachers. Some teachers set up video cameras to record themselves so they could do self-observations. Some teachers, who felt comfortable doing so, invited students to give them feedback as well as a way of simultaneously raising their awareness of gendered narratives.

- As a way of grounding data in her own community, Dr. Q asked her Math department to work with students on a special project tracking gender equity data from their school to create infographics for the community. These are presented together with the infographics on national trends on the website and in physical locations in school with the question, "Are we doing better?" This creates interest and motivation to focus on the issue and take steps to improve gender equity in school.

- The teachers have proposed parents' in-service sessions that can be held on weekends or evenings to reach out to as many families as possible.

GUIDING QUESTIONS

- Which of the tactics and programs described above strike you as most salient and applicable to your school community?
- In these examples, which of the key principles do you see:
  - Interdepartment Collaboration
  - Experiential Tactics or Projects
  - Student-Centered Projects
  - Community Inclusion and Engagement
  - Documentation
- Do you see ways to adapt any of these tactics and programs to apply to other dimensions of diversity beyond gender?

Applications Across PreK–12

While the case study is set in a high-school context, the three main strategies for transformative practice to address gender inequities are translatable to elementary and middle school settings. Elementary and middle school leaders can implement the first two strategies of using data, especially in the form of strongly visual infographics, and of developing a reflective practice with teachers and staff to surface and address gendered assumptions and narratives. Many tactics in the third strategy of involving students can be adapted to different ages and abilities by paying attention to the operating principles listed above.

Some Examples of Projects or Tactics in Lower Grades

- Have children explore children's books and do a simple counting exercise to see how many times different genders and people of color are shown as main characters. They can make simple posters to present this information.
- Ensure each classroom has storybooks that present fewer gendered perspectives or that question gendered perspectives, such as *The Paperbag Princess*, *Ballerino Nate,* or *Oliver Button Is a Sissy*.
- Run the same *5 Minutes for 5 Weeks* tactic in classes as above, but provide a more structured frame for conversation around the concept of how people are different. Pick one specific topic, for example, "bullying" or "girly girls and tomboys," rather than have students come up with something.
- Make a collective art project that celebrates variation, diversity, and being different. Help children make a list or collage of words and images to celebrate all the ways in which human beings are different—gender, race, height, hair type, hair color, favorite games, etc. In one class, the teacher put this on a bulletin board in the hallway and other children and classes added to it.
- Have upper-grade children do simple research projects on gender (for example, famous women) and do classroom visits to lower grades to share their stories.

CONCLUSION

This case study reinforces the importance of keeping a long-term focus on gender using all possible resources, including state and local data. Without the proactive guidance of school and district leaders, counternarratives to gender stereotypes will not be offered and/or embraced. Leaders should take every opportunity to present data showing the gender similarities of academic performance to parents and other community members. Regarding mathematics, leaders should emphasize that gender differences are so small that stereotypical beliefs are more likely to affect girls' self-efficacy than ability (Hyde & Lindberg, 2007). Leaders must disaggregate test score and other achievement data by gender and race/ethnicity to help teachers learn how females and males across different groups perform in math, science, and related subject areas (Lacampagne, Campbell, Damarin, Herzig, & Vogt (2007). Collecting and analyzing data disaggregated by race/ethnicity, gender, and socioeconomic status is necessary to address the inequities that would otherwise not be revealed simply by focusing on one of the marginalizing factors. Dyslexia is a case in point. Klein et al. (2007) argue that since dyslexia occurs three-and-a-half times more often in boys than girls, collecting such data allows leaders to provide appropriate resources to their reading teachers and to discover cases of over- or under-representation in the school population.

As research on classrooms and school buildings indicates (DiPrete & Buchmann, 2013), gender identities constructed in the classrooms and reinforced in schools affect students' interactions and approaches to learning. Our earlier anecdotal evidence from voices in the community reinforced this understanding. Compliant behavior and enthusiasm for school will continue to be mistaken for learning. Stromquist and Fischman (2009) advocate recurrent gender training to all educators, and to parents and communities through what they call "undoing gender" to create contexts and agency that are "less dichotomous in terms of masculinity and femininity and more democratic, demanding equal rights for all" (p. 469). Therefore, once sensitized to the gendering practices enacted in these arenas, school principals and other instructional coaches who spend large amounts of time observing teachers and students must make the effort to shed light on what is going on. Without deliberate intervention, under the weight of local cultures and societal gender stereotypes, gendered learning environments will surely be perpetuated to no one's advantage. As Dr. Q hopes to accomplish in our case study, principals who attend to gender using disaggregated data, resources, and dialogue are likely to contribute to the power of education to provide all students with the optimal learning opportunities based on individual passions and interest instead of on limiting notions of femininities and masculinities.

We began this chapter noting how gendered identities were part of the Enlightenment narratives of rationality used in the educational imperatives in founding this nation. This reinforces historical gendered cultural memes that permeate all aspects of society and that shape our perceptions and actions. Gendered responses are not easy to become aware of and harder still to shift. We articulate our lives as gendered beings. However, as educators preparing our students for their futures, we can help change the game for them. In fact, since schools provide a large part of the environment in which gender identities and perceptions are formed starting in kindergarten, then, they are powerful spaces in which we can counter negative social narratives of gender. School offers some of the best opportunities for shifting values and changing mindsets in ways that will not only enhance how both boys and girls learn and achieve scholastically, but will also prepare them to be more informed and ethical citizens of the world. And in many ways, if we succeed in creating greater gender equity in school, we will actually be truly realizing the principles of equality and freedom. Our imperative as leaders, then, is to first become aware and then to act in order to help our communities move toward more mindful and intentional responses toward gender in our classrooms and homes. The important thing to bear in mind is that these ancient and deep-seated gendered values and perceptions are not inevitable. We do have a choice in how we shape gender narratives for the future.

EQUITY AUDIT QUESTIONS

There are many equity audit questions related to gender that we recommend school leaders use. The final chapter of this text describes a comprehensive equity audit process. See the gender section and full equity audit detailed in Chapter 10 and online (www.routledge.com/cw/theoharis). Getting answers to these questions allows leaders, staff, and stakeholders to lay the groundwork for creating inclusive schools with regards to gender through a data-informed process.

NOTES

1 Banksy is the pseudonym of a white street artist and political activist in the U.K. His work has received global acclaim.
2 The terms Latino/a and Hispanic are used interchangeably in this chapter.
3 The standards were based on a report, *Greatness by design: Supporting outstanding teachers to sustain a golden state*, by the Educator Excellence Task Force that was commissioned by the California Department of Education (2012) and the Commission on Teacher Credentialing.
4 Infographics or information graphics are visual ways of representing any kind of data in order to show patterns and trends, which are easier for the mind to process visually. They are also sometimes known as "edugraphics." Graphs, charts, maps, symbols, and images are combined with clear text that all together present a single point or "story" about something. Edward Tufte's (1982) seminal book *The Visual Display of Quantitative Information* describes the graphic or visual display of data as being more revealing than conventional presentations of statistical information, especially when working with large amounts of data. Some examples can be found in the Resource List.

REFERENCES

AAUW. (2010). *Improve girls' and women's opportunities in science, technology, engineering, and math.* Retrieved from http://www.aauw.org/files/2013/02/position-on-STEM-education-111.pdf

Arms, E. (2007). Gender equity in co-educational and single sex educational environments. In S. Klein, B. Richardson, D. A. Grayson, L. H. Fox, C. Kramarae, D. Pollard, & C. A. Dwyer (Eds.), *Handbook for achieving gender equity through education* (2nd ed., pp. 171–190). Florence, KY: Erlbaum.

Ashcraft, C., Eger, E., & Friend, M. (2012). *Girls in IT: The facts.* Retrieved from http://www.ncwit.org/resources/girls-it-facts

Bogotch, I. E. (2002). Educational leadership and social justice: Practice into theory. *Journal of School Leadership, 12,* 138–156.

California Department of Education. (2012). *Greatness by design: Supporting outstanding teaching to sustain a golden state.* Retrieved from http://www.cde.ca.gov/eo/in/documents/greatnessfinal.pdf

Ceci, S.J., & Williams, W.M. (2011). Understanding current causes of women's underrepresentation in science. *Proceedings of the National Academy of the Science, 108*(8), 3157–3162, doi: 10.1073/pnas.1014871108

Connell, R. (2009). *Gender* (2nd ed.). Malden, MA: Polity Press.

Corbett, C., Hill, C., & St. Rose, A. (2008). *Where the girls are: The facts about gender equity in education.* Washington, DC: AAUW.

Cott, N. F. (1997). *The bonds of womanhood* (2nd ed.). New Haven, CT: Yale University Press.

Curran, E., & Murray, M. (2008). Transformative learning in teacher education: Building competencies and changing dispositions. *Journal of the Scholarship of Teaching and Learning, 8*(3), 108–118.

Datnow, A., & Hubbard, L. (2002). *Gender in policy and practice: Perspectives on single-sex and coeducational schooling.* New York: Routledge Falmer.

DiPrete, T.A., & Buchmann, C. (2013). *The rise of women.* New York: Russell Sage Foundation.

Fine, C. (2010). *Delusions of gender: How our minds, society and neurosexism create difference.* New York: W. W. Norton & Company.

Foley, D., Levinson, B.A., & Hurtig, J. (2000). Anthropology goes inside: The new ethnographer of ethnicity and gender. *Review of Research in Education, 25,* 37–97.

Frattura, E., & Capper, C. (2007). *Leadership for social justice in practice: Integrated comprehensive services for all learners.* Thousand Oaks, CA: Corwin Press.

Furman, G. (2012). Social justice leadership as praxis: Developing capacities through preparation programs. *Educational Administration Quarterly, 48*(2), 191–229.

Grogan, M. (1999). Equity/equality issues of gender, race and class. *Educational Administration Quarterly, 35*(4), 518–536.

Hansen, A. (2014, April). *The link between teen pregnancy and high school dropouts.* Retrieved from http://stateimpact.npr.org/ohio/2014/04/03/the-link-between-teen-pregnancy-and-high-school-dropouts/

Hill, C., & Kearl, H. (2011). *Crossing the line: Sexual harassment at school.* Washington, DC: AAUW.

Hoff Summers, C. (2000). *The war against boys: How misguided feminism is harming our young men.* New York: Simon & Schuster.

Hyde, J., & Lindberg, S.M. (2007). Facts and assumptions about the nature of gender differences and the implications for gender equity. In S. Klein, B. Richardson, D.A. Grayson, L. H. Fox, C. Kramarae, D. Pollard, & C.A. Dwyer (Eds), *Handbook for achieving gender equity through education* (2nd ed., pp. 19–32). Florence, KY: Erlbaum.

Hyde, J. S. & Mertz, J. E. (2009). Gender, culture, and mathematics performance. *Proceedings of the National Academy of Sciences, 106*(2), 8801–8807.

Jones, S., & Dindia, K. (2004). A meta-analytic perspective on sex equity in the classroom. *Review of Educational Research, 74*(4), 443–471.

Kerber, L. K. (1980). *Women of the republic: Intellect and ideology in revolutionary America.* Chapel Hill: University of North Carolina Press.

Klein, S.S. (2008). *Gender equity information on state education agency (SEA) websites.* Retrieved from http://www.feminist.org/education/Title%20IX%20on%20State%20Education%20Websites%20Report%20603.pdf

Klein, S., Homer, E.A., Kramarae, C., Nash, M.A., Burger, C.J., & Shevitz, L. (2007). Summary and recommendations for achieving gender equity in and through education. In S. Klein, B. Richardson, D.A. Grayson, L.H. Fox, C. Kramarae, D. Pollard, & C.A. Dwyer (Eds), *Handbook for achieving gender equity through education* (2nd ed., pp. 655–682). Florence, KY: Erlbaum.

Lacampagne, C., Campbell, P.B., Damarin, S., Herzig, A., & Vogt, C. (2007). Gender equity in mathematics. In S. Klein, B. Richardson, D.A. Grayson, L.H. Fox, C. Kramarae, D. Pollard, & C.A. Dwyer (Eds). *Handbook for achieving gender equity through education* (2nd ed., pp. 235–254). Florence, KY: Erlbaum.

Langer, E.J. (1997). *The power of mindful thinking.* Boston, MA: DeCapo Press.

Langer, E.J., & Moldoveanu, M. (2000). The construct of mindfulness. *Journal of Social Issues, 56*(1), 1–9.

Mangel, L. (2010, October). *Teen pregnancy, discrimination and the dropout rate.* Retrieved from https://aclu-wa.org/blog/teen-pregnancy-discrimination-and-the-dropout-rate

Marshall, C. (1993). The new politics of race and gender. In C. Marshall (Ed.), *The new politics of race and gender: The 1992 yearbook of the politics of education association* (pp. 1–6). Washington, DC: Falmer.

Miettinen, R. (2000). The concept of experiential learning and John Dewey's theory of reflective thought and action. *International Journal of Lifelong Education, 19*(1), 54–72.

Moller, S., Stearns, E., Southworth, S., & Potochnick, S. (2013). Changing course: The gender gap in college selectivity and opportunities to learn in the high school curriculum. *Gender and Education, 25*(7), 851–871.

Morris, E. W. (2007). "Ladies" or "loudies"?: Perception and experiences of black girls in classrooms. *Youth Society, 38*(4), 490–515.

Morris, E. W. (2012). *Learning the hard way: Masculinity, place, and the gender gap in education.* New Brunswick, NJ: Rutgers University Press.

National Coalition for Women and Girls in Education (NCWGE). (2012). *Title IX at 40: Working to ensure gender equity in education.* Retrieved from http://ncwge.org/TitleIX40/TitleIX-print.pdf

National Coalition for Women and Girls in Education (NCWGE). (2014). Retrieved from http://ncwge.org/STEM.html

Noguera, P. (2008). *The trouble with black boys: . . . And other reflections on race, equity and the future of public education.* San Francisco, CA: Jossey-Bass.

Office of Adolescent Health. (2014, June). *Trends in teen pregnancy and childbearing.* Retrieved from http://www.hhs.gov/ash/oah/adolescent-health-topics/reproductive-health/teen-pregnancy/trends.html

Paludi, M. A., Martin, J., & Paludi, C. A. (2007). Sexual harassment: The hidden gender equity problem. In S. Klein, B. Richardson, D. A. Grayson, L. H. Fox, C. Kramarae, D. Pollard, & C. A. Dwyer (Eds), *Handbook for achieving gender equity through education* (2nd ed., pp. 215–230). Florence, KY: Erlbaum.

Perkins, L. M. (1997). The African American female elite: The early history of African American women in the Seven Sister Colleges, 1880–1960. *Harvard Educational Review, 67*(4), 718–756.

Ridgeway, C. (1993). Gender, status and the social psychology of expectations. In P. England (Ed.), *Theory on gender: Feminism on theory* (pp. 175–198). New York: Aldine De Gruyter.

Riordan, C. (1990). *Girls and boys in school. Together or separate?* New York: Teachers College Press.

Robinson, J. P., & Lubienski, S. T. (2011). The development of gender achievement gaps in mathematics and reading during elementary and middle school: Examining direct cognitive assessments and teacher ratings. *American Educational Research Journal, 48*(2), 268–302.

Rush, B. (1787). *Thoughts upon female education.* Philedelphia: Prichard & Hall.

Sadker, M., & Sadker D. (1994). *Failing at fairness: How our schools cheat girls.* New York: Scribner.

Sadker, D., Sadker, M., & Zittleman, K. (2009). *Still failing at fairness: How gender bias cheats girls and boys in school and what we can do about it.* [Kindle iPad version]. doi: 8086862–4492121

Sax, L. (2007). *Boys adrift.* New York: Basic Books.

Scanlan, M., & Lopez, F. (2012). Vamos! How school leaders promote equity and excellence for bilingual students. *Educational Administration Quarterly, 48*(4), 583–625.

Shields, C. M. (2011). Transformative leadership: An introduction. In C. M. Shields (Ed.), *Transformative leadership: A reader* (pp. 1–20). New York: Peter Lang Publishing.

Stromquist, N. P., & Fischman, G. E. (2009). Introduction—from denouncing gender inequities to undoing gender in education: Practices and programs toward change in the social relations of gender. *International Review of Education, 55*, 463–482. doi: 10.1007/s11159–009–9146-z

Theoharis, G. (2007). Social justice educational leaders and resistance: Towards a theory of social justice leadership. *Educational Administration Quarterly, 43*(2), 221–258.

Theoharis, G., & O'Toole, J. (2011). Leading inclusive ELL: Social justice leadership for English language learners. *Educational Administration Quarterly, 47*(4), 646–688.

Tufte, E. R. (1982). *The visual display of quantitative information.* Cheshire, CT: Graphics Press.

US Department of Education. (2012). *Gender equity in education: A data snapshot.* Retrieved from http://www2.ed.gov/about/offices/list/ocr/docs/gender-equity-in-education.pdf

Vasudevan, L., & Campano, G. (2009). The social production of adolescent risk and the promise of adolescent literacies. *Review of Research in Education, 33*, 310–353.

West, C., & Fenstermaker, S. (1993). Power, inequality and the accomplishment of gender: An ethnomethodological view. In P. England (Ed.), *Theory on gender: Feminism on theory* (pp. 151–174). New York: Aldine De Gruyter.

Wortham, S. (2004). The interdependence of social identification and learning. *American Educational Research Journal, 41*(3), 715–750.

CHAPTER 8

Inclusive Leadership and Religion

Joanne M. Marshall

> Religion and education share a characteristic that so many human activities lack: they matter.
> (Carter, 1993)

PART 1: THE CURRENT CONTEXT OF RELIGION IN SCHOOLS

Religious belief is one of the United States' hot-button topics. It matters, as Stephen Carter says above, to a lot of people. In this chapter I unpack how it matters for inclusive leadership in schools. I begin with a short review of US history and demographics, which illuminates how religion and public schooling began together, and how religion gets enacted in public schooling now.

History, in Brief

The Puritans, who were Protestant Christians dissenting from the practices of the Church of England, founded a version of public schools in 1647 for the purpose of teaching children to read the Bible (Nord, 1995). Horace Mann (1855, 1872), who is credited for establishing the state-wide, publicly funded model of public schools that we know today, argued in the mid-1800s that such schools were needed both to create democratic citizens and to create *good Christians* (emphasis added). Mann defined "good Christian" only as "non-sectarian," which was code then for "not Mormon."

This dominant vision of non-sectarianism was challenged by waves of Catholic immigrants (mostly German and Irish) who questioned the daily practice in schools of reading from the Protestant Bible. Shouldn't their Bible also be included? Anti-Catholic and anti-immigrant sentiment was strong. At its worst, in 1844, when the Philadelphia school board ruled that Catholic students could use the Catholic Bible, riots broke out killing 13 people, burning two Catholic churches and several homes, and wounding more than 50 (Ahlstrom,

1972; Nord, 1995). Eventually, in the face of continued Protestant opposition, Catholic leaders formed a separate system of parochial schools, which remains today.[1]

Because of the public funding model, and because of the way schools are usually governed by locally elected boards, schools continue to be closely tied to their communities. The savvy school leader will analyze her community's religious demographics as closely as she analyzes its social demographics and tax base.

Changing Religious Demographics and Non-Homogeneous Groups

The United States is a country that is more religious than most others in the world, whether measured by weekly attendance at a religious service or measured by religious belief (Kelley & de Graaf, 1997; Norris & Inglehart, 2011). It is largely Christian, as claimed by 73% of the adult population in 2010, though what used to be a Protestant majority has been slowly shrinking (Pew Forum on Religion and Public Life, 2012b). Compared to the rest of the world, the United States is "moderately" diverse religiously, ranking 68th of the 232 countries and territories measured by the Pew Forum on Religion and Public Life (2014). Our diverse ethnic groups have contributed to this religious diversity (Eck, 2001; Kosmin & Lachman, 1993; Marshall, 2006), though most new immigrants are Christian (Pew Forum on Religion and Public Life, 2013b).

The biggest change in religious demographics has been a steadily increasing group, now at nearly 20%, of people who do not claim a religious affiliation (Pew Forum on Religion and Public Life, 2012b). Sociologists have speculated about why the number of people "unaffiliated" with religion has been increasing. The most common theory is that young people are less religious, so that as the US population ages, fewer people claim a religious affiliation (Kosmin, Keysar, Cragun, & Navarro-Rivera, 2008). It's not clear why young people are less religious, but "unaffiliated" belief is correlated with similar belief of one's parents, peers, and social networks (Baker & Smith, 2009). Regardless of cause, those who identify as "unaffiliated" have diverse beliefs. For example, about two-thirds of people who say they are unaffiliated also say they believe in God (Pew Forum on Religion and Public Life, 2012b). Unaffiliated people may have religious belief but are not part of an organized religious group. They may belong to a "diffuse" religious tradition, such as Confucianism, rather than an institutionalized religion (Tang, in press; Yang, 1961) They may claim to be spiritual but not religious. The important fact to note is that they are not a homogeneous group.

In fact, no religious group is homogeneous. As with people in other demographic categories, such as race or gender or social class, religious people within one group are not all alike. People may belong to a religious group because one or both parents practice it. They may belong because they are born into a particular ethnic tradition, like Judaism or Greek Orthodoxy. They may belong because they have married into a faith tradition, or because they have studied a tradition and adopted it as their own. They may have changed their beliefs over time, retaining elements of one tradition, adopting new ones, and discarding others.

While sociologists can track religious demographics by affiliation, people within that affiliation are not homogeneous because individuals can have different beliefs and practices. One person identifying as Catholic could attend Mass once a month, serve each week in the church soup kitchen, disagree with the Church's position on birth control and celibacy, and be unsure whether God exists. Another person identifying as Catholic may have grown up attending Catholic schools, married a non-Catholic, pray every day, and attend services only at Christmas and Easter. Is one person more Catholic than the other? While this example is from Catholicism, other religions ask similar questions about religious identity and what key elements are essential to it (see, for example, Pew surveys about core Jewish and Muslim beliefs: Pew Research Center for the People and the Press, 2011; Pew Forum on Religion and Public Life, 2013a). Religious belief or nonbelief in the United States is complex and individualized and contains an element of choice. It is about both belief and practice. One cannot simply label someone as "X" and assume that they hold particular religious beliefs or practice in certain ways.

So while a school leader will seek to discover the religious demographics of her community, she will not make assumptions about everyone's beliefs. Instead, she'll seek to create a school environment that is inclusive of religious belief or nonbelief. This is easy to say, but can be complicated in practice, partly because of the extreme politicization and polarization of religion.

Why Religion Is a Hot-Button Issue

Because religious belief is a deeply personal matter, a combination of one's upbringing and one's choice, people tend to have strong opinions about it. In addition, two social forces make religion particularly contentious. First, while Protestant Christianity has been embedded in US public schooling from the schools' founding, courts have been interpreting the First Amendment to make public schools less explicitly religious (McCarthy, 2009; Russo, 2003). Many baby boomers, for example, grew up saying the (Christian) Lord's Prayer in school, a practice ruled unconstitutional in *School District of Abington Township, Pennsylvania v. Schempp* (1963). The second force at work is the politicization of religious belief, which occurred in the 1980s as the religious right was created as a coalition for the Republican party (for a history of the religious right in education, see Lugg, 2000; and Lugg & Robinson, 2009). The link between politics and religion is central to what James Hunter (1991) termed "the culture wars." In this case, the culture wars are about the place of religion in a democratic and pluralistic society. To portray the sides in very broad strokes: one side feels that we as a society are not religious enough, that our religious freedoms are constrained, that many of our social ills are due to a lack of morality, and that the social ills could be solved if we as a nation would return to the religious values upon which our government was (supposedly) founded. The other side feels that most talk about loss of religious freedom is really only about evangelical Protestant Christian freedom and no one else's, that religion is responsible for wars across the world and does not belong in government at all, and that our nation was actually founded on the separation of church and state, or the freedom *from* religion. This conflict, and its accompanying incivility, is evident on talk shows and in social media, in debates over marriage equality and about reproductive coverage in the Affordable Care Act. It is also aligned with political party, with (very broadly speaking) Republicans ascribing to the first view and Democrats ascribing to the second. According to the Pew Research Center for the People and the Press (2012a), the polarization between Republicans and Democrats is higher now than it has been for the last 25 years.

Naturally, this cultural conflict spills over to all schools, public and private. And understandably, many school leaders want absolutely nothing to do with the conflict, choosing instead to try to preserve neutrality in their schools, often by ignoring religion entirely, especially in a public school. However, ignoring religion or religious belief is a mistake. School leaders have the opportunity to establish a *different* culture in their schools, one that includes religion as a topic and includes people of all beliefs. If schools are instruments of change, then an inclusive school can be an example of how people can discuss religious topics civilly and treat one another's beliefs respectfully. Moreover, if religious belief or unbelief is an important dimension of identity for many individuals, inclusive school leaders must attend to this alongside all the other salient dimensions (as discussed throughout this book).

PART 2: WHAT WE KNOW ABOUT INCLUDING RELIGION AND RELIGIOUS BELIEFS: THE LITERATURE

There are several reasons to include religion or religious belief in schools; in this section I discuss two. The first is about including religion as a topic in curriculum. The second is about including religious or non-religious beliefs of people; about making sure students, staff, and families of all religious beliefs or nonbelief feel a part of the school. I review key literature pertaining to both of these topics. I conclude this section by discussing how religion and religious belief intersect with several other dimensions of diversity.

Including Religion as a Topic in the Curriculum

Several educators and associations have written about the importance of including religion as a topic in the school curriculum. For example, the First Amendment Center (2008) has a *Teacher's Guide to Religion in the Public Schools* and *Teaching about Religion in National and State Social Studies Standards* (Douglass, 2000). In his opinion on the court case that made school prayer unconstitutional, Justice Clark wrote that "one's education is not complete without a study of comparative religion or the history of religion and its relationship to the advancement of civilization" (School District of Abington Township, Pennsylvania v. Schempp, 1963). However, despite world events and the role that religion has played in them, and despite what Nord has called "national consensus" (2010, p. 5) that the study of religion in schools would be valuable, very few K–12 schools offer a comparative religion course. Few offer a course on the Bible as literature, even though understanding Biblical allusions is necessary to understand many Western literary classics. Few include religion as a topic in their curriculum outside of history classes. From equity audits on religion conducted by my students, I can say that hardly any of their school libraries include a religious text other than the Bible. Lugg and Tabbaa-Rida (2006) have written that many educators have confused religious neutrality with silence. When courses or texts do mention religion, they mention only Christianity, thus making that silence "selective" (p. 135).

All of this ignoring of religion as a subject area has led to religious illiteracy, as argued by Prothero (2007) and evidenced by Pew's more recent finding that on average, Americans correctly answer half (16 of 32) of questions about religious knowledge (Pew Forum on Religion and Public Life, 2010).[2] Atheists, agnostics, Jews, and Mormons score best, at 20 out of the 32 correct, on average. At 62% accuracy, most educators' grading scales would evaluate even these higher scores as, at best, barely passing.

Relegating religion to the margins of the curriculum overlooks the force that it is in American society. It ignores its influence in history, politics, law, social structure, culture, and economics. Could Reagan have been elected president without the religious right? Would the Civil Rights movement have occurred without the participation of the Black Church? Would we have acted differently in a War on Terror if we knew more about Islam? Our students can't answer these questions if we are not discussing religion in the curriculum. Our ignorance as a nation is thus perpetuated.

There is some empirical evidence that teaching about world religions in a public school could inform student beliefs, which in turn could influence school culture. Modesto, California's required nine-week religion course not only increased students' knowledge about religion, but also increased their "passive tolerance" and "active respect" for people of other religious beliefs (Lester & Roberts, 2011). The superintendent of that school speculated that a long-term effect of the course might be to help students become better citizens, while the researchers speculated that the pedagogy of the course modeled civil discussion about religion and religious belief. Teachers of this course were given approximately 30 hours of training, including visiting local religious leaders and institutions. While survey results in this study were statistically significant, the researchers wondered if they might be even greater if the course were longer than nine weeks.

Another study that might address that question comes from the United Kingdom, where researchers (Francis & Village, 2014) compared the attitudes toward religious diversity from students who attended religious schools (Catholic, Anglican, joint Anglican and Catholic) with the attitudes of students who attended non-religious schools. Presumably, students in religious schools would have more extensive religious education, at least about their school's stated religion, than the nine-week course taught in Modesto. However, Francis and Village found no difference in attitudes toward diversity based on schooling type. They found more difference at the level of the individual student, where religious students, regardless of the type of school they attended, were more likely to have positive attitudes about religious diversity than non-religious students. Francis and Village conclude that religious schools, as institutions, do just as good a job of preparing students to enter a diverse society as non-religious ones. Both of these studies are limited to students' self-reports about their attitudes about religious diversity, and we have little idea of how those students interacted with people of diverse faiths in daily life. However, they are an attempt to quantify the long-term social effects of religious education on students, with an eye toward how those students might eventually function in a pluralistic society.

Other scholars have written more extensively about ways to include religion throughout the curriculum. Three examples are: *Taking Religion Seriously Across the Curriculum* (Nord & Haynes, 1998), *Does God Make a Difference? Taking Religion Seriously in Our Schools and Universities* (Nord, 2010), and *Teaching about Religions: A Democratic Approach for Public Schools* (Lester, 2011). All of these book-length works posit that religious knowledge is essential to being a well-educated, informed citizen.

Before launching an initiative to incorporate religion into the curriculum I pose some guiding questions for a school leader to ponder or discuss with staff.

GUIDING QUESTIONS

- Where are we already addressing religion in the curriculum? (See the Equity Audit on page 214.)
- How might religion in the curriculum help us meet our current mission or goals?
- Where might religion fit naturally (subject, grade level, unit, assignments)? How can we incorporate it throughout the curriculum in an authentic way instead of as a one-time lesson to be checked off?
- What kind of training would teachers need to have, both in content and in facilitation? How would they get this training, and how much would it cost?
- What local resources (e.g., faith leaders, educational institutions) are available to us and to our students? How might we use or create community partnerships?
- How might family or community fears about the way their own religion is portrayed be allayed?

Including Religious and Non-Religious People

Religious belief is an important part of human identity and development. Yet in teacher and leadership preparation programs and in schools we typically ignore religious belief as an element of identity. In the same way some people still ignore race or ethnicity, claiming to be "color blind," we are "belief blind." Theoharis (2009) has written that the social justice-oriented, inclusive leader is one who "creates a climate of belonging." It is impossible to create such a climate if one is steadfastly ignoring the religious beliefs of students, staff, and families.

Religion, Spirituality, and Identity Development

One does not have to be a religious person to engage in existential questions about one's meaning and purpose in life. Religious people answer these questions from the perspectives of their traditions, but most everyone asks them. Toshalis (2008), who writes about adolescent development, says that adolescents typically ask questions such as:

- Who am I?
- Why am I here?
- What is my purpose?
- How do I make moral decisions?
- Whom should I love and how should I love them?
- What is sacred and what is taboo?
- In what or whom should I place my trust?

(pp. 190–191)

Clearly these existential questions *can* be answered in a religious way. My own tradition, for example, answers the "who am I?" question in its catechism with, "I am a child of God." However, they do not *have to* be answered religiously. Thus, there is a distinction between religion and "faith" or "spirituality." Faith and spirituality are about these deep questions of meaning and purpose. They are more inclusive than religion, which answers the same questions, but through the lens of a particular set of shared beliefs, usually beliefs shared in a particular faith-based community.

Many scholars have argued persuasively that schools are not soulless buildings where students are produced like widgets, but that they are spiritual places where people find meaning and purpose and where they learn to interact with each other and with the world larger than themselves (see, for example, Dantley, 2003; Lantieri, 2001; Palmer, 1983; Purpel, 1989). Others, like Milligan (2000), have pointed out that the distinction between what is religious and what is secular is relatively recent. Some communities, such as the African American community, especially value spirituality, even in school roles (e.g., Dillard, Abdur-Rashid, & Tyson, 2000; Jones, 2010; Witherspoon & Taylor, 2010). If one conceptualizes spirituality as being concerned with meaning and purpose, then schools can function as a spiritual community, where people work together toward a common, even moral, purpose, caring for each other and those around them. Inclusive leaders can be spiritual leaders as defined by Fullan (2002), those who are engaged with a "deeper sense of purpose," which "invites everyone to be a moral/spiritual contributor . . . in a thousand small ways through everyday behavior."

Including Communities of Belief

In addition to the community formed within a school, school leaders recognize the importance of partnering with community groups outside the school to share resources and gain trust (see Scanlan and Johnson, next chapter). Those community partnerships can include local religious communities. The research on social capital indicates that religious communities can be an important resource for students, because they provide an additional network of people who care about and support the student (Bauch, 2001; Bryk, Lee, & Holland, 1993; Jordan & Nettles, 1999; McGrath, Swisher, Elder, & Conger, 2001; Muller & Ellison, 2001). Religious communities can be especially supportive for students of color, perhaps because of the values and beliefs imparted and reinforced by a religious social system (Brown & Gary, 1991), or perhaps because parents who are involved in a religious community have better relationships with and stronger educational aspirations for their children (Sikkink & Hernández, 2003), or perhaps the church provides role models and celebrations of success (Barrett, 2010). One study found that churchgoing by African American students' friends and family was positively associated with students' GPAs and negatively related to school suspensions (Williams, Davis, Saunders, & Williams, 2002). The causes for these positive religious effects are not fully understood by religious sociologists, but Christian Smith (2003), who has studied the religion of adolescents extensively, has developed a theoretical model outlining nine contributing factors.

It may be more difficult for leaders to engage with members of some religious communities than others. It is easy to reach out to an Interfaith Alliance or Ecumenical Council, with clerics or representatives from many groups. It is harder if a school family seems to be the only local practitioner of a faith tradition, or if the tradition itself may or may not be associated with a religious institution. Some families are also going to practice their faith privately. For example, while there may or may not be a Hindu temple nearby, 78% of Hindu families keep a shrine in their home (Pew Forum on Religion and Public Life, 2012a). However, if an inclusive leader has created a space for all beliefs to be welcomed and all voices to be heard, these more private families will still feel included.

Religious communities can and should be included in school activities. However, it is vital to provide guidelines for participation. While, for example, school tragedy often leads to calling in religious grief counselors, those occasions are not intended to be opportunities for converting someone from one belief to another.

School leaders also need to be aware of the public nature of their role, recognizing that their own beliefs and practices are public, particularly in smaller communities. If they belong to a faith tradition, for example, that excludes women from leadership, they should be aware of how others' perception of that tradition might influence their own relationships with women in their school and community. School and local communities also sometimes expect their school leader to be involved in a religious organization as a symbol of her community involvement, whether or not the leader is religious. One school leader I know, who does not consider himself religious, rotates his weekly church attendance among the congregations in his school district, appearing at each one to meet and greet students and their families. He believes this rotation improves school and community connections.

A spiritual autobiography tool for a leader to reflect on his or her own practices is included later in the chapter. The following Guiding Questions can help inclusive school leaders reflect on how to engage with their communities around these matters.

GUIDING QUESTIONS

- What is the moral purpose of our school community? Is it shared across constituencies?
- What faith groups are institutionalized and visible in my faith community (see the Equity Audit on page 214)? Which ones might I be missing? Who can tell me?

- Which belief groups are dominant in this community? What can I do to ensure I listen to and involve those who are less dominant?
- Is there a local Interfaith Alliance or similar group with whom I could work? How can I involve them in the moral purpose of our school community?

Intersections Across Communities: Religion and Race/Ethnicity, Language, and Sexual Orientation

While this section has discussed religious demographics and practices across the nation and in schools, it is worth noting that religion intersects with other dimensions of identity identified in this book, such as race/ethnicity, language, gender, and socioeconomic status. A few key intersectionalities are discussed below.

The Intersection of Religion and Race/Ethnicity

Religion is inextricably linked to ethnic identity, often because religions are formed in a particular geographic region. Native Americans, Punjab Sikhs, Scottish Presbyterians, or Tibetan Vajrayanan Buddhists all hail from a specific place and share other cultural characteristics such as language. Immigration and geographic mobility are two of the factors that have contributed to the United States' religious pluralism. However, as mentioned earlier, Christianity is still the dominant religion both within the United States and within public schools.

A 2006 special issue of *Equity and Excellence in Education* addresses ethnoreligious oppression, or the "interactions of ethnic identity with religious oppression in schools and in society" (Joshi, 2006a, p. 178). For example, Joshi (2006b) has written about the racialization of religion, where religion and physical features are conflated. Using South Asian Americans as an example, she notes that

> The ascription of "X" racial features to the tenets of religion "Y" leads easily to the presumption that all people who look like "X" share a belief in "Y." Hinduism, Sikhism, and Islam are presumed to be theologically similar because their adherents are racially similar. Of course, nothing could be further from the truth.
>
> (p. 219)

She also cautions that people should not lump faith traditions together as "Eastern":

> Used most often to connote Islam, Hinduism, Sikhism, and Buddhism, the phrase ["Eastern religions"] represents a host of flawed and troubling assumptions. It implies that religions with widely divergent practices, beliefs, and scriptures are theologically similar or even derivative of one another. By ascribing geography to theology, it inaccurately characterizes Islam, diminishing it from a global religion followed by people of all races—and, indeed, one of the three Abrahamic faiths—to something merely distant and exotic.
>
> (p. 219)

The inclusive school leader will try to learn as much as possible about religions, especially those represented within her school.

Members of minority religions have experienced discrimination in their school communities since the tragedies of 9/11 (Ghaffar-Kucher, 2012; Guo, 2011; Jandali, 2012; Sirin & Katsiaficas, 2011; Zehr, 2001). But the negative experiences of students and staff who are not Christian predate 9/11. Zine (2000), for example, analyzed the resistant strategies of Islamic students to being marginalized in Canadian schools, and called then for inclusive schools, which, she said, move "beyond bland celebrations of diversity found within multicultural paradigms and involve a critical approach to issues of social justice and ethno-cultural equity in education" (p. 312). Zine's challenge to inclusive leaders is as relevant now as it was then.

In addition to the intersection of religion with ethnicity, religion intersects broadly with race and racial history in the United States. The African American experience, for example, is closely entwined with the Black Church, largely Protestant Christian.[3] In establishing a community of leaders, operating its own (sometimes secret) schools, and mobilizing against political and economic oppression from Whites, the Church has been a strong social force (see, for example, Anderson, 1988; Fraser, 1999; Frazier & Lincoln, 1974; Lincoln & Mamiya, 1990; Perry, Steele, & Hilliard, 2003). The Church has continued to be active in communities. In their study of the activism of the Church, Billingsley and Caldwell (1991) found that nearly 70% of Black churches were operating one or more programs in their communities, 60% operated two or more programs, and nearly half operated three or more programs; 76.5% of the churches reported that they were cooperating with local schools. This activism may seem like more than that of White congregations. In an analysis comparing the community involvement of Black and White churches, Chaves and Higgins (1992) found that congregations were generally equally active, but that Black congregations were more active in civil rights and in serving meals, community development, and health education. An update of the Chaves and Higgins study (Tsitsos, 2003) again found no difference in level of activity between Black and White congregations, and more mixed results about the types of community activities congregations choose. School leaders can work with local African American congregations and know that their members have a long and effective history of community activism. Jeynes (2012) has identified three types of opportunities for schools and congregations to work together: mentoring, supplementary courses such as tutoring or technology, and summer programs.

The Intersection of Religion and Language

Related to the intersection of religion and ethnicity is the intersection of religion and language, particularly for new immigrants. Participation in a religious group can be a way for new immigrants to feel "at home" in the United States. Ebaugh (2003) summarizes the role of religious participation in a new country:

> Religious institutions provide social and physical space and social networks that help the immigrants reproduce and maintain their values, traditions, and customs in the midst of an often alienating and strange American society. Religion is intricately interwoven with cultural values and practices so that it becomes a way of reproducing many aspects of immigrants' native cultures for themselves and their children.
>
> (p. 230)

The networks, or social capital, that religious communities provide for immigrants is one explanation Akresh (2010) offers for her finding that immigrants tend to increase their religious attendance as they are in the United States longer, even when controlling for the frequency of their past practice in their home country. The space that immigrants create, whether "informal places of worship, including house churches, scriptural study groups, paraliturgical groups, domestic altars, and neighborhood festivals" (Ebaugh, 2003, p. 227) or formal places of worship, serve dual purposes of providing religious ritual and socialization.

Knowing this pattern of religious socialization and the types of religious and social spaces that immigrants create can help the inclusive school leader establish relationships with these families in his community. Establishing those relationships can help make families feel more welcome and foster their involvement in schools, both of which are recommended by Scanlan (2011) for meeting the needs of linguistically diverse students.

Ebaugh (2003) has commented that many new arrivals, particularly Hindus and Buddhists, do not perceive social services as the work of a religious community, so do not expect their own religious and social spaces to deliver them. Instead, those services tend to be delivered by Interfaith Alliances and mainline Protestant congregations. These other, native-born religious organizations are a second religiously based entry point for a school leader to serve linguistically diverse students, particularly if that wise leader has already been communicating and working with his Interfaith Alliance and local congregations about issues and families they share in common.

The Intersection of Religion and Sexual Orientation

Social justice leaders must also balance the two sometimes-competing issues of religious belief and sexual orientation. Although some Christian religious traditions are deliberately inclusive of lesbian, gay, bisexual, transgender, and questioning (LGBTQ) people, the two largest US Christian traditions, Catholicism and evangelical Protestant Christianity, are not. However, as noted already, individuals sharing a common religious affiliation may represent a wide array of beliefs. More Catholics support same-sex marriage (52% vs. 37%) even though the Catholic Church officially does not; whereas more White evangelical Protestants (74%) and Black Protestants (62%) are against it (Pew Research Center for the People and the Press, 2012b). But even when there is a clear majority opinion within a religious affiliation, as just mentioned, 30% to 40% of people within the same denomination disagree. So a school leader cannot immediately assume—not that she would leap to such an assumption anyway—that since this person goes to that church or comes from that background, he must be homophobic. However, there is a solid research base indicating that one of the strongest predictors of anti-gay attitudes in the general American public has been how strong a person's religious belief and practice are, or how important religious belief is to him, regardless of faith tradition (Cotten-Huston & Waite, 1999; Herek, 1994; Hicks & Lee, 2006; Whitley, 2009), and it would be disingenuous to overlook that research base.

The tension between religious belief and sexual orientation has surfaced in my own classroom of future school leaders, as I've written with Frank Hernandez elsewhere (Marshall & Hernandez, 2013). I've learned to address that tension head-on by acknowledging that it is a conflict for some people, and affirming the importance of religious belief, if that is something someone holds dear, for sustaining one's own well-being as an administrator. I tell my students that the conflict makes me worry about the safety and social dynamics of my own classroom. I tell them the story of a former student years ago who stated emphatically that he didn't think he could work with a gay person, while, unbeknownst to him, he sat next to a student who had come out to me personally, but not to the rest of the class. Ironically, he had *already* been working with a person who was gay. I ask them to consider how that person might have felt. I ask myself, and them, if perhaps that person had not come out to the rest of the class because s/he knew it wasn't a safe space, or that s/he would face condemnation like this from a colleague?

We've had good conversations thus far. In their reflections on sexual orientation and their reflections on religion, my students have noted that they will undoubtedly face resistance from some of their community members if they advocate for their students who are LGBTQ, but that they see it as their duty to do so.

The First Amendment Center has partnered with various organizations, including the American Association of School Administrators, Christian Educators Association International, and the Gay, Lesbian and Straight Education Network (GLSEN) to endorse a dialogue guide for finding common ground on issues of sexual orientation, which inclusive school leaders might find helpful (First Amendment Center & BridgeBuilders, 2006).

In this section I discussed the literature base regarding: (a) including religion as a topic in the curriculum; and (b) including religious or non-religious beliefs of people, as well as the intersection of religion with several other dimensions of diversity. I now turn to describe in greater detail the implications of this literature for inclusive leadership.

PART 3: INCLUSIVE LEADERSHIP AROUND RELIGION

The role of the leader in creating an inclusive school around religion is the same as it is for other marginalized areas: to make all people feel welcome, to create a climate and culture conducive to learning, and to advocate for equity. Multiple scholars in the leadership and social justice literature have identified these tasks as the role of the inclusive leader, though my students find extremely helpful Table 10.1 from *The School Leaders Our Children Deserve: Seven Keys to Equity, Social Justice, and School Reform*, which differentiates between "good leadership" and "social justice leadership" (Theoharis, 2009, p. 160). Being a social justice leader requires extra effort. My contribution to this already-strong conversation is to demand that leaders also consider religious beliefs when creating social justice climates and advocating for students. I want us to *find* our religion again, to borrow from the R.E.M. song. The question, of course, is how to do that. In this section I describe three strategies and examples focused at the personal, school, and district levels. I follow this with case studies to illustrate such leadership.

Tool 1: Personal Reflection—The Spiritual Autobiography

I begin our class session on religion and spirituality with a brief lecture. Its first slide is the statement, "We lead who we are," which is adapted from Parker Palmer's (1998) quote that "who you are inwardly is what you teach outwardly" (p. 2). The decisions we make, the way we treat people, our purpose for going to school and working each day are all spiritual issues. I review the difference between religion and spirituality, and then ask them to reflect upon two questions as they review the upcoming slides: (1) Where do you see yourself?; and (2) Where do you see your students, staff, families, and community?

The slides following that introduction highlight some of the information provided earlier in this chapter. The first reviews the spiritual life cycle, which is derived from research on the sociology of religion. The second reviews national and state-wide religious demographics, as found in the Pew Religious Landscape Survey (Pew Forum on Religion and Public Life, 2008). Pew's website (http://religions.pewforum.org/maps) has an interactive feature with a drop-down menu that lets users sort data by state so that one can find, for example, what percentage of Iowans attend a religious service at least once a week, or who are certain there is a God, or who pray every day. Because so much of our state is Christian, the third slide summarizes survey data from *Christianity Today* on "5 Kinds of Christians"

(Lee, 2007). The fourth summarizes some of the demographic data on spirituality and ethnicity and immigration. We pause then to reflect upon and discuss the two questions identified at the beginning of the lecture.

The next step is to hand out a sheet of landscape-formatted paper (so there's more room to write) with a simple timeline on it that looks like Figure 8.1.

Birth   Now

Figure 8.1 Spiritual Autobiography Timeline

The sheet is titled "Your Spiritual Autobiography" and has these questions at the top:

- Key spiritual events? Changes?
- Where are you in the spiritual life cycle?
- What do you believe?
    - Meaning, purpose, call
    - How you treat other people
- How did you come to believe what you believe?

I ask people to put key events from their life on the timeline and to answer the questions. They complete it individually and then leave the room to discuss their answers in pairs. They return and we discuss it as a group.

I've used this tool both with my class and in a professional development session with our state's affiliate of the American Association of School Administrators. It provokes interesting discussion about how people journeyed to where they are spiritually, as well as lively discussion comparing where they are and where their communities are.

Tool 2: School-Level Religious Inclusion Equity Audit

As discussed throughout this book, and developed fully in Capper and Young's chapter, an essential tool for evaluating the current state of inclusion in a school is an equity audit. In their book, *Meeting the Needs of Students of ALL Abilities*, Capper, Frattura, and Keyes (2000) provide a "Demographic Data Questionnaire" for school teams to use to establish information about current programs and services for students in the areas of social class, race and ethnicity, gender, sexual orientation, and disability. The final chapter of this text describes a comprehensive equity audit process. See the religion section and full equity audit detailed in Chapter 10 and online (www.routledge.com/cw/theoharis).

This addition of religion to the Demographic Data Questionnaire helps my students think about the religious makeup of their communities, such as who the majority is and who the minority is. As Abo-Zena (2011) has observed about minority religious students, there is rarely achievement data available sorted by religious affiliation, but leaders in some smaller communities are able, for example, to identify the religious affiliation of members of the National Honor Society. They write in their reflections that they'd never noticed how many houses of worship there are, and that they find it helpful to engage their school librarians in conversations about what religious materials are available to students. Collecting this data is often the first time they've thought about religion within their school communities.

Tool 3: District-Level Analysis of Current Practices

I've written in another article (Marshall, 2008) about the "blurry Christianity" that remains in some schools as a result of their Protestant history. Schools often don't question these practices, since "we've always done it this way." Four questions can help school leaders to identify, evaluate, and discuss religious practices in their district. They are:

1.   What religious-related practices are in place in our district?
2.   What educational purpose does this school practice serve?
3.   Does that educational purpose violate anyone's religious or nonreligious belief?
4.   How can we reconcile majority and minority religious viewpoints when they conflict?

As a result of these questions, current leaders and students in my classes are able to identify some of the residually Christian practices of their schools, such as no activities on Sundays. Whether or not they change those practices is up to them and their knowledge of the local context, but knowing and questioning are the first steps toward change.

Case Studies

The news sends us a *negative* example of religious inclusion—call it religious *exclusion*—nearly every week. A Florida chapter of Fellowship of Christian Athletes files suit against its school because it is excluded from announcements and the yearbook (National School Boards Association, 2014). A Buddhist family sues a Louisiana school district (which settles) for harassing their daughter and including prayer in classes and Bible verses on the school marquee (Associated Press, 2014). An Ohio principal tells a gay teen he can't wear a T-shirt with "Jesus is not a homophobe" on it; the student sues (Horn, 2012). The goal of the following case studies is to provide some positive examples of leadership around religion, yet examples controversial enough for intriguing discussion.

It is easy for students to become bogged down in these discussions by what their legal obligations are in these situations. However, I encourage readers to think in addition about the moral obligations of an inclusive, social-justice-oriented leader. A solely legal orientation limits leaders in their ethical decision-making, keeping them focused on an ethic of justice rather than of critique, care, or professionalism (Starratt, 1991; Stefkovich & Begley, 2007). Instead, think about more complicated ways to make decisions such as:

What is right?
What is right for an individual? What is right for the organization?
How do you resolve competing rights?

CASE STUDY 1
The Praying Leader

As a first-year superintendent, Todd Nilsson moved into a rural community. Having dutifully completed his religious equity audit before taking the job, he was sure that he knew where his religious communities were, and he knew that all of them—*all*—were Christian. A devout Lutheran himself, he believed in the power of prayer. "What if," he thought, "I created a prayer team for my school? I know I'm going to need all the help I can get. I'll ask for it."

Todd sent a letter to the pastor of each congregation introducing himself and asking for volunteers for the Midlands School Prayer Team. He included a sign-up sheet, which he asked that each pastor return to him. All but one of the churches returned a sign-up sheet to him, with at least one name—and from one church a dozen names—and e-mail addresses on it.

He felt more comfortable knowing that people were praying for him and the district. Shortly after the school year began, he sent his first e-mail message to the prayer team:

Dear Midlands School Prayer Team:

Thank you for volunteering for praying for me and for our school. I want to be the best leader I can possibly be for the Midlands community, and I appreciate all the help I can get. I'd appreciate it if this time you'd pray for our teachers and students and me as we start the school year. I want us all to get off on the right foot and stay safe in this heat. Thank you again.

Sincerely, Superintendent Nilsson

He heard nothing back from anyone on the team, but was quickly absorbed into tasks. A month later, he sent another message, similar to the first, but asking for wisdom on budgeting for the next school year. He continued in this vein throughout his first year. He did hear from members of his team—occasionally he'd get back an e-mail message saying, "Praying for you!" Sometimes people would stop him in the grocery store to tell him that they were praying for him. One elderly woman told him that she hadn't been involved with the schools since her children had grown, but that praying for him made her feel involved again. But Todd's favorite response was from his wife, who said that she felt especially welcome in Midlands, and that not only the Lutheran women, but several of their friends, had introduced her around and included her in their social activities.

GUIDING QUESTIONS

- Do you think Todd's prayer team is "good leadership"? (Use the criteria from Table 10.1 from Theoharis' *The School Leaders Our Children Deserve: Seven Keys to Equity, Social Justice, and School Reform*.)
- Again using Table 10.1, is Todd's prayer team good practice for a social justice leader committed to religious inclusion?

CASE STUDY 2
The Memorial Day Ceremony

Emily MacDonald was the new middle school principal in suburban Greenlee. Toward the end of the school year, her band director, Ms. Pattison, let her know that one of the Greenlee traditions was for the middle school band to march in the city's Memorial Day parade. The parade ends at the local cemetery, and is followed by a brief ceremony honoring Greenlee's service personnel, both living and deceased. "Not only is the ceremony very nice," said Ms. Pattison, "but I could use an extra adult to sit with me and the middle-schoolers. Since it's Memorial Day, not all of them will be there, and this is technically an optional event, but most of them will be there anyway because they like to be in the parade and we have school the next day." Emily agreed.

The day of the parade was sunny and beautiful, one of those glorious May days that makes everyone think of the approaching summer break. The middle school band marched mostly in-step, wearing their school T-shirts, and played "My Country 'Tis of Thee" and "America the Beautiful" mostly on-key. Emily wore red, white, and blue, and met the band and Ms. Pattison at the cemetery, where folding chairs were set up for them. She nodded and smiled to families she recognized in the crowd. She wondered if her superintendent was there.

The ceremony opened with a cute 10-year-old singing the national anthem, and with a flyover from the Air National Guard. The mayor asked the crowd to stand for the Pledge of Allegiance, while a color guard of veterans stood by. Emily wondered idly what the current legal status of saying the Pledge in school was, while keeping an eye on the middle-schoolers, who were beginning to fidget. The next speaker, however, brought everyone to attention. He began with a prayer thanking God for the sacrifice of the brave men and women who had died in the service of our country, and then began to get louder and more emphatic as he prayed that the GLORY of the LORD would be reVEALED and that God would have MERcy on this GREAT NATION despite its SINS ("Oh dear," thought Emily), such as HOMOSEXUALITY AND ABORTION, and that the NEXT GENERATION, such as THESE FINE YOUNG PEOPLE IN THE BAND (Emily sat up straighter and wished she were anywhere but here) would KNOW and LOVE and FEAR the LORD as their forefathers had BEFORE them, so that if they are CALLED upon to give their LIVES, they will NOT FEAR going to HELL, but enjoy the wonders of HEAVEN with OUR SAVIOUR, in whose name we PRAY, AMEN.

"Psst! Ms. MacDonald!" hissed the eighth-grade girl behind her, "Did you hear that guy? My uncle's gay. And that guy thinks he's going to hell! I don't think that!"

Emily was not as attentive for the next ten minutes of the service, as she started planning what she was going to say to her superintendent as soon as she was free to call.

GUIDING QUESTIONS

- What should Emily say to her superintendent when she calls him?
- What should she say to the family of the eighth-grade girl whose uncle is gay?
- What other information would you want if you were Emily?

CASE STUDY 3
The Ecumenical Holiday Shrub

It was the beginning of December, and Principal Dwayne Jackson was standing in a stairwell talking with one of his teachers. His cell phone buzzed with a call from his administrative assistant: Mr. Vitale had brought him a pre-holiday present. Wondering what in the world this was about,

Dwayne returned to his office to find an enormous Scottish pine tree blocking the door. Behind the tree he could just glimpse Louie Vitale, a local insurance salesman he knew through Rotary, and the father of two students in the school.

"Thought I'd brighten up your office," said Louie, edging around the tree.

That it would. The tree was already decorated, with bright lights and ornaments in the green and gold colors of the school sports teams, the Giants.

Dwayne thanked Louie, said coffee was on him next time, waved at his assistant, and headed back out to visit one of his new math teachers.

By the next morning, his assistant had moved the tree to a corner of the front office, where it blinked in the window overlooking the front hallway. Dwayne forgot about it, except when students shouted "Go Giants!" as they passed the tree. During the lunch hour, Dwayne looked up to see two girls standing in his doorway, clearly nervous but determined.

Girl 1:   "Principal Jackson? Isn't that a Christmas tree?"

Girl 2:   "Isn't that against school rules? Because it's about Christmas and we're a public school?"

Girl 1:   "I don't like it. It makes me feel . . . it just reminds me that I don't really belong here."

Girl 2:   "I already feel left out of Christmas. My family doesn't celebrate it, and there have been decorations in the stores since, I don't know, like, before Halloween, at least. I'm sick of it."

Dismayed, Principal Jackson stammered, "Well, it's really just a school spirit tree. Really. It doesn't have much to do with Christmas. How about we think of it as an ecumenical holiday shrub with Giants decorations. Would that help?"

GUIDING QUESTIONS

- What principles of good leadership conflict here?
- What principles of social justice leadership apply?
- What should Dwayne say next?
- What should Dwayne do with the tree?

CONCLUSION

My students often tell me that my class session on religion and spirituality in school leadership is the only time in their professional education that they have talked about these topics. That is a sad commentary on our ability as a profession to engage with these globally important ideas. I urge you, gentle reader, to work so that together we can change that.

As we do that, we must remember that social justice leadership presumes an ethic of critique, which Starratt (1991) has suggested includes asking questions such as "Who benefits by these arrangements?" and "Who defines the way things are structured here?" (p. 189). The inclusive leader must apply those critical questions with an eye toward the ways in which religion is included in the curriculum and the ways in which people of all beliefs are included or excluded.

NOTES

1   In fall 2011, private school enrollment was about 5.3 million students. Of those, about 40% were enrolled in Catholic schools, 38% in other religious schools, and 23% in non-sectarian schools (National Center for Education Statistics, 2013).
2   If you'd like to take the quiz yourself and compare your knowledge to that of national participants, the quiz is at http://www.pewforum.org/quiz/u-s-religious-knowledge/.
3   Pew's *Religious Portrait of African Americans* (2009) categorizes African Americans as the most Protestant of US racial and ethnic groups, at 78% (compared with 53% of Whites, 27% of Asians, and 23% of Latino/as). They also state that more than three-fourths of those Protestants belong to historically Black Protestant denominations such as the National Baptist Convention or the African Methodist Episcopal Church. For a far more detailed portrait, see *Religious service attendance and distress: Moderating role of life events and race/ethnicity* (Tabak & Mickelson, 2009) from the Program for Research on Black Americans (http://www.rcgd.isr.umich.edu/prba/).

REFERENCES

Abo-Zena, M. M. (2011). Faith from the fringes. *Phi Delta Kappan, 93*(4), 15–19.
Ahlstrom, S. E. (1972). *A religious history of the American people.* New Haven, CT: Yale University Press.
Akresh, I. R. (2010). Immigrants' religious participation in the United States. *Ethnic and Racial Studies, 34*(4), 643–661. doi:10.1080/01419870.2010.526719
Anderson, J. D. (1988). *The education of Blacks in the South, 1860–1935.* Chapel Hill: University of North Carolina Press.
Associated Press. (2014, March 14). Settlement in suit involving La. Buddhist student. *USA Today.*
Baker, J. O., & Smith, B. G. (2009). The nones: Social characteristics of the religiously unaffiliated. *Social Forces, 87*(3), 1251–1263.
Barrett, B. D. (2010). Faith in the inner city: The urban Black church and students' educational outcomes. *The Journal of Negro Education, 79*(3), 249–262. doi:10.2307/20798347
Bauch, P. A. (2001). School-community partnerships in rural schools: Leadership, renewal, and a sense of place. *Peabody Journal of Education, 76*(2), 204–221.
Billingsley, A., & Caldwell, C. H. (1991). The church, the family, and the school in the African American community. *The Journal of Negro Education, 60*(3), 427–440.
Brown, D. R., & Gary, L. E. (1991). Religious socialization and educational attainment among African Americans: An empirical assessment. *Journal of Negro Education, 60*(3), 411–426.
Bryk, A. S., Lee, V. E., & Holland, P. B. (1993). *Catholic schools and the common good.* Cambridge, MA: Harvard University Press.
Capper, C. A., Frattura, E. M., & Keyes, M. W. (2000). *Meeting the needs of students of all abilities: How leaders go beyond inclusion.* Thousand Oaks, CA: Corwin Press.
Carter, S. L. (1993). *The culture of disbelief: How American law and politics trivialize religious devotion.* New York, NY: BasicBooks, Harper Collins.
Chaves, M., & Higgins, L. M. (1992). Comparing the community involvement of Black and White congregations. *Journal for the Scientific Study of Religion, 31*(4), 425.
Cotten-Huston, A. L., & Waite, B. M. (1999). Anti-homosexual attitudes in college students. *Journal of Homosexuality, 38*(3), 117–133. doi:10.1300/J082v38n03_07
Dantley, M. E. (2003). Critical spirituality: Enhancing transformative leadership through critical theory and African American prophetic spirituality. *International Journal of Leadership in Education, 6*(1), 3–17.
Dillard, C. B., Abdur-Rashid, D., & Tyson, C. A. (2000). My soul is a witness: Affirming pedagogies of the spirit. *Qualitative Studies in Education, 13*(5), 447–462.
Douglass, S. L. (2000). Teaching about religion in national and state social studies standards. Fountain Valley, CA, & Nashville, TN: Council on Islamic Education & First Amendment Center.

Ebaugh, H. R. (2003). Religion and the new immigrants. In M. Dillon (Ed.), *Handbook of the sociology of religion* (pp. 225–239). Cambridge, UK: University of Cambridge.

Eck, D. L. (2001). *A new religious America: How a "Christian country" has now become the world's most religiously diverse nation.* New York, NY: HarperSanFrancisco.

First Amendment Center. (2008). *A teacher's guide to religion in the public schools.* Nashville, TN: First Amendment Center.

First Amendment Center & BridgeBuilders. (2006). Public schools and sexual orientation: A First Amendment framework for finding common ground. Retrieved from http://www.firstamendmentcenter.org/madison/wp-content/uploads/2011/03/sexual.orientation.guidelines.pdf

Francis, L. J., & Village, A. (2014). Church schools preparing adolescents for living in a religiously diverse society: An empirical enquiry in England and Wales. *Religious Education, 109*(3), 264–283. doi:10.1080/00344087.2014.911623

Fraser, J. W. (1999). *Between church and state: Religion and public education in a multicultural America.* New York, NY: St. Martin's Press.

Frazier, E. F., & Lincoln, C. E. (1974). *The Negro church in America.* New York, NY: Schocken Books.

Fullan, M. (2002). Moral purpose writ large. *School Administrator, 59*(8), 14–16.

Ghaffar-Kucher, A. (2012). The religification of Pakistani-American youth. *American Educational Research Journal, 49*(1), 30–52. doi:10.3102/0002831211414858

Guo, Y. (2011). Perspectives of immigrant Muslim parents: Advocating for religious diversity in Canadian schools. *Multicultural Education, 18*(2), 55–60.

Herek, G. M. (1994). Assessing heterosexuals' attitudes toward lesbians and gay men: A review of emprical research with the ATLG scale. In B. Greene & G. M. Herek (Eds.), *Lesbian and gay psychology: Theory, research, and clinical applications* (pp. 206–228). Thousand Oaks, CA: Sage.

Hicks, G. R., & Lee, T.-T. (2006). Public attitudes toward gays and lesbians. *Journal of Homosexuality, 51*(2), 57–77. doi:10.1300/J082v51n02_04

Horn, D. (2012, April 4). School lifts ban on gay teen's shirt. *Cincinnati.com.* Retrieved from http://news.cincinnati.com/apps/pbcs.dll/article?AID=/AB/20120404/NEWS/304040165/

Hunter, J. D. (1991). *Culture wars: The struggle to define America.* New York, NY: Basic.

Jandali, A. K. (2012). Muslim students in post-9/11 classrooms. *School Administrator, 69*(9), 32–35.

Jeynes, W. (2012). Reaching out to make a difference. *Phi Delta Kappan, 93*(5), 80.

Jones, A. D. (2010). *Leadership and spirituality: The indivisible leadership of African American school administrators as pastors* (Doctoral dissertation). Iowa State University, Ames, IA.

Jordan, W. J., & Nettles, S. M. (1999). *How students invest their time out of school: Effects on school engagement, perceptions of life chances, and achievement.* Washington, DC: Center for Research on the Education of Students Placed at Risk.

Joshi, K. Y. (2006a). Guest editor's introduction. *Equity and Excellence in Education, 39*(3), 177–180.

Joshi, K. Y. (2006b). The racialization of Hinduism, Islam, and Sikhism in the United States. *Equity and Excellence in Education, 39*(3), 211–226.

Kelley, J., & de Graaf, N. D. (1997). National context, parental socialization, and religious belief: Results from 15 nations. *American Sociological Review, 62*(4), 639–659.

Kosmin, B. A., Keysar, A., Cragun, R. T., & Navarro-Rivera, J. (2008). *American nones: The profile of the no religion population.* Hartford, CT: Trinity College.

Kosmin, B. A., & Lachman, S. P. (1993). *One nation under God: Religion in contemporary American society.* New York, NY: Harmony Books.

Lantieri, L. (2001). *Schools with spirit: Nurturing the inner lives of children and teachers.* Boston, MA: Beacon Press.

Lee, H. (2007). 5 kinds of Christians. *Leadership Journal.* Retrieved from http://www.christianitytoday.com/le/2007/fall/1.19.html

Lester, E. (2011). *Teaching about religions: A democratic approach for public schools.* Ann Arbor: University of Michigan Press.

Lester, E., & Roberts, P. S. (2011). Learning about world religions in Modesto, California: The promise of teaching tolerance in public schools. *Politics and Religion, 4*(2), 264–288. doi:10.1017/S1755048311000174

Lincoln, C. E., & Mamiya, L. H. (1990). *The Black church in the African-American experience*. Durham, NC: Duke University Press.

Lugg, C. A. (2000). Reading, writing, and reconstructionism: The Christian right and the politics of public education. *Educational Policy, 14*(5), 622–637.

Lugg, C. A., & Robinson, M. N. (2009). Religion, advocacy coalitions and the politics of U.S. Public schooling. *Educational Policy, 23*(1), 242–266.

Lugg, C. A., & Tabbaa-Rida, Z. (2006). Social justice, religion, and public school leaders. In C. Marshall & M. Oliva (Eds.), *Leadership for social justice: Making revolutions in education* (pp. 130–144). Boston, MA: Allyn & Bacon.

Mann, H. (1855). *Lectures on education*. Boston, MA: Ide and Dutton.

Mann, H. (1872). *Thoughts selected from the writings of Horace Mann*. Boston, MA: Lee and Shepard.

Marshall, J. M. (2006). Nothing new under the sun: A brief history of ethnoreligious oppression in the United States. *Equity and Excellence in Education, 39*(3), 181–194.

Marshall, J. M. (2008). Whose religious values? Managing changing religious demographics in a school community legally and pro-actively. *The School Administrator, 65*(5), 28–32.

Marshall, J. M., & Hernandez, F. (2013). "I would not consider myself a homophobe": Learning and teaching about sexual orientation in a principal preparation program. *Educational Administration Quarterly, 49*(3), 451–488. doi:10.1177/0013161X12463231

McCarthy, M. M. (2009). Beyond the wall of separation: Church-state concerns in public schools. *Phi Delta Kappan, 90*(10), 714–719.

McGrath, D. J., Swisher, R. R., Elder, G. H., Jr., & Conger, R. D. (2001). Breaking new ground: Diverse routes to college in rural America. *Rural Sociology, 66*(2), 244–267.

Milligan, J. A. (2000). Mapping the road to Bethlehem: Parameters for the discourse on the relationship between religion and public education. *Educational Policy, 14*(5), 685–702.

Muller, C., & Ellison, C. G. (2001). Religious involvement, social capital, and adolescents' academic progress: Evidence from the national longitudinal study of 1988. *Sociological Focus, 34*, 155–183.

National Center for Education Statistics. (2013). Table 205.20. Enrollment and percentage distribution of students enrolled in private elementary and secondary schools, by school orientation and grade level: Selected years, fall 1995 through fall 2011. *Digest of education statistics, 2001*. Washington, DC: Institute of Education Sciences, U.S. Department of Education.

National School Boards Association. (2014). Christian student club sues Florida district seeking greater access to school resources. *Legal Clips*. Retrieved from http://legalclips.nsba.org/2014/04/17/christian-student-club-sues-florida-district-seeking-greater-access-to-school-resources/

Nord, W. A. (1995). *Religion and American education: Rethinking a national dilemma*. Chapel Hill: University of North Carolina Press.

Nord, W. A. (2010). *Does God make a difference? Taking religion seriously in our schools and universities*. New York, NY: Oxford University Press.

Nord, W. A., & Haynes, C. C. (1998). *Taking religion seriously across the curriculum*. Alexandria, VA: Association for Supervision and Curriculum Development.

Norris, P., & Inglehart, R. (2011). *Sacred and secular: Religion and politics worldwide*. New York, NY: Cambridge University Press.

Palmer, P. J. (1983). *To know as we are known: A spirituality of education*. San Francisco, CA: Harper and Row.

Palmer, P. J. (1998). *The courage to teach: Exploring the inner landscape of a teacher's life*. San Francisco, CA: Jossey-Bass.

Perry, T., Steele, C., & Hilliard, A. G. (2003). *Young, gifted, and Black: Promoting high achievement among African-American students*. Boston, MA: Beacon Press.

Pew Forum on Religion and Public Life. (2008). *U.S. religious landscape survey*. Washington, DC: Pew Research Center.

Pew Forum on Religion and Public Life. (2010). *Religious knowledge*. Washington, DC: Pew Research Center.

Pew Forum on Religion and Public Life. (2012a). *Asian Americans: A mosaic of faiths*. Washington, DC: Pew Research Center.

Pew Forum on Religion and Public Life. (2012b). *"Nones" on the rise: One-in-five adults have no religious affiliation*. Washington, DC: Pew Research Center.

Pew Forum on Religion and Public Life. (2013a). *A portrait of Jewish Americans*. Washington, DC: Pew Research Center.

Pew Forum on Religion and Public Life. (2013b). *The religious affiliation of U.S. immigrants: Majority Christian, rising share of other faiths*. Retrieved from http://www.pewforum.org/2013/05/17/the-religious-affiliation-of-us-immigrants/

Pew Forum on Religion and Public Life. (2014). *Global religious diversity: Half of the most religiously diverse countries are in Asia-Pacific region*. Washington, DC: Pew Research Center.

Pew Research Center for the People and the Press. (2011). *Muslim Americans: No signs of growth in alienation or support for extremism*. Washington, DC: Pew Research Center.

Pew Research Center for the People and the Press. (2012a). Partisan polarization surges in Bush, Obama years. *Trends in American Values: 1987–2012*. Washington, DC: Pew Research Center.

Pew Research Center for the People and the Press. (2012b). *Religion and attitudes toward same-sex marriage*. Washington, DC: Pew Research Center.

Prothero, S. R. (2007). *Religious literacy: What every American needs to know—and doesn't*. San Francisco, CA: HarperSanFrancisco.

Purpel, D. E. (1989). *The moral and spiritual crisis in education: A curriculum for justice and compassion in education*. New York, NY: Bergin and Garvey.

Russo, C. J. (2003). Religion and public schools: A forty year retrospective. *Religion and Education, 30*(2), 1–22.

Scanlan, M. (2011). How school leaders can accent inclusion for bilingual students, families, and communities. *Multicultural Education, 18*(2), 4–9.

School District of Abington Township, Pennsylvania v. Schempp, 374 U.S. 203 (1963).

Sikkink, D., & Hernández, E. I. (2003). *Religion matters: Predicting schooling success among Latino youth*. Notre Dame, IN: Institute for Latino Studies, University of Notre Dame.

Sirin, S. R., & Katsiaficas, D. (2011). Religiosity, discrimination, and community engagement. *Youth & Society, 43*(4), 1528–1546. doi:10.1177/0044118x10388218

Smith, C. (2003). Theorizing religious effects among American adolescents. *Journal for the Scientific Study of Religion, 42*(1), 17–30.

Starratt, R. J. (1991). Building an ethical school: A theory for practice in educational leadership. *Educational Administration Quarterly, 27*(2), 185–202.

Stefkovich, J. A., & Begley, P. T. (2007). Ethical school leadership: Defining the best interests of students. *Educational Management Administration Leadership, 35*(2), 205–224. doi:10.1177/1741143207075389

Tabak, M. A., & Mickelson, K. D. (2009). Religious service attendance and distress: The moderating role of stressful life events and race/ethnicity. *Sociology of Religion, 70*(1), 49–64.

Tang, W. (in press). The worshipping atheist: Institutional and diffused religiosities in China. *China: An International Journal*.

Theoharis, G. (2009). *The school leaders our children deserve: Seven keys to equity, social justice, and school reform*. New York, NY: Teachers College, Columbia University.

Toshalis, E. (2008). A question of "faith". In M. Sadowski (Ed.), *Adolescents at school: Perspectives on youth, identity, and education* (2nd ed., pp. 189–205). Cambridge, MA: Harvard Education Publishing Group.

Tsitsos, W. (2003). Race differences in congregational social service activity. *Journal for the Scientific Study of Religion, 42*(2), 205–215. doi:10.1111/1468–5906.00173

Whitley, J. B. E. (2009). Religiosity and attitudes toward lesbians and gay men: A meta-analysis. *International Journal for the Psychology of Religion, 19*(1), 21–38. doi:10.1080/10508610802471104

Williams, T. R., Davis, L. E., Saunders, J., & Williams, J. H. (2002). Friends, family, and neighborhood: Understanding academic outcomes of African American youth. *Urban Education, 37*(3), 408–431. doi:10.1177/00485902037003006

Witherspoon, N., & Taylor, D. L. (2010). Spiritual weapons: Black female principals and religio-spirituality. *Journal of Educational Administration and History, 42*(2), 133–158.

Yang, C. K. (1961). *Religion in Chinese society: A study of contemporary social functions of religion and some of their historical factors*. Berkeley: University of California Press.

Zehr, M. A. (2001, September 26). Islamic schools and Muslim youngsters report harassment. *Education Week, 21*(4), 13.

Zine, J. (2000). Redefining resistance: Towards an Islamic subculture in schools. *Race Ethnicity and Education, 3*(3).

CHAPTER 9

Inclusive Leadership on the Social Frontiers

Family and Community Engagement

Martin Scanlan and Lauri Johnson

This chapter focuses on inclusive service delivery and the role of leadership promoting social justice, but departs from emphasizing a specific area of difference within K–12 schools, shifting toward the broader context: the school as nested in a wider community. Attending to this broader context is a vital extension of inclusive leadership for social justice. How do school leaders engage families and external community members in their efforts to craft school communities that are inclusive? How does this engagement shape the ways that school leaders notice and work with other stakeholders to eliminate barriers to inclusion? These are the types of questions we examine here.

The premise of this chapter is that inclusive leadership for social justice extends beyond the schoolhouse doors. Previous chapters have honed in on inclusion across multiple dimensions of diversity within schools, describing ways to ameliorate the educational inequities that students who have been historically marginalized experience. Complementing these chapters, we turn here to argue that inequities within schools cannot be understood without considering the various out-of-school influences (Berliner, 2014). Hence, school leaders must take a holistic, or "ecological" approach to unpacking these inequities (Duncan & Murnane, 2011). This means seeing the developing child nested in a family that is in turn nested in a neighborhood. It means working with others to connect the intersections of these various sectors. Our students' families are diverse, with parents and caregivers coming into children's lives in many different ways. The communities with which school leaders seek to engage are multifaceted as well, comprising a wide range of organizations and institutions. In this chapter we argue that building socially just, inclusive schools entails a holistic approach of school leaders apprehending and appreciating the pluralism inherent to this broader context. Referring to this context as "social frontiers," this chapter describes how school leaders committed to fostering educational equity and inclusivity can navigate this terrain as boundary spanners, border crossers, and advocates.

PART 1: THE CURRENT CONTEXT OF SOCIAL FRONTIERS IN SCHOOLS

What is a social frontier? Sociologist Ronald Burt (1992) coined this term to describe places where different social worlds collide, forcing the interaction of people who would otherwise tend to be isolated from one another. Interpersonal relationships "that cross the frontier involve continual negotiation" (p. 163), Burt argues, since commonly held expectations and cultural norms do not exist.

The metaphor of social frontiers is a useful one for school leaders to apply to the complexities inherent to building productive relationships with families and with communities (Miller, Scanlan, & Wills, 2014; Miller, Wills, & Scanlan, 2013). Schools themselves are such frontiers to the degree that they create a space in which diverse families are forced together to negotiate different notions of teaching and learning, the *why* of schooling (Rose, 2009). But more than this, school administrators—particularly building-level principals—are uniquely positioned to engage with others—such as neighborhood residents, community activists, and colleagues in local businesses, government, and faith communities—to find and build common ground and pursue shared goals. Such relationships are formed on social frontiers.

By their nature, social frontiers are heterogeneous, bringing together individuals from different backgrounds, cultures, races, and so forth. Here are some snapshots to illustrate:

* At a home-school meeting, a Hmong mother meets a Jewish mother. They bond over shared concerns about the school's cafeteria, and in the process discover that their children share a homeroom.
* At a neighborhood meeting, a principal meets a local store owner. The principal, who is Black, American-born, and middle class, does not live in the neighborhood. The store owner is Korean, a first-generation immigrant, and a working-class resident of the neighborhood.
* A local university holds a workshop for local professions on depression, mental health, and suicide prevention. Over lunch, a high school principal and counselor encounter a social worker whose office is right up the road from their school.
* The director of a local shelter for the homeless comes to school to meet with the leadership team. Concerned with the rising incidence of itinerant and homeless families in the area, she is seeking to partner with the school to more effectively meet the educational needs of children in these families.

Intersections: Boundaries and Borders

All of these snapshots can be considered social frontiers: in each of them people have new encounters, coming together over shared interests or, perhaps, shared conflicts. Social frontiers bring out boundaries: places of intersection. Boundaries are ambiguous middle grounds, where something is held in common, while much remains apart. These snapshots illustrate Akkerman and Bakker's (2011) point that "Boundaries simultaneously suggest a sameness and continuity in the sense that within discontinuity two or more sites are relevant to one another in a particular way" (p. 133). So the school cafeteria is relevant to the two mothers, and a safe neighborhood is relevant to the principal and store owner alike. The particular shared interest creates a point of intersection, creates a social frontier.

Increasingly, scholarship in educational leadership emphasizes the importance of boundary spanning. As Miller (2008) asserts, "To varying degrees all educational leaders are called to serve as boundary spanners" (p. 356). We extend this notion by claiming that these leaders are also called to serve as border crossers. Miller characterizes boundary-spanning leaders as "institutional infiltrators organizing for community advancement" who are "in" and "of" their communities (Miller, 2008, p. 372), and operate as "flexible organizational navigators" and "knowledgeable information brokers" (Miller, 2009, p. 619).

Sometimes boundaries are permeable, allowing one to stand with one foot on both sides. Other times they act as borders, where crossing over requires leaving one context and joining another. The notion of boundary spanners implies that the individual has connections to more than one world or organization and can act as a link between. In contrast, the notion of border crossers implies leaving behind one's assumptions, privileges, and expectations in order to enter a new space.

Using the distinction of borders and boundaries, Erickson (2007) recommends that schools reframe cultural borders as cultural boundaries, so that students do not need to leave behind dimensions of their cultural identity in order to belong to the school community. We are making a different point here: leadership on social frontiers does not necessarily entail reframing borders into boundaries, but navigating both. Sometimes school leaders span boundaries, standing with individuals who come from very different places and helping them address a common concern. Other times school leaders must cross a border on social frontiers, leaving behind what is familiar and comfortable and putting themselves in a new space. In the process they often must confront their own sociocultural differences and power dynamics in their work with diverse communities.

Returning to the snapshots above, how often are the Hmong and Jewish mothers in the same room and *not provided opportunities to discuss common concerns*? What brings the Black principal and Korean businesswoman *together to work for the benefit of the larger community*? Are these intersections borders or boundaries? The challenge is for school leaders to navigate these intersections in ways that respect the voices and perspectives of each participant.

Advocacy at Intersections

Toward this end, school leaders for social justice are called to be not only boundary spanners and border crossers, but also advocates. Advocacy signifies standing with others—particularly those who are being marginalized—providing support and solidarity. In boundary spanning and border crossing one *encounters* others on social frontiers, forming relationships. Advocacy deepens these relationships to alliances. As an advocate, I not only know the other, but identify as an ally.

Literature describing educational leadership for social justice and inclusivity frequently emphasizes the importance of advocacy skills (Theoharis, 2007). As Cambron-McCabe and McCarthy (2005) put it:

> Within a social justice context, school leaders are being called on to take up the role of transformative intellectuals, public intellectuals, or critical intellectuals—that is, individuals who engage in critical analysis of conditions that have perpetuated historical inequities in schools and who work to change institutional structures and culture.
>
> (p. 202)

Lopez, Gonzalez, and Fierro (2006) argue that "Educational leaders who cross cultural borders engage their work in fundamentally different ways . . . In a nutshell, they are social *activists* as well as educators who seek to challenge and change the world through their praxis" (pp. 67–68, emphasis added). At times this puts principals in the uncomfortable position of advocating for parent and community groups against school district authorities. Anderson (2009) argues that educational leaders in positional power—such as principals and superintendents—need to be "motivated primarily through their advocacy for children and their communities" (p. 8) and pursue this "advocacy in alliance with other groups, such as teachers, parent and community leaders, unions, policy advocates, and other emerging civil society groups" (p. 2). The type of advocacy leadership that Anderson calls for is a "more politicized notion of leadership that acknowledges that schools are sites of struggle over material and cultural resources and ideological commitments" (p. 13).

Boundary Spanners, Border Crossers, and Advocates

These concepts—social frontiers, crossing boundaries and borders, and advocacy leadership—weave together to form a conceptual framework for this chapter. Our fundamental argument is that creating inclusive, socially just schooling demands that school leaders develop the knowledge, skills, and dispositions to navigate as boundary spanners, border crossers, *and* advocates. In this sense, our conceptual framework aligns with the argument Lopez and colleagues (2006) make:

> [I]n addition to having a thorough understanding of race, gender, sexual orientation, disability, class, and other areas of difference and how such factors impact the schooling process for everyone within the organization . . . [school leaders] must have a keen awareness of school-community relations, group dynamics, intercultural tolerance, politics and power, team building, and community engagement and how to effectively bridge these "borders" in order to collectively work toward success.
>
> (p. 66)

This framework is distinct from how educational administrators have been trained to think about school-community relations. Traditionally, school-community relations has been treated largely as a matter of public relations. Relatedly, it has also been primarily approached in a school-centric manner. In our framework, emphasizing the role of school leaders as boundary spanners, border crossers, and advocates, we are shifting the focus and moving well beyond this traditional approach to school-community relations. This framework asks school leaders to recognize how power is shared with families and organizations beyond the schoolhouse doors, and to explore how their educational goals for students intersect with the interests and goals of families and neighborhood residents. In the next section we ground our thesis in empirical and conceptual literature, before turning to the main point of the chapter: operationalizing this.

PART 2: WHAT WE KNOW ABOUT SOCIAL FRONTIERS: THE LITERATURE

Several key strands of literature are important for school leaders to understand when considering how to foster inclusivity on these social frontiers through crossing borders and boundaries and through advocacy. These include literature on culturally responsive leadership, parent engagement, and community engagement.

Culturally Responsive Leadership

The first strand of literature examines the development of the concept of culturally responsive leadership. This involves those leadership practices that emphasize high expectations for student achievement; incorporate the history, values, and cultural knowledge of students' home communities in the school curriculum; work to develop a critical consciousness among both students and faculty to challenge inequities in the larger society; and create inclusive organizational structures at the school and district level that empower students and parents from diverse racial and ethnic communities. Similar terms such as culturally proficient leadership, culturally relevant leadership, multicultural leadership, and diversity leadership have been used to describe these leadership practices that support students from diverse ethnic and cultural backgrounds and create inclusive schooling environments.

The concept of culturally responsive leadership arises from inquiry into culturally oriented teaching practices. Ladson-Billings (1994) coined the term *culturally relevant pedagogy* 20 years ago in *The Dreamkeepers*, her now classic study of eight exemplary teachers of African American students. This instructional approach is based on studies that noted a cultural mismatch between students from culturally diverse backgrounds and their White middle-class teachers, particularly in terms of language and verbal participation structures. In Ladson-Billings' (1995a; 1995b) view, culturally relevant pedagogy rests on three propositions: (1) students must experience academic success; (2) students must develop and/or maintain cultural competence; and (3) students must develop a critical consciousness through which they challenge the status quo of the social order. Other authors (Gay, 2010, Villegas & Lucas, 2001) include additional teacher practices such as developing effective cross-cultural communication and embracing constructivist views of teaching. In sum, most approaches to culturally relevant or culturally responsive instruction not only utilize students' culture as a vehicle for learning, but also advocate teaching students how to develop a broader sociopolitical consciousness that enables them to critique the cultural norms, values, mores, and institutions that produce and maintain social inequities (Ladson-Billings, 1995b, p. 162). Recently, in an effort to embrace a more dynamic view of culture (youth cultures in particular), some researchers have extended the conceptualization of assets-based pedagogies to what they term *culturally sustaining pedagogy* (Paris, 2012; Paris & Alim, 2014). Paris (2012) argues that instruction should do more than relate to a student's culture; it should "support young people in sustaining the cultural and linguistic competence of their communities while simultaneously offering access to dominant cultural competence" (p. 95).

While assets-based approaches have generally been applied to classroom teaching, some researchers have used a culturally responsive framework to study the practices of school leaders. These studies have identified culturally responsive principals as those who emphasize high expectations for student academic achievement, exhibit an ethic of care or "empowerment through care," and maintain a commitment and connection to the larger community (e.g., Reitzig & Patterson, 1998; Scheurich, 1998; Johnson, 2006; 2007). In her review of the literature on the principal's role in creating inclusive schools, Riehl (2000) also identifies three tasks that determine whether school leaders are prepared to respond to diversity and demonstrate multicultural leadership. These include fostering new definitions of diversity; promoting inclusive instructional practices within schools by supporting, facilitating, or being a catalyst for change; and building connections between schools and communities.

Because all students and their families engage in a variety of cultural practices, culturally responsive leadership focuses on improving the educational experiences and outcomes for all students, but particularly those who have been historically marginalized in schools. To become culturally responsive, school leaders need to move beyond a "food and festival approach" to cultural diversity that focuses on sharing cultural contributions to an analysis of the ways that schools may reinforce inequalities and blame students and their families for realities beyond their control (see further Horsford & Clark, this volume).

Parent Engagement

A second strand of literature focuses on engaging parents in authentic partnerships. Individuals who parent are varied, extending to a wide range of individuals including guardians, extended family, and other caregivers. Over the past few decades, literature on parent engagement has evolved. Epstein (Epstein, 1986, 1990; Epstein & Salinas, 2004) articulates a typology of different types of involvement of parents and community members in schools. Many of these may seem fundamental, such as parents providing health and safety for children, parents volunteering in schools and extending the learning from school to the home (e.g., homework), and schools communicating effectively with parents about the teaching and learning goals and progress toward these goals. Others are more sophisticated, such as schools providing opportunities for parents to actively influence decision-making in the school and assisting families in accessing support services from community agencies and organizations (e.g., healthcare, tutoring, economic development).

Efforts to engage parents—even when ostensibly seeking to empower those who have traditionally been marginalized—can effectively reinforce the power of the privileged. As Anderson (1998) notes, "In socioeconomically diverse schools, those who have the time, interest, and cultural capital to participate in schools tend to be middle-class parents whose class socialization is similar to that of school personnel, many of whom are themselves parents" (p. 581). School leaders, accordingly, must critically examine how power relations shape partnerships. Fine (1993) points out that parents (and community members) frequently "feel and are typically treated as 'less' than the professionals" (p. 684). Given this dynamic, Fine asserts that "Rich and real parental involvement requires a three-way commitment—to organizing parents, to restructuring schools and communities toward enriched educational and economic outcomes, and to inventing rich visions of educational democracies of difference" (p. 474). Auerbach (2012) makes a similar point, calling for "respectful alliances among educators, families, and community groups that value relationship building, dialogue across difference, and sharing power in pursuit of a common purpose in socially just, democratic schools" (p. 29). Auerbach points out that this can challenge school norms: "Despite the rhetoric of partnership, the literature suggests that many educators don't want parents or community groups as equal partners with agency and voice" (p. 32). Moreover, this plays out differently across school settings. Principals in schools with high concentrations of families living in poverty tend to be less proactive and effective at engaging parents than their counterparts serving schools with higher concentrations of families who are economically privileged (Rogers, Freelon, & Terriquez, 2012).

An ecological perspective toward parent engagement attends to these dynamics of power by seeing parents as "authors and agents" and their involvement as "a dynamic, interactive process in which parents draw on multiple experiences and resources to define their interactions with schools and among school actors" (Calabrese Barton, Drake, Perez Carreon, St. Louis, & George, 2004, p. 3). This perspective recognizes that parental interactions with schooling occur in both school-based spaces (some academic, others nonacademic) and home/community spaces (e.g., church-based groups, community organizations). Schools successful at engaging parents—particularly those traditionally marginalized—hold themselves accountable to engaging with and meeting the needs of parents across this variety of spaces (Lopez, Scribner, & Mahitivanichcha, 2001). This begins with developing processes to carefully listen to and communicate respectfully with parents (Ramirez, 2003; Scanlan, 2008) and a willingness to meet with families outside of schools in community spaces, which provide a more level playing field for relationships. Evidence suggests that building trusting, collaborative relationships with families and community members, recognizing and addressing families' diverse needs, and sharing power and responsibility in authentic partnerships are all features of schools where parent engagement correlates with growth in student learning (Henderson & Mapp, 2002).

Community Engagement

A third strand of literature is community engagement. In ways this literature parallels and overlaps with literature on parent engagement. Concentrated poverty and accompanying adverse social conditions create barriers for student learning (Noguera, 2011). These barriers include reduced academic and social supports available to students outside school as well as adverse conditions diminishing students' health, safety, and well-being. Research shows several trends of productive ways to foster community engagement to overcome such obstacles.

Toward this end, Warren (2005) describes three different approaches to collaboration between schools and community-based organizations. First, the service model—epitomized in community schools—uses schools as hubs that house a range of support services for families. For instance, community schools frequently include health clinics and provide adult education classes. Second, the development model involves the community sponsoring a new school, investing resources in creating the school as a vital organization in the neighborhood. Third, the organizing model uses schools as one partner amongst many local organizations working in a concerted manner to reform the quality of life in a neighborhood. As Warren (2005) summarizes:

> All three models seek to build new, stronger, and more collaborative relationships between and among parents, educators, and community members. In conceptual terms, they work to build social capital and relational power. But each model does so in different ways, which gives them distinctive strengths and weaknesses.
>
> (p. 163)

One lesson across all the models is the importance of investing resources in building social capital. For instance, schools with staff dedicated to engaging community and parent partners are much more successful. In addition, independent community organizations that bring together parents and school personnel across racial and economic diversity play an important role in developing *bridging* social capital across organizational boundaries, which strengthens relations between school personnel and families (Johnson, Carter, & Finn, 2011). Finally, conflicts around relational power, including racial tensions and competing organizational self-interests, often accompany all these models.

Place-Based Initiatives

Increasingly these models of community engagement are blended in place-based initiatives—such as Promise Neighborhoods and Neighborhood Educational Opportunity Zones—with substantial support from both federal grants and private foundations (Miller et al., 2013; Scanlan & Miller, 2013). Place-based initiatives function as social frontiers when they bring together people of different professions and social worlds, such as PreK–12 schools, child care agencies, providers of social service and health care, and economic development agencies. As Miller and colleagues (2014) describe:

> While still teaming with others who are predominantly like themselves (e.g., principals collaborating with other school personnel) or pursuing organization-specific goals/outcomes (e.g., principals focusing upon student achievement and school resource allotment), leaders on social frontiers are also challenged to expand their collaborative orientations and core objectives.

(p. 3)

These place-based initiatives typically target urban neighborhoods that, due to extreme concentrations of poverty, can be characterized as "truly disadvantaged" (Williams, 1987). Yet they also are directed toward rural, including tribal, contexts (Miller et al., 2013). Across these contexts, place-based initiatives strive to be guided by the collaborative efforts of people who are rooted, through work and residency, in the area. This stands in contrast to efforts of outsiders to come into communities to "solve their problems."

In these different formats, community engagement has many benefits. For instance, it can help children start school better prepared to learn, foster participation from more stakeholders in support of the school, and build public support for education (Warren, 2005). A central critique of efforts by schools to promote community engagement is that these efforts frequently focus primarily on improving schools, not communities, and encourage only token participation and decision-making by community stakeholders (Schutz, 2006). Schutz argues that more balanced and collaborative partnerships between schools and community organizations and residents have the *potential* to contribute not only to advance academic achievement within schools but also to evolve schools' core understandings of their "role in promoting a more equal and more democratic society" (p. 693).

Intersections

These three strands of literature—culturally responsive leadership, parent engagement, and community engagement—intersect to create a foundation for inclusive leadership on social frontiers. Each of these literatures describes different requisite knowledge, skills, and dispositions for school leaders to create productive relationships with colleagues and stakeholders beyond the schoolhouse doors. Together they necessitate the recognition that effective culturally responsive strategies to engage and work collectively with parents and community members may vary across different ethnic, cultural, and geographic communities. Advocacy by school leaders designed to challenge inequities must also be attuned to the particular community contexts in which they work.

Inclusive leadership *within schools* requires attending to the multiple, intersecting dimensions of diversity of students in order to cross cultural borders and integrate service delivery to meet needs associated with these dimensions. In a parallel manner, the inclusive leadership *on social frontiers* that we address requires attending to the multiple, intersecting dimensions of diversity in the broader familial and community context. Moreover, developing the knowledge and skills requires that aspiring and novice school leaders have access to authentic experiences working with parents and community organizations in equal status relationships. We now turn to apply these bodies of literature by describing specific examples of inclusive leadership on social frontiers.

PART 3: INCLUSIVE LEADERSHIP ON SOCIAL FRONTIERS IN SCHOOLS

As discussed at the outset, inclusive leadership on social frontiers is manifest through the practices of boundary spanning, border crossing, and advocacy. In order to illustrate specific ways this can look, we weave in examples of how parent and community organizations in different communities have engaged with schools and school leaders. We organize this into three themes:

- Tripping Equity Traps
- Fostering Relational Networks
- Building Partnerships

The themes are meant to help you, as a school leader or aspiring school leader, conceptualize these possible examples, as opposed to an exhaustive list.

At the outset of this section, we want to be clear about a point that we will weave throughout: these strategies for inclusive leadership on social frontiers are not ancillary. Rather, they are central to effective, innovative leadership that builds social justice. Abundant evidence shows that effectively engaging families and communities is an essential support for organizing schools to be effective learning environments (Bryk, Sebring, Allensworth, Luppescu, & Easton, 2010; Wahlstrom, Louis, Leithwood, & Anderson, 2010).

Tripping Equity Traps

Practicing boundary spanning, border crossing, and advocacy entails overcoming equity traps. McKenzie and Scheurich (2004) describe equity traps as "patterns of thinking and behavior that trap the possibilities for creating equitable schools for children of color. In other words, they trap equity; they stop or hinder our ability to move toward equity in schooling" (p. 603). For instance, some equity traps are deficit orientations toward students and families and refusal to face race, racism, and White privilege. In our experience, inclusive leadership on social frontiers entails "tripping"—or dismantling—these equity traps. Put differently, it requires acknowledging and overcoming patterns of thinking and behavior that hinder educators from moving toward engaging as boundary spanners, border crossers, and advocates for parents and community members.

Asset Orientations

One fundamental equity trap to inclusive leadership on social frontiers is deficit orientations (Schutz, 2006). Tripping this trap involves replacing deficit orientations with asset orientations. We know that students are more likely to succeed when educators hold and communicate ambitious expectations for students within schools (McKenzie & Scheurich, 2004). Deficit orientations are the antithesis of this (Valencia, 1997). In schools, directly confronting and dispelling myths of intellectual inferiority of people of color is an important step to interrupting deficit orientations and adopting a culturally responsive leadership approach (T. Perry, 2003a, 2003b). A practical step toward "tripping" this equity trap is by creating counternarratives (Delgado, 1989; I. Perry, 2011). The counternarrative to seeing communities as laden with deficits is to recognize, affirm, and build from assets in ways that join community resources with the school. Two examples of creating counternarratives is by recrafting space and by using schools as sites for continuing education.

Recrafting Space

Since the communities in which schools are located are often seen as places defined by their deficits, one way to interrupt this narrative is by seeing these communities through new perspectives.

Recrafting Outdoor Spaces at Schools

An example of creating this counternarrative is collaboratively recrafting outdoor spaces at schools. Several schools with which we have worked in both the United States and England have engaged in initiatives to transform sections of asphalt playgrounds into neighborhood vegetable gardens, rain gardens, native plant gardens, and outdoor spaces to house small animals (i.e., chickens and rabbits), that were cared for by the students. In each of these cases, the school communities were situated in densely populated urban areas with relatively few public green spaces. By leveraging resources from local foundations and businesses, these schools were able to fund the necessary materials to create community garden spaces. In each case, local residents were central to planning the space and implementing the change. This support was central to the gardens' success, as none of the schools were year-round, so school personnel were not around to tend to the space during the prime growing season.

Public gardens on playgrounds create counternarratives by inverting the traditional view of school playgrounds as separate, gated space reserved for school usage to shared, communal spaces that serve multiple audiences. A boundary between school and community that was formerly impervious has grown porous, and space that was once viewed as belonging solely to the school is now shared. This *process* of working together to recraft the school's outdoor space illustrates boundary spanning. As school personnel, parents, and other community members built the garden, they developed and deepened their relationships, but the educators do not need to leave their familiar roles and spaces to do so.

Recrafting Space in Neighborhoods

Another example of recrafting space is collaborative efforts to improve neighborhoods. For instance, one school with which we worked engaged in raising awareness about the need to protect a local waterway from pollutants. Using resources from a local foundation, students and community members stenciled storm drains with messages to inform the public about how these drain to a local waterway. They also created signage for a park about the history and health of the watershed. In another community, a local community organization converted abandoned plots of land into urban orchards, community vegetable gardens, and apiaries for beekeeping. The community group then welcomed schools to these spaces for field trips. In a third urban neighborhood students worked with the school's community liaison and other community residents to clean up a city park near the school that was filled with abandoned tires and garbage. Again, these serve as a counternarratives by inverting the common assumption that densely populated urban areas are necessarily disconnected from the natural environment. This example reflects not only boundary spanning, but culturally responsive advocacy as well: action by school personnel who challenge the status quo and work alongside community groups to advocate for the improvement of the neighborhood.

Continuing Education

A second example of creating counternarratives to deficit orientations is through using schools as sites for continuing education of parents and community members. Many schools innovatively use their resources to foster continuing education. Some efforts are long-term, such as providing space for English-as-a-Second-Language courses and African-centered cultural programs. Others are targeted, short-term initiatives, such as health and wellness workshops or legal clinics on immigration. When school leaders partner with community groups to provide continuing education, they create counternarratives to the destructive myths that people living in poverty are unmotivated or unable to use their agency to improve their communities. It also serves to refashion the school building as a community learning center that serves all ages.

Connecting to the Core Role as School Leader

You can create counternarratives in these (and other) ways in manners that both directly and indirectly connect back to the core teaching and learning in the school community. For instance, the process and products of recrafting space around the school are opportunities to integrate authentic curricular materials for addressing science, social studies, and writing standards. In addition, continuing education opportunities build the capacity of parents and caregivers to support and extend the learning of their children outside the schoolhouse doors.

GUIDING QUESTIONS

- How do you imagine the educators who establish continuing education in their school or are working to recraft the outdoor spaces in their school are practicing boundary spanning, border crossing, and advocacy?
- What are the challenges that educators face as they practice boundary spanning, border crossing, and advocacy?
- In your experience, what are other counternarratives that promote asset orientations to local communities?

Antiracism

A second equity trap to inclusive leadership on social frontiers is the reluctance of school personnel to directly and proactively confront racism and white privilege (McKenzie & Scheurich, 2004). Importantly, antiracism should be considered as a piece within the broader context of critically and proactively confronting all examples of oppression, ranging from ableism to misogyny to classism to heteronormativity to religious and linguistic prejudices. The biases operating at the personal level along with structures operating at institutional levels perpetuate these oppressions, and the chapters throughout this book elucidate the implications of these for school leadership. In the context of social frontiers, however, we focus on race because of its profound and persistent role impacting communities. Many—perhaps most—aspects of the residential neighborhoods in which students and families in our schools live are racialized. In other words, when considering a whole host of community aspects, from quality of life indicators to crime rates to housing to employment rates, practices of racial inequality persist (I. Perry, 2011).

In many urban areas a racial and ethnic mismatch exists between school personnel, many of whom are White, and neighborhood residents, who are often people of color. Addressing racism—both at the personal and institutional level—is frequently something that school personnel are reluctant to do. A practical way to trip this equity trap is to engage in antiracist training. School leaders can play a catalytic role in this, as Case Study 1 illustrates.

CASE STUDY 1
Bryce Elementary Grows Antiracist

Bryce Elementary (a pseudonym) is an elementary school in Chicago serving 350 students. Over the course of five years, Bryce developed an antiracist mission, vision, and identity. The school principal, Ms. Megan, spearheaded this effort. Ms. Megan had two decades of administrative experience, and had been at Bryce for six years. She was struck by the complexities that Bryce was experiencing as it went through a demographic transformation.

Most educators in Bryce—including Ms. Megan—were White and monolingual, and the population of teachers was relatively stable. In contrast, the student and neighborhood population had transformed in the past decade from being primarily White and native English speaking to being predominantly Latino, native Spanish speaking, and from several different national origins. This transformation was leading to increased tensions within the school community around language, race/ethnicity, and school identity.

As Ms. Megan considered this she became interested in antiracism. She started at the personal level, engaging in extensive training and reflection to raise her own awareness of racism and White privilege. She slowly undertook the process of critiquing this and developing an understanding and commitment to antiracism. This personal process of confronting her own racism and White privilege laid the foundation for Ms. Megan to consider how to address racism in Bryce as a school community. She began a deliberative, thoughtful process of working with teachers on developing the knowledge, skills, and dispositions of antiracism.

Just as the personal transformation was not a quick fix, but a methodical shift in orientation, so too was the institutional transformation. By steadily supporting teachers in on-going reflections and professional development, Bryce developed a deep and widespread commitment to antiracism. This resulted in a faculty-led process of recreating the school mission to explicate an antiracist identity. Importantly, while this antiracist commitment began at the behest of Ms. Megan, it grew to be widely shared. This led directly to increased engagement of parents within the school community, and laid a foundation for increased engagement with community members on shared initiatives.

As Case Study 1 suggests, educators can move across a continuum of boundary spanning, border crossing, and advocacy on social frontiers. In this case, the principal's initial movement toward antiracism was boundary crossing. By enrolling in a professional development course on antiracism she stretched outside her comfort zone, but did so on relatively familiar ground. But as she continued this journey, she also experienced border crossing by moving from predictable modes of learning (e.g., formal professional development activities) into interactions in which she was more vulnerable. Attending neighborhood meetings, for instance, placed her off her own "turf" and out of a position of authority. Yet this was a vital step to forging deeper relationships across race, ethnicity, and culture. Finally, she embraced advocacy by affirmatively embracing antiracism in the school policies and mission.

GUIDING QUESTIONS

- How do you identify with the educators in these examples practicing boundary spanning, border crossing, and advocacy?
- In your experience, what are other antiracist initiatives that apply to leadership on social frontiers?
- Asset orientations and antiracist initiatives are two ways to trip equity traps. Consider these as examples, not an exhaustive list. What are other equity traps—other patterns of thinking and behavior that trap the possibilities of inclusive schooling on social frontiers?

Fostering Relational Networks

In addition to tripping equity traps, a second way to pursue inclusive leadership on social frontiers is in fostering relational networks with families and community partners, which develop new understandings about community issues. We describe several examples of how school leaders can effectively build these relationships in their schools and how aspiring school leaders can learn network-building skills through their leadership preparation courses. Again, we emphasize the roles of boundary spanning, border crossing, and advocacy on these social frontiers.

Home Visits

The value of building personal relationships with families by having school personnel conduct home visits is not a new idea. Research has found this strategy to be valuable for engaging many traditionally marginalized populations in both urban and rural contexts (Henderson & Mapp, 2002; Lopez et al., 2001). Sometimes home visits are promoted by the district level with a well-defined process and goals (e.g., The Parent-Teacher Home Visit Project, http://www.pthvp.org/). At other times these are initiatives that arise within individual schools, or even just from particular teachers in schools. Home visits can be a way to learn about and highlight the "funds of knowledge" that are present in students' home environments (Gonzalez, Moll, & Amanti, 2005).

As a school leader, one important role you play is ensuring that home visits support productive learning. One barrier to productive learning is when individuals engaged in home visits work in isolation, without having opportunities to process and share their learning. As a result, the benefits of the visits are idiosyncratic and limited to individuals, rather than shared and systematic. Another more insidious threat to productive learning is that if educators are not well prepared and provided opportunities to process them, home visits can actually reinforce negative, deficit orientations toward families and communities.

Mindful of these barriers, school leaders must ensure productive learning from home visits. There are several ways to do this. First and most fundamentally, home visits must be resourced. When home visits are not adequately resourced, then they are only available to those who are able to volunteer additional time to participate. Providing meaningful professional development opportunities to prepare teachers and staff to develop an assets-based mindset for conducting home visits is another important strategy. This should include regular occasions for those making home visits to share successes and challenges they are experiencing with one another and with the broader school community. In addition, school leaders should gather and analyze data from all participants, including families, regarding what is beneficial and what can be improved about home visits. For instance, questions about home visits could be included on regular school climate surveys. E. Johnson (2014) provides school leaders with specific activities to help guide teachers through the process—before, during, and after the visit—that focus on procedures to help teachers use the home visits to develop deeper relationships with families (see Table 9.1, "Home Visit Procedural Framework").

Table 9.1 Home Visit Procedural Framework

Phase 1: Before the visit
* ★ Inquire about administrative policy on home visits.
* ★ Find school or community assistance with translation of documents or phone calls.
* ★ Send letters home with all students describing purpose of home visits.
* ★ Talk to parents about home visits in person when informal occasions arise.
* ★ Set up visits according to appropriate days/time for the family.
* ★ Research culturally appropriate etiquette for visits.
* ★ Collect home visit props (work samples, photographs, games, food, etc.).
* ★ Compile a list of community resources that might be useful to the family.

Phase 2: During the visit
* ★ When introducing yourself, let the family know what name they can use with you (e.g., Ms./Mr. Xyz or first name).
* ★ Greet everyone present, including young children.
* ★ Accept refreshments, though provide information about allergies if you cannot consume something being offered.
* ★ Discuss topics that are not related to school, if possible—use your props as a prompt for conversation.
* ★ Inquire about the family's home, customs, children, and so on.
* ★ Take pictures if appropriate—start by asking if it is OK to get a photo of you and your student (include siblings, pets, friends, etc.).
* ★ Mention to parents that you enjoy having parents visit your class, and extend an invitation if they seem interested.

Phase 3: After the visit
* ★ Record details of visit and develop a "funds of knowledge" list.
* ★ Share your experiences with faculty and administrators.
* ★ Send a thank-you note home with the student, and include photographs of the visit.
* ★ Post photographs in classroom on a "home visit wall" for other students and faculty to see (after getting permission from student).
* ★ Contact other parents about visits, especially those who know the families whom you have already visited.
* ★ Maintain informal communication—for example, send a personal note home to one family per week, or drop by the families' homes periodically for brief greetings.
* ★ Invite an administrator or colleague to accompany you on a subsequent visit.
* ★ Offer to accompany a colleague on a home visit.

Adapted from Johnson (2014).

Note that home visits provide a structure that may help educators move from boundary spanning into border crossing. Boundary spanning involves fostering relational networks with diverse partners, including parents, but can be done from within a familiar space. Border crossing asks educators to leave their familiar spaces and enter new ones.

GUIDING QUESTIONS

- How might some educators experience home visits as boundary spanning and others experience it as border crossing? How might discussing these differences in experience be helpful in a school community?
- How can home visits create opportunities for developing skills in advocacy?
- Who in your school community would be (or is) the biggest champion of home visits? Who would be (or is) the biggest critic? How can you, as a school leader, learn from people at both ends of this spectrum?

Community Walks and Story Mapping

Alongside home visits, two other strategies for fostering relational networks on social frontiers are community walks and story mapping. Community walks are designed to help educators develop some basic familiarity with the neighborhoods of school families. When done well, community walks provide a forum for learning about a variety of topics, such as housing issues, business and community organizations, religious institutions, and community-based advocacy organizations. A vital component to successful community walks is that educators hear from the perspective of community residents. This serves as a conscious-raising activity to provide educators with an insider's view about both assets and challenges present in the neighborhoods surrounding their school. A community resident can act as a "cultural broker" who brings familiarity with the neighborhood and a willingness to help teachers and administrators view the neighborhood in a new light. Case Study 2 provides an illustration of how a community walk can work.

CASE STUDY 2
Community Walks in Boston

In Spring 2014, as part of a Family and Community Engagement course at Boston College, local teachers and aspiring school leaders participated in "community walks" in diverse communities throughout the greater Boston metropolitan area, including Dorchester, Jamaica Plain, Allston-Brighton, Framingham, and Waltham. Modeled after the neighborhood walk activity described in the *UCEA Preparing Leaders to Support Diverse Learners* module on Family and Community Engagement (see http://ucea.org/neighborhood-walk-ple/), participants organized themselves into small groups of three to five participants. Some explored community institutions in the neighborhood where they taught while others elected to walk a Boston neighborhood quite culturally and ethnically different from their school neighborhood. As a culminating project each group produced a photo essay or digital story of the neighborhood and wrote a reflection about their experiences.

High school students served as the cultural brokers in two of the groups. One student high-lighted community sites that she deemed significant to neighborhood youth (e.g., the local park where they played sports and the Caribbean convenience store where they congregate with their friends after school). Another student leader discussed local divisions along class and race lines and the unfair stereotypes about crime associated with his neighborhood. Although some stops on the community walks were predetermined, each group also experienced serendipitous experiences along the way, such as a conversation with a community organizer at City Life, a storefront organization in Jamaica Plain that fights banks on behalf of residents who have fallen prey to "predatory lending practices" that result in foreclosure. Some groups later used the contacts they made during their community walk for a follow-up class inquiry project, which required them to collect data about a neighborhood issue from the perspective of at least two stakeholder groups.

Story Mapping

A related activity to community walks that also can help foster relational networks is *story mapping*. The goal of story mapping is to uncover, recover, and retell the stories and assets of community members in order to develop a road map for future advocacy. In the story mapping process there are multiple ways to develop community stories (see Table 9.2).

In May 2014 a story mapping process was modeled in Pittsburgh at the 7th Annual Duquesne Educational Leadership Symposium. The theme of the symposium was "Rivers of Justice, Bridges of Love: What is the new steel upon which we re-imagine a healthier, more equitable Pittsburgh community?" Duquesne University graduate students, visiting university professors from around the country, and community residents worked in teams of three to collect stories in the Hill District and West Pittsburgh neighborhoods over a two-day period. Community residents conducted the interviews, and Duquesne University students (many of whom are Pittsburgh school leaders) and visiting university professors served as notetakers and critical friends. Shifting the power relationships in the story

Table 9.2 Story Mapping Strategies

1. Use a pre-determined prompt

   A prompt asks the storyteller to consider a particular event and tell the story of a conflict or dilemma. That may be followed by reflective questions that support deeper reflection. Those stories help the storyteller talk through a dilemma and come to some ideas about how to address an issue.

2. Create a digital story

   A digital story asks the director/writer to frame a story around an individual or collective or community autobiography, biography, or issue. The story is told through the eyes, research, images, and perspective of the person or team constructing the script and choosing the images for the story.

3. Interview community members

   An interview can provide the framework for a story. Begin with guiding questions to start the interview, and continue with probing questions in response to what the storyteller says. That story emerges as a dialogue between the interviewer and the interviewee. When multiple persons are interviewed in a community, this helps the group map the story of the community through several stories and experiences.

mapping process provides an authentic border-crossing experience where school leaders learn to take leadership from community residents who identify what issues in the neighborhood matter, and what advocacy school leaders might provide in the neighborhood improvement process. Short one-page stories were written up based on the interviews and shared across the groups for further reflection. These story mapping techniques, which are part of Community Learning Exchanges developed by the Center for Ethical Leadership, are designed to honor collective leadership by local residents for sustainable community change (see more detail at http://www.communitylearningexchange.org).

GUIDING QUESTIONS

- How do story mapping and neighborhood walks foster relational networks in different ways than home visits?
- How might some participants experience community walks and story mapping as boundary spanning and others experience these as border crossing? How might discussing these differences in experience be helpful in a school community?
- How can these create opportunities for developing skills in advocacy?
- Who in your school community would be (or is) the biggest champion of neighborhood walks and story mapping? Who would be (or is) the biggest critic? How can you, as a school leader, learn from people at both ends of this spectrum?

Building Partnerships

Alongside tripping equity traps and fostering relational networks, a third way to pursue inclusive leadership on social frontiers is building partnerships across organizations. Partnerships are linkages—some more formalized, others less so—that connect individuals working in these different sectors into common pursuits. We briefly discuss three organizational levels that we have seen catalyzing these partnerships: PreK–12 educational institutions, institutes of higher education, and community-based organizations. Organizational structures promote and facilitate partnerships across these levels. These structures support practices of boundary spanning, border crossing, and advocacy.

PreK–12 Educational Institutions

First, educational institutions—at the school and district level—often catalyze partnerships. Often developed through coalitions between community advocates and their school district allies, the development of inclusive structures and dedicated staff positions serve to provide official sanction and recognition of the importance of parent and community engagement. These structures also create culturally responsive avenues to assist both families and educators to both span cultural boundaries and cross cultural borders. In Case Study 3 we describe examples from the Boston Public Schools (BPS) and the Toronto District School Board (TDSB) that underscore the importance of these structures at both the building and district levels for providing parents and community members a "place at the table" in educational decision-making.

CASE STUDY 3
Schools and Districts Catalyzing Partnerships

In Boston, parent organizations such as BPON (the Boston Parent Organizing Network) targeted the appointment of a full-time Parent Liaison or Community Partnership Coordinator in every Boston public school as a key community organizing issue. As noted in their mission statement, BPON "organizes, develops and supports parents and families who are marginalized by class, race, language, disabilities and immigration status to work with and hold accountable the Boston Public School system to provide an excellent education for all students." (For more information on BPON, see http://bpon.org) BPON successfully advocated with school district leadership to establish these building-level positions, as well as a cabinet-level position for Assistant Superintendent for Family and Student Engagement. A former parent organizer from BPON, Michele Brooks, was hired to fill the district position. Her office also sponsors a student advocacy group (the Boston Student Advisory Council), whose members advocated for a new Student Disciplinary Code and were active in recent neighborhood forums to identify the qualities that parents and community members are looking for in a new superintendent for BPS. The partnerships established between advocacy organizations such as BPON and their school district allies legitimate advocacy as part of the school improvement process.

TDSB first established consultative committees (e.g., Black Consultative Committee, Portuguese Consultative Committee) in the late 1970s to provide parents and community members from particular ethnic communities a forum to discuss with school officials issues that affected their ethnic community. Historically these committees worked with the Toronto school district officials to draft and monitor the first Race Relations Policy in a North American school district in 1979 and advocate for more teachers of color and multicultural curriculum in the Toronto schools. The establishment of the district position of Executive Officer for Student and Community Equity in 2005, filled by longtime equity advocate Lloyd McKell, provided a cabinet-level position to collect data on the racial achievement gap in relation to African Canadian students, and the establishment of a parent-district task force, which led to the development of Toronto's first Afri-centric Public Elementary School in 2009. As immigration to Toronto has shifted in recent years to include East African families, a new Somali Consultative Committee was established. Over the years, these consultative committees have provided an official space where parents and school district officials could work together to make the Toronto schools more culturally responsive.

Institutes of Higher Education

While sometimes PreK–12 schools and districts prompt partnerships, at other times institutes of higher education (IHEs) are the instigators. There are several advantages for school leaders who look to colleagues in IHEs to facilitate partnerships. First, IHEs can play the role of being neutral players who bridge relationships amongst institutions on social frontiers which otherwise would be isolated or even in competition with one another. Secondly, IHEs bring different types of resources—such as content-area expertise in a variety of fields—that can prove valuable in crafting productive partnerships. Finally, IHEs often enjoy a strong reputation in the extended community that schools and community partners can exploit to help establish the credibility of nascent partnerships. In Case Study 4 we describe an example of this.

CASE STUDY 4
An IHE Catalyzing Partnerships

The Center for Urban Research and Learning (CURL) was established in 1996 at Loyola University in Chicago with a mission to create "innovative solutions that promote equity and opportunity in communities throughout the Chicago metropolitan region" (http://www.luc.edu/curl/Mission. shtml). In contrast to most centers that promote collaboration with community groups to examine research that is driven by the interests and agendas of faculty, CURL operates on a team model of research. "A primary element in CURL's mission is to bring the community's eyes, ears, and voice to the metaphorical or real 'research table'" (Nyden, 2009, p. 2). Community members serve as integral team members proposing and designing any research project. Nyden (2009), a founding member and director of CURL, describes the fluid process of conceptualizing new partnership ideas:

> The venues for conceptualization vary. They have been breakfasts with community leaders where emerging community needs are discussed. They have been meetings with executive directors and/or staff of social service agencies related to pressing internal evaluation needs. In other instances, collaborative research projects themselves have generated new research ideas. When new issues emerge out of ongoing research, CURL often convenes "think tank" meetings of potentially interested faculty, community leaders, and policy makers to discuss facets of an issue and how additional information—either existing data or newly collected data—may be useful in addressing that issue.
>
> (pp. 2–3)

The innovative structure of CURL includes recognizing that community partners need not only a seat at the table, but compensation as well:

> To provide a more level playing field in collaborative research, CURL has always worked to build in compensation for community partners. While this can take the form of paying for community organization office space or other project expenses, it most often means salary support for staff members involved in the research team. CURL offers community fellowships which range from $5,000 to $10,000 in a given year.
>
> (Nyden, 2009, p. 7)

CURL partnerships engage Loyola faculty and students to work with community and nonprofit organizations, civic groups, and government agencies to address specific issues, which range widely, including homelessness, hunger and nutrition, community health and safety, and job training and placement.

Community-Based Organizations

Finally, community-based organizations (CBOs) at times are the catalysts for building partnerships on social frontiers. As opposed to partnerships that originate with PreK-12 schools or IHEs, partnerships that emerge from CBOs are most naturally based in the needs of the community members. Here the roles are reversed: schools are invited to the table, as opposed to being the hosts who invite others.

Examples of partnerships that originate in CBOs abound. Sometimes local foundations provide the start-up funding for such partnerships. For instance, the Zilber Neighborhood Initiative has funded several CBOs focusing on sustained neighborhood transformation efforts in Milwaukee, Wisconsin (Zilber Family Foundation, n.d.). At other times, state governments provide this funding. For instance, the Department of Human Services in Dane County, Wisconsin, has created a series of 16 offices—nine urban, seven rural—that coordinate "voluntary, community-based, supportive service that helps families address their basic human needs" (Joining Forces for Families, n.d.). Teams from various sectors, including public health nurses, social workers, school personnel, clergy, and others work "to support efforts to make their community a safer, healthier place to live." Examples of this include creating job fairs, hosting immunization clinics, helping families register and prepare children for school, and organizing citizens to problem-solve public safety concerns.

Another way to partner with CBOs is via community-based internships. Such internships require aspiring school leaders to engage with diverse families and community-based projects for an extended period of time. Leadership preparation programs typically require the completion of 300–500 practicum hours working in schools in order to provide hands-on experience to learn leadership skills. Some states, such as Massachusetts, have added Family and Community Engagement as one of the state-wide leadership standards and instituted performance-based assessments, which all candidates must complete before qualifying for their principal licensure. Community-oriented internships provide practicum experiences where aspiring school leaders can learn boundary spanning and advocacy skills by apprenticing with principals who are deeply connected to their local community, or work under the leadership of parents and neighborhood leaders in community-based improvement projects. For example, this might involve working with the Community Partnership Coordinator at a full-service middle school to assess student and parent needs regarding the high school choice process, or an internship at a local community center that is providing outreach and advocacy for families who are displaced because of school closures in their urban neighborhood. To be most effective, these internships should be coupled with seminars where aspiring school leaders can dialogue and critically reflect on how their experiences in diverse communities intersect with issues of race, culture, and power (Auerbach, 2009; Johnson & Campbell-Stephens, 2013).

Roles of School Leaders

The differing levels from which partnerships originate—PreK–12 schools and districts, IHEs, or CBOs—influence how school leaders engage in roles of boundary spanning, border crossing, and advocacy. Partnerships structured via schools and districts tend to promote boundary spanning opportunities, facilitating relationships from within traditional roles. Partnerships activated by CBOs are more apt to provide opportunities for border crossing and advocacy, as they require educators to give up more control to enter. Partnerships rooted in IHEs run the gamut. Across all levels, however, a key component to remember is that the structures, such as specific roles and committees (see Case Study 3) or new organizations (see Case Study 4), play an important role in shaping these roles. For instance, CURL could have been structured in a manner that facilitated boundary spanning. Yet as configured, it is much more likely that the partnerships it spurs result in advocacy as well.

Returning to a point we made earlier, the role of school leaders in such partnerships is a departure and expansion on the traditional emphasis in school-community relations on public relations. Being a boundary spanner, border crosser, and advocate is a stance. School leaders take this stance when they engage with community organizers proactively. One motivation for this is a recognition that this stance can enhance the teaching and learning directly in their school communities—such as by providing new opportunities to meet the needs of students or families. Another motivation is a recognition of the indirect effects of such partnerships, such as strengthened alliances with stakeholders in the community. In other words, some of the benefits are more immediate and tangible, while others are delayed and less tangible.

GUIDING QUESTIONS

- Reflect on the partnerships between schools and other organizations with which you have participated. Have these been catalyzed by PreK–12 schools or districts, IHEs, or CBOs? Have they promoted roles of boundary spanning, border crossing, or advocacy?
- What are the low-hanging fruit for building partnerships in your context?

EQUITY AUDIT QUESTIONS

Projects like equity audits (see Chapter 10 in this volume) where achievement gaps and differences in teacher quality are compared across local school districts can help uncover how schools reinforce social inequality. These audits might also include analyzing the curriculum to investigate whose culture is included (or not) in textbooks, school assemblies, extra-curricular activities, and parent involvement programs. The final chapter of this text describes a comprehensive equity audit process. See the social frontiers section and full equity audit detailed in Chapter 10 and online (www.routledge.com/cw/theoharis).

CONCLUSION

In this chapter, we have explored how school leaders engage families and external community members in their efforts to craft school communities that are inclusive in the context of social frontiers. We have emphasized that school leaders navigate these social frontiers by being boundary spanners, border crossers, and advocates, applying these roles to the practices of tripping equity traps, fostering relational networks, and building partnerships. This is substantively different from traditional approaches to community relations. As boundary spanners, border crossers, and advocates, school leaders recognize that while their central responsibility resides in the school, authentic partnerships with families and community members need not exclusively focus on the school as the center, and that power in envisioning and enacting such partnerships should be distributed across key stakeholders.

A key implication that we want to underscore in this conclusion is how engaging in these roles beyond the schoolhouse doors complements inclusive leadership *within* the school community. These are complementary in many ways, two of which we focus on here.

First, by practicing boundary spanning, border crossing, and advocacy with families and community groups, school leaders enhance skills that also apply to working with students and families each day inside the school. Each of us is more familiar and comfortable with some dimensions of diversity more than others. Clearly we play to these advantages when building relationships on social frontiers. For example, if I am a native Spanish speaker and have a bilingual family, I am going to be more adept at working with my Latino community members. But I cannot stop there, ignoring the other stakeholders with whom I am less accustomed. As we have discussed throughout this chapter, school leaders need to learn ways to engage with *all* their families and community partners, not just the ones that come easily. In a parallel manner, within our schools we typically are more comfortable with some dimensions of diversity and less so with others. For instance, if I identify as a heterosexual woman and have a brother who identifies as gay, I may find myself very much at ease engaging with the Gay-Straight Alliance at the middle school where I am the principal. But I may find that—since I identify as an atheist—I have a strong reluctance to discuss religious pluralism in the school community. Thus, growing my skills at boundary spanning, border crossing, and advocacy on the social frontier can help strengthen my practices at engaging across the multiple dimensions of diversity within my school.

Second, since the practices of boundary spanning, border crossing, and advocacy are all asset-oriented, these may provide novel insights into community resources that can support my efforts at inclusion within the school. Throughout the other chapters in this text authors have focused on building asset-oriented approaches to inclusion across multiple dimensions of diversity—from race to language to gender to socioeconomic status to sexual orientation to disability to religion. Either implicitly or explicitly, many of the strategies suggested in these chapters involve not just drawing upon existing resources within the school, but engaging community members in bringing new resources to the school. Tripping equity traps, fostering relational networks, and building partnerships are specific strategies for identifying and securing such resources.

REFERENCES

Akkerman, S., & Bakker, A. (2011). Boundary crossing and boundary objects. *Review of Educational Research, 81*(2), 132–169.

Anderson, G. (1998). Toward authentic participation: Deconstructing the discourses of participatory reforms in education. *American Educational Research Journal, 35*(4), 571–603.

Anderson, G. (2009). *Advocacy leadership: Toward a post-reform agenda in education*. New York, NY: Routledge.

Auerbach, S. (2009). Walking the walk: Portraits in leadership for family engagement in urban schools. *The School Community Journal, 19*(1), 9–32.

Auerbach, S. (2012). Conceptualizing leadership for authentic partnerships. In S. Auerbach (Ed.), *School leadership for authentic family and community partnerships: Research perspectives for transforming practice* (pp. 29–51). New York, NY: Routledge.

Berliner, D. (2014). Effects of inequality and poverty vs. teachers and schooling on America's youth. *Teachers College Record, 116*(1).

Bryk, A., Sebring, P.B., Allensworth, E., Luppescu, S., & Easton, J. (2010). *Organizing schools for improvement: Lessons from Chicago*. Chicago, IL: University of Chicago Press.

Burt, R. (1992). *Structural holes: The social structure of competition*. Cambridge, MA: Harvard University Press.

Calabrese Barton, A., Drake, C., Perez Carreon, G., St. Louis, K., & George, M. (2004). Ecologies of parental engagement in urban education. *Educational Researcher, 33*(4), 3–12.

Cambron-McCabe, N., & McCarthy, M. (2005). Educating school leaders for social justice. *Educational Policy, 19*(1), 201–222.

Delgado, R. (1989). Storytelling for oppositionists and others: A plea for narrative. *Michigan Law Review, 87*(8), 2411–41.

Duncan, G., & Murnane, R. (2011). Introduction: The American dream, then and now. In G. Duncan & R. Murnane (Eds.), *Whither opportunity?* (pp. 3–23). New York, NY: Russell Sage Foundation.

Epstein, J. (1986). Parents' reactions to teacher practices of parent involvement. *The Elementary School Journal, 86*, 277–294.

Epstein, J. (1990). School and family connections: Theory, research, and implications for integrating sociologies of education and family. *Marriage & Family Review, 15*(2), 99–126.

Epstein, J., & Salinas, K. C. (2004). Partnering with families and communities. *Educational Leadership, 61*(8), 12–18.

Erickson, F. (2007). Culture in society and in educational practices. In J. A. Banks & C. A. M. Banks (Eds.), *Multicultural education* (6th ed., pp. 33–61). Danvers, MA: John Wiley & Sons, Inc.

Fine, M. (1993). [Ap]parent involvement: Reflections on parents, power, and urban public schools. *Teachers College Record, 94*(4), 682–710.

Gay, G. (2010). *Culturally responsive teaching: Theory, research, and practice* (2nd ed.). New York, NY: Teachers College Press.

Gonzalez, N., Moll, L. C., & Amanti, C. (2005). *Funds of knowledge: Theorizing practices in households, communities, and classrooms.* Mahwah, NJ: Erlbaum.

Henderson, A., & Mapp, K. L. (2002). *A new wave of evidence: The impact of school, family, and community on student achievement.* Austin, TX: Southwest Educational Development Laboratory.

Johnson, E. (2014). From the classroom to the living room: Eroding inequities through home visits. *Journal of School Leadership, 24*(2), 357–385.

Johnson, L. (2006). "Making her community a better place to live": Culturally responsive urban school leadership in historical perspective. *Leadership and Policy in Schools, 5*, 19–37.

Johnson, L. (2007). Rethinking successful school leadership in challenging U.S. schools: Culturally responsive practices in school-community relationships. *International Studies in Educational Administration, 35*(3), 49–57.

Johnson, L., & Campbell-Stephens, R. (2013). Beyond the colorblind perspective: Centering issues of race and culture in leadership preparation programs in Britain and the United States. In I. Bogotch & C. Shields (Eds.), *International handbook of educational leadership and social [in]justice* (pp. 1169–1185). Dordrecht, Netherlands: Springer.

Johnson, L., Carter, J., & Finn, M. (2011). Parent empowerment through organizing for collective action. In C. Hands & L. Hubbard (Eds.), *Including families and communities in urban education* (pp. 69–95). Charlotte, NC: Information Age.

Joining Forces for Families. (n.d.). Retrieved June 1, 2014, from https://danecountyhumanservices.org/Family/JoiningForcesForFamilies/introduction.aspx

Ladson-Billings, G. (1994). *The dreamkeepers: Successful teachers of African American children.* San Francisco, CA: Jossey-Bass.

Ladson-Billings, G. (1995a). Toward a theory of culturally relevant pedagogy. *American Education Research Journal, 32*(3), 465–491.

Ladson-Billings, G. (1995b). But that's just good teaching! The case for culturally relevant pedagogy. *Theory Into Practice, 34*(3), 159–165.

Lopez, G. R., Gonzalez, M. L., & Fierro, E. (2006). Educational leadership along the U.S.—Mexico border: Crossing borders/embracing hybridity/building bridges. In C. Marshall & M. Oliva (Eds.), *Leadership for social justice: Making revolutions in education* (pp. 64–84). Boston, MA: Pearson.

Lopez, G. R., Scribner, J. D., & Mahitivanichcha, K. (2001). Redefining parental involvement: Lessons from high-performing migrant-impacted schools. *American Educational Research Journal, 38*(2), 253–288.

McKenzie, K. B., & Scheurich, J. J. (2004). Equity traps: A useful construct for preparing principals to lead schools that are successful with racially diverse students. *Educational Administration Quarterly, 40*(5), 601–631.

Miller, P. M. (2008). Examining the work of boundary spanning leaders in community contexts. *International Journal of Leadership in Education, 11*(4), 353–377.

Miller, P. M. (2009). Boundary spanning in homeless children's education: Notes from an emergent faculty role in Pittsburgh. *Educational Administration Quarterly, 45*(4), 616–630.

Miller, P.M., Scanlan, M., & Wills, N. (2014). Leadership on the social frontier: Principals' roles in comprehensive reform settings. *Principal's Research Review, 9*(2), 1–6.

Miller, P.M., Wills, N., & Scanlan, M. (2013). Educational leadership on the social frontier: Developing promise neighborhoods in urban and tribal settings. *Educational Administration Quarterly, 49*(4), 543–575.

Noguera, P. (2011). A broader and bolder approach uses education to break the cycle of poverty. *Phi Delta Kappan, 93*(3), 9–14.

Nyden, P. (2009). *Collaborative university-community research teams.* Chicago, IL: Center for Urban Research and Learning.

Paris, D. (2012). Culturally sustaining pedagogy: A needed change in stance, terminology, and practice. *Educational Researcher, 41*(3), 93–97.

Paris, D., & Alim, S. (2014). What are we seeking to sustain through culturally sustaining pedagogy? A loving critique forward. *Harvard Education Review, 84*(1), 85–100.

Perry, I. (2011). *More beautiful and more terrible.* New York: New York University Press.

Perry, T. (2003a). Tackling the myth of black students' intellectual inferiority. *The Chronicle Review, 49*(18), B10–B12.

Perry, T. (2003b). Young, gifted and black: Promoting high achievement among African American students. In T. Perry, C. Steele, & A. Hilliard (Eds.), *Young, gifted and black: Promoting high achievement among African American students* (pp. 131–165). Boston, MA: Beacon Press.

Ramirez, A.Y.F. (2003). Dismay and disappointment: Parental involvement of Latino immigrant parents. *The Urban Review, 35*(2), 93–110.

Reitzig, U. C., & Patterson, J. (1998). "I'm not going to lose you!" Empowerment through caring in an urban principal's practice with students. *Urban Education, 33,* 150–181.

Riehl, C. (2000). The principal's role in creating inclusive schools for diverse learners: A review of normative, empirical, and critical literature on the practice of educational administration. *Review of Educational Research, 70*(1), 55–81.

Rogers, J., Freelon, R., & Terriquez, V. (2012). Enlisting collective help. In S. Auerbach (Ed.), *School leadership for authentic family and community partnerships: Research perspectives for transforming practice* (pp. 55–77). New York, NY: Routledge.

Rose, M. (2009). *Why school?* New York, NY: New Press.

Scanlan, M. (2008). Caregiver engagement in religious urban elementary schools. *Marriage & Family Review, 43*(2), 308–337.

Scanlan, M., & Miller, P.M. (2013). In fits and starts: Learning to create a neighborhood educational opportunity zone. *Teachers College Record, 115*(5), 1–44.

Scheurich, J. (1998). Highly successful and loving, public elementary schools populated mainly by low SES children of color: Core beliefs and cultural characteristics. *Urban Education, 33*(4), 451–491.

Schutz, A. (2006). Home is a prison in the global city: The tragic failure of school-based community engagement strategies. *Review of Educational Research, 76*(4), 691–743.

Theoharis, G. (2007). Social justice educational leaders and resistance: Toward a theory of social justice leadership. *Educational Administration Quarterly, 43*(2), 221–258.

Valencia, R. (Ed.). (1997). *The evolution of deficit thinking: Educational thought and practice.* Washington, DC: Falmer Press.

Villegas, A. M., & Lucas, T. (2001). *Educating culturally responsive teachers: A coherent approach.* Albany: State University of New York Press.

Wahlstrom, K., Louis, K.S., Leithwood, K., & Anderson, S. (2010). *Investigating the links to improved student learning: Executive summary of research findings.* Washington, DC: Wallace Foundation.

Warren, M. (2005). Comunities and schools: A new view of urban education reform. *Harvard Educational Review, 75*(2), 133–173.

Williams, W.J. (1987). *The truly disadvantaged: The inner city, the underclass, and public policy.* Chicago, IL: University of Chicago Press.

Zilber Family Foundation. (n.d.). Zilber Neighborhood Initiative. Retrieved from http://www.znimilwaukee.org/

The Equity Audit as the Core of Leading Increasingly Diverse Schools and Districts

Colleen A. Capper and Michelle D. Young

Educators "overwhelmingly do not have a clear, accurate, or useful understanding of the degree of inequity present in their own schools and school districts."

(Skrla, McKenzie, & Scheurich, 2009, p. 5)

The past two decades have witnessed significant change within the field of education. Among the most influential changes is the increased emphasis on educational accountability within individual states and the nation as a whole. Policy-makers across the United States expect all schools to ensure that all children meet or exceed state academic performance standards (Skrla et al., 2009). This emphasis has been marked both by increased levels of policy activity and by a growing body of scholarship focused on accountability and its impact. Within this literature, scholars have developed a robust conversation focused on equity audits.

Although the use of equity audits is relatively new within the field of educational administration, they have a significant history in education and other professional fields (Skrla, et al., 2009). Their most significant application has been to determine compliance with a number of civil rights statutes that prohibit discrimination in programs and activities receiving federal funding. As the name suggests, such audits involve the collection and systematic review of a variety of data sources, including but not limited to accountability data. According to Skrla et al. (2009), equity audits provide a systematic way for educational leaders to leverage accountability toward equitable and high-achieving schools for all students.

Given the essential role educational leaders play in fostering positive school culture, developing teacher effectiveness and supporting student learning, addressing equity and opportunity gaps must be a chief concern of educational leaders and those that prepare them (Capper, Theoharis & Sebastian, 2006). Opportunities to learn will not become more equitable until this becomes a priority for school leaders and they have the knowledge and skills needed to respond effectively. Eliminating equity and opportunity gaps and ensuring a high-quality education for all student populations depends chiefly upon the capacity of educational leaders. However, it also depends upon the capacity of local universities to prepare and support educational leaders who can achieve such results, even in the most challenging school contexts.

In this chapter, we position the equity audit as the primary equity practice in schools, providing insight for both educational leaders and those that prepare them. We begin with an overview of scholarly literature focused on equity audits. We then delineate the six phases we consider essential to an effective equity audit: (1) identify integrated practices as measured by proportional representation as the anchoring philosophy for equity audits; (2) establish the equity audit team; (3) design the audit; (4) collect and analyze data; (5) set and prioritize data-based goals; and (6) develop an equity implementation plan.

EQUITY AUDITS AS A FOCUS OF SCHOLARSHIP

Educational scholars have long employed the methods of equity audits. The process was introduced to the educational leadership community by Capper, Frattura, and Keyes (2000), who offered a Demographic Questionnaire as a key tool in leading beyond inclusion and which included detailed and key components of later equity audits. In the mid-2000s a group of researchers in Texas (Skrla, Scheurich, Garcia, & Nolly, 2004; Skrla et al., 2009) formally introduced the term *equity audits* to the field, and Capper and Frattura (2009) further revised their equity audit for leaders. Since that time, scholars have engaged in a variety of inquiry and development projects involving equity audits, many seeking to expand the focus of equity audits or to more explicitly define the methods used to conduct equity audits and to make the best use of equity audit results. The published literature on equity audits, as a result, can be organized into two general categories: (1) literature that features the implementation of full or partial equity audits; and (2) literature that explores the preparation of leaders to engage in equity audits.

Exploring the Use of Equity Audits

Questions about compliance anchored the purposes of many of the first-generation audit processes, including curriculum audits and civil rights investigations. For example, the civil rights program audits provided a detailed method of determining the degree of compliance with a number of requirements designed to prohibit discrimination in educational programs and activities receiving federal funding. However, such processes, as Skrla and colleagues (2009) point out, produce large volumes of data, and as a result, have limited utility for the typical educational leader. In response, a number of scholars, including Capper et al. (2000; Capper & Frattura, 2009; Frattura & Capper, 2007) and Skrla and colleagues (2009), have suggested scaled-back versions that can be implemented in shorter time frames and with fewer resources.

The scaled-back version developed by Skrla and colleagues (2009) examines three key equity issues: (1) teacher quality; (2) programmatic equity; and (3) achievement equity, which they argue are the most important indicators of educational equity. Their audit involves five phases, including: (1) bringing together stakeholders; (2) gathering the data and presenting it to the group; (3) openly discussing the data and the equity gaps that were revealed; (4) developing solutions; and (5) implementing solutions and monitoring results. These scholars note that "the power of . . . equity auditing is in the process itself—the process of making the choices about how to proceed, of gathering the data, of discussing the presentation of the results, of grappling with the meaning of what is revealed by the audit, and of planning for change" (p. 25).

Bleyaert (2011) also learned about the importance of the equity process itself when she piloted an equity audit instrument and process in five high schools diverse by size and across the urban, suburban, rural spectrum. These schools were all required by a state equity mandate to strengthen math requirements across all students. In this study, schools emerged as "mission schools" that leveraged the state mandate and equity audit process to strengthen the equity work they were already doing. "Compliance schools" that failed to address many of the equity audit questions viewed the equity audit process and the state mandate as a "bookkeeping headache" (p. 7), and ". . . the language used by leaders in the compliance-focused schools often suggested an expectation of student failure and a focus on planning directly related to that expected failure" (p. 9).

McKenzie and Scheurich (2004) delineated a number of different equity traps that educational leaders may encounter in their schools, including holding deficit perspectives, engaging in racial erasure, and avoiding and employing "the gaze." According to these authors, equity traps are assumptions that prevent educators from believing that their students can be successful learners. One of several strategies suggested for understanding and eliminating equity traps was the equity audit. The authors described the audit process as "a simple way to start a discussion of inequities within a school or district" (p. 618), and explained that it involved gathering, analyzing, and discussing data and then devising and implementing solutions. As such, the data become the basis for analyzing problematic situations, discussing how to address the situation, and then devising actions to challenge the inequities. They further note that "the process of analyzing, discussing and devising solutions makes teachers aware of the need to focus positively" on student differences (p. 618).

McKenzie and Skrla (2011) extended their work on school-level equity audits to focus equity audits at the classroom level that interrogate classroom teaching and learning. Filled with practical strategies that can help teachers and leaders transform classroom learning for all students, they suggest how to conduct equity audits for teaching and learning, discipline, parent involvement, and programmatic equity. Johnson and Avelar LaSalle (2010) provide an additional detailed guide for gathering equity data to uncover and address hidden inequities in schools. Importantly, their data process is also grounded in inclusive integrated, heterogeneous classrooms and schools. This same theme anchors both the equity audits we present later in this chapter, as well as the chapters throughout this book.

Brown (2010) relied on an equity audit process to examine data associated with state-recognized "Honor Schools of Excellence" in North Carolina. Results revealed a fair amount of equity in the schools with regard to teacher quality and program access; however, the results also revealed great disparities between the achievement of students in different school types. In addition to their practicality and ease of use, Brown notes the utility of audits in developing objective assessments of equity, particularly in complex school contexts. Similarly, Sailes (2008) examined factors that contributed to the achievement gap between different student groups and, based on the data analysis, discussed the importance of such audit processes in addressing academic disparities. More limited in scale, Bustamante, Nelson, and Onwuegbuzie (2009) focused their equity audit on the cultural competence of educational leaders. Their primary tool for gathering data, the Schoolwide Cultural Competence Observation Checklist, supplemented other school-level data to audit the school culture broadly and the views of the school leader specifically. Although the typical focus of equity audits is urban schools, Cleveland et al. (2012) describe the use of the audit process within rural Appalachian schools. They were particularly interested in understanding the relationship between equity, school culture, and student academic performance.

As the popularity of the equity audit has grown, its uses have evolved. For example, Lewis, James, Hancock, and Hill-Jackson (2008) used what they referred to as a "quasi equity audit in that it reviews national achievement data as a means to begin a conversation on test score gaps as an indicator of inequality" (p. 131). Grounded in critical race theory, their work sought to frame ideological positions of success and failure for African American students in urban school settings. Clearly, this study holds implications for the development of larger-scale equity audits at the state and national level.

Preparing Leaders to Conduct Equity Audits

The second area of literature we examined for this review considers how leaders should be prepared to conduct or lead equity audits. The question of "how do we prepare leaders to engage in the equity audit process?" is an important one. A growing body of research demonstrates a strong relationship between quality program content and learning experiences and graduates' leadership practices (Darling-Hammond, LaPointe, Meyerson, & Orr, 2007; Young, Crow, Murphy, & Ogawa, 2009). Specifically, research indicates that educational leaders are best prepared through curriculum and learning experiences that are well-defined, purposeful, and coherent, and which include challenging and reflective content (Darling-Hammond et al., 2007; Young et al., 2009). Given these findings, we would expect that strategically designed and focused opportunities to learn about and to implement equity audits could yield improvement in leader practices.

The scholarship in this area includes descriptions of equity audits in educational leadership preparation programs and publications that incorporate equity audits as preparation tools, such as case studies for classroom use. Interestingly, a few publications also capture the use of equity audits to examine equity issues within educational leadership preparation programs. For example, Karanxha, Agosto, and Bellara (2013) describe a process of program self-assessment attuned to equity and justice, with a specific focus on the policies and practices that affect candidate diversity, such as candidate selection. Capper (2014) has developed and is piloting an equity audit instrument and process specifically designed for teacher and leadership preparation programs that aligns with effective leadership and teaching practices in high-achieving, inclusive, equitable schools.

Boske's (2012) description of how her program prepares future educational leaders noted the use of equity audits in her leadership for social justice course. Boske highlighted both the challenges and opportunities involved in conducting equity audits as part of the leadership preparation experience. Focusing on the doctoral level, Harris and Hopson (2008) describe their use of an equity audit as part of their social justice leadership preparation. Following the culmination of the audit, the researchers administered a survey to their students to capture the perceived value of the process and impact on the candidates' schools. Results indicated that the equity audit fostered powerful learning among the leadership candidates, including candidates making equity changes in their schools during and after the course, thus enhancing their capacity to become social justice leaders. Bustamante et al.'s (2009) study compliments Harris and Hopson's findings. Specifically, they found that the process of engaging in audits enhances leaders' culturally responsive skills and knowledge, their ability to assess school-wide cultural competence, and their willingness to examine personal biases, privilege, and beliefs about others who are different.

Two cases in the *Journal of Cases in Educational Leadership* explicitly incorporate the equity audit process. Rodríguez (2012) suggests the equity audit be used in an exploration of teacher expectations of Latino student success. Green and Dantley (2013), in contrast, focus the case around an equity audit conducted by a White female principal within an urban high school. These authors challenge readers to consider the privilege and beliefs of those who are conducting equity audits and suggest practices that can avoid the perpetuation of racism and inequities as a result of equity audits. Shakeshaft and Sherman (2013), who participated in the University Council for Educational Administration's Leaders Supporting Diverse Learners initiative created an entire instructional module focused on equity audits. The module includes five powerful learning experiences that introduce the candidate to the equity audit process and then guide him or her through an actual equity audit at the candidate's school.

If, indeed, school principals are essential to school improvement, teacher quality, and student learning, it is essential that educational leadership faculty, who train and certify the majority of those who lead schools, ensure that their graduates know how to facilitate the creation of schools in which all students are successful. The scholarship presented in this section contributes in important ways to the ability of leadership preparation programs to deliver learning experiences that build leaders' knowledge of and skills for supporting the education of diverse student populations. Coupled with the larger base of scholarship on the use of equity audits, we are gaining a much clearer picture of how equity audits can be used to support equitable practices in schools.

THE EQUITY AUDIT PROCESS

Building off this literature and the chapters throughout this book, in the following section we present an equity audit process that includes six key phases which we believe support the comprehensiveness and effectiveness of a school based equity audit (Table 10.1). We describe each of these phases in turn.

Phase 1: Identifying Integrated/Inclusive Practices as Measured by Proportional Representation as the Anchoring Philosophy of the Equity Audit

Integrated/inclusive practices as measured by proportional representation as a means for high achievement for all students must anchor the equity audit. This anchoring philosophy addresses the question: To what end are we conducting an equity audit? Integrative practices achieved through proportional representation that anchor the equity audit we present here distinguish it from the other equity audit literature we reviewed. Without this anchoring philosophy, educators run a high risk of conducting an equity audit that perpetuates the marginalization of students. We have already seen this to be the case with the No Child Left Behind Act (2001), which has required schools to collect and disaggregate equity data since 2001, yet low achievement among all students, achievement gaps, and the segregation and tracking of students remain. Further, nearly all districts and schools are involved in data

Table 10.1 Six Phases of a Comprehensive Equity Audit

1. Identify integrated/inclusive practices as measured by proportional representation as the anchoring philosophy of the equity audit.
2. Establish the team to conduct the audit.
3. Design the audit.
4. Collect and analyze the data.
5. Set and prioritize goals based on the data.
6. Develop an implementation plan to reach the goals that includes review of the goals and plan.

collection and analysis and data retreats, yet these data collection and analysis activities are not targeted toward integrated/inclusive practices and high achievement for each student.

Proportional representation means that the demographics of the school are reflected in every classroom, course, activity, setting, or experience within the school. For example, if 12% of students are labeled with a disability, then no more than 12% of students in any classroom, course, activity, setting, or experience are students labeled with a disability. Proportional representation applies to grade levels when assigning students labeled with disabilities, students who are linguistically diverse, and students labeled gifted. That is, if 12% of the students in the school are labeled with a disability and 20% of the students in the school are linguistically diverse, and there are six third-grade classrooms, then no more than 12% of students in each third-grade classroom has a disability and no more than 20% of students in each classroom are culturally and linguistically diverse. Students who are linguistically diverse and students who have disabilities are equally assigned across these six classrooms to reflect their proportion in the school.

Some schools claim to be inclusive when they have eliminated all their pullout class-rooms for students with disabilities and students who are linguistically diverse, but then, continuing the example, segregate students with disabilities into particular third-grade classrooms, segregate students who are linguistically diverse into other third-grade class-rooms that do not have students with disabilities, and then assign students labeled gifted to yet another third-grade classroom that does not include students with disabilities or stu-dents who are linguistically diverse. The result is that students with disabilities and students who are linguistically diverse are over-represented in, and thus segregated into particular third-grade classrooms (that is, the number of students with disabilities and number of students who are linguistically diverse in these classrooms exceeds their proportion in the school). Instead, with an anchoring philosophy of integrated/inclusive practices defined by proportional representation, the number of students with disabilities and students who are linguistically diverse would be mixed and equally assigned across the third-grade class-rooms to reflect their proportion in the school.

Many educators compromise on proportional representation, even educators deeply committed to inclusive practices, by allowing percentages that exceed proportional represen-tation in the classroom. For example, instead of committing to proportional representation, educators will allow up to 30% of classrooms to include students labeled with disabilities when 14% of the students in the school are labeled with disabilities. Similarly, they will allow, for example, up to 40% of a class to be students who are linguistically diverse when these students may only compose 30% of the students enrolled in the school. Often, these educators term this practice "clustering" and defend the practice as a more efficient means for educators to serve students with these labels by reducing the number of classrooms that require support staff. Based on adult needs rather than student needs, "clustering" students in classrooms in these ways is another form of segregation and enables and prevents educa-tors from doing the hard work of effectively educating a broad range of student needs in the classroom. This prevents the establishment of diverse communities of students learning alongside each other. Once these inclusive compromises have been allowed and made, the slippery slope of segregation has been set. We have never seen a school work toward a fully proportional representative school in these conditions and in fact, educators in these schools then find additional reasons to segregate students further (e.g., establish behavior rooms, entire classrooms set aside for tracked reading interventions, etc.).

At the same time, proportional representation does not apply to achievement mea-sures such as achievement scores on standardized tests or participating in ACT exams and Advanced Placement (AP) courses. For example, per proportional representation, at least 12% of students taking the ACT should be students labeled with disabilities, yet with achievement measures such as the ACT, proportional representation is the minimal goal. That is, the ultimate goal should be that 100% of students labeled with disabilities who do not have a cognitive disability participate in the ACT exams and AP courses, and to score in the top range on standardized state achievement tests.

At times, equity data may show, for example, that Latino students are under-represented in special education. The question then, under the principle of proportional representation, is should more Latino students be labeled for special education? The answer is no. When typically marginalized students are under-represented in school remedial systems—such as special education, Response to Intervention (RTI), at-risk programs, alternative programs, remedial programs, or lower-tracked classes—that is a good thing. Similarly, when typically marginalized students are under-represented in truancy or discipline data such as suspensions or expulsions, that is a good thing. Decades of outcome data on remedial systems show how these systems do not ameliorate inequities, but instead perpetuate them. Thus, the fewer students referred into these systems, the better. In sum, the anchoring philosophy of proportional representation must undergird all aspects of the equity audit from data collection through data analysis, goal setting, and implementation.

Phase 2: Establishing the Team to Conduct the Equity Audit

Because of the size and scope of the equity audit, the audit cannot be the responsibility of one person in the school or district. Rather, a team should be established to conduct the audit. To ensure that equity stays at the center and forefront of the district and school work, the team should comprise the existing leadership team at the district or school level with the addition of a few key community members. At the school level, the team of no more than 8–10 individuals should include the principal and representative teachers, including special education, bilingual education, general education, support staff (e.g., school psychologist), and a community member associated with students of color at the school. The school should also have grade-level teams and one teacher from each of these teams should be on the leadership team. At the district level, the team should include a representative from each of the building leadership teams, though again, the size should be kept to about 10–12 individuals. The team should also include the superintendent, director of special education, curriculum director, and at least one community member representing students of color in the district. These teams should complete all the steps of the equity audit process and regularly share progress with the rest of the school, district, and community.

Phase 3: Designing the Audit

Most of the equity audit literature does not provide an actual audit form. Instead the literature suggests that the audit be designed around equity questions that educators would like to be addressed in their school/district. However, based on the literature and practice, we provide an example of an entire equity audit instrument at the end of this chapter that can help educators get started on conducting the audit. The equity audit we suggest includes two key features: (a) the extent to which students are labeled in the school; and (b) equity related to specific areas of difference, including social class, race, language, ability, gender, sexual orientation/gender identity, and religion. With regards to social class, race, language, and ability, data are collected in four major areas:

1. Percent of students of that identity in the school and how that compares to other schools in the district.

2. Percent of students labeled for special education, gifted (including Honors, AP, and related programs), and receiving RTI (and other programs that address "at-risk" including remedial courses) who are of that identity.
3. Rates of truancy and suspensions/expulsions for students who are of that identity.
4. Achievement data disaggregated by that identity, including participation in and scores on the ACT and graduation rates.

We include space at the end of each area of difference for the team to add additional questions they wish to address pertinent to their situation, such as participation in extra-curricular activities and parent/family organizations, among others.

Sexual orientation, gender, and religious identity require a different set of data, given that students are not asked to self-identify in this way. Thus, the equity audit form we provide includes questions to measure equitable practices for these students in three areas: (a) law and policy; (b) school culture; and (c) curriculum. For instance, questions address whether the school's anti-harassment policy specifically addresses sexual orientation and gender identity; the extent to which teasing, bullying, and harassment data are collected, including specifically in relation to sexual orientation and gender identity; and whether or not the school supports a Gay-Straight Alliance.

Finally, social frontier data expand the scope of the equity audit to examine partner-ships and links in the broader community (see further Scanlan & Johnson, this volume).

Phase 4: Collecting and Analyzing the Data

Unfortunately and somewhat surprisingly, for most districts and schools equity audit data is not easily available and the equity audit we describe here is the first time many schools have collected such data. Further, many educators report that though their school/district col-lects some data, these data are often not analyzed nor used to inform instruction or change educator practice toward equitable ends. Thus, the first time that the equity audit data are collected using the form we suggest, educators learn that finding some of the data is dif-ficult because either the district or state does not require the collection of such data (e.g., the percent of students labeled with disabilities who are from low-income homes) or the data is collected by the school or district but not housed in one single place. For example, the district may collect data on the percent of students of color in special education and also data on the percent of students of color who take the ACT, but the former data are collected and stored by the special education department and the ACT data are collected and stored by the curriculum department. Schools and districts should take advantage of the equity audit process to establish a centralized, efficient database system for equity data that allows all educators in the district to have instant access to equity data that are regularly updated.

We suggest that the leadership team coordinate the data collection with perhaps each team member being responsible for each identity section; for example, one team member collects data on social class, while another team member collects data on race. Another way to divide up the data collection is for each team member to collect disaggregated data on the four dimensions of the equity audit that we previously described.

As the equity audit form we provide suggests, data are collected and disaggregated for the four major sections of the audit. The audit form requires the data to be disaggregated by social class, race, ability, language, and gender. Further, the audit form requires that racial data (or "ethno-racial" classification data [Richomme, 2009]) be disaggregated, including African American, Asian, Caucasian, Latino, Native American, and multi-racial.[1] Disag-gregating racial data can uncover additional racial inequities that can be masked when only examining data by race in general. For example, the data may show that students of color are not over-represented in RTI. However, when disaggregating the race data further, African American students may be over-represented in this program. Further, in districts who enroll Hmong students from southeast Asia, the data for Asian students should be further disaggregated between students who are from southeast Asia and students who are not.

Because proportional representation anchors the equity audit (as discussed above), the equity audit form requires that data collection include fractions along with percentages to be able to measure proportional representation. For example, of 100 students labeled with disabilities, if 70 of these students receive free and reduced-priced lunch, then the fraction for this data is 70/100 and the percent is 70%. This data can then be compared to the percent of students in the school who are receiving free and reduced-price lunch, which in this example is 210 students out of 600 (210/600 = 35%). Thus, in this example, at this school, we know that students from low-income homes are twice as likely to be labeled for special education, and thus are over-represented in special education. Proportional representation of students from low-income homes in special education should be 35% or less.

Phase 5: Setting and Prioritizing Goals Based on the Data

With all the data gathered, the team must then prioritize goals based on the data. We suggest identifying three to five measurable goals that can be achieved over a one- to three-year period. The goals should begin with achievement in reading and math. The primary goal should be for 100% of all students who do not have severe cognitive disabilities to be advanced in reading and math. Many schools find that the percent of all students advanced in reading and math falls far below 100%. They also find that reading and math achievement for students from low-income homes, students with disabilities, students who are linguistically diverse, and students of color falls far below that for students from middle- to upper-income families, White students, students for whom English is their home language, and students without disability labels. Thus, in this case, reading and math achievement goals should be written for all students, and sub-goals written for each of the typically marginalized student groups. It is critical to write sub-goals for each typically marginalized group of students because our educational history shows that when we aim reform to "all students" without specifying specific goals or practices for typically marginalized students, the students who benefit most from educational reform are White, middle- to upper-class students without disabilities and for whom English is their home language.

We suggest a format for writing goals that includes: (a) a focus goal (e.g., reading or math); (b) present level of performance; (c) future level of performance; (d) over what period of time; and (e) the measure that will be used to determine whether the goal was attained. Thus, we suggest the following template: Increase (what?) from (present level of performance) to (future level of performance) over (period of time) as measured by (what). As an example for this template, we suggest "Increase reading achievement from 45% of all students proficient/advanced to 100% of students proficient/advanced over three years as measured by the state reading assessment."

We suggest goals and working toward achieving them to be about three years. This provides enough time for educators to make the necessary changes to increase achievement, but not too much time that the momentum and energy is lost while working toward the goal. We also suggest that targeted goals be established for each year of the three years leading up to 100%. Thus, in this example, educators must increase reading achievement by 55% over three years, or about 19% per year. Thus, at the end of year one, 64% of students should be proficient/advanced in reading, and by the end of year two, about 83% of students should be proficient/advanced. Similar three-year goals should then be set for students with disabilities, students from low-income homes, and students of color (disaggregated by race).

Once clear reading and math achievement goals have been established, then additional goals can be addressed and prioritized based on the equity data, such as decreasing the percent of students labeled for special education, or more specifically decreasing the percent of students from low-income homes or students of color (specifically by race) in special education; decreasing the percent of students labeled for RTI to 0%; or increasing attendance. Again, we suggest limiting the goals to no more than five to seven and ensuring all goals are measurable.

Educators need to also be clear about: (a) the difference between establishing goals and identifying strategies to reach them; and (b) the link between goals and student achievement. For the former, "increase teacher collaboration time" cannot be a goal as it is difficult to measure. Rather, increasing teacher collaboration time focused on reading could be a strategy that will help raise student reading achievement—collaboration time is a strategy, not a goal. Further, all goals should link back to student achievement goals. For example, increasing student attendance (disaggregated by race, social class, ability, and language, if appropriate) will support reading and math achievement goals. Thus, rather than making a list of disparate goals, educators should make it clear how all goals link back to student achievement.

Phase 6: Developing an Implementation Plan

Finally, for each measurable goal, educators should then identify specific strategies to reach that goal. The strategies should include a timeline, who will be involved, and what measure will be used to measure progress toward the goal. We have included an example of a planning template to help educators map out implementation plans to reach the goals.

CONCLUSION

The achievement gap cannot be substantially narrowed unless we eliminate the significant equity gaps that inhibit students' opportunities to learn (Frattura & Capper, 2007). Moreover, achieving educational equity requires that school leaders have the knowledge and skills to understand educational inequity, to identify its causes, and to transform practices and conditions in schools. As increasing numbers of educational leadership programs include equity audits in their preparation curriculum, aspiring leaders will be better prepared to lead schools that effectively serve diverse student populations. Perhaps more importantly, by strengthening educational leaders' knowledge of and skills for understanding, identifying, and transforming inequity, we anticipate significant and positive changes in our nation's school system.

NOTE

1   We understand that race and ethnicity are distinct concepts (see further Horsford & Clark, this volume). In this chapter we use "race" to include the "Latino" category, since, from an equity audit perspective, it does not operate differently from other groups (see further Richomme, 2009).

REFERENCES

Bleyaert, B. (2011). Is compliance "trumping" mission? Findings from an equity audit pilot. *International Journal of Educational Leadership Preparation, 6*(4), 1–11.

Boske, C. (2012). Sending forth tiny ripples of hope that build the mightiest of currents: Understanding how to prepare school leaders to interrupt oppressive school practices. *Planning and Changing, 43*(1/2), 183–197.

Brown, K.M. (2010). Schools of excellence and equity? Using equity audits as a tool to expose a flawed system of recognition. *International Journal of Education Policy & Leadership, 5*(5), 1–12.

Bustamante, R.M., Nelson, J.A., & Onwuegbuzie, A.J. (2009). Assessing schoolwide cultural competence: Implications for school leadership preparation. *Educational Administration Quarterly, 45*(5), 793–827.

Capper, C.A. (2014, May). *An equity audit of teacher and leadership preparation/development.* Paper presented at the Department of Public Instruction Institute for Higher Education Conference, Green Bay, WI.

Capper, C.A. & Frattura, E. (2009). *Meeting the needs of all students: Leading beyond inclusion* (2nd ed.). Thousand Oaks, CA: Corwin Press.

Capper, C.A., Frattura, E., & Keyes, M.A. (2000). *Meeting the needs of all students: Leading beyond inclusion.* Thousand Oaks, CA: Corwin Press.

Capper, C.A. Theoharis, G., & Sebastian, J. (2006). Toward a framework for preparing leaders for social justice. *Journal of Educational Administration, 44*(3), 209–224.

Cleveland, R., Chambers, J., Mainus, C., Powell, N., Skepple, R., Tyler, T., & Wood, A. (2012). School culture, equity, and student academic performance in a rural Appalachian school. *Kentucky Journal of Excellence in College Teaching and Learning, 9*(4), 35–42.

Darling-Hammond, L., LaPointe, M., Meyerson, D., & Orr, M. (2007). *Preparing school leaders for a changing world: Lessons from exemplary leadership development programs.* Stanford, CA: Stanford University.

Frattura, E., & Capper, C.A. (2007). *Leading for social justice: Transforming schools for all learners.* Thousand Oaks, CA: Corwin Press.

Green, T.L., & Dantley, M.E. (2013). The great white hope? Examining the white privilege and epistemology of an urban high school principal. *Journal of Cases in Educational Leadership, 16*(2), 82–92.

Harris, S., & Hopson, M. (2008). Using an equity audit investigation to prepare doctoral students for social justice leadership. *Teacher Development, 12*(4), 341–352.

Johnson, R.S., & Avelar LaSalle, R.L. (2010). *Data strategies to uncover and Eeliminate hidden inequities: The wallpaper effect* (Paperback). Thousand Oaks, CA: Corwin Press.

Karanxha, Z., Agosto, V., & Bellara, A.A. (2013). The hidden curriculum: Candidate diversity in educational leadership preparation. *Journal of Research on Leadership Education, 9*(1), 1–25.

Lewis, C.W., James, M., Hancock, S., & Hill-Jackson, V. (2008). Framing African American students' success and failure in urban settings: A typology for change. *Urban Education, 43*(2), 127–153.

McKenzie, K.B., & Scheurich, J.J. (2004). Equity traps: A useful construct for preparing principals to lead schools that are successful with racially diverse students. *Educational Administration Quarterly, 40*(5), 601–632.

McKenzie, K.B., & Skrla, L. (2011). *Using equity audits in the classroom to reach and teach all students.* Thousand Oaks, CA: Corwin Press.

Moll, L., Amanti, C., Neff, D., & González, N. (1992). Funds of knowledge for teaching: Using a qualitative approach to connect homes and classrooms. *Theory Into Practice, 31*(2), 132–141.

No Child Left Behind (NCLB) Act of 2001, Pub. L. No. 107-110, § 115, Stat. 1425 (2002).

Richomme, O. (2009). The role of "ethno-racial" classification in the Americanization Process. *Cercles, 9*, 1–17.

Rodríguez, M.A. (2012). "But they just can't do it": Reconciling teacher expectations of Latino students. *Journal of Cases in Educational Leadership, 15*(1), 25–31.

Sailes, J. (2008). School culture audits: Making a difference in school improvement plans. *Improving Schools, 11*(1), 74–82.

Schmidt, R. (2014). *Equity audit of Greenhill Elementary School*. Unpublished manuscript.

Shakeshaft, C., & Sherman, W. (2013). *Preparing leaders to examine the allocation of resources using equity audits*. Retrieved from http://ucealee.squarespace.com/marshaling-and-using-resources/

Skrla, L., McKenzie, K. B., & Scheurich, J. J. (2009). *Using equity audits to create equitable and excellent schools*. Thousand Oaks, CA: Corwin Press.

Skrla, L., Scheurich, J. J., Garcia, J., & Nolly, G. (2004). Equity audits: A practical leadership tool for developing equitable and excellent schools. *Educational Administration Quarterly, 40*(1), 133–161.

Yosso, T. (2005). Whose culture has capital? A critical race theory discussion of community cultural wealth. *Race, Ethnicity and Education, 8*(1), 69–91.

Young, M. D., Crow, G., Murphy, J., & Ogawa, R. (2009). *The Handbook of research on the education of school leaders*. New York, NY: Routledge.

APPENDIX

Equity Audit Data Collection and Analysis

Colleen A. Capper, Michelle D. Young, Carmen Campuzano, Julie Causton, Christine Clark, Shamini Dias, Anne Dudley-Marling, Curt Dudley-Marling, Don Fraynd, Margaret Grogan, Frank Hernandez, Sonya Douglass Horsford, Isabel Kelsey, Francesca López, Joanne M. Marshall, Martin Scanlan, George Theoharis, and Casey Woodfield

Adapted from *Leading for Social Justice: Transforming Schools for All Learners* (2007), Colleen A. Capper and Elise M. Frattura. Thousand Oaks, CA: Corwin Press. Reprinted with Permission.

General Directions: (1) This instrument was developed for school-level data, thus all questions apply to a particular school; however, the instrument can be adapted to the district, regional, or state levels. (2) All data should be reported as a fraction and percent. For example, if the question asks for how many students in the school receive free and reduced-price lunch, then the fraction would be 200/400, and the percent would be 50%.

GENERAL DATA (REPORT TOTAL NUMBER, FRACTION, AND PERCENTAGE)

1. Number of students in your district:	
2. Number of staff in your school (certified and noncertified):	
3. Number of students in your school:	

4. Fraction and percentage of staff in your school who are associated with student services (e.g., special education, special education assistants, counselors, psychologists, nurses, bilingual specialists, reading specialists, gifted and talented specialist, etc.):	
Status of Labeling at Your School (report total number, fraction, and percentage)	
1. Students labeled "gifted":	
2. How are students labeled gifted served (in class, out of class)? Are students labeled gifted proportionally represented in all classes/courses/learning experiences?	
3. Students receiving Tier 2 and Tier 3 RTI interventions:	
4. How are students receiving Tier 2 and Tier 3 interventions served?	
5. Students labeled with a disability:	
6. Students labeled ESL or bilingual:	
7. Students who attend an alternative school/setting:	
8. Students with any other kind of label (include the label):	
9. Total students who are labeled:	

STUDENTS LABELED WITH DISABILITIES (REPORT FRACTION AND PERCENTAGE)

1. Students labeled with disabilities in your school:	
2. Students labeled with disabilities in each grade level in your school:	
3. Students by disability label (i.e., behavioral challenges, cognitively disabled, learning disabled, severely disabled, etc.) in your school:	
4. Students labeled with disabilities in your district:	
5. Special education referrals each year. How has this changed over time?	
6. Of those students referred, what fraction/percentage were then identified for special education?	
7. Do all students with disabilities in your school community attend the school they would attend if they were not labeled? Explain.	
8. To what extent are students labeled with disabilities proportionally represented in all classes, courses, etc., in your school?	

9. Do some students with (dis)abilities who do not live in your attendance area attend your school or district? Explain.	
10. Which/how many students with (dis)abilities are educated primarily in a special education setting/classroom? Disaggregate by race, social class, ELL label, and gender.	
11. Which/how many students with (dis)abilities are educated primarily in the general education setting/classroom? Disaggregate by race, social class, ELL label, and gender.	
Disability—Discipline Data	
12. Students who were suspended in the past year. Divide by in-school and out-of-school suspensions and compare students with disabilities with students without disabilities:	
13. Students who were expelled in the past year. Compare students with disabilities with students without disabilities:	
14. Students who were placed in an Alternative Interim Placement in the past year. Compare students with disabilities with students without disabilities:	
15. If your district has an alternative educational setting, compare the students labeled with disabilities in this setting to the percent of students labeled with disabilities in the district or high school:	
16. Low attendance and/or truancy. Compare students with disabilities with students without disabilities:	
17. Other relevant discipline data:	
Disability—Achievement Data	
18. Reading and math achievement. Compare students with disabilities with students without disabilities:	
19. Graduation rate. Compare students with disabilities with students without disabilities:	
20. Graduated with a four-year academic diploma. Compare students with disabilities with students without disabilities:	
21. Dropout rate. Compare students with disabilities with students without disabilities:	
22. Participation in ACT, SAT, Advanced Placement exams. Compare students with disabilities with students without disabilities:	
23. Test results of ACT, SAT, Advanced Placement exams. Compare students with disabilities with students without disabilities:	

24. Collect (dis)ability information in at least two other areas in your school/setting and compare to students without disabilities:	
25. Disability Data Analysis. Do not exceed two double-spaced pages. (University students, support the analysis thoroughly with the literature.) What do these disability data mean? In your analysis, include the strengths and areas for improvement in serving students labeled with disabilities within your school's curriculum, instruction, and other learning opportunities. Identify concrete, specific actions for eliminating inequities by disability.	

SOCIAL CLASS (REPORT FRACTION AND PERCENTAGE) (FREE/REDUCED-PRICE = LOW SOCIAL CLASS)

1. Students receiving free/reduced-price lunch:	
2. Students receiving free/reduced-price lunch in other schools in your district at the same level (elementary, middle, secondary):	
3. Students identified for special education (all categorical areas):	
4. Of the number of students identified for special education, what fraction and what percentage receive free/reduced-price lunch? Note: We have found that most districts do not gather or report this information. It may be possible, however, to find such data or to calculate this information by hand. Compare to the % of students receiving free/reduced-price lunch in the school. What social class myths support these data?	
5. Students identified as "gifted" (e.g., TAG) or placed in high academic classes in your setting who receive free/reduced-price lunch. Compare to the % of students receiving free/reduced-price lunch in the school. (If students are not labeled gifted, investigate related student groups in the school, such as Academic Decathlon, Advanced Placement classes, algebra classes.)	
6. Students receiving RTI interventions or who are identified as "at risk" in your setting who receive free/reduced-price lunch. Compare to the % of students receiving free/reduced-price lunch in the school. (If students are not labeled "at risk," investigate related student groupings in the school, such as remedial reading, summer school, general math.)	
7. Do all students have opportunities to learn challenging content? For example, are low-achieving students focused exclusively on low-level skills (e.g., word-level reading skills or computational skills)?	
8. Do all students have opportunities to draw on their language and cultural resources and experience in support of their learning?	

9. Are students' languages and cultural experiences represented in the classroom environment and classroom materials? For example, the reading materials authentically reflect the diverse ways in which people live their lives.	
Social Class—Discipline Data	
10. Students who were suspended in the past year. Disaggregate these data by free/reduced-price lunch; divide into in-school and out-of-school suspensions, compare to the % of students receiving free/reduced-price lunch in the school.	
11. Students who were expelled in the past year. Disaggregate by free/reduced-price lunch, compare to the % of students receiving free/reduced-price lunch in the school.	
12. Students who were placed in an Alternative Interim Placement in the past year. Disaggregate by free/reduced-price lunch, compare to the % of students receiving free/reduced-price lunch in the school.	
13. If your district has an alternative educational setting, compare the students receiving free-reduced priced lunch in this setting with the % of students receiving free/reduced-price lunch in the district or high school.	
14. Low attendance and/or truancy. Disaggregate by free/reduced-price lunch, compare to the % of students receiving free/reduced-price lunch in the school.	
15. Other relevant discipline data:	
Social Class—Achievement Data	
16. Reading and math achievement data comparing low social class with not low social class students:	
17. Graduation rate comparing low social class with not low social class students:	
18. Graduated with an academic diploma comparing low social class with not low social class students:	
19. Dropout rate comparing low social class with not low social class students:	
20. Participation in ACT, SAT, Advanced Placement exams comparing low social class with not low social class students:	
21. Test results of ACT, SAT, Advanced Placement exams comparing low social class with not low social class students:	
22. Collect social class comparison data on at least two other areas in your school/setting (e.g., parent-teacher organization, student council, safety patrol, band, extra-curriculars), comparing low social class with not low social class students:	
23. Social Class Analysis—See Disability Data Analysis for directions.	

RACE AND ETHNICITY (REPORT FRACTION AND PERCENTAGE)

1. Students of color in your school. Disaggregate by race:	
2. Students of color in the total district. Disaggregate by race:	
3. Students labeled for special education:	
4. Of the number of students labeled for special education, what fraction and percentage are students of color? Disaggregate by race. Compare to the % of students of color in the school and by each race:	
5. Of the number and percentage of students labeled to receive RTI interventions or labeled "at-risk" (such as remedial reading, summer school, general math), what fraction and percentage are students of color? Disaggregate by race. Compare to the % of students of color in the school and by each race:	
6. Students identified as "gifted" (e.g., TAG) or placed in high academic classes in your setting who are of color. Disaggregate by race. Compare to the % of students of color in the school and by each race. (If students are not labeled gifted, investigate related student groups in the school, such as Academic Decathlon, Advanced Placement classes, algebra classes.)	
7. Total staff who are people of color in your school. Compare to the % of students of color in the school and by each race:	
8. Certified staff who are people of color in your school. Compare to the % of students of color in the school and by each race:	
9. Uncertified staff who are people of color in your school. Compare to the % of students of color in the school and by each race:	
10. People of color serving on the school board. Compare to the % of students of color in the school and by each race:	
Race—Discipline Data	
11. Students who were suspended in the past year. Divide into in-school and out-of-school suspensions and disaggregate these data by race. Further disaggregate by each race, and compare to the % of students of color in the school and by each race:	
12. Students who were expelled in the past year. Disaggregate these data by race. Further disaggregate by each race, and compare to the % of students of color in the school and by each race:	
13. Students who were placed in an Alternative Interim Placement in the past year. Disaggregate these data by race. Further disaggregate by each race, and compare to the % of students of color in the school and by each race:	
14. If your district has an alternative educational setting. Compare the students who are of color in this setting, further disaggregated by each race with the % of students of color in the district or high school and by each race:	

15. Low attendance and/or truancy. Disaggregate these data by race and further disaggregate by each race, and compare to the % of students of color in the school and by each race:	
16. Other relevant discipline data:	
Race—Achievement Data	
17. Reading and math achievement data comparing students of color with White students and report for each race:	
18. Graduation rate comparing students of color with White students and report for each race:	
19. Graduated with a four-year academic diploma comparing students of color with White students and report for each race:	
20. Dropout rate comparing students of color with White students and report for each race:	
21. Participation in ACT, SAT, Advanced Placement exams comparing students of color with White students and report for each race:	
22. Test results of ACT, SAT, Advanced Placement exams comparing students of color with White students and report for each race:	
23. Collect race/ethnicity comparison data on at least two other areas in your school/setting, comparing students of color with White students and report for each race:	
24. To what extent are we using "funds of knowledge" (Moll, Amanti, Neff, & González, 1992, p. 132) and "community cultural wealth" (Yosso, 2005, p. 69) informed approaches, based on the normative experiences of the black/Latino/a students, to develop new curriculum for all students based on these experiences?	
25. We know what works educationally, the question is do we have the will to do it for all students? Do we really want to close the proverbial achievement gap between White and Asian students, and black and Latino/a students?	
26. If eradicating racial disparity in public education is really our goal, why are we so uncomfortable considering only race-conscious strategies for achieving this goal?	
27. Analyze the amount/percent of school funds targeted toward race, social class, language, gender, sexual identity, and in comparison to the general school programs:	
28. How does where you allocate your resources compare to the performance of students with these demographics?	
29. Where are our commitments lowest, needs greatest, and performance poorest among these demographic groups?	

30. How could resources be reallocated to where commitments are lowest, needs are greatest, and performance is poorest?	
31. Race and Ethnicity Data Analysis. See Disability Data Analysis for directions. Include the following: Discuss the problems with the phrase, "I don't even see the person's color," and, "But we do not have, or have very few, students of color in our school/district, so race isn't an issue here."	

STUDENTS WHO ARE LABELED ENGLISH-LANGUAGE LEARNERS (REPORT FRACTION AND PERCENTAGE)

1. How many ELLs are in your school, what languages do they speak, and how many speak each language? How does this compare to other schools in your district?	
2. How many ELLs are in each grade at your school?	
3. How many ELLs are in the district?	
4. How many students are labeled for special education?	
5. Of the number of students labeled for special education, what fraction and percentage are ELLs? Compare to the % of ELLs in the school:	
6. Of the number of students receiving RTI interventions or labeled "at-risk" (such as remedial reading, summer school, general math), what fraction and percentage are students are ELL? Compare to the % of ELLs in the school:	
7. Of the number and percentage of students labeled "gifted" (e.g., TAG) or placed in high academic classes in your setting, what fraction and percentage are ELLs? Compare to the % of ELLs in the school:	
8. Do all students labeled ELL in your district attend the school they would attend if they were not labeled? Explain:	
9. What is the ELL service delivery model used in your school? To what extent are students who are ELL proportionally represented in classrooms, courses, programs, activities?	
10. How many bilingual people serve on the school board? Compare to the % of students labeled ELL in your school:	
ELL—Discipline Data	
11. Students who were suspended in the past year. Divide into in-school and out-of-school suspensions. Compare students who are ELL with students who are not ELL:	
12. Students who were expelled in the past year. Compare students who are ELL with students who are not ELL:	

13. Students who were placed in an Alternative Interim Placement in the past year. Compare students who are ELL with students who are not ELL:	
14. If your district has an alternative educational setting, compare the students labeled ELL in this setting with the percent of students labeled ELL in the district or high school:	
15. Low attendance and/or truancy. Compare students who are ELL with students who are not ELL:	
16. Other relevant discipline data:	
ELL—Achievement Data	
17. Identify the English proficiency levels (beginning, intermediate, proficient) for each student. How many at each level are in each grade?	
18. What assessments are used to determine proficiency in the student's home language? How are these assessments used to inform home language instruction? Report the data for these assessments:	
19. What assessments are used to determine English proficiency? How are these assessments used to inform instruction? Report the data that show the number/percent of students who are becoming more English proficient:	
20. Reading and math achievement data comparing students who are ELL with students who are not ELL:	
21. Graduation rate comparing students who are ELL with students who are not ELL:	
22. Graduated with a four-year academic diploma comparing students who are ELL with students who are not ELL:	
23. Dropout rate comparing students who are ELL with students who are not ELL:	
24. Participation in ACT, SAT, Advanced Placement exams comparing students who are ELL with students who are not ELL:	
25. Test results of ACT, SAT, Advanced Placement exams comparing students who are ELL with students who are not ELL:	
26. Collect student ELL comparison data on at least two other areas in your school/setting and compare to students who are not ELL:	
27. ELL and Bilingual Data Analysis. See Disability Data Analysis for directions.	

SEXUAL ORIENTATION AND GENDER IDENTITY

Law and Policy	
1. Do all staff understand and apply federal and state law associated with sexual orientation and gender identity to leverage integrated, high-achieving schools/districts?	
2. Does your district have any active policies that address sexual orientation? Gender identity? Are these policies clearly communicated to the school community?	
3. Does your school/district provide domestic partner benefits to its employees?	
4. Assess your school or district's anti-harassment policy. To what extent does it address sexual orientation? Gender identity?	
5. To what extent are school enrollment forms inclusive of same-gender families?	
6. To what extent do school hiring and enrollment forms include the range of gender demographics including male, female, transgender, intersex, and other?	
7. Does your school provide gender-neutral bathrooms for all students to use?	
Sexual Orientation and Gender Identity— School Culture	
8. How many staff are open about their lesbian, gay, bisexual, transgender, or questioning (LGBTQ) identity to other staff? To students? To families and community? (This is an estimate.)	
9. What percentage of teachers in your school would be proactive in supporting LGBTQ staff, students, and families? What percentage would be neutral? What percentage would oppose being supportive of LGBTQ staff, students, and families? (Estimate these percentages.)	
10. To what extent are invitations to school functions, staff gatherings, and so forth, inclusive of LGBTQ relationships?	
11. To what extent are students teased or called names because of their gender identity or sexual orientation in your school? How do you know? To what extent is data collected on this? How do staff respond?	
12. To what extent are students at your school required to adhere to a gender-specific dress code (e.g., at holiday concerts, are girls required to wear dresses and boys required to wear suits?)?	

13. Which activities or programs are currently in use at your school or other schools in your district related to LGBTQ students?	
14. Do you have students in your school who are gender non-conforming (e.g., biological boys who are stereotypically more feminine and biological girls who are stereotypically more masculine)? How are you ensuring these students are supported and protected from teasing, harassment, or pressure from students or staff to be gender conforming?	
Sexual Orientation/Gender Identity—Curriculum	
15. How and to what extent does your school's curriculum integrate LGBTQ history, events, and/or persons across it?	
16. For students and staff, are sexual orientation and gender identity and their intersections always included when listing diversity/equity identities, such as gender, race, class, etc.?	
17. If a group of students approached your building principal and requested to begin a Gay-Straight Alliance, how would your principal or district respond?	
18. Does your middle/high school have a Gay-Straight Alliance? If not, why not? If so, assess the efforts of this group:	
19. Assess your school's library/media holdings related to sexual orientation and gender identity. To what extent do students in your school have access to information about sexual orientation and gender identity, and what is the nature of this information?	
20. To what extent has professional development addressed sexual orientation and gender identity?	
21. To what extent do students at the elementary level receive information about and have access to information about same-gender families (i.e., when the early elementary grades complete family units, how many books and materials are available to these classrooms about same-gender families?)?	
22. Provide two additional data points related to sexual orientation and gender identity:	
Sexual Orientation and Gender Identity— Community Context	
23. How many hate crimes have occurred in your community in the last five years?	
24. How many "out" community leaders, school leaders, or politicians are there in your community or district?	
25. What is the social climate like in your state and local community? For example, are there pride festivals, anti-gay/ anti-hate groups, or marriage equality laws?	
26. Sexual Orientation Data Analysis. See Disability Data Analysis for directions.	

GENDER (REPORT FRACTION AND PERCENTAGE)

1. Females on the teaching staff at the elementary level, middle school level, and high school level:	
2. Females teaching science and math classes at the middle/high school level:	
3. Females teaching English (and related courses) at the middle/high school level:	
4. Females teaching history (and related courses) at the middle/high school level:	
5. Females teaching the highest level of math students at your school:	
6. Females teaching Advanced Placement courses at the high school:	
7. Females/males on the administrative team:	
8. Females/males at the elementary, middle, and high school administrative level:	
9. Females/males on the school board:	
Gender—Discipline	
10. Students labeled for emotional disabilities:	
11. Students who were suspended in the past year. Divide by in-school and out-of-school suspensions and compare females and males:	
12. Students who were expelled in the past year and compare females and males:	
13. Students who were placed in an Alternative Interim Placement in the past year and compare females and males:	
14. If your district has an alternative educational setting, compare the percent of females and males with the percent of females and males in the district or high school:	
15. Low attendance and/or truancy. Compare females and males:	
16. Other relevant discipline data:	
Gender—Achievement Data	
17. Reading and math achievement. Compare females and males:	
18. Graduation rate. Compare females and males:	
19. Graduated with a four-year academic diploma. Compare females and males:	
20. Dropout rate. Compare females and males:	

21. Participation in ACT, SAT, Advanced Placement exams. Compare females and males:	
22. Test results of ACT, SAT, Advanced Placement exams. Compare females and males:	
23. Collect gender comparison data on at least two other areas in your school/setting and compare female with male students:	
Gender—Policy	
24. Does the school have explicit, written policies on gender issues with clear protocols on how to handle issues that arise for staff, teachers, and students?	
25. Are these policies clearly communicated and available to the school community?	
26. Are there budget allocations that support initiatives for professional development and school-wide student programs that address gender issues?	
Gender—Professional Development	
27. Are teachers and paraprofessionals sensitized to the effects of name-calling and use of gendered slang in school hallways, playgrounds, etc.?	
28. Are teachers and school staff trained in specific ways to deal with gender issues they encounter? How often is this training offered? Is the training mandatory?	
29. Are there initiatives with teachers to facilitate conversations and self-assessments that raise awareness of gendering discourse and actions?	
30. Is gender bias, especially inadvertent gender bias, part of staff and faculty meeting agendas?	
Gender—Assessment and Evaluation	
31. Are gender bias and stereotypes taken into consideration in selecting school resources and images presented to the school community?	
32. Is there a point person whose job it is to look out for and bring gender bias in school resources to the principal's attention?	
33. In classroom observations tools, are there items that focus on gendering actions and ways of speaking?	
Gender—Student Programs	
34. Does the school have initiatives integrated into the curriculum that address gender issues? Are these offered by one subject area, or do they cut thematically across the curriculum?	

35. Are there programs for students that help raise awareness of gender issues and how to negotiate them? Are these programs during school and mandatory, or after school and optional?	
36. Does the school know of and work with local non-profit organizations that offer special STEM-based programs for girls?	
37. Does the school know of and work with local non-profit organizations that offer programs for students to deal with other kinds of gender inequities?	
Gender—Family and Community Outreach	
38. What are the different ways in which gender issues are proactively brought into conversations with parents?	
39. Does the school have a protocol for working with families to address gender-based issues that challenge students?	
40. How does the school reach out to and educate its community on proactively seeking help with gender issues such as sexual harassment, bullying, teen pregnancy, and academics?	
Gender—District & Leadership Support	
41. Does the school/district have a Title IX coordinator and, if so, who is that person? Does the school have an active relationship with its Title IX coordinator?	
42. Are gender issues on the agenda at district-level meetings?	
43. Do school leaders have access to leadership development opportunities that specifically address gender issues in educational settings?	
44. Gender Data Analysis. See Disability Data Analysis for directions.	

RELIGION

1. How many formal houses of worship or practice are in your community? ____ churches ____ synagogues ____ mosques ____ temples ____ meditation centers ____ other (specify)	
2. Does your district have any active policies related to religion?	
3. Are there any religious-related practices in place in the district?	
4. How and to what extent does your district's curriculum provide instruction related to religion (e.g., what grades, subjects)?	

5. If a group of students approached your building principal and requested space for a Bible study, how would your principal and/or district respond? What if an atheist's club wanted to meet?	
6. Does your school library contain sacred texts for each world religion? ____ Protestant Bible ____ Catholic Bible ____ Book of Mormon ____ Hebrew Bible ____ Talmud ____ Qur'an ____ Bahá'í ____ Buddhism ____ Vedas ____ Other	
7. Are religious organizations involved in your school (e.g., grief counselors on call, youth pastors at lunch, volunteers at events)?	
8. How does your school handle major Christian religious holidays like Christmas and Easter? Are other religious holidays acknowledged?	
9. Are there any academic achievement data related to religion?	
10. Collect religion/non-religion information in at least two other areas in your school/setting. For example, you could compare the numbers of students who participate in Fellowship of Christian Athletes with the percentage of the total number of athletes in the school:	
11. Religion Data Analysis. See Disability Data Analysis for directions.	

SOCIAL FRONTIERS

1. Who are the current partners with whom the school works? List organizations and key features, including: How long has partnership lasted? Which students does the partnership serve? What resources does the school provide toward the partnership? What resources do others provide toward the partnership?	
2. What potential partners exist in the enrollment zones of the school? List organizations, including community-based organizations, for-profit businesses, and faith-based communities that exist in the enrollment zone. Identify which of these organizations is currently partnering with the school in some manner. Identify which of these organizations is not currently partnering with the school but which should be:	
3. What ways do partnerships privilege certain students and families and marginalize others? Considering the multiple dimensions of diversity addressed throughout this book (race, language, socioeconomic status, disability, gender, sexual orientation, and religion), analyze the data gathered in questions 1 and 2 to identify whether the level of partnerships are disproportionately addressing some dimensions of diversity while ignoring others:	
4. Social Frontier Data Analysis. See Disability Data Analysis for directions.	

EQUITY AUDIT SAMPLE IMPLEMENTATION PLAN
(ADAPTED FROM SCHMIDT, 2014)

Goal	Action Step	People Involved	Purpose	How It Will Happen	When It Will Happen	Support in Place	Evidence of Progress

About the Contributors

George Theoharis is Department Chair for the Teaching and Leadership Department and an Associate Professor in Educational Leadership and Inclusive Elementary Education at Syracuse University. He has extensive field experience in public education as a principal and as a teacher. He served as the university liaison to the Say Yes to Education collaboration, and directed the urban education initiatives. George teaches classes in educational leadership and elementary/early childhood teacher education. His interests, research, and work with K–12 schools focuses on issues of equity, justice, diversity, inclusion, leadership, and school reform. His books titled *The School Leaders Our Children Deserve*, *What Every Principal Needs to Know to Create Excellent and Equitable Schools*, and *The Principal's Handbook for Leading Inclusive Schools* focus on issues of leadership and creating more equitable schools. George's published works appear in such journals as *Teachers College Record*, *The School Administrator*, *Educational Administration Quarterly*, *Educational Leadership*, *Urban Education*, the *Journal of School Leadership*, *Remedial and Special Education*, the *Journal of Special Education Leadership*, *The International Journal of Inclusive Education*, and *Equity & Excellence in Education*. He co-runs a summer leadership institute for school administrators focusing on issues of equity and inclusion as well as a school reform project called Schools of Promise. He consults with leaders, schools, and districts around issues of leadership, equity, diversity, and inclusive reform. His PhD is in Educational Leadership and Policy Analysis from the University of Wisconsin–Madison.

Martin Scanlan is an Associate Professor in Educational Policy and Leadership at Marquette University. He is currently serving as a Visiting Associate Professor of Research in the Lynch School of Education at Boston College, with his work focusing on supporting the formation of TWIN-CS. His current research focuses on how to strengthen the communities of practice in schools to promote inclusion of students across multiple dimensions of diversity.

Carmen Campuzano is celebrating 40 years as an educator. She has dedicated her professional life to serving those communities with the highest numbers of families with lower socioeconomic status and communities with large numbers of Hispanic children and large numbers of English-language learners. She comes from a long line of educators in her family; both of her parents had teaching experience in Mexico, and her grandmother, her mentor, gave 50 years of her life to teaching. Carmen currently serves as the principal of a unique "magnet" school with a focus on Spanish immersion for all children, including ELLs. The Davis Spanish Immersion model has been successful for the last 30 years and annually has a waiting list of families who love and support the program. The Davis model has a unique focus on celebrating cultural diversity and social justice, and culturally relevant topics are infused throughout the curriculum. Davis children continuously score above the district average in reading on state assessments. Bilingual education works! Even in Arizona, there is a light at the end of the dark tunnel, which currently continues to "segregate our ELL students" and Carmen hopes to be one of many key players holding that light.

Colleen A. Capper is Professor in the Department of Educational Leadership and Policy Analysis at the University of Wisconsin–Madison. She has published extensively on leadership for social justice and equity. She is the editor of the book series *Educational Leadership for Equity and Diversity* (Routledge), and author of the forthcoming book in the series *Organizational Theory for Equity and Diversity*. She also published three best-selling books: *Leading for Social Justice: Transforming Schools for All Learners*, *Meeting the Needs of Students of All Abilities: Leading Beyond Inclusion* (2nd ed.) (both with Elise Frattura), and *Educational Administration in a Pluralistic Society*. Capper co-directs the annual National Leadership for Social Justice Institute. She received the Master Professor Award from the University Council for Educational Administration and has chaired over 60 PhD dissertations to completion. More than a dozen of her former students now serve as professors at universities around the world.

Julie Causton is an Associate Professor in the Inclusive and Special Education Program in the Department of Teaching and Leadership at Syracuse University. Her teaching, research, and consulting are guided by a passion for inclusive education. She teaches graduate and undergraduate courses focused on including students with disabilities, supporting behavior, differentiation, special education law, lesson design, and adaption. A former elementary, middle, and high school special education teacher herself, Julie knows firsthand how inclusion leads to better outcomes for students. Julie's research and writing focus on best practices in inclusive education that promote belonging in schools. Her published works have appeared in over 30 journals, including *Exceptional Children*, *Teaching Exceptional Children*, the *Journal of Research in Childhood Education*, the *International Journal of Inclusive Education*, *Behavioral Disorders*, *Studies in Art Education*, *Camping Magazine*, *Remedial and Special Education*, and *Equity & Excellence in Education*. She has published four books on inclusive education: *The Paraprofessional's Handbook for Effective Support in Inclusive Classrooms*, *The Principal's Handbook for Leading Inclusive Schools*, *The Speech-Language Pathologist's Handbook for Inclusive School Practices*, and *The Occupational Therapist's Handbook for Inclusive School Practices*. Julie works as a consultant with administrators, teachers, and paraprofessionals to help promote and improve inclusive practices.

Christine Clark is Professor of Curriculum and Instruction, Senior Scholar for Multicultural Education, and Founding Vice President for Diversity and Inclusion at the University of Nevada, Las Vegas. Clark is a two-time Fulbright Senior Scholar (Mexico and Guatemala), a Fulbright Senior Specialist, and served as the Council for the International Exchange of Scholars/U.S. Department of State Office of Cultural Affairs 2004 Visiting Fulbright Scholars Conference coordinator. Clark is the series editor for the six-volume *PK-12 Multicultural Curriculum Transformation Handbook Series* (2015–2017, Rowman & Littlefield), lead co-editor of *Occupying the Academy: Just How Important Is Diversity*

Work in Higher Education? (2012, with Brimhall-Vargas and Fasching-Varner, Rowman & Littlefield), and an invited entry author for *Multicultural America: A Multimedia Encyclopedia* (Cortés, 2013, Sage) and the *Encyclopedia of Diversity in Education* (Banks, 2012, Sage). Clark was a member of the Board of Directors of the National Association for Multicultural Education (NAME) for seven years and has served on the Editorial Board for the organization's journal, *Multicultural Perspectives*, since 1998. Clark is also the Associate Editor for the Higher Education section of *Multicultural Education*, serves on the Editorial Board for the *Journal of Diversity Management* (since 2006), and served on the Editorial Board of the *Journal of Praxis in Multicultural Education* (from 2005–2009); she is also a regular reviewer for the *Journal of Diversity in Higher Education*, the *Journal of Educational Philosophy and Theory*, the *Journal of Negro Education*, *Action in Teacher Education,* and the *National Association for Bilingual Education (NAME) Journal of Research and Practice*. In 2010 and 2013, Clark was appointed/reappointed to the National Advisory Committee of the National Conference on Race and Ethnicity (NCORE).

Shamini Dias received her PhD in Education from Claremont Graduate University, and her MA and BA in Literature and Linguistics from the National University of Singapore. Shamini has been an educator and teaching artist for over 20 years, working in early childhood through higher education contexts as well as in organizational settings. Her research and practice focus on capacity-building in teachers and learners through leadership identity development, specifically through a complexity-based framework for developing creative adaptive capacity. She also researches and advocates for arts-based interventions to improve teaching, learning, and self-development. Shamini currently directs the Preparing Future Faculty program at Claremont Graduate University.

Sonya Douglass Horsford is an Associate Professor of Education in the Graduate School of Education and College of Education and Human Development at George Mason University. Her research interests include the political and policy contexts of education leadership with a focus on school desegregation and education reform in the post-Civil Rights Era. Her work has been funded by The Spencer Foundation and published in numerous journals and edited volumes, including *Educational Administration Quarterly, Teachers College Record, Theory Into Practice, The Urban Review,* and the *Handbook on Critical Race Theory in Education*. She is editor of three books and author of *Learning in a Burning House: Educational Inequality, Ideology, and (Dis)Integration* (Teachers College Press, 2011), which received a 2013 Critics Choice Books Award from the American Educational Studies Association.

Anne Dudley-Marling is currently a Master's student in the Clinical Mental Health Counseling program at The University of Dayton. Prior to returning to school, Anne worked for the Office of Head Start Center on Cultural and Linguistic Responsiveness. In this role she worked to ensure culturally responsive practices for Head Start children and their families and trained administrators, teachers, and families on models of responsiveness. Anne also has a Master's Degree in Applied, Developmental and Educational Psychology from Boston College.

Curt Dudley-Marling is Professor Emeritus at Boston College. His teaching and scholarship has focused on language and literacy development and disability studies. Overall, his work stands as a critique of the deficit thinking that pathologizes the language, culture, and communities of children for whom school is often a struggle, including students with disabilities and children living in poverty. Dudley-Marling has written extensively on alternatives to pedagogical practices based on deficit thinking, including the recently published volume, *High-Expectation Curricula: Helping All Students Succeed with Powerful Learning* (edited with Sarah Michaels), which illustrates the power of rich, engaging curricula in high-poverty schools and special education classrooms.

Don Fraynd, PhD, started his career as a teacher and mid-level administrator and then studied educational leadership and policy analysis at the University of Wisconsin-Madison focusing on the politics of education, leadership for equity, and organizational theory. Upon graduating, he served as a high school principal, the chief school improvement officer for one of the nation's largest school districts, and now CEO of TeacherMatch, an organization that seeks to transform the selection and support of teachers.

Margaret Grogan is currently Professor of Educational Leadership and Policy in the School of Educational Studies at Claremont Graduate University, California. Originally from Australia, she received a Bachelor of Arts degree in Ancient History and Japanese Language from the University of Queensland. She taught high school in Australia, and was a teacher and an administrator at an international school in Japan, where she lived for 17 years. After graduating from Washington State University with a PhD in Educational Administration, she taught in principal and superintendent preparation programs at the University of Virginia and at the University of Missouri-Columbia. Among the various leadership positions she has held at her institutions and professional organizations, she served as Dean of the School of Educational Studies from 2008–2012, Chair of the Department of Educational Leadership and Policy Analysis at the University of Missouri–Columbia from 2002–2008, and she was President of the University Council for Educational Administration in 2003/4. A frequent keynote speaker, she has also published many articles and chapters and has authored, co-authored, or edited six books, including *Women and Educational Leadership* (2011) with Charol Shakeshaft, and the *Jossey Bass Reader on Educational Leadership* (2013). Her current research focuses on women in leadership, gender and education, the moral and ethical dimensions of leadership, and leadership for social justice.

Frank Hernandez is the Dean of the College of Education at the University of Texas of the Permian Basin. His research interests include the intersection of identity and school leadership and Latina/os and school leadership. He has conducted several national research projects with Latino school leaders and is one of the founding scholars of the National Latino Leadership Project. Frank has also written about racial identity development and its impact on leadership practice. Most recently, his work has focused on ways in which school leaders create inclusive communities for lesbian, gay, bisexual, transgendered, and questioning (LGBTQ) youth. His work has been published in *Educational Administrative Quarterly*, *Education and the Urban Society*, and the *Journal of Research in Leadership Education*. He holds a PhD from the Department of Educational Leadership and Policy Analysis at the University of Wisconsin–Madison.

Lauri Johnson is an Associate Professor and Educational Leadership program coordinator at the Lynch School of Education at Boston College. She focuses on investigating culturally responsive leadership practices and preparation programs in national and international contexts, and examining the historical role of parent and community activism in urban school reform. She is a member of the original US team of the International Successful School Principalship Project, a 15-nation study that has conducted cross-national research on successful school leaders since 2002. She has published extensively on these topics in national and international journals and three books. Before entering academic life in 1999 she was a special education and reading teacher in Oregon and New York State, and an administrator with the New York City Board of Education, where she directed professional and curriculum development on issues of diversity for teachers and school leaders in more than 200 schools. In addition to teaching leadership courses with an equity and social justice focus, she coordinates the Educational Leadership program area and the EdD program for practicing administrators from throughout Massachusetts (PSAP). She is Boston College's principal investigator for the Carnegie Project on the Education Doctorate (CPED), a national effort involving 55 institutions, which aims to reform the education practice doctorate to focus on high-impact problems of practice in local school districts.

Isabel Kelsey has taught K–5 for 19 years in diverse classroom settings: mainstream, bilingual, and ELL. She's currently a teacher at Davis Bilingual Magnet Elementary. She is a doctoral student in the Department of Educational Leadership at the University of Arizona. Her research interest is focused on providing ELL students with a socially just, culturally responsive curriculum.

Francesca López is an associate professor in the Educational Psychology Department at the University of Arizona. She began her career in education as a bilingual (Spanish/English) elementary teacher, and later as an at-risk high school counselor, in El Paso, Texas. After completing her PhD in Educational Psychology at the University of Arizona (2008), she served on the faculty of the Educational Policy and Leadership Department at Marquette University (2008–2013). Her research is focused on the ways educational settings promote achievement for Latino youth and has been funded by the American Educational Research Association Grants Program and the Division 15 American Psychological Association Early Career Award; she is a 2013 National Academy of Education/Spencer Postdoctoral Fellow. She has served on the editorial board of the *Journal of Psychoeducational Assessment* and is currently an associate editor for *Reading and Writing Quarterly*.

Joanne M. Marshall (EdD, Administration, Planning, and Social Policy, Harvard University) is an associate professor of educational administration at Iowa State University, where she serves as program coordinator. Her research agenda focuses on how people's internal values and beliefs relate to their public school roles, particularly in the areas of religion/ spirituality, moral and ethical leadership, philanthropy, social justice pedagogy, and work-life balance. A former high school English teacher, she has published articles in *The Journal of School Leadership*, *Equity and Excellence in Education*, *Educational Administration Quarterly*, *The School Administrator*, and *Phi Delta Kappan*. She is the lead editor of *Juggling Flaming Chainsaws: Faculty in Educational Leadership Try to Balance Work and Family* and editor of the Work-Life Balance book series from Information Age Publishing. Her website is http:// www.public.iastate.edu/~jmars/.

Casey Woodfield is a doctoral candidate in the Inclusive and Special Education Program in the Department of Teaching and Leadership at Syracuse University. She also holds a Master's degree in Cultural Foundations of Education and a Certificate of Advanced Study in Disability Studies from Syracuse University. Her academic, professional, and personal interests most closely align with the field of Disability Studies in Education and an emphasis on inclusion for people with disabilities in all aspects of society. Her research focuses on inclusive strategies for individuals who use augmentative and alternative communication; transition, independence, self-determination, and self-advocacy; peer relationships;

creative non-fiction writing; and narrative. She is most interested in exploring the voices and experiences of students as critical agents of advocacy and change.

Michelle D. Young, PhD, is the Executive Director of the University Council for Educational Administration (UCEA) and a Professor of Educational Leadership at the University of Virginia. Through her work with UCEA, an international consortium of research universities with programs in educational leadership, Michelle has fostered research on leadership preparation and brought that research to bear on the work of policy-makers. Young's scholarship focuses on how university programs, educational policies, and school leaders can support equitable and quality experiences for all students and adults who learn and work in schools. She is the recipient of the William J. Davis Award for the most outstanding article published in a volume of *Educational Administration Quarterly*. Her work has also been published in the *Review of Educational Research,* the *Educational Researcher*, the *American Educational Research Journal*, the *Journal of School Leadership*, the *Journal of Educational Administration* and *Leadership and Policy in Schools*, among other publications. She recently edited, with Murphy, Crow, and Ogawa, the first *Handbook of Research on the Education of School Leaders*.

Index

Page references in italic refer to figures and tables.

Abo-Zena, M.M. 153
ACT exam data 191–2, 193
Adams, A.D. 48
African Americans: and religious affiliations 150, 158n3; see also race and inclusive leadership
Agosto, V. 189
Akkerman, S. 163
Akresh, I.R. 150
American Association of School Administrators 152
American Association of University Women (AAUW) 121, 126
Anderson, G. 165, 167
anti-bullying policies 106, 113
Anyon, Jean 42
Apple, M.W. 85
Arizona: exclusionary educational policies in 88; Move on When Reading (MOWR) law 93; Proposition 199, 85, 90, 96
Auerbach, S. 167
Avelar LaSalle, R.L. 188

Bakker, A. 163
Banks, J.A. 96
Beecher, Catherine 121
Bell, Derrick 72–3
Bell, R. 43
Bellara, A.A. 189
The Bell Curve Wars (Fraser) 72
Bereiter, C. 41
Biklen, Doug 15
Bilingual Education Act (1968) 82–3

bilingual schools *see* English learners and inclusive leadership
Billingsley, A. 150
Birkett, M. 106
bisexual students *see* LGBTQ affiliation and inclusive leadership
Bleyaert, B. 188
Boaler, J. 45
book circles 72–3
Books, S. 39
Boske, C. 189
Boston College: Family and Community Engagement course 176–7
boundary-spanning leaders, defined 164
BPON (Boston Parent Organizing Network) 179
Brooks, Michele 179
Brown, K.M. 188
Brown v. Board of Education (1954) 61–2, 77, 119
Buchmann, C. 127, 128
bullying 106–07, 129
Burke, Jamie 15–16
Burns, M.S. 42
Burris, C.B. 44
Burt, Ronald 163
Bustamante, R.M. 188

Caldecott Medal books 124
Caldwell, C.H. 150
California: nine-week religion course, Modesto 149–50; Quality Professional Learning Standards 133, 139n3

Cambron-McCabe, N. 164
Camp, P. 43
Campano, G. 127
Canada: Toronto District School Board (TDSB) 178–9
Capper, C.A. 86, 153, 187, 189, 198
Carter, Stephen 142
case studies: disability and inclusive leadership 30–5, *31*, *34*; English learners and inclusive leadership 89–94; family and community engagement 173–82; gender and inclusive leadership 132–37; LGBTQ affiliation and inclusive leadership 114–15; poverty and inclusive leadership 50–4; race and inclusive leadership 64–68; religion and inclusive leadership 154–57
Cass, V.C. 108–09
Catchings, B. 105
Ceci, S.J. 121
Center for Ethical Leadership 178
Center for Public Education 60
Chaves, M. 150
children's books and gender representation 124–5
Children's Defense Fund 62
Christian Educators Association International 152
Civil Rights Act (1964) 83
Civil Rights Act (1978) 126
Civil Rights Movement 58
Clark, Tom C. 145
Cleveland, R. 188
"common sense" rhetoric 86, 87, 89, 96
community-based organizations (CBOs) 181
community engagement 168–9; *see also* family and community engagement
Community Learning Exchanges (Center for Ethical Leadership) 178
companion website 28
competence, presumption of *see* disability and inclusive leadership
content integration (Banks) 96
COP sociogram 7
Corbett, C. 127–8
critical curriculum leadership (Ylimaki) *see* English learners and inclusive leadership
Critical Race Theory 63, 66
Cultural Ecological Theory 63
culturally and linguistically diverse (CLD) students *see* English learners and inclusive leadership
culturally relevant pedagogy (Ladson-Billings) 48–9, 166
culturally responsive theories of education 46–49

Culture-Centered Theory (CCT) 63–4
culture of poverty (Payne) 41–2
culture wars (Hunter) 144

Dantley, M.E. 189
Datnow, A. 128
D'Augelli, A.R. 108
Day of Silence 110, 111–12
deficit thinking *see* poverty and inclusive leadership
De Jong, E. 87
detracking *see* poverty and inclusive leadership
Dewey, J. 86
dialogue: defined 68–9; facilitating 69–70; as foundational strategy 70–1, *70*; stages of social development 69
Diaz, E.M. 106
Diprete, T.A. 127, 128
disability and inclusive leadership 13–35; aligning school structures 26–7; building instructional teams 27–8; case studies 30–5, *31*, *34*; collaborative planning and implementation 22–3; and community feedback 14–16; current context in schools 13–16; efficacy of inclusive services 19–20; leaders' vision of full inclusion 21–2; literature review 16–17; monitor/adjust/celebrate 29; presumption of competence 19–20; reducing fragmentation of initiatives 28-29–1; response to intervention (RTI) 19; school climate goals 26; service delivery maps 23–5, *24–6*; social construction of 17–18; structure goals 25
disability studies (DS) 17
disability studies education (DSE) 17
Does God Make a Difference? Taking Religion Seriously in Our Schools and Universities (Nord and Haynes) 146
Donnellan, Anne 20
The Dreamkeepers (Ladson-Billings) 166
dropout rates 44, 85, 130
Du Bois, W.E.B. 59
Dudley-Marling, Curt 50
dyslexia 138

Ebaugh, H.R. 150–1
Education Trust 40
Engelmann, S. 41
English as a Second Language (ESL) 87
English learners and inclusive leadership 82–97; academic vigor via Funds of Knowledge 88; accountability 88–89; analyzing "common sense" rhetoric 86, 87, 89, 96; best practices 89; case studies 89–94; and community feedback 84–5; culturally responsive curriculum

87–88, 96; current context in schools 82–3;
curriculum leadership framework (Ylimaki)
86–88, 95; history of meeting needs of 83–4;
inclusive school reform 94–6; literature
review 85–6; professional development
95–6
Epstein, J. 167
Equal Educational Opportunity Act (1974) 83
Equity and Excellence in Education, on ethnoreligious oppression 149
equity audits 186–213, *190*; audit design
192–3; data collection and analysis 193–4,
198–212; goal setting and prioritization
194–5; implementation plans 195, 213; leader
preparation 189–190; LGBTQ affiliation and
inclusive leadership 112–13; literature review
187–90; proportional representation measures
190–2; purpose of 23; team formation 192;
use of 187–9
Erickson, F. 164
ethnicity, use of term 58–9
Eurocentric cultural norms 63
Evans, N.J. 110

Failing at Fairness: How Our Schools Cheat Girls
(Sadker and Sadker) 125
family and community engagement 162–83;
advocacy at intersections 164–5; antiracism
training 172–4; asset vs. deficit orientation
170–1; building partnerships 178–82; case
studies 173–82; community-based organizations 181; community engagement 168–9;
community walks 176–7; continuing education 172; culturally responsive leadership
166–7; current context in schools 163–5;
fostering relational networks 174–78; home
visits 174–78, *175*; literature review 167–69;
overcoming equity traps 170–3; parent
engagement 167–8; recrafting neighborhood spaces 171–2; recrafting outdoor school
spaces 171; school leaders, roles of 181–2;
social justice leadership 164–5; story mapping
177–8, *177*
Family Stories Project 47
Fellowship of Christian Athletes 154
Fenstermaker, S. 124
Fierro, E. 164–5
Figueroa, R. 47
Fine, C. 125
Fine, M. 167
First Amendment 144
First Amendment Center 152; *Teacher's Guide
to Religion in the Public Schools* and *Teaching
about Religion in National and State Social Studies
Standards* 145

Fischman, G.E. 138
Fishkin, J. 75
Francis, L.J. 146
Fraser, Steven 72
Frattura, E.M. 86, 153, 187, 198
Fraynd, Don 102–4, 113, 114
Fullan, M. 147
Funds of Knowledge 46–7, 88,
93–4
Furman, G. 91

Garcia, O. 91
Gay, Lesbian, & Straight Education Network
(GLSEN) 102, 105, 106, 112, 152
Gay-Straight Alliances (GSAs) 102, 103, 106,
110, 112, 113
gay students *see* LGBTQ affiliation and inclusive
leadership
Gee, J.P. 42
gender and inclusive leadership 119–39;
academic performance and career preparation
127–8; case studies 132–37; and community
feedback 121–4; current context in schools
120–4; curriculum 126–7; intersectionality
of 17, 123–4, 126–8, 129, 130; legislation
125–26; literature review 124–30; pregnancy
and parenting 129–0; preK-12 projects 137;
professional development 132–37; sexual
harassment 129, 131; social justice leadership
130–2
gender identity, defined 104
Gibson, P. 108
Gong Lum v. Rice (1927) 58, 77
Gonzalez, M.L. 164–5
Gould, Stephen Jay 72
Green, T.L. 189
Greytak, E.A. 106
Griffin, P. 42–3

Hall, Meredith 64, 65–6
Hancock, S. 188–9
harassment rates 106–07
Harris, S. 189
Harry, Beth 72–3
Hart, B. 41
Hatzenbuehler, M. 103
Haycock, Kati 40
HB 1070 deportations 96
Hernandez, Frank 102–4, 112–13,
151
Higgins, L.M. 150
Hill, C. 129
Hill-Jackson, V. 188–9
Hopson, M. 189
Horsford, S.D. 59, 64–68, 70

Hubbard, L. 128
Hunter, James 144

identity development model (Cass) 108–09, *109*
inclusive school reform: definition of 21; practices to avoid *34*
Individuals with Disabilities Education Improvement Act (2004): Individualized Education Program (IEP) 14; least restrictive environment (LRE) principle, defined 13–14
infographics 133–4, 139*n*4
Inheriting Shame (Selden) 72
institutes of higher education (IHEs), as partners 179–80
intersectionality in educational leadership 1–10; building networked social justice communities 8–10, *9*; communities of practice 5–6; expectations of leaders 1–4; leadership practices 4–5; shared repertoire 8; social justice and leadership standards 2–4, *3*; social justice leadership 6–8, *6–7*
Interstate School Leaders Licensure Consortium (ISLLC) Standards 2–3, *2*

Jackson, Dwayne 156–7
James, M. 188–9
Jenkins, Patrice 114
Jeynes, W. 150
Johnson, E. 175
Johnson, R.S. 188
joint enterprise, defined 6
Joshi, K.Y. 149
Journal of Cases in Educational Leadership, on equity audit process 189–90

Karanxha, Z. 189
Kearl, H. 129
Keyes, M.W. 153, 187
Kilingner, Jeanette 72–3
King, Lawrence 101
Klein, S.S. 126, 138
Koschoreck, J. 110
Kosciw, J.G. 106
Kozol, Jonathan 73

Ladson-Billings, G. 48, 76, 166
Langer, E. 132
language, intersectionality with religion 150–1
Laughter, J.C. 48
Lau v. Nichols (1974) 83
Lawrence, Charles 70
least dangerous assumption (Donnellan) 20
least restrictive environment (LRE) principle, defined 13–14

Lee, C. 112
lesbian students *see* LGBTQ affiliation and inclusive leadership
Lewis, C.W. 188–89
LGBTQ affiliation and inclusive leadership 101–15; case studies 114–15; and community involvement 113; countering heteronormative perspectives 110–11; current context in schools 101–4; definitions of terms 104–5; and district policies 113; equity audits 112–13; identity development theories and research 108–09, *109*; intersectionality of 105, 107, 151–2; literature review 104–09, *107*, *109*; professional development 111; sexual harassment 129, 131; sexually degrading name-calling 107–08; social justice leadership 109–10; supportive activities 111–12
Lopez, G.R. 164–5
Loyola University: Center for Urban Research and Learning (CURL) 180, 182
Lubienski, S.T. 126
Lugg, C.A. 104, 145
Lyon, Mary 119

MacDonald, Emily 155–6
Macgillivray, I. 106
magnet schools 88, 90–3, 97, 103
Mann, Horace 142
Marshall, Catherine 131
Martin, J. 129
Massachusetts: Boston Public Schools (BPS) 178–79; Family and Community Engagement leadership standard 181
McCarthy, M. 164
McInerney, Brandon 101
McKell, Lloyd 179
McKenzie, K.B. 170, 188
McKnight, C.C. 43
Meeting the Needs of Students of ALL Abilities (Capper, Frattura, and Keyes) 153, 198
Mendez v. Westminster (1956) 58
mental retardation, use of term 17–8
Michaels, Sarah 50
Miller, P.M. 164, 169
Milligan, J.A. 147
minoritized, use of term 77
The Mismeasure of Man (Gould) 72
Moll, L.C. 46
Morris, E.W. 126–7
Murphy, J. 42
Murray, Charles 52
mutual engagement, defined 6
My Brother's Keeper Initiative (2014) 62

National Assessment of Educational Progress (NAEP) 39–40, 62, 120

National Coalition for Dialogue and Deliberation or the Social Justice Training Institute 70

National Coalition for Women and Girls in Education (NCWGE) 126, 131

Neighborhood Educational Opportunity Zones 168

Nelson, J.A. 188

neoliberal groups 85–6, 89

networked social justice communities, defined 8–10, *9*

Nieto, S. 76

Nilsson, Todd 154–5

No Child Left Behind Act (2001) 14, 60, 83, 84, 88, 90, 91, 130, 190–1

No Name-Calling Week 110, 111–12

Nord, W.A. 145

North Carolina: Honor Schools of Excellence equity audit 188

Oakes, J. 42, 43

Obama, Barack: My Brother's Keeper Initiative (2014) 62

online tools 28

Onwuegbuzie, A.J. 188

Optimum Learning Environment (OLE) project 49

Ormseth, T. 43

O'Toole, J. 131

Palmer, D. 97

Palmer, Parker 152

Paludi, C.A. 129

Paludi, M.A. 129

parent involvement initiatives 75–86 *see also* family and community engagement

Parker, Carl 114–15

parochial schools 142–3, 146, 158n1

Payne, Ruby 41–2

Perez, Carlos 64, 66–7, 68

Perkins, L.M. 119

Perkins Act (1984) 121

Pew Forum on Religion and Public Life 143–4, 145, 152; Pew Religious Landscape Survey 152; *Religious Portrait of African Americans* 158n3

Pew Research Center for the People and the Press 144

Plessy v. Ferguson (1896) 58

political party polarization 144

poverty and inclusive leadership 39–54; case studies 50–4; culturally relevant pedagogy 48–9; current context in schools 39–41;

dismantling tracking and ability grouping 44–5; Funds of Knowledge approach to teaching 46–7; high-expectation curriculum 44, 49–50; intersectionality of 16; literature review 41–3; pregnant teen dropouts 130; Shared Inquiry discussions 49–3

Precious Knowledge (documentary) 67

pregnancy and parenting *see* gender and inclusive leadership

Preuss School (UCSD campus) 45

The Principal's Perspective: School Safety, Bullying and Harassment (Markow and Dancewicz) 106

professional development: English learners and inclusive leadership 95–6; gender and inclusive leadership 132–37; LGBTQ affiliation and inclusive leadership 111

Professional Learning Communities (PLCs) 95–6

Promise Neighborhoods 168

proportional representation, defined 191

Prothero, S.R. 145

race, use of term 58

race and inclusive leadership 58–77; overview 58–60; book circles 72–3; case studies 64–68; current context in schools 60–61; and dialogue 68–71, *70*; history of exclusion 58, 77; inclusion and justice 76–7; intersectionality of 16–17, 61, 77, 149–54; literature review 61–4; multicultural curriculum transformation seminars 73–5; parent outreach and programming 75–6; video/film screenings 71

race-consciousness progression (Horsford) 59, 64–68

RACE: The Power of an Illusion (PBS) 71

Race to the Top competition 84

racial literacy, defined 65

racial realism, defined 66

racial reconciliation, defined 67

racial reconstruction, defined 66

Ravitch, Diane 40

religion and inclusive leadership 142–58; case studies 154–57; and communities of belief 147–48; current context in schools 142–5; equity audits 153–4; history of 142–3; and identity development 147; intersectionality of 147–52; literature review 145–52; personal reflection/spiritual biography 152–3; religion as curriculum topic 145–46; social justice leadership 152–4

response to intervention (RTI), defined 19

Riehl, C. 166

rigor, use of term 88
Riojas-Cortez, M. 46–7
Risely, T.R. 41
Robinson, J.P. 128
Rodríguez, M.A. 189
Rorty, R. 68
Rufte, Edward 141n4
Ruiz, N.T. 49
Ruiz, R. 84
Rush, Benjamin 119

Sadker, D. 121, 125, 126
Sadker, M. 121, 125, 126
Savage Inequalities (Kozol) 73
Sax, L. 127
Scanlan, M. 151
Scheurich, J. 169, 170, 188
Schmidt, W.H. 43
School District of Abington Township, Pennsylvania v. Schempp (1963) 144, 145
Schoolwide Cultural Competence Observation Checklist 188
Schott Foundation 62
science, technology, engineering, and math (STEM) *see* gender and inclusive leadership
segregation, government-sanctioned 77
Selden, Steven 72
service delivery maps 23–5, *24–6*
Seven Sisters colleges 119
sexual harassment 129, 131
Sexuality Matters: Paradigms and Policies for Educational Leaders (Koschoreck and Tooms) 110
sexual orientation: intersectionality with religion 151–2; *see also* LGBTQ affiliation and inclusive leadership
Shakeshaft, C. 189–90
Shared Inquiry discussions 49–53
shared repertoire, defined 6, 8
Sheltered Instruction 87; *see also* English learners and inclusive leadership
Sherman, W. 189–90
Short, L. 106
Silent Covenants: Brown v. Board of Education and the Unfulfilled Hopes for Racial Reform (Bell) 72–3
Skrla, L. 186, 187, 188
Smith, Christian 148
Snow, C.E. 42
social activists, defined 164–5
social frontiers *see* family and community engagement
The Souls of Black Folk (Du Bois) 59
The Space Traders unit 48–9
Staples, M. 45

Starratt, R.J. 157
Steele, Claude M. 72
Still Failing at Fairness: How Gender Bias Cheats Girls and Boys in Schools and What We Can Do About It (Sadker and Sadker) 125
story mapping 177–8
Stromquist, N.P. 138
Structured English Immersion (SEI) model 86, 89, 91
suicide 101, 103, 108
Swearer, S.M. 107

Tabbaa-Rida, Z. 145
Taking Religion Seriously Across the Curriculum (Nord and Haynes) 146
Taylor, Damilola 101
Teacher's Guide to Religion in the Public Schools and *Teaching about Religion in National and State Social Studies Standards* (Douglass) 145
Teaching about Religions: A Democratic Approach for Public Schools (Lester) 146
Theoharis, G. 105–6, 131, 152
The School Leaders Our Children Deserve (Theoharis) 152
Thousand, J.S. 20, 147
Title IX (1972) 120, 129, 130, 131
tools for teachers 28
Tooms, M. 110
Toronto District School Board (TDSB) 178–9
Toshalis, E. 147
tracking and ability grouping *see* poverty and inclusive leadership
transgendered students *see* LGBTQ affiliation and inclusive leadership

United States: religion demographics 143–4
University Council for Educational Administration's Leaders Supporting Diverse Learners initiative 189–90
University of California, San Diego (UCSD): Preuss School 45
US Department of Education 124; Office for Civil Rights study 62

Vargas, Manuel 64–5, 67–68
Vasudevan, L. 127
Villa, R.A. 20
Village, A. 146
The Visual Display of Quantitative Information (Tufte) 139n4

Warren, M. 168
Washington, Mabel 64, 66, 68
Watanabe, M. 42

Watkins, William 73
Welner, K. 44
West, C. 124
Whistling Vivaldi: How Stereotypes Affect Us and What We Can Do (Steele) 72
The White Architects of Black Education (Watkins) 73
Why Are So Many Minority Students in Special Education? (Harry and Kilingner) 72–3
Wiley, E. 44
Willard, Emma 121
Williams, W.M. 121

Wisconsin: Department of Human Services 185; Zilber Neighborhood Initiative 181
Women's Educational Equity Act (1974) 120, 125, 126
Wortham, S. 127

Ylimaki, R. 82, 86–88, 89, 95, 97
Young, M.D. 153

Zilber Neighborhood Initiative 181
Zine, J. 150